Finance Act Handbook 2020

Finance Act Handbook 2020

Contributors

Rebecca Combes
Bill Dodwell, LLB, LLM,
CTA (Fellow), ACA
Eile Gibson
Andrew Goodall
Louise Hemmingsley
Andrew Hubbard, BMus, PhD,
CTA (Fellow), ATT (Fellow)
Ali Kazimi
Martin Lavender
John Lindsay
BA, FCA, FTII

Lisa Macpherson
Pete Miller, CTA (Fellow)
Nicola Pitcher
Lynne Poyser
BMedSc (Hons), ATT, CTA
Dilpa Raval
Philip Ridgway
David Rudling, CTA
David Smailes, FCA
Matt Stringer
Edd Thompson
Kevin Walton

Tolley®

LexisNexis UK & Worldwide

United Kingdom	RELX (UK) Limited trading as LexisNexis, 1–3 Strand, London WC2N 5JR and 9–10 St Andrew Square, Edinburgh EH2 2AF
LNUK Global Partners	LexisNexis® encompasses authoritative legal-publishing brands dating back to the 19th century including; Butterworths® in the United Kingdom, Canada, the Asia-Pacific region, Les Editions du Juris Classeur in France and Matthew Bender® worldwide. Details of LexisNexis® locations worldwide can be found at www.lexisnexis.com

© 2020 RELX (UK) Limited

Published by LexisNexis

This is a Tolley title

A CIP Catalogue record for this book is available from the British Library.

ISBN 9781474314305

Typeset by Letterpart Limited, Caterham on the Hill, Surrey CR3 5XL

Printed and bound by CPI Group (UK) Ltd, Croydon, CR0 4YY

Visit LexisNexis at www.lexisnexis.co.uk

FOREWORD

On 22 July 2020, Royal Assent was given to Finance Act 2020 and a further 200 or so pages were added to the statute book. The Bill went through the normal stages, although the Covid-19 pandemic meant that some of the hearings were by video rather than in person. Despite its relatively short length, it contains a number of controversial measures.

Section 1 of the new Act is a joy 'Income tax is charged for the tax year 2020–21.' This continues the unnecessary pretence that income tax is an annual tax, renewed each year by Parliament. No one can possibly consider there is any reality in this; it is surely time for income tax to be placed on a perpetual basis.

Possibly the biggest change – in terms of money – comes in one of the shorter clauses. The decision to reverse the planned cut in corporation tax to 17% is simply enacted by specifying that the rate for 2020/21 shall be 19%. This raises £4.6 billion in 2020/21, rising to £6–7 billion in subsequent years.

Moving now to the more controversial measures, the first is the enactment – from 6 April 2021 – of the off-payroll working rules for large and medium-sized engagers outside the public sector. The rules were deferred a year from the intended start date due to the pandemic. Larger engagers were more prepared than smaller ones to operate the new rules from 2020, which in some cases will put up costs for engagers and in others put up tax/national insurance for freelancers. The Finance Bill sub-committee of the House of Lords Economic Affairs committee urged greater deferral and more work done to improve the rules; however, the Chancellor and the Treasury ignored the protests. The Office of Tax Simplification has recommended that the Government consider enacting a new statutory definition of employment to make it easier for engagers and contractors to understand clearly which side of the line they fall. The underlying issue remains the substantial differences in tax/national insurance treatment between employees and the self-employed, combined with engagers desire for flexible working. It remains to be seen whether any changes are made before 2021.

The Government accepted almost all the recommendations of Sir Amyas Morse in relation to the loan charge and the Act contains the necessary legislation. A cross-party campaign continued to seek even more changes, but in the end, Parliament approved the measures. The changes to the original measures are estimated to cost £750 million. The loan charge has given rise to two further reviews: one into how HMRC uses its powers and a second into the tax advisory and agent market. Sir Amyas expressed considerable concern that variants of loan charge schemes continued to be marketed and HMRC gave firm warnings to NHS workers and others not to enter into them.

The third new area is the Digital Services Tax, which takes effect from April 2020. This – and similar taxes from European countries – have prompted a fierce reaction from the United States, where the majority of companies liable to pay the tax are headquartered. The UK has said that it would prefer a global agreement but until one is reached, will proceed with its own tax.

The Conservative party had included in its manifesto a commitment to review and reform entrepreneur's relief – and the Act gives effect to that commitment. The relief is renamed Business Asset Disposal relief, which is easy prey for opponents of any form of tax relief in this area. The level is cut from £10 million to £1 million – which was the level introduced by Alistair Darling in 2008. There are quite draconian anti-forestalling provisions which apply where the disposal giving rise to the relief had not been completed before Budget Day

(11 March 2020). The relief has traditionally benefitted about 45–50,000 business owners every year and the changes will cut the cost by £1–1.8 billion every year.

The Act gives HMRC authority to start preparing for a plastic packaging tax, which is expected to raise several hundred million pounds when in force from April 2022 – although the main intention is to reduce the use of such packaging.

In a sign of the times, the final schedule of the Act provides that coronavirus support payments are taxable in almost all circumstances. It says something for the complexity of tax that this takes ten pages to achieve. It includes a 100% charge where a person has received payments in excess of any entitlement.

As always, I would like to congratulate the publishers in preparing this book so quickly and the authors of the commentary in the speed of their analysis, which I hope will aid those charged with considering the changes introduced by this Act.

Bill Dodwell
July 2020

CONTENTS

Schedules

RELEVANT DATES AND ABBREVIATIONS

11 March 2020	Budget Statement
19 March 2020	Finance Bill
22 July 2020	Royal Assent

ABV	=	alcohol by volume
ACS	=	authorised contractual schemes
AIM	=	Alternative Investment Market
ALDA 1979	=	Alcoholic Liquor Duties Act 1979
APD	=	air passenger duty
ATT	=	Association of Taxation Technicians
BADR	=	business asset disposal relief
BEPS	=	Base Erosion and Profit Shifting
CA 2006	=	Companies Act 2006
CAA 2001	=	Capital Allowances Act 2001
CFC	=	controlled foreign company
CGT	=	capital gains tax
Ch	=	Chapter (of a part of an Act)
CIOT	=	Chartered Institute of Taxation
CTA 2009	=	Corporation Tax Act 2009
CTA 2010	=	Corporation Tax Act 2010
DPT	=	diverted profits tax
DST	=	digital services tax
EEA	=	European Economic Area
EU ETS	=	EU Emissions Trading Scheme
FA	=	Finance Act
FCA	=	Financial Conduct Authority
FTT	=	First-tier Tribunal
GGY	=	gross gaming yield
HMRC	=	Her Majesty's Revenue and Customs
IHT	=	inheritance tax
IHTA 1984	=	Inheritance Tax Act 1984
IIP	=	interest in possession
ITA 2007	=	Income Tax Act 2007
ITEPA 2003	=	Income Tax (Earnings and Pensions) Act 2003
ITTOIA 2005	=	Income Tax (Trading and Other Income) Act 2005
LLPs	=	limited liability partnerships
MTF	=	multilateral trading facility
MVL	=	members' voluntary liquidation
OECD	=	Organisation for Economic Co-operation and Development
para	=	paragraph (of a Schedule to an Act)
PAYE	=	pay as you earn
PPR	=	principal private residence (relief)
Pt	=	part (of an Act or of a Schedule to an Act)
R&D	=	research and development
reg	=	regulation (of an SI)
RNRB	=	residence nil rate band
s	=	section (of an Act)
SBA	=	structures and buildings allowance
Sch	=	Schedule (to an Act)
SI	=	Statutory Instrument (since 1948)
ss	=	sections (of an Act)
STC	=	Simon's Tax Cases
sub-para	=	sub-paragraph
sub-s	=	subsection
TCGA 1992	=	Taxation of Chargeable Gains Act 1992
TIOPA 2010	=	Taxation (International and Other Provisions) Act 2010
TMA 1970	=	Taxes Management Act 1970

TPDA 1979	=	Tobacco Products Duty Act 1979
VATA 1994	=	Value Added Tax Act 1994
VED	=	vehicle excise duty
VERA 1994	=	Vehicle Excise and Registration Act 1994
WLTP	=	worldwide harmonised light vehicles test procedure

ABOUT THE AUTHORS

Rebecca Combes

Rebecca Combes joined Smith & Williamson in 2004 after managing the global tax affairs of WS Atkins plc. Previously, she worked as a chemical engineer before training as a chartered accountant with Deloitte in London. She manages a wide portfolio of clients, including listed manufacturing companies, tech start-ups, professional partnerships and not-for-profit organisations. Her areas of expertise are: corporation tax; research and development (R&D) tax relief; patent box; investor reliefs; partnerships; not-for-profit.

Rebecca has written the commentary for FA 2020, ss 28, 36 and 110.

Bill Dodwell, LLB, LLM, CTA (Fellow), ACA

Bill Dodwell is Tax Director at the Office of Tax Simplification and a past president of the Chartered Institute of Taxation.

Bill has written the Foreword to the handbook.

Eile Gibson

Eile Gibson qualified as a lawyer in 1997 and trained as a tax expert whilst employed as a solicitor in a number of London based firms. She was also a qualified Chartered Tax Adviser. She started her own legal tax practice in 2008. Her expertise encompassed corporate tax, property tax and transactional taxes. Having stepped back from providing legal advice she has continued to use her expertise of some 20 years in editing and providing commentary in tax publications including for LexisNexis.

Eile has written the commentary for FA 2020, ss 76 to 79, 101 and Sch 14.

Andrew Goodall

Andrew Goodall is a freelance writer specialising in UK tax policy, law and administration. He is a regular contributor to Tax Notes, published by Tax Analysts. His work has been published by several LexisNexis UK titles including Simon's Tax Intelligence, Tolley's Tax Guide and Tax Journal. He is a non-practising member of the Chartered Institute of Taxation.

Andrew has written the commentary for FA 2020, ss 8–14, s 102 and Sch 15, ss 103–105, s 106 and Sch 16, and ss 111–112.

Louise Hemmingsley

Louise Hemmingsley is an in-house writer responsible for writing and updating the VAT content for a number of Tolley products. Louise has specialised in VAT since 1993 and has worked for HMC&E, the top four firms of accountants and in-house for Siemens, Nortel Networks and Williams Lea as their sole VAT manager. During her time with PwC, Louise worked for their US practice providing international VAT advice for their US clients.

Louise has written the commentary for FA 2020, ss 82, 85, 89, 92, 93, 96 and Sch 11.

Andrew Hubbard, BMus, PhD, CTA (Fellow), ATT (Fellow)

Andrew Hubbard is the editor-in-chief of Taxation magazine. He is a long-term contributor to Tolley's Tax Planning and Finance Act Handbook. In 2006 he won the tax writer of the year award at the Taxation Awards and is a former president of both the CIOT and the ATT. He is well known as a writer and lecturer on tax matters. He has recently retired as a partner in the Nottingham office of RSM where he specialised in tax dispute resolution and the taxation of entrepreneurial businesses. Andrew originally trained as a musician before joining the Inland Revenue as an Inspector of Taxes.

Andrew has written the commentary for FA 2020, ss 15 to 21 and Sch 2.

Ali Kazimi

Ali Kazimi is the managing director of Hansuke Consulting. Ali is a leading authority in the field of banking and securities taxation having held successive leadership roles with Big4 firms and as head of tax at Barclays Global Investors (now BlackRock). Ali has contributed regularly to several LexisNexis UK publications and webinars on FATCA, CRS, DAC6 and tax integrity. Ali is a graduate chartered accountant and a long-standing member of the Chartered Institute for Securities and Investment, International Fiscal Association, and the Association of Corporate Treasurers.

Ali has written the commentary for FA 2020, ss 33, 35.

Martin Lavender

Martin Lavender is a technical writer with LexisNexis, where he is responsible for pensions content on a variety of sources, including Simon's Taxes and TolleyGuidance. Prior to joining LexisNexis, he worked for HMRC and as a pensions technical consultant for both Mercer and Legal & General.

Martin has written the commentary for FA 2020, ss 22 and 108.

John Lindsay, BA, FCA, FTII

John Lindsay is a consultant in the tax department of Linklaters LLP. He advises on all corporate taxes with a focus on the taxation of capital market and securitisation transactions. John is a contributor to Simon's Taxes, Simon's Tax Planning and Tolley's Tax Planning and is also a co-author of the Taxation of Companies and Company Reconstructions (Sweet & Maxwell, 2009). He is a member of both the CIOT Technical Policy and Oversight Committee and the CIOT Corporate Tax Committee and is also a member of a number of HMRC working groups.

John has written the commentary for FA 2020, ss 31, 32, Sch 6.

Lisa Macpherson

Lisa Macpherson is the Head of Tax Technical at PKF Francis Clark, supporting the firm's teams on tax policy and technical issues across its offices and also across the wider PKF network. She has more than 20 years' experience working in all areas of taxation including compliance and consultancy. For the last fifteen years Lisa has specialised in dealing with inheritance tax planning, onshore and offshore trust taxation, residence and domicile issues, capital gains tax and pre-owned assets tax for a number of high net worth clients.

Lisa has written the commentary for FA 2020, ss 73 to 75.

Pete Miller, CTA (Fellow), Partner, The Miller Partnership

Pete Miller has worked in tax for 31 years, starting as an Inspector of Taxes where he had roles in Policy and Technical Divisions and was the Inland Revenue's expert on distributions. He spent 11 years in 'Big 4' firms, specialising in corporate transactions, before founding The Miller Partnership, which advices other advisers on transactions in securities, reorganisations, reconstructions, distributions, partnerships, Patent Box, HMRC clearances and intangible assets. Pete speaks and writes regularly on tax and is General Editor of Whiteman and Sherry on Capital Gains Tax and on Income Tax and is on the Editorial Boards of Taxation, and Tax Journal.

Pete has written the commentary for FA 2020, ss 5, 6, 25, 26, 34 and Schs 4, 7.

Nicola Pitcher

Nicola Pitcher is a Chartered Accountant and a self-employed employment tax consultant who has specialised in employment taxes for more than 25 years, having worked both in industry and in the Big 4. She has particular expertise in the recruitment sector and contingent workforce matters and has been extensively involved in helping businesses deal with employment tax legislation in this area – most recently the changes to IR35.

Nicola has written the commentary for FA 2020, s 7 and Sch 1.

Lynne Poyser, BMedSc (Hons), ATT, CTA

An expert in personal taxation with over 15 years' experience, Lynne joined Tolley from BDO, where she worked in the private client team and the national tax training department, having previously worked for Grant Thornton and Arthur Andersen. Lynne has written for TolleyGuidance, Simon's Taxes, Taxwise 1, Taxation magazine, Tax Adviser magazine and has been a tutor for Tolley Exam Training. She is also the former Chairman of the London branch of ATT and CIOT.

Lynne has written the commentary for FA 2020, ss 1 to 4, 27, 38, 109.

Dilpa Raval

Dilpa Raval is a Senior Associate in the Employee Incentives team at CMS, specialising in share schemes and employee incentive arrangements. She has experience of working with both listed and private companies, advising on executive remuneration and the design of incentive structures, including the drafting and implementation of shares schemes and bonus plans. She also has experience of dealing with the share schemes aspects of large corporate transactions.

Dilpa has written the commentary for FA 2020, s 107.

Philip Ridgway

Philip Ridgway joined Temple Tax Chambers when he returned to the Bar in June 2007 and advises on all areas of revenue law, both corporate and personal. Philip has a special expertise in the taxation of insolvent companies, members' voluntary liquidations (including s 110 schemes) and bankruptcy, and lectures regularly to R3 and is a member of the R3/HMRC liaison group which meet regularly to discuss issues of conflict between insolvency law and tax law. He is a Member of the Association of Business Recovery Professionals (MABRP) having passed the JIEB examinations.

Philip has written the commentary for FA 2020, ss 99 to 100 and Sch 13.

David Rudling, CTA
David Rudling is a technical writer with LexisNexis. Before joining LexisNexis he worked for HMRC, in industry, and for a Big Four firm of accountants. He specialises in VAT and is involved in the production of De Voil Indirect Tax Service, Tolley's VAT Planning, Tolley's VAT Handbook and Tolley's VAT cases.

David has written the commentary for FA 2020, ss 80, 83, 86, 90, 91.

David Smailes, FCA
David Smailes is a senior tax writer on the staff of LexisNexis and is the current author of Tolley's Income Tax. His career in tax publishing has taken in many publications, and he previously worked full-time in tax practice with medium to large professional firms.

David has written the commentary for FA 2020, ss 29, 30, and Sch 5 and the Introduction to this book.

Matt Stringer
Matt Stringer is the Head of International Tax at Grant Thornton UK. He has a decade of experience in large corporate and international tax, working with both inbound and outbound multinational groups. Matt has particular expertise in cross border structuring matters and the OECD BEPS initiatives, with recent experience across Diverted Profits Tax, Anti-Hybrid rules and structuring opportunities for US multinationals in light of US tax reform measures. Matt writes for Tax Adviser magazine in the UK, with recently published articles on Diverted Profits Tax, State Aid and the new UK Digital Services Tax.

Matt has written the commentary for FA 2020, ss 39 to 72, and Schs 8 to 10.

Edd Thompson
Edd Thompson is a Chartered Accountant and Chartered Tax Adviser. He trained and worked in a top 10 accountancy firm for a number of years where he provided indirect tax advice to a broad range of clients including large corporates, owner managed businesses, public bodies and not-for-profits. He now works for Tolley as a technical writer where he contributes to several publications including De Voil Indirect Tax Service.

Edd has written the commentary for FA 2020, ss 81, 84, 87, 91,97, and Sch 12.

Kevin Walton
Kevin Walton is an in-house writer with Tolley. He is the author of Tolley's Capital Gains Tax, Tolley's Corporation Tax and Tolley's Capital Allowances.

Kevin has written the commentary for FA 2020, ss 23, 24 and Sch 3.

INTRODUCTION TO FINANCE ACT 2020

This edition brings to an end something of a hiatus for the Finance Act Handbook. Finance Act 2019 received Royal Assent as long ago as 12 February 2019. Some 17 months later, and in what may feel to many like a different world, Finance Act 2020 has now reached the statute book. The PDF weighs in at 208 pages, which seems relatively few, though this compares to 176 pages when the Finance Bill was first presented to Parliament on 18 March 2020. One clause and one schedule were added at Committee Stage. A further eight clauses and one more schedule were then added at Report Stage. Of course, that original Bill was based on an 11 March Budget delivered to a packed House of Commons with no thoughts yet of lockdown or social distancing. All of the clauses added to the original Bill contain measures that are designed to relieve the impact of the COVID-19 (coronavirus) pandemic or are taken in consequence of non-tax measures implemented to relieve that impact. For example, the extension of the off-payroll working rules to the private sector was meant to commence on 6 April 2020 and would presumably have been in the original Finance Bill. The decision to delay the commencement for one year due to coronavirus led to its being omitted from that original Bill and added at Committee Stage. The largest single measure in Finance Act 2020 though is the new Digital Services Tax first announced in 2018, accounting for 34 sections and three schedules.

Royal Assent was given on 22 July 2020.

PART 1   INCOME TAX, CORPORATION TAX AND CAPITAL GAINS TAX

Income tax charge, rates etc

Section 1 imposes the charge to income tax for the year 2020/21.

Section 2 sets the main rates of income tax for 2020/21; these remain at 20% (basic rate), 40% (higher rate) and 45% (additional rate). The basic rate limit and higher rate limit remain unchanged at £37,500 and £150,000. These rates apply to the 'non-savings, non-dividend income' of taxpayers of England and Northern Ireland. For Scottish and Welsh taxpayers (both as defined), those rates are set by the Scottish Parliament and Welsh Assembly respectively. The rates set by the Scottish Parliament are as follows.

	Band of income	Rate of income tax
Starter rate	0 to £2,085	19%
Scottish basic rate	£2,086 to £12,658	20%
Intermediate rate	£12,659 to £30,930	21%
Higher rate	£30,931 to £150,000	41%
Top rate	Above £150,000	46%

The Welsh Assembly again chose to align its rates with those applicable to England and Northern Ireland taxpayers.

Section 3 sets the default and savings rates for the year 2020/21, which are unchanged from 2019/20 and thus remain the same as the main rates of income tax. The savings rates, i e the rates chargeable on savings income, apply to Scottish and Welsh taxpayers as they do to other UK taxpayers.

Section 4 disapplies the automatic indexation of the starting rate limit for savings, and thus freezes the starting rate limit at £5,000 for 2020/21.

Corporation tax charge and rates

Section 5 sets the main rate of corporation tax at 19% for financial year 2020 (the year beginning 1 April 2020), replacing the intended rate of 17% that had been set by F(No 2)A 2015, s 7(2).

Section 6 imposes the charge to corporation tax for financial year 2021 (the year beginning 1 April 2021) and sets the main rate of corporation tax for that year at 19%.

Employment income and social security income

Section 7 introduces **Schedule 1**, which makes provision about workers' services provided through intermediaries. It aligns the tax treatment for payments made for workers' services thus provided to the private sector with the pre-existing treatment for payments made for workers' services thus provided to the public sector. It does not, however, apply where the private sector client qualifies as small or does not have a UK connection. Where these exceptions are in play, the engagement remains within the regime ('the normal IR35 rules') at ITEPA 2003, Pt 2 Ch 8 (ss 48–61).

Where the client is in the public sector, the pre-existing regime in ITEPA 2003, Pt 2 Ch 10 (ss 61K–61X) shifts responsibility for operating the rules, and deducting any tax and national insurance contributions due, from the individual to the organisation, agency or other third party paying the individual's personal service company or other intermediary. This is the regime now extended, with the exceptions mentioned above, to cases where the client is in the private sector. Subject to some transitional rules, the new rules have effect where the deemed direct payment (see ITEPA 2003, s 61Q) falls to be treated as made (see ITEPA 2003, s 61N(3), (4)) on or after 6 April 2021.

Schedule 1 is split into four parts. Part 1 (paras 1–6) makes the amendments to ITEPA 2003, Pt 2 Ch 8 required to take engagements out of the normal IR35 rules. This includes the introduction of the exceptions mentioned above. Part 2 (paras 7–17) amends the public sector regime at ITEPA 2003, Pt 2 Ch 10 so as to bring private sector engagements within its remit and provide some extra rules in consequence of doing so. Part 3 (paras 18–23) makes consequential and miscellaneous amendments to pre-existing tax legislation. Finally, Part 4 (paras 24–34) provides the detailed commencement rules and the transitional provisions. The transitional provisions are intended to remove services performed by the worker before 6 April 2021 from the new private sector regime (paras 30–32).

The question of whether a client qualifies as small for a tax year for the purposes of the above exceptions is determined under new ITEPA 2003, ss 60A–60H (inserted by Sch 1, para 5). As to whether a client has a UK connection for a tax year is determined under new ITEPA 2003, s 60I (also inserted by Sch 1, para 5).

The client will be required to provide a statement of status determination (new ITEPA 2003, s 60NA (inserted by Sch 1, para 13)) to the worker. The statement must be to the effect that the client has reached a conclusion as to whether or not the worker would be regarded as an employee of the client if the services were provided under a contract directly between client and worker; it must state that conclusion and explain the reasons for it. The legislation also makes provision for a new client-led status disagreement process and provides a duty for a client to withdraw a status determination statement if it begins to qualify as small (new ITEPA 2003, ss 60T, 60TA (substituted/inserted by Sch 1, para 16)).

Section 8 applies, for 2020/21 onwards, a new regime (the worldwide harmonised light vehicles test procedure (WLTP)) for calculating a car's CO_2 emissions in order to determine the appropriate percentage for the car. The appropriate percentage is used in calculating the cash equivalent of the benefit, and thus the taxable benefit, of a car made available by reason of an employment for the employee's private use. The new regime is applied to all cars first registered after 5 April 2020, and replaces emissions testing under the New European Driving Cycle (NEDC). NEDC emissions values continue to apply to cars first registered between 1 October 1999 and 5 April 2020 inclusive. See also sections 9 and 10.

Section 9 applies in determining the appropriate percentage for a car for 2020/21 only. To support the introduction of the WLTP regime (see section 8), appropriate percentages for cars measured under WLTP are set to be generally two percentage points fewer for 2020/21 than those for other cars. For zero emissions cars, whether registered before or on or after 6 April 2020, the appropriate percentage is set at 0%. See also section 10.

Section 10 applies in determining the appropriate percentage for a car for 2021/22 only. Following on from section 9, and to continue to support the introduction of the WLTP regime, appropriate percentages for cars measured under WLTP are set to be generally one percentage point fewer for 2021/22 than those for other cars. For zero emissions cars, whether registered before or on or after 6 April 2020, the appropriate percentage is set at 1%; this will revert to 2% for 2022/23 under pre-existing legislation at ITEPA 2003, s 140.

Section 11 inserts a new ITEPA 2003, s 254A, which provides, for 2020/21 onwards, an income tax exemption for apprenticeship bursaries paid to persons leaving local authority care. A similar exemption for Class 1 NIC is to be introduced by regulations. For payments made before the exemptions took effect, HMRC will use its collection and management discretion and will not seek to collect tax and NIC otherwise due. This exemption is to do with one-off £1,000 bursaries paid since 2018 by the Education and Skills Funding Agency to persons aged between 16 and 24 who leave local authority care to enter an apprenticeship.

Section 12 provides, for 2020/21 onwards, an income tax exemption for three new social security benefits payable by the Scottish Government.

Section 13 gives the Treasury power to henceforth exempt particular social security benefits from income tax by means of regulations. This will avoid the need for primary legislation each time a new benefit intended to be tax-exempt is introduced.

Section 14 inserts a new ITEPA 2003, s 299B, which provides that no liability to income tax arises on a payment to a person holding a voluntary office if the payment is in respect of reasonable expenses incurred in carrying out the duties of that office. This gives statutory footing for 2020/21 onwards to a long-standing HMRC practice. A corresponding exemption for Class 1 NIC has been introduced by regulations (SI 2020/320).

Loan charge

Section 15 is the first of seven sections that give effect to the Government's decision to implement changes to the loan charge provisions introduced by F(No 2)A 2017. This followed an independent review of the policy by Sir Amyas Morse. Whilst many will associate the loan charge with disguised remuneration from employment (F(No 2)A 2017, Sch 11), it should be borne in mind that a separate but similar charge applies in relation to disguised remuneration schemes used by the self-employed (F(No 2)A 2017, Sch 12). This group of sections applies in both these cases.

The loan charge originally applied to loans made on or after 6 April 1999. Section 15 removes loans made before 9 December 2010 from the scope of the charge. It also introduces **Schedule 2, Part 1**, which makes amendments consequential to this change.

Section 16 enables an irrevocable election to be made by the person chargeable to spread the charge over the three tax years 2018/19 to 2020/21 by splitting the chargeable amount into three equal parts. The election must be made before 1 October 2020. Section 16 also introduces **Schedule 2, Part 2**, which makes amendments consequential to this change.

Section 17 provides for a reduction in amounts treated as chargeable where a reasonable case could have been made that, for 2015/16 or any earlier year, a person was chargeable to tax on an amount referable to the loan or quasi-loan in question, reasonable disclosure of the loan had been made and HMRC did not take steps prior to 6 April 2019 to recover the tax. No reduction applies for 2015/16 and earlier years where a reasonable disclosure was not made, and for 2016/17 onwards irrespective of whether there has been reasonable disclosure or HMRC had taken steps to recover the tax.

Section 18 gives relief from late payment interest where the chargeable person files a 2018/19 tax return, including a complete and accurate self-assessment, before 1 October 2020. If before 1 October 2020 the person discharges their liability to income tax and capital gains tax (CGT) for 2018/19, or enters into an agreement with HMRC for the discharge of their liability, any amount paid (before 1 October 2020) in discharging that liability (other than a self-assessment payment on account) is to be taken as not carrying interest. There is also relief from interest on self-assessment payments on account for 2019/20 in this situation, but by the end of January 2021 the person must either have discharged their liability to income tax and CGT for 2019/20 or entered into an agreement with HMRC for its discharge.

Section 19 amends the date by which loan charge information must be provided to HMRC. The original legislation specified a date of 1 October 2019 but this is now revised to 1 October 2020.

Section 20 gives effect to the Government's agreement following the Morse review that HMRC should repay voluntary restitution, that has been made by individuals and employers under settlement agreements, if the loan was made before 9 December 2010 (see section 15) or if the loan was made before 6 April 2016 and circumstances similar to those in section 17 apply. The settlement agreement must have been made between 16 March 2016 and 11 March 2020 inclusive. The Commissioners for HMRC must establish a scheme under which they may, on an application made to them before 1 October 2021, repay or waive amounts paid under such settlement agreements.

Section 21 provides more detail of how the scheme mentioned in section 20 will operate, including how applications under the scheme are to be made and determined.

Pensions

Section 22 amends the tapered annual allowance provisions in FA 2004, s 228ZA. The point at which a high-income individual's adjusted income becomes high enough to cause the annual allowance to be tapered is increased from £150,000 to £240,000. The income threshold at which someone is classed as a high-income individual is increased from £110,000 to £200,000. The minimum tapered annual allowance is reduced from £10,000 to £4,000. These amendments have effect for 2020/21 onwards.

Chargeable gains

Section 23 introduces **Schedule 3**, which reduces the capital gains tax entrepreneurs' relief lifetime limit from £10 million to £1 million for disposals on or after 11 March 2020. Schedule 3 also provides against forestalling arrangements where either these are based on the rules determining date of disposal or there was a reorganisation of share capital or an exchange of shares or securities between 6 April 2019 and 10 March 2020 inclusive. It also renames entrepreneurs' relief, which is henceforth to bc known as business asset disposal relief.

Section 24 makes various changes to capital gains tax principal private residence relief, generally in relation to disposals on or after 6 April 2020. The final period of exemption is reduced from 18 months to 9 months; this does not affect those who are disabled or in a care home, for whom the final period of exemption remains at 36 months. Lettings relief is restricted to circumstances where the owner of the property is in shared-occupancy with a tenant. Two extra-statutory concessions, D21 and D49, are given statutory effect. Job related accommodation relief is extended to certain serving members of the armed forces who are required to live away from home. The rules on transfers of an interest in a dwelling between spouses or civil partners are clarified.

Section 25 introduces **Schedule 4**. Part 1 of the Schedule expands the corporate income loss restriction (introduced by F(No 2)A 2017, Sch 4 and amended by FA 2019, Sch 10) to now include carried-forward capital losses from previous accounting periods. A company will only be able to offset up to 50% of chargeable gains using carried-forward capital losses. The main provision is set out in a new CTA 2010, s 269ZBA. There is special provision for insolvent companies (new CTA 2010, s 269ZWA) and companies without a source of chargeable income (new CTA 2010, s 269ZYA).

Schedule 4, Part 2 provides that during a financial year where a company has more than one very short accounting period where the company is only within the charge to corporation tax because of chargeable gains, it can set off allowable losses against any chargeable gains accruing in the same financial year, even if this is effectively a carry back of the losses, and without any restriction under the corporate loss restriction regime. Part 2 also clarifies the rules relating to life insurance companies.

Schedule 4, Part 3 contains the commencement rules. It provides that Schedule 4 has effect for accounting periods beginning on or after 1 April 2020, with special rules for accounting periods straddling that date. There are anti-forestalling rules applying to arrangements made on or after 29 October 2018, the date of the original announcement of the expanded restriction.

Section 26 amends the Corporation Tax (Instalment Payments) Regulations 1998 (SI 1998/3175) in relation to accounting periods beginning on or after 11 March 2020. The payment by instalment rules are more stringent for 'very large' companies than for 'large' companies. This amendment provides that a company that is chargeable to corporation tax for an accounting period only because of a chargeable gain is treated as large rather than very large. HMRC previously applied this treatment informally.

Section 27 is concerned with the relief for loans to traders in TCGA 1992, s 253. With effect in relation to loans made on or after 24 January 2019, it abolishes the rule that a loan qualifies for relief only if the borrower is UK resident, thus complying with EU treaty rules.

Reliefs for business

Section 28 increases the research and development (R&D) expenditure credit available to companies from 12% to 13% of qualifying R&D expenditure. This has effect in relation to expenditure incurred on or after 1 April 2020.

Section 29 amends the structures and buildings allowance code in CAA 2001, Pt 2A (ss 270AA–270IH). It increases the annual rate of relief from 2% to 3% and reduces the writing-down period from 50 years to $33\frac{1}{3}$ years. The increase in the annual rate has effect on and after 1 April 2020 for corporation tax and 6 April 2020 for income tax, with chargeable periods straddling 1 or 6 April being split into two separate notional chargeable periods.

Section 30 introduces **Schedule 5**, which makes miscellaneous amendments to the operation of structures and buildings allowances (SBAs). Paragraph 2 of Schedule 5 deals with the interaction of SBAs and research and development capital allowances. Paragraph 3 covers SBAs due to a person who has contributed to another's expenditure ('contribution allowances'). The amendments made by these paragraphs apply broadly from 11 March 2020. Paragraphs 4–7 make minor amendments to ensure that various rules operate as intended, and these amendments are treated as always having had effect.

Section 31 runs to nine pages and amends the intangible fixed asset regime in CTA 2009, Pt 8 (ss 711–906). In particular it adds new Chapters 16A (ss 900A–900I) and 16B (ss 900J–900O) to Part 8. The amendments made by section 31 have effect in relation to accounting periods beginning on or after 1 July 2020, with an accounting period straddling that date being treated as two separate accounting periods for this purpose.

New Chapter 16A contains special rules affecting the debits to be brought into account by a company for tax purposes in respect of an intangible fixed asset that is a restricted asset. New sections 900B–900D set out three cases in which an intangible fixed asset is a restricted asset. Broadly, the special rules are intended to prevent transactions between related parties being used to obtain a tax advantage by bringing assets into Part 8 at market value. They apply in the specified circumstances to a company that acquires a pre-FA 2002 asset or a restricted asset from a related party; either directly or indirectly such as through a licence arrangement. The special rules limit the amount of debit relief available to the acquiring company by restricting the costs that can be recognised for the purposes of the relevant Chapters of Part 8.

New Chapter 16B provides a self-contained set of rules to deal with fungible assets, ie assets of a type that can be dealt in without identifying the particular assets involved. The pre-existing sections on fungible assets (CTA 2009, ss 858, 890 and 891) are accordingly repealed. Chapter 16B makes new provision for fungible assets to be treated as restricted assets in appropriate cases.

Miscellaneous measures affecting companies

Section 32 introduces **Schedule 6**, which makes amendments to the rules introduced by FA 2019 under which non-UK resident companies are chargeable to corporation tax (as opposed to income tax) in respect of UK property income on and after 6 April 2020. FA 2019, Sch 5 is to have effect as if the amendments now made had at all times been incorporated into the provision made by that Schedule. The amendments are described as minor amendments designed to ensure that the FA 2019 rules work as intended to ensure a smooth transition of the taxation of UK property profits from the income tax to the corporation tax regime.

In particular, Schedule 6 inserts a new CTA 2009, s 330ZA, under which companies will be able to bring into account in the first accounting period of their UK property business a net amount of loan relationship debits referable to the seven previous years. It also inserts a new CTA 2009, s 607ZA, which makes similar provision for derivative contract debits.

Section 33 makes amendments to CTA 2010, Pt 7A Ch 4 (ss 269D–269DO) which contains provision for, and in connection with, a surcharge on the profits of banking companies. It introduces an adjustment to surcharge profits. The adjustment denies relief against the surcharge for allowable losses transferred to a banking company from a non-banking company in the same group. This has effect in relation to an allowable loss, or any part of an allowable loss, deducted from a chargeable gain accruing on a disposal made on or after 11 March 2020.

Section 34 introduces **Schedule 7**, which makes provision for the deferral of payment of corporation tax arising in connection with certain transactions involving companies resident in a European Economic Area (EEA) State. Schedule 7 inserts a new TMA 1970, Sch 3ZC under which companies liable to pay corporation tax on certain transactions with an EEA resident can defer payment by entering into a CT payment plan with HMRC. Plans can be entered into in respect of transactions occurring in accounting periods ending on or after 10 October 2018.

Section 35 amends FA 2019, Sch 14 (leases: changes to accounting standards etc). The amendments are to the transitional rules applicable where a lessee treats a lease as a right-of-use asset under IFRS 16 and had not previously accounted for the lease as a finance lease. The amendments simply remove ambiguities and are treated as always having had effect.

Investments

Section 36 amends the EIS approved fund rules in ITA 2007, s 251 to focus investment on knowledge-intensive companies. The amendments also give approved funds a longer period over which to invest fund capital. They have effect on and after 6 April 2020 in relation to funds which, on or after that date, close for the acceptance of further investments.

Section 37 makes changes to income tax top slicing relief, which applies to gains from chargeable events on life policies etc and has effect in relation to chargeable event gains occurring on or after 11 March 2020. Firstly, the personal allowance to be included in the computation of tax payable on the annual equivalent is determined as if the chargeable event gain is limited to the annual equivalent. In practice, HMRC will apply this change to all gains arising in 2019/20 onwards. Secondly, in each of the computations made for the purpose of top slicing relief, deductible reliefs and allowances are to be set against the chargeable event gain or annual equivalent only to the extent that they cannot be set against other income.

Section 38 is concerned with share loss relief. In relation to disposals made on or after 24 January 2019, the requirement that the shares be in a company carrying on its business wholly or mainly in the UK is abolished, thus complying with EU treaty rules and widening the availability of relief.

PART 2   DIGITAL SERVICES TAX

Introduction

Section 39 introduces a new tax, to be known as digital services tax (DST), on UK digital services revenues arising to a person in an accounting period. The DST was first announced at Budget 2018. It is a new tax on the revenues of large digital businesses to ensure that the amount of tax paid in the UK is reflective of the value derived from UK users. It applies to groups providing social media platforms, internet search engines and online marketplaces. By virtue of section 61, DST has effect on and after 1 April 2020.

Digital services revenues, UK digital services revenues etc

Section 40 defines the digital services revenues of a group as being the total revenues arising to members of the group in connection with any digital services activity of any member of the group.

Section 41 defines a group's UK digital services revenues as being so much of its digital services revenues as are attributable to UK users. It sets out five cases in which revenues are attributable to UK users. Cases 1 to 3 are where the revenues are online marketplace revenues which arise in connection with: an online market-place transaction to which a UK user is a party; particular accommodation or land in the UK; or online advertising for particular services, goods etc where the advertising is paid for by a UK user. Case 4 is where the revenues are online advertising revenues, are not within any of Cases 1 to 3, and the advertising is viewed or otherwise consumed by UK users. Case 5 covers any other situation where the revenues arise in connection with UK users. As regards Cases 4 and 5 the revenues, where they relate to both UK users and others, are to be allocated to UK users to such extent as is just and reasonable.

Section 42 supplements section 41 by setting out when online marketplace revenues arise in connection with accommodation or land.

Section 43 defines 'digital services activity' for the purposes of this Part (see, for example, section 40) as a social media service, an internet search engine or an online marketplace. The section also defines each of these expressions.

Section 44 qualifies the meaning of 'user', and defines 'UK user' for the purposes of this Part (see, for example, section 41) as any user who, in the case of an individual, is normally in the UK and, in any other case, is established in the UK.

Section 45 excludes an online financial marketplace (as defined) from being an online marketplace for these purposes.

Charge to tax

Section 46 sets out threshold conditions that must be met before a group is subject to DST. The total digital services revenues arising to members of the group in an accounting period must exceed £500 million, and total UK digital services revenues arising to group members in that period must exceed £25 million. Both figures are proportionately reduced if an accounting period is less than a year.

Section 47 provides that, where the threshold conditions are met for an accounting period, each member of the group is liable to DST in respect of UK digital services revenues arising in the accounting period. It sets out the steps to be taken in order to calculate the DST liability for each member of the group. Step 1 is to take the total UK digital services revenues of the group; Step 2 is to deduct a £25 million allowance from that total; Step 3 is to take 2% of what is left, which gives the 'group amount'. The group member's liability to DST is the appropriate proportion of the group amount, meaning such proportion of the total UK digital services revenues arising to members of the group in the accounting period as is attributable to that member.

Section 48 provides an alternative basis of charge. This is intended to be of value where activity in a particular category has a very low or negative UK operating margin. The group must elect in its DST return for an accounting period to use the alternative basis for that period. The election must be made for a specific category or categories of revenue, the categories of revenue being those from social media, an internet search engine and online marketplaces. Section 48 sets out the steps to be taken in order to calculate the DST liability for each member of the group where an election has been made.

Section 49 supplements section 48 by providing a definition of 'relevant operating expenses' of a group in relation to a specified category of revenues. The amount of the relevant operating expenses is used in calculating the operating margin for the purposes of section 48.

Section 50 gives relief for relevant cross-border transactions. The relief is dependent on a claim for relief being included in the group's DST return for an accounting period. A relevant cross-border transaction is an online marketplace transaction where: the online marketplace is provided by a member of the group; a foreign user is a party to the transaction; and all or part of any revenues arising to a group member in connection with the transaction are subject to a charge under the law of the foreign user's country which is comparable to DST.

Section 51 provides that DST in respect of an accounting period is due and payable nine months and one day after the end of that accounting period.

Duty to submit returns etc

Section 52 provides that 'the responsible member' of a group for the purposes of the DST legislation is the parent of the group or a corporate group member nominated by the parent. The responsible member will generally be the point of contact between HMRC and the group, and will have various obligations regarding DST including the making of returns. Section 52 sets out the conditions under which a company may be nominated and for the continued validity of the nomination.

Section 53 provides for the continuity of obligations and liabilities where there is a change in the responsible member of the group.

Section 54 imposes a duty to notify HMRC when the threshold conditions (see section 46) are met. This applies to the first accounting period of a group in respect of which the threshold conditions are met or are once more met. The notification must be made by the responsible member within 90 days after the end of the accounting period.

Section 55 imposes a duty to notify HMRC when there is any change in information provided to it by virtue of section 54. The notification must be made by the responsible member within the 90 days beginning with the date of change.

Section 56 imposes a duty to file DST returns. Where the threshold conditions are met for an accounting period, a return must be filed for that and each subsequent accounting period. However, HMRC may, on the application of the responsible member and if it is satisfied that the threshold conditions are no longer met, direct that the duty to deliver DST returns no longer applies. The duty to file is restored if and when the threshold conditions are once more met.

Section 56 also introduces **Schedule 8**, which runs to 60 paragraphs and contains provision about returns, enquiries, assessments etc. A DST return for an accounting period must be filed within one year after the end of the accounting period, and must include a self-assessment of the amount of tax payable by the group (including a breakdown showing the amount payable by each member). It may be amended by the responsible person within twelve months after the statutory filing date. Other matters covered by Schedule 8 include: a duty to keep and preserve records (paras 4 and 5); provision regarding enquiries into returns (paras 6–15); HMRC determinations of tax payable where no return delivered (paras 16–18); discovery assessments (paras 19–23); claims for repayment of overpaid tax (paras 24–32); appeals against HMRC decisions (paras 33–51); and penalties (paras 52–60). The penalties comprise late filing penalties (both flat-rate and tax-related), with a reasonable excuse defence, and a penalty for failure to keep and preserve records.

Groups, parents and members

Section 57 defines a group as being a relevant entity (see section 58) and its subsidiaries (if any).

Section 58 defines a relevant entity for the purposes of section 57 as a company or as any entity the shares or other interests in which are listed on a recognised stock exchange and are 'sufficiently widely held' (as defined).

Section 59 applies for the purpose of determining whether a group at any time is the same group as a group at any earlier time.

Section 60 provides a rule for where two or more entities would be the parent of a group and are stapled to each other.

Accounting periods, accounts etc

Section 61 effectively provides the commencement rules for DST. It provides that a group's first accounting period for DST purposes begins on 1 April 2020 and ends on the first subsequent accounting date of the group or, if earlier, on 31 March 2021. In the case of a group formed after 1 April 2020, its first accounting period for DST purposes begins on the date on which it is formed and ends on its first accounting date or, if earlier, one year after it begins.

Section 62 provides for time apportionment of revenues and expenses in cases where a group's actual period of account does not coincide with a DST accounting period.

Section 63 interprets 'revenues arising to members of a group in a period' and 'expenses of members of a group recognised in a period'. For any period of account of the group for which its accounts are produced in accordance with the applicable accounting standards (see section 63), these expressions refer to revenues (however described) and expenses recognised in the income statement (or in profit and loss) for that period (or which would have been so recognised if no consolidation exemption applied). In other cases, International Accounting Standards are applied.

Section 64 gives the meaning of 'applicable accounting standards' used in section 63, and does so by reference to generally accepted accounting practice.

Supplementary

Section 65 provides that any tax advantage that would otherwise arise from relevant avoidance arrangements (as defined) is to be counteracted by the making of such adjustments as are just and reasonable. The adjustments (whether or not made by HMRC) can be made by way of an assessment, the modification of an assessment, amendment or disallowance of a claim, or otherwise.

Section 66 applies where any DST liability (including any liability to a DST penalty) relating to a group for an accounting period is unpaid at the end of three months after the relevant date. The relevant date is generally that on which the tax becomes due and payable, but varies depending on such matters as whether the DST return is delivered after the filing date, whether an enquiry is opened, whether HMRC makes an assessment or a determination, and whether an appeal is made. If the DST liability arose because of a penalty, the relevant date is the date on which the notice of the penalty is issued. A designated HMRC officer may give a notice (a 'payment notice') to any member, requiring that member, within 30 days of the giving of the notice, to pay all unpaid DST liabilities relating to the group for the accounting period. A payment notice cannot be given more than three years and six months after the relevant date.

Section 66 also introduces **Schedule 9**, which makes further provision about payment notices. It provides, in particular, that the recipient of a payment notice can appeal against the notice, within 30 days of its being given, on the ground that the recipient was not a member of the group in the accounting period concerned. Where an appeal is made, anything required by the notice to be paid is due and payable as if there had been no appeal. If the recipient pays any amount in pursuance of the notice, the recipient may recover that amount from the person liable to pay it.

Section 67 provides that DST carries late payment interest from the date the tax becomes due and payable until payment is made.

Section 68 provides for repayment interest to be paid by HMRC on overpaid DST. It also provides for the recovery by HMRC of overpaid repayment interest.

Section 69 provides that a DST liability is recoverable as a debt due to the Crown.

Section 70 introduces **Schedule 10**, which makes minor and consequential amendments pursuant to this Part. In particular, it provides that the penalty provisions of FA 2007, Sch 24 (inaccuracies in returns) and FA 2008, Sch 41 (failure to notify chargeability), as well as the information and inspection powers in FA 2008, Sch 36, apply to DST.

Section 71 requires the Treasury to conduct in due course a review of DST, prepare a report of that review, and present it to Parliament. This must be completed before 1 January 2026.

General

Section 72 is a signpost to the definitions of various expressions used in this Part.

PART 3   OTHER TAXES

Inheritance tax

Section 73 provides that additions of property by individuals domiciled in the UK to trusts made when they were non-UK domiciled cannot be excluded property and are therefore within the scope of inheritance tax. In relation to any chargeable transfer made on or after the date of Royal Assent to this Act, the amendments made by this section are treated as always having been in force.

Section 74 introduces new tests to determine whether property transferred between trusts is excluded property; this will now depend on the current domicile of the settlor (or other person) that caused the property to move to the other trust. In relation to any chargeable transfer made on or after the date of Royal Assent, the amendments made by this section are treated as always having been in force.

Section 75 provides that one-off compensation payments of €2,500 made, from the Kindertransport Fund established by the Federal Republic of Germany, to survivors of the Kindertransport will not be subject to inheritance tax. It has effect in relation to deaths occurring on or after 1 January 2019, which is when the Fund opened.

Stamp duty land tax

Section 76 enables individuals to obtain a repayment of the higher rates of stamp duty land tax (SDLT) for additional dwellings where exceptional unforeseen circumstances, including (but not limited to) exceptional circumstances related to the coronavirus pandemic, have resulted in the sale of their previous main residence taking place outside of the statutory three-year period allowed. An application to HMRC to extend the permitted period must be made within twelve months after the sale. This has effect where the purchase of the new main residence occurs on or after 1 January 2017 and the disposal of the previous main residence occurs on or after 1 January 2020.

Stamp duty and stamp duty reserve tax

Section 77 extends the stamp duty market value rule to the transfer of unlisted securities to connected companies for consideration. This has effect in relation to instruments executed on or after the date of Royal Assent to this Act. The market value rule was introduced by FA 2019, s 47.

Section 78 performs a similar function to section 77 but in relation to the stamp duty reserve tax (SDRT) market value rule introduced by FA 2019, s 48. It broadly has effect in relation to agreements to transfer made on or after Royal Assent date.

Section 79 amends FA 1986, s 77A, which qualifies the relief available under FA 1986, s 77 on instruments transferring shares in one company (the target company) to another company (the acquiring company) where the acquiring company issues shares as consideration for the transfer to all the shareholders of the target company. Section 79 provides that an arrangement for a change of control of an acquiring company will not prevent the relief from applying where certain conditions are met. This has effect in relation to instruments executed on or after the date of Royal Assent.

Value added tax

Section 80 runs to six pages and makes the changes to UK law required by Council Directive (EU) 2018/1910 to simplify the VAT treatment of call-off stock moved from the UK to another member State or vice versa. It inserts a new Schedule 4B into VATA 1994, which applies where stock is moved on or after 1 January 2020. During the Brexit Implementation Period the UK is still obliged under EU law to implement the Directive. The position after Implementation Period completion day, expected to be 31 December 2020, will be determined by the outcome of negotiations on UK's future economic partnership with the EU.

Call-off stock refers to goods removed by a supplier from an origin State to a destination State where, at the time of removal, the supplier knows the identity of the customer to whom these goods will be supplied ('called-off') after they have arrived in the destination State. Before section 80 took effect, this gave rise to a deemed supply and acquisition of the goods by the supplier (in the destination State), followed by a 'domestic' supply to the customer which required the supplier to register for VAT in the destination State. To avoid this, the new rules provide that, subject to conditions, the supply and acquisition is delayed until the goods are called-off. The new rules should not ordinarily alter the total amount of VAT collected, but they delay the time when the VAT must be brought into account on the transaction as well as removing the need for the supplier to register in the destination State. They do require additional records to be kept and for additional reporting requirements on the part of the supplier. There is no obligation on suppliers to structure transactions so as to meet the conditions. If they do not, pre-existing rules will apply.

Alcohol liquor duties

Section 81 amends the Alcoholic Liquor Duties Act 1979 to introduce sanctions for post-excise duty point dilution of wine or made-wine which, if carried out before the duty point, would have resulted in a higher amount of duty being payable. It has effect in relation to any addition of water or other substance to the wine or made-wine on or after 1 April 2020.

Tobacco products duty

Section 82 increases the rates of excise duty on tobacco products. The changes are treated as having come into force at 6pm on 11 March 2020.

Vehicle taxes

Section 83 makes changes to certain rates of vehicle excise duty (VED) with effect in relation to licences taken out on or after 1 April 2020. It affects vehicles first registered before 1 March 2001, light passenger vehicles, light goods vehicles and motorcycles

Section 84 makes amendments to Vehicle Excise and Registration Act 1994, Sch 1 (annual rates of duty) to facilitate implementation of the worldwide harmonised light vehicles test procedure (WLTP), which is the new regime for calculating a car's CO_2 emissions. It has effect in relation to licences taken out on or after 1 April 2020.

Section 85 exempts all registered zero-emission light passenger vehicles registered on or after 1 April 2017 from the vehicle excise duty (VED) supplement for light passenger vehicles with a list price exceeding £40,000. This has effect on and after 1 April 2020 but not so as to affect licenses in force immediately before that date.

Section 86 provides for new motorhomes which are type approved M1SA to be taxed in the Private/Light Goods or Private HGV VED class from 12 March 2020. Motorhome manufacturers and dealers will no longer need to provide a CO_2 emissions figure when they register such a vehicle.

Section 87 exempts purpose-built vehicles used by medical courier charities, commonly referred to as blood bikes, from vehicle excise duty (VED). This has effect on and after 1 April 2020.

Section 88 suspends the collection of the heavy goods vehicle (HGV) road user levy for the twelve months beginning 1 August 2020. This is to support the haulage sector as it recovers from the impact of the coronavirus pandemic. Non-UK hauliers are entitled to a rebate for levy already paid in respect of any part of the twelve-month exemption period. No equivalent provision is required for UK hauliers, who will benefit from the full twelve months suspension when they renew their VED licence.

Hydrocarbon oil duties

Section 89 introduces **Schedule 11.** The Schedule amends Hydrocarbon Oil Duties Act 1979 so as to make provision about the use of rebated fuel in private pleasure craft. It comes into force on such day or days as are appointed by the Treasury via regulations. The new legislation is in response to a Court of Justice of the European Union (CJEU) judgment that it is contrary to the Fuel Marker Directive for the UK to allow red diesel to propel private pleasure craft, even though the user of the fuel pays their supplier the duty differential between the rates for red diesel and white diesel on the amount used to propel their craft.

Air passenger duty

Section 90 increases the rates of air passenger duty for flights to Band B destinations in relation to the carriage of passengers beginning on or after 1 April 2021. Rates for flights to Band A destinations are unchanged. Band A includes destinations whose capital is up to 2,000 miles from London, and Band B includes all other destinations.

Gaming duty

Section 91 increases, in line with inflation, the gross gaming yield bands for gaming duty for accounting periods beginning on or after 1 April 2020.

Environmental taxes

Section 92 amends the main rates of the rates of climate change levy (CCL) and the rates for reduced-rate supplies with effect in relation to supplies of fuels treated as taking place on or after 1 April 2020. It also amends, with similar effect, the formula used to calculate the reduced rate of CCL paid by businesses that participate in the Climate Change Agreement scheme.

Section 93 performs the same functions as section 92 but with effect in relation to supplies of fuels treated as taking place on or after 1 April 2021.

Section 94 increases, in line with inflation, the standard and reduced rates of landfill tax with effect in relation to disposals made (or treated as made) on or after 1 April 2020.

Section 95 introduces **Schedule 12**, which amends FA 2019, Pt 3 (ss 69–79) to make further provision about carbon emissions tax (which is not yet in force). If the Government decides to use the tax as its carbon pricing policy after the Brexit Implementation Period, the tax would be commenced on 1 January 2021. The amendments made by Schedule 12 include updating references to other legislation that has been amended since FA 2019 received Royal Assent, and adding provisions relating to penalties. In line with the Withdrawal Agreement, the UK will remain in the EU Emissions Trading System (ETS) until Implementation Period completion date, expected to be 31 December 2020. As set out in the UK's Approach to Negotiations, the UK would be open to considering a link between any future UK Emissions Trading System (ETS) and the EU ETS if it suited both sides' interests. In the event that no link is agreed, the UK will introduce an alternative carbon pricing policy. The Government is therefore preparing both a standalone emissions trading system and a carbon emissions tax. An amendment is made to FA 2009, Sch 56, para 1, from a date to be appointed, so as to add carbon emissions tax to the list of taxes on which late payment penalties can be charged.

Section 96 gives the Treasury the power to make regulations which provide for the allocation of emissions allowances in return for payment under any future UK Emissions Trading System (see section 95), and sets out what those regulations may contain.

Import duty

Section 97 will enable the Government to make regulations to vary the rate of import duty on goods when a dispute or other issue has arisen between the UK and the country from which the goods originate. The rate will be varied only after the UK Government has had regard to its international obligations and considers it appropriate to do so. Previously the rate could be varied only if the UK was authorised to do so under international law. The change has effect from the date of Royal Assent to this Act.

PART 4   MISCELLANEOUS AND FINAL

Insolvency

Section 98 amends the preferential debts provisions of Insolvency Act 1986 and corresponding legislation covering Scotland and Northern Ireland. It gives HMRC priority in the recovery in insolvency proceedings of certain taxes owed by companies and other businesses. It does so by making HMRC a secondary preferential creditor in relation to any such tax. Section 98 applies only to taxes collected and held by businesses in relation to other taxpayers. Examples are VAT, income tax under PAYE, employee national insurance contributions, construction industry scheme deductions, and student loan deductions. It has effect for insolvency proceedings beginning on or after 1 December 2020.

Section 99 is linked to section 98, and they are intended to operate together. Section 99 gives the Treasury power to make regulations: specifying the taxes to be included in the ambit of section 99; and providing that only amounts referable to such period as is specified in the regulations can be classed as secondary preferential debts.

Joint and several liability

Section 100 introduces **Schedule 13**. Together, they enable HMRC to issue a notice (a 'joint liability notice') to individual directors or shadow directors of a company, or to individual participators in a company, making them jointly and severally liable for the company's tax liabilities or penalties. Such a notice is not restricted to corporation tax but can apply to any tax or penalty payable by the company to HMRC, including liabilities under a contract settlement. The provisions apply also to limited liability partnerships (LLPs), with references to a director, shadow director or participator being read as references to members or shadow members of the LLP. The provisions apply to tax liabilities for periods ending on or after the date of Royal Assent to Finance Act 2020 and to other tax liabilities (ie those not related to a period) arising from an event or default occurring on or after that date.

HMRC can issue a joint liability notice only when the liability arises, or is expected to arise, from tax avoidance, tax evasion, repeated insolvency or non-payment, or a penalty for facilitating avoidance or evasion; and where the company begins insolvency proceedings, or is expected to do so, so that some or all of that liability will be lost to HMRC. An individual will have a right of appeal against a joint liability notice. Where the company has appealed against the liability in question, the individual is entitled to be a party to the proceedings, and may continue the appeal if the company is unable or unwilling to do so.

General anti-abuse rule

Section 101 introduces **Schedule 14**, which makes procedural and technical amendments to the general anti-abuse rule (GAAR) with effect from the date of Royal Assent to this Act. The primary change is the repeal of FA 2013, ss 209A–209F (provisional counteraction notices) and their replacement with new FA 2013, ss 209AA–209AC (protective GAAR notices), which provide for what is intended to be a procedurally simpler system. Provisional counteraction notices issued before the date of Royal Assent are not affected. Schedule 14 also introduces some minor procedural and technical amendments to the legislation to remove ambiguity and to ensure that where HMRC decides not to pursue the GAAR, enquiries can still be pursued using technical non-GAAR arguments.

Compensation schemes etc

Section 102 introduces **Schedule 15**, which provides an exemption from income tax for payments made under or otherwise referable to the Windrush Compensation Scheme and payments under the Troubles Permanent Disablement Payment Scheme. In each case, the exemption is effective from the date of launch of the scheme.

Administration

Section 103 puts beyond doubt that functions given to an officer of HMRC may be carried out by HMRC using automated processes or other means. It follows a number of judicial challenges to HMRC's ability to automate certain functions, for example the giving of notice to file a tax return, the opening of an enquiry and the imposition of a penalty. It is treated as always having been in force, but not so as to interfere with any court or tribunal decision made before 11 March 2020.

Section 104 is an anti-avoidance measure enabling HMRC to deal as necessary with returns where a limited liability partnership (LLP) has delivered a return on the basis that it carried on business with a view to profit but did not, in fact, do so. The measure is treated as always having had effect, but does not apply to any return where, before 11 March 2020, a court or tribunal decided in the LLP's favour on the point.

Section 105 gives the Treasury power to specify liabilities that will not accrue late payment interest if payment is deferred. Examples of its use during the 2020 coronavirus pandemic are in relation to the deferral of the second self-assessment payment on account for 2019/20 otherwise due on 31 July 2020 and the deferral of VAT payments between 20 March 2020 and 30 June 2020.

Coronavirus

Section 106 defines 'coronavirus support payment' as a payment made (whether before or after the passing of Finance Act 2020) under any of a number of specified schemes. These include the coronavirus job retention scheme (CJRS), the self-employment income support scheme (SEISS), the coronavirus statutory sick pay rebate scheme and coronavirus business support grant schemes such as the small business grant fund (SBGF). Section 106 then introduces Schedule 16, which provides for the taxation of coronavirus support payments.

Schedule 16, para 1 confirms that coronavirus support payments made to businesses, individual partners of firms and employers are within the scope of tax as income and must be brought into account as revenue receipts in calculating the profits of the business for income tax or corporation tax purposes. Para 2 provides that a payment that relates to a business that has ceased will be taxed as a post-cessation receipt. If this is not possible, because the business is not a trade, profession or property business, the business to which the payment relates will be treated as if it is being carried on by the recipient at the time of receipt. Para 3 makes provisions further to paras 1 and 2. Para 4 deals with the interaction between coronavirus support payments and certain pre-existing exemptions, reliefs and deductions.

Schedule 16, para 5 provides for income tax to be charged on coronavirus support payment under an employment-related scheme where the employment costs are deductible for tax purposes by another person. Para 6 provides for tax to be charged on a coronavirus support payment, other than a payment made under an employment-related scheme or the SEISS, if at the time the coronavirus support payment was received, the recipient did not carry on a business whose profits are charged to tax and to which the payment could be referable. The CJRS and the coronavirus statutory sick pay rebate scheme are employment-related schemes.

Schedule 16, para 7 gives the Treasury regulation-making powers to modify tax legislation that may affect the application of paras 1, 2, 5 and 6 above.

Schedule 16, para 8 imposes a charge to income tax on a recipient of a coronavirus support payment, other than under a coronavirus business support grant scheme or the coronavirus statutory sick pay rebate scheme, who was not entitled to the payment in accordance with the scheme under which it was made. An example would be where a CJRS payment was not used for the purposes for which it was made. Para 9 provides for the making of assessments of tax chargeable under para 8. Para 10 provides for the tax due under para 8 to be included at Step 7 of ITA 2007, s 23 (calculation of income tax liability). Para 11 deals with the situation where the person chargeable under para 8 is a company within the charge to corporation tax. Para 12 imposes a duty to notify chargeability by virtue of para 8, and paras 13 and 14 impose penalties for failure to notify chargeability. Para 15 provides for certain officers of an insolvent company to be jointly and severally liable for the company's tax liabilities arising from a deliberate act to claim or retain amounts of coronavirus support payments to which the company was not entitled.

Section 107 gives relief from disqualifying events under ITEPA 2003, s 535 in relation to enterprise management incentive (EMI) share options. It seeks to ensure that a disqualifying event does not occur purely as a result of an individual taking leave, being furloughed or working reduced hours because of the coronavirus pandemic. It has effect in relation to the period 19 March 2020 to 5 April 2021 inclusive.

Section 108 provides that retired individuals can be re-employed by their former employer (or a connected employer) without losing the benefit of a protected pension age. This is to encourage certain retired members of public service pension schemes, such as police, fire fighters and other uniformed service personnel, to rejoin the workforce to aid in the coronavirus pandemic. Re-employment must commence during the period 1 March 2020 to 1 November 2020 inclusive.

Section 109 makes modifications to the statutory residence test in connection with the coronavirus pandemic. It has effect for the purposes of determining whether an individual was UK resident for 2019/20 and, if an individual was not UK resident for 2019/20, whether that individual is UK resident for 2020/21. It provides relaxations to the various tests where days were spent in the UK within the period 1 March 2020 to 1 June 2020 inclusive on certain activities related to the detection, treatment or prevention of coronavirus disease.

Section 110 prevents relief under the enterprise investment scheme (EIS) or the seed enterprise investment scheme (SEIS) from being reduced or withdrawn in a case where, on or after 20 May 2020, an EIS or SEIS shareholder enters into a convertible loan agreement under the Future Fund with a company and subsequently receives value from the company under the agreement. The Future Fund was set up as part of the Government's support to companies impacted by the coronavirus pandemic.

Preparing for new tax

Section 111 gives the Commissioners for HMRC the power to make preparations for the introduction of a new tax to be charged in respect of certain plastic packaging. The Government aims to introduce the tax in Finance Act 2021.

Local loans

Section 112 increases the statutory lending limit on the issuance of local loans through the Public Work Loans Board (PWLB). It comes into force on a day to be appointed by the Treasury via regulations.

Other

Section 113 gives the meaning of abbreviations for a number of Acts referred to in this Finance Act.

Section 114 provides for this Act to be cited as the Finance Act 2020.

FINANCE ACT 2020

2020 Chapter 14

ARRANGEMENT OF SECTIONS

PART 1—INCOME TAX, CORPORATION TAX AND CAPITAL GAINS TAX

Income tax charge, rates etc

PART 4—MISCELLANEOUS AND FINAL

SCHEDULES

An Act To Grant certain duties, to alter other duties, and to amend the law relating to the national debt and the public revenue, and to make further provision in connection with finance.

[22 July 2020]

PART 1
INCOME TAX, CORPORATION TAX AND CAPITAL GAINS TAX
Income tax charge, rates etc

1   Income tax charge for tax year 2020–21

Income tax is charged for the tax year 2020–21.

COMMENTARY ON SECTION 1

Section 1 imposes the charge to income tax for 2020/21. Income tax is an annual tax, and the charge must be renewed by statute each year (ITA 2007, s 4).

---

2   Main rates of income tax for tax year 2020–21

For the tax year 2020–21 the main rates of income tax are as follows—

    (a)   the basic rate is 20%,
    (b)   the higher rate is 40%, and
    (c)   the additional rate is 45%.

COMMENTARY ON SECTION 2

Section 2 sets out the main rates at which income tax is charged for 2020/21. These are unchanged from 2019/20, so the basic rate is 20%, the higher rate is 40% and the additional rate is 45% (ITA 2007, s 6(1), (2)).

The main rates apply to an individual who is resident in the UK and is not subject to the Scottish rates of income tax or the Welsh rates of income tax (ITA 2007, ss 6(3), 11A, 11B). The main rates apply to all of the individual's taxable income apart from savings income and dividend income, each of which have their own rates (see ITA 2007, ss 7, 7A, 8 and the commentary under sections 3 and 4 below).

The Scottish rates of income tax for 2020/21 also remain the same as in 2019/20, so the starter rate is 19%, the basic rate is 20%, the intermediate rate is 21%, the higher rate is 41% and the top rate is 46%. The rates are set via a resolution in the Scottish Parliament and apply to Scottish taxpayers, as defined under Scotland Act 1998, ss 80D–80F.

The Welsh rates of income tax for 2020/21 remain the same as the UK rates, ie the basic rate is 20%, the higher rate is 40% and the additional rate is 45%. Unlike in Scotland, where the Scottish Parliament has the power to set and create income tax bands as well as rates, the Welsh Parliament only has limited powers to set its own basic rate, higher rate and additional rate. The rates are set via a resolution in the Welsh Parliament and apply to Welsh taxpayers, as defined under Government of Wales Act 2006, ss 116E–116H.

---

3   Default and savings rates of income tax for tax year 2020–21

(1)   For the tax year 2020–21 the default rates of income tax are as follows—

    (a)   the default basic rate is 20%,
    (b)   the default higher rate is 40%, and
    (c)   the default additional rate is 45%.

(2)   For the tax year 2020–21 the savings rates of income tax are as follows—

    (a)   the savings basic rate is 20%,
    (b)   the savings higher rate is 40%, and
    (c)   the savings additional rate is 45%.

COMMENTARY ON SECTION 3

Section 3(1) provides that for 2020/21 the default basic rate is 20%, the default higher rate is 40%, and the default additional rate is 45% (ITA 2007, s 6C). This means that the default rates for 2020/21 are the same as the main rates of income tax.

The default rates of income tax apply to the non-savings and non-dividend income of taxpayers who are not subject to either the UK main rates of income tax, the Scottish rates of income tax or the Welsh rates of income tax (ITA 2007, s 11C). These include trustees (other than where the trust rates in ITA 2007, s 9 apply) and non-UK resident individuals.

Section 3(2) provides that for 2020/21 the savings basic rate is 20%, the savings higher rate is 40%, and the savings additional rate is 45% (ITA 2007, s 7A).

The savings rates are charged on the savings income of any individual liable to UK income tax, including Scottish and Welsh taxpayers and non-UK resident individuals (ITA 2007, s 11D). Savings income is defined in ITA 2007, s 18. Generally speaking, savings income is treated as the highest part of an individual's total income apart from dividend income, subject to the ordering rules in ITA 2007, s 1012 (ITA 2007, s 16).

The savings rates have effect only after the starting rate for savings and the savings nil rate have been applied (ITA 2007, ss 12, 12A).

4   Starting rate limit for savings for tax year 2020–21

Section 21 of ITA 2007 (indexation) does not apply in relation to the starting rate limit for savings for the tax year 2020–21 (so that the starting rate limit for savings remains at £5,000 for that tax year).

COMMENTARY ON SECTION 4

Section 4 disapplies the indexation uplift in ITA 2007, s 21 from the starting rate limit for savings. It sets the starting rate limit for 2020/21 at £5,000, the same as for 2019/20 (ITA 2007, s 12). The starting rate for savings remains 0% in 2020/21 and applies before considering the savings nil rate (ITA 2007, ss 7, 12A).

Corporation tax charge and rates

5   Main rate of corporation tax for financial year 2020

(1)   For the financial year 2020 the main rate of corporation tax is 19%.

(2)   Accordingly, omit section 7(2) of F(No.2)A 2015 (which is superseded by the provision made by subsection (1)).

COMMENTARY ON SECTION 5

The corporation tax rate is set at 19% for FY 2020 (ie the year to 31 March 2021).

6   Corporation tax: charge and main rate for financial year 2021

(1)   Corporation tax is charged for the financial year 2021.

(2)   The main rate of corporation tax for that year is 19%.

COMMENTARY ON SECTION 6

The corporation tax rate is set at 19% for FY 2021 (ie the year to 31 March 2022).

These rates have been known for some time but they still represent something of a reversal from previous announcements. The Summer Budget of 2015 included announcements that the rate of corporation tax would be 19% for the years starting 1 April 2017, 2018 and 2019, then reduce to 18% for the year from 1 April 2020 and to 17% from 1 April 2021. FA 2016 then reduced the 2020/21 rate to 17%, before the Prime Minister's announcement in November 2019 that the rate from 1 April 2020 onwards would remain at 19%.

The retention of the 19% rate for FY 2020 and FY 2021 did not come as a surprise to many observers. Indeed, since the onset of the coronavirus emergency a few days after the 2020 Budget speech, it would not be much of a surprise if corporation tax rates rose sharply from April 2021 and, possibly, even from April 2020. While this would involve some degree of retrospection, this is not unprecedented, as FA 1991 made a retrospective change to the corporation tax rates for FY 1990.

Employment income and social security income

7   Workers' services provided through intermediaries

Schedule 1 makes provision about workers' services provided through intermediaries.

COMMENTARY ON SECTION 7, SCHEDULE 1
[See Commentary note for Schedule 1]

8   Determining the appropriate percentage for a car: tax year 2020–21 onwards

(1)   Chapter 6 of Part 3 of ITEPA 2003 (taxable benefits: cars etc) is amended as follows.

(2)   In section 136 (car with a CO_2 emissions figure: post-September 1999 registration)—

    (a)   in subsection (2A)—

        (i)   after "figure" insert "in a case where the car is first registered before 6 April 2020",

        (ii)   for "light-duty" substitute "light", and

        (iii)   for "an EC certificate of conformity" substitute "the EC certificate of conformity or UK approval certificate", and

    (b)   after subsection (2A) insert—

"(2B)   For the purpose of determining the car's CO_2 emissions figure in a case where the car is first registered on or after 6 April 2020, ignore any values specified in the EC certificate of conformity or UK approval certificate that are not WLTP (worldwide harmonised light vehicle test procedures) values."

(3)   In section 137 (car with a CO_2 emissions figure: bi-fuel cars)—

    (a)   in subsection (2A)—

        (i)   after "figure" insert "in a case where the car is first registered before 6 April 2020",

        (ii)   for "light-duty" substitute "light", and

        (iii)   for "an EC certificate of conformity" substitute "the EC certificate of conformity or UK approval certificate", and

    (b)   after subsection (2A) insert—

"(2B)   For the purpose of determining the car's CO_2 emissions figure in a case where the car is first registered on or after 6 April 2020, ignore any values specified in the EC certificate of conformity or UK approval certificate that are not WLTP (worldwide harmonised light vehicle test procedures) values."

(4)   In section 139 (car with a CO_2 emissions figure)—

    (a)   for subsection (2) substitute—

"(2)   For the purposes of subsection (1) and the table—

    (a)   if a CO_2 emissions figure is not a whole number, round it down to the nearest whole number, and

    (b)   if an electric range figure is not a whole number, round it up to the nearest whole number.", and

    (b)   after subsection (5) insert—

"(5A)   For the purpose of determining the electric range figure for a car first registered before 6 April 2020, ignore any WLTP (worldwide harmonised light vehicle test procedures) values specified in an EC certificate of conformity, an EC type-approval certificate or a UK approval certificate.

(5B)   For the purpose of determining the electric range figure for a car first registered on or after 6 April 2020, ignore any values specified in an EC certificate of conformity, an EC type-approval certificate or a UK approval certificate that are not WLTP (worldwide harmonised light vehicle test procedures) values."

(5)   The amendments made by this section have effect for the tax year 2020–21 and subsequent tax years.

COMMENTARY ON SECTION 8

Sections 8 to 10 fix the 'appropriate percentage' used in determining, under ITEPA 2003, s 121, the cash equivalent of the benefit of a company car.

Budget 2018 announced a review of the impact of the worldwide harmonised light vehicles test procedure (WLTP) on vehicle excise duty and 'company car tax' (CCT). Noting that WLTP aims to provide 'a closer representation of "real-world" fuel consumption and CO2 emissions' than the previous New European Driving Cycle (NEDC), the Government said it sought to strike a balance between protecting consumers and meeting climate change commitments. Reported emissions were generally expected to be higher under WLTP.

Following the review, HM Treasury observed in July 2019 that the introduction of WLTP emissions values in 2017 had provided an opportunity to 'strengthen the link between the vehicle tax system and the true environmental impact of car purchasing decisions'.

The Treasury announced (see https://tinyurl.com/yybdzvno) that, for cars first registered from 6 April 2020, most 'CCT rates' (ie appropriate percentages) would be reduced by 2 percentage points in 2020/21 in order to smooth the transition to WLTP, before returning to planned rates over the following two years – increasing by 1 percentage point in 2021/22 and by a further 1 percentage point in 2022/23. To accelerate a shift to zero emission cars, all zero emission models would attract a reduced appropriate percentage of 0% in 2020/21 and 1% in 2021/22, before returning to the planned 2% rate in 2022/23.

Section 8 amends ITEPA 2003, ss 136, 137 and 139 for 2020/21 onwards. Subsection (2) amends ITEPA 2003, s 136 so that WLTP values are used for cars first registered on or after 6 April 2020, while NEDC values continue to be used for cars first registered before that date. Subsection (3) makes similar amendments to ITEPA 2003, s 137 for bi-fuel cars; and subsection (4) makes similar amendments to ITEPA 2003, s 139, which sets the appropriate percentage for cars with a CO2 emissions figure. The diesel car supplement (ITEPA 2003, s 141) is unchanged.

9   Determining the appropriate percentage for a car: tax year 2020–21 only

(1)   For the tax year 2020–21, Chapter 6 of Part 3 of ITEPA 2003 (taxable benefits: cars etc) has effect with the following modifications.

(2)   In section 139 (car with a CO_2 emissions figure: the appropriate percentage)—

(a)   in the table in subsection (1), in the second column of the entry for a car with a CO_2 emissions figure of 0, for "2%" substitute "0%", and

(b)   in subsection (7) before paragraph (a) insert—

"(za) section 139A (recently registered cars),".

(3)   After section 139 insert—

"139A   Section 139: recently registered car with CO_2 emissions figure

In its application in relation to a car that is first registered on or after 6 April 2020, section 139 has effect as if—

(a)   for the table in subsection (1) there were substituted—

"Car	Appropriate percentage
Car with CO_2 emissions figure of 0	0%
Car with CO_2 emissions figure of 1–50	
Car with electric range figure of 130 or more	0%
Car with electric range figure of 70–129	3%
Car with electric range figure of 40–69	6%
Car with electric range figure of 30–39	10%

Car with electric range figure of less than 30	12%
Car with CO_2 emissions figure of 51–54	13%
Car with CO_2 emissions figure of 55–59	14%
Car with CO_2 emissions figure of 60–64	15%
Car with CO_2 emissions figure of 65–69	16%
Car with CO_2 emissions figure of 70–74	17%"

   (b) in subsection (3)(a) for "20%" there were substituted "18%"."

(4) In section 140 (car without a CO_2 emissions figure: the appropriate percentage) in subsection (3)(a) for "2%" substitute "0%".

COMMENTARY ON SECTION 9

Section 9 amends ITEPA 2003, ss 139 and 140 for 2020/21 only. It reduces from 2% to 0% the appropriate percentage for cars having an emissions figure of zero; and it inserts new ITEPA 2003, s 139A, setting out in a new table the appropriate percentages for cars first registered on or after 6 April 2020.

---

10 Determining the appropriate percentage for a car: tax year 2021–22 only

(1) For the tax year 2021–22, Chapter 6 of Part 3 of ITEPA 2003 (taxable benefits: cars etc) has effect with the following modifications.

(2) In section 139 (car with a CO_2 emissions figure: the appropriate percentage)—

   (a) in the table in subsection (1), in the second column of the entry for a car with a CO_2 emissions figure of 0, for "2%" substitute "1%", and

   (b) in subsection (7) before paragraph (a) insert—

   "(za) section 139A (recently registered cars),".

(3) After section 139 insert—

"139A Section 139: recently registered car with CO_2 emissions figure

In its application in relation to a car that is first registered on or after 6 April 2020, section 139 has effect as if—

   (a) for the table in subsection (1) there were substituted—

"Car	Appropriate percentage
Car with CO_2 emissions figure of 0	1%
Car with CO_2 emissions figure of 1–50 Car with electric range figure of 130 or more Car with electric range figure of 70–129 Car with electric range figure of 40–69 Car with electric range figure of 30–39 Car with electric range figure of less than 30	1% 4% 7% 11% 13%
Car with CO_2 emissions figure of 51–54	14%
Car with CO_2 emissions figure of 55–59	15%
Car with CO_2 emissions figure of 60–64	16%
Car with CO_2 emissions figure of 65–69	17%
Car with CO_2 emissions figure of 70–74	18%

(b) in subsection (3)(a) for "20%" there were substituted "19%".

(4) In section 140 (car without a CO_2 emissions figure: the appropriate percentage) in subsection (3)(a) for "2%" substitute "1%".

COMMENTARY ON SECTION 10

Section 10 amends ITEPA 2003, ss 139 and 140 for 2021/22 only. It reduces from 2% to 1% the appropriate percentage for cars having an emissions figure of zero; and inserts new ITEPA 2003, s 139A, setting out in a new table the appropriate percentages for cars first registered on or after 6 April 2020.

11 Apprenticeship bursaries paid to persons leaving local authority care

(1) In Part 4 of ITEPA 2003 (employment income: exceptions), in Chapter 4 (exemptions: education and training), after section 254 insert—

"Persons leaving local authority care

254A   Apprenticeship bursaries paid to persons leaving local authority care

(1) No liability to income tax arises in respect of a care leaver's apprenticeship bursary payment.

(2) A care leaver's apprenticeship bursary payment is a payment—

(a) payable out of the public revenue,

(b) to a care leaver (see subsection (3)),

(c) made in connection with the person's employment as an apprentice (see subsection (4)), and

(d) in respect of which any conditions specified in regulations made by the Treasury are met.

(3) A person is a care leaver if they are a person—

(a) who is, or was, a child looked after—

    (i) by a local authority in England within the meaning of section 22 of the Children Act 1989 (general duty of local authority in relation to children looked after by them);

    (ii) by a local authority in Wales within the meaning of the Social Services and Well-being (Wales) Act 2014 (anaw 4) (see section 74 of that Act (child or young person looked after by a local authority));

    (iii) by a local authority in Scotland within the meaning of Chapter 1 of Part 2 of the Children (Scotland) Act 1995 (see section 17(6) of that Act (duty of local authority to child looked after by them));

    (iv) by an authority in Northern Ireland within the meaning of the Children (Northern Ireland) Order 1995 (SI 1995/755 (NI 2)) (see Article 25 of that Order (children looked after by an authority: interpretation)), and

(b) in respect of whom any other conditions specified in regulations made by the Treasury are met.

(4) "Apprentice" has the meaning specified in regulations made by the Treasury.

(5) Regulations under this section—

(a) may make provision framed by reference to a scheme (however described or named), or document, as it has effect from time to time,

(b) may make different provision for different purposes,

(c) may make different provision for different areas, and

(d) may make retrospective provision."

(2) The amendment made by this section has effect in relation to the tax year 2020–21 and subsequent tax years.

COMMENTARY ON SECTION 11

Section 11 inserts new ITEPA 2003, s 254A, introducing an income tax exemption for a care leaver's apprenticeship bursary paid by the Education and Skills Funding Agency on or after a date to be specified in regulations to be made after Royal

Assent. 'This legislation will confirm HMRC's current position that care leavers' bursaries are tax exempt, including those paid prior to the 2020/21 tax year,' the Government said at Budget 2020.

The exemption applies to payment that is payable out of public revenue to a person leaving local authority care, if the payment is made in connection with the person's employment as an apprentice and it meets the conditions to be specified in the regulations.

'Young people who are in care or have left care who choose to start an apprenticeship receive a £1,000 bursary to help them to make the transition to the workplace for their practical studies. The extra financial support is for those aged 16 to 24 and living in England,' Financial Secretary to the Treasury Jesse Norman said during a finance bill committee debate on 4 June 2020. Regulations will introduce a corresponding disregard for Class 1 NICs, he said in a 5 June 2020 letter to committee member Wes Streeting.

12   Tax treatment of certain Scottish social security benefits

(1)   Table B in section 677(1) of ITEPA 2003 (UK social security benefits wholly exempt from income tax) is amended as follows.

(2)   In Part 1 (benefits payable under primary legislation etc), insert each of the following at the appropriate place—

"Disability assistance for children and young people	SS(S)A 2018	Sections 24 and 31"
"Job start	ETA 1973	Section 2".

(3)   In Part 2 (benefits payable under regulations), insert the following at the appropriate place—

"Scottish child payment	SS(S)A 2018	Section 79".

(4)   The amendments made by this section have effect for the tax year 2020–21 and subsequent tax years.

COMMENTARY ON SECTION 12

Section 12 amends Table B in ITEPA 2003, s 677(1) to confirm, for 2020/21 onwards, that three new social security benefits – the job start payment, disability assistance for children and young people, and the Scottish child payment – are exempt from income tax.

The Scottish Government's fiscal framework, agreed by the UK and Scottish Governments, provides that new benefits will not be deemed to be income for tax purposes unless they top up a benefit that is deemed taxable.

13   Power to exempt social security benefits from income tax

(1)   The Treasury may by regulations amend Chapter 4 or 5 of Part 10 of ITEPA 2003 (social security benefits: exemptions) so as to provide that no liability to income tax arises on social security benefits of a description specified in the regulations.

(2)   Regulations under this section may make—

(a)   different provision for different cases;
(b)   retrospective provision;
(c)   incidental or supplementary provision;
(d)   consequential provision (which may include provision amending any provision made by or under the Income Tax Acts).

(3)   In section 655 of ITEPA 2003 (structure of Part 10), in subsection (2), at the end insert ";

section 13 of FA 2020 (power to exempt social security benefits from income tax)."

COMMENTARY ON SECTION 13

Section 13 creates a new power enabling HM Treasury to exempt social security benefits (introduced by either the UK Government or the devolved administrations) from income tax, by means of regulations amending ITEPA 2003, Pt 10, Ch 4 or 5. The regulations may be retrospective.

14   Voluntary office-holders: payments in respect of expenses

(1)   After section 299A of ITEPA 2003 insert—

> **"299B   Voluntary office-holders: payments in respect of expenses**
>
> (1)   No liability to income tax arises in respect of a payment to a person who holds a voluntary office if the payment is in respect of reasonable expenses incurred in carrying out the duties of that office.
>
> (2)   It does not matter whether—
>
> > (a)   the payment is an advance payment or a reimbursement;
> > (b)   the person who makes the payment is the person with whom the office is held.
>
> (3)   Subsections (2) and (3) of section 299A apply for the purposes of subsection (1) of this section as they apply for the purposes of subsection (1) of that section."

(2)   In section 299A(3)(a) of ITEPA 2003 (voluntary office-holders: compensation for lost employment income) after "payment" insert "(whether an advance payment or a reimbursement)".

(3)   The amendments made by this section have effect for the tax year 2020–21 and subsequent tax years.

COMMENTARY ON SECTION 14

Section 14 inserts new ITEPA 2003, s 299B, introducing an income tax exemption for payments to a voluntary office-holder in respect of 'reasonable expenses incurred in carrying out the duties of that office'.

The measure ensures that 'reasonable out-of-pocket private expenses paid or reimbursed to voluntary office holders and which are linked to the duties of the office remain tax exempt', HMRC said in a policy paper on 11 July 2019. It puts existing HMRC practice on a statutory footing for 2020/21 onwards.

HMRC noted that there are about 11,500 special constables and 21,500 magistrates in the UK, and that there are office-holders elsewhere in the voluntary sector including 168,000 registered charities.

ITEPA 2003, s 299A already provides that no income tax liability arises where a 'relevant authority' makes a payment to a voluntary office-holder representing compensation for loss of income.

Loan charge

15   Loan charge not to apply to loans or quasi-loans made before 9 December 2010

(1)   In Schedule 11 to F(No.2)A 2017 (employment income provided through third parties: loans etc outstanding on 5 April 2019) in paragraph 1 (person to be treated as taking a relevant step for the purposes of Part 7A of ITEPA 2003 by reason of making a loan or quasi-loan) in sub-paragraph (1)(b) for "6 April 1999" substitute "9 December 2010".

(2)   In Schedule 12 to F(No.2)A 2017 (trading income provided through third parties: loans etc outstanding on 5 April 2019) in paragraph 1 (application of sections 23A to 23H of ITTOIA 2005 in relation to certain loans and quasi-loans) in sub-paragraph (2)(a)(i) for "6 April 1999" substitute "9 December 2010".

(3)   Part 1 of Schedule 2 makes further amendments to F(No.2)A 2017 in consequence of this section.

COMMENTARY ON SECTIONS 15 TO 21

The loan charge introduced in F(No 2)A 2017, Sch 11 has been one of the most controversial of all recent tax measures. As originally enacted it would have imposed an income tax charge on the amount of any loan provided through a third party (typically an employee trust) which was outstanding on 5 April 2019 where the loan had been made on or after 6 April 1999. The provision was introduced as part of an attempt by HMRC to bring to an end all existing enquiries into employee benefit trust (EBT) arrangements but it gradually became clear that its impact would be much wider, and in particular would affect many contractors and others who had been 'remunerated' via loan arrangements for many years without HMRC having challenged their tax position.

The Treasury undertook a review of the loan charge in 2019 but this did not satisfy many of the more vocal critics and an independent review of the charge was commissioned from Sir Amyas Morse, formerly Comptroller and Auditor General and Chief Executive of the National Audit Office (NAO). His report (www.gov.uk/ government/publications/disguised-remuneration-independent-loan-charge-review/ guidance) supported some of the broad principles of the charge but made a number of criticisms of the way in which it operated, particular the quasi-retrospective effect of the decision to include within the charge loans made as far back as April 1999. The Government accepted many, though not all, of the recommendations in his report and sections 15–21 enact the legislation which gives effect to those changes.

Section 15 enacts the main change to the existing legislation. Previously the loan charge had applied to all loans, and quasi loans, made on or after 6 April 1999. The charge will now only arise in respect of loans and quasi loans made on or after 9 December 2010. That was the date on which the disguised remuneration provisions in ITEPA 2003, Pt 7A originally came into effect.

Subsection (2) introduces a similar provision for the parallel rules in relation to trading income provided through third parties in ITTOIA 2005, ss 23A et seq.

Subsection (3) introduces Schedule 2, which makes further amendments in relation to the loan charge. These amendments are virtually all consequential drafting amendments with no substantive effect.

16   Election for loan charge to be split over three tax years

(1)   Schedule 11 to F(No.2)A 2017 (employment income provided through third parties: loans etc outstanding on 5 April 2019) is amended as follows.

(2)   In paragraph 1 (person to be treated as taking a relevant step for the purposes of Part 7A of ITEPA 2003 by reason of making loan or quasi-loan)—

    (a)   after sub-paragraph (6) insert—

"(6A)   Sub-paragraph (4) is subject to paragraph 1A(5).", and

    (b)   in sub-paragraph (7)—

        (i)   in the words before paragraph (a) after "paragraph" insert "and paragraph 1A", and

        (ii)   in paragraph (a) for "the following provisions of this Schedule" substitute "paragraphs 3 to 18".

(3)   After paragraph 1 insert—

"**1A** (1)   This paragraph applies where—

    (a)   a person ("P") is treated as taking a relevant step within paragraph 1 ("the initial step") by reason of making a loan or quasi-loan, and

    (b)   an election has been made by A for the purposes of this paragraph.

(2)   P is treated as taking two further relevant steps for the purposes of Part 7A of ITEPA 2003.

(3)   P is treated as taking one of the further steps on the first anniversary of the date on which P is treated as taking the initial step.

(4)   P is treated as taking one of the further steps on the second anniversary of the date on which P is treated as taking the initial step.

(5)   For the purposes of section 554Z3(1) of ITEPA 2003 (value of relevant step), the initial step and each of the further steps is to be treated as involving a sum of money equal to one third of the amount of the loan or quasi-loan that is outstanding at the time P is treated as taking the initial step.

(6)   References in this Schedule and in Part 7A of ITEPA 2003 to a relevant step within paragraph 1A of this Schedule are to be read as references to a relevant step which a person is treated by this paragraph as taking.

(7)   An election for the purposes of this paragraph—

    (a)   may be made at any time before 1 October 2020, and .

    (b)   may be made at a later time if an officer of Revenue and Customs allows it.

(8)   But a person who is under a duty imposed by paragraph 35C of this Schedule or paragraph 22 of Schedule 12 may not make an election for the purposes of this paragraph until that duty has been complied with.

(9)   An election for the purposes of this paragraph may not be revoked.

(10)   A person who has made an election for the purposes of paragraph 1(3A) of Schedule 12 is to be treated as having made an election for the purposes of this paragraph.

(11)   The Commissioners for Her Majesty's Revenue and Customs may by regulations provide that sub-paragraph (7)(a) applies to a specified class of persons as if the reference to 1 October 2020 were to such later date as is specified.

(12)   In sub-paragraph (11) "specified" means specified in the regulations."

(4)   Schedule 12 to F(No.2)A 2017 (trading income provided through third parties: loans etc outstanding on 5 April 2019) is amended as follows.

(5)   In paragraph 1 (application of sections 23A to 23H of ITTOIA 2005 in relation to certain loans and quasi-loans)—

- (a)   in sub-paragraph (1) for the words from "as a" to the end substitute "for the purposes of sections 23A to 23H of ITTOIA 2005 as a relevant benefit that arises immediately before the end of 5 April 2019.",
- (b)   in sub-paragraph (3)—
  - (i)   in the words before paragraph (a), after "applies" insert "and T has not made an election for the purposes of sub-paragraph (3A)",
  - (ii)   in paragraph (a) for the words from "immediately" to the end substitute "at the time the relevant benefit is treated as arising, and", and
  - (iii)   for paragraphs (b) and (c) substitute—

  "(b)   where T ceases to carry on the relevant trade before the tax year in which the relevant benefit is treated as arising, as if section 23E(1)(b) were omitted and as if section 23E(1) provided that the relevant benefit amount is treated for income tax purposes as a post-cessation receipt of the trade received in that tax year.", and

- (c)   after sub-paragraph (3) insert—

"(3A)   Where section 23E of ITTOIA 2005 applies in relation to a relevant benefit which is a loan or quasi-loan in relation to which sub-paragraph (2) applies and T has made an election for the purposes of this sub-paragraph, section 23E has effect—

- (a)   as if the "relevant benefit amount" were one third of the amount of the loan or quasi-loan that is outstanding at the time the relevant benefit is treated as arising,
- (b)   as if section 23E(1)(a) specified the tax year in which the relevant benefit is treated as arising and each of the two subsequent tax years, and
- (c)   where T ceases to carry on the relevant trade before any tax year so specified in section 23E(1)(a), as if section 23E(1)(b) were omitted and as if section 23E(1) provided that the relevant benefit amount is to be treated for income tax purposes as a post-cessation receipt of the trade received in that tax year.

(3B)   An election for the purposes of sub-paragraph (3A)—

- (a)   may be made at any time before 1 October 2020, and
- (b)   may be made at a later time if an officer of Revenue and Customs allows it.

(3C)   But a person who is under a duty imposed by paragraph 22 of this Schedule or paragraph 35C of Schedule 11 may not make an election for the purposes of sub-paragraph (3A) until that duty has been complied with.

(3D)   An election for the purposes of sub-paragraph (3A) may not be revoked.

(3E)   A person who has made an election for the purposes of paragraph 1A of Schedule 11 is to be treated as having made an election for the purposes of sub-paragraph (3A) of this paragraph.

(3F)   The Commissioners for Her Majesty's Revenue and Customs may by regulations provide that sub-paragraph (3B)(a) applies to a specified class of persons as if the reference to 1 October 2020 were to such later date as is specified.

(3G)   In sub-paragraph (3F) "specified" means specified in the regulations."

(6)   Part 2 of Schedule 2 makes amendments in consequence of this section.

COMMENTARY ON SECTION 16

One of the major criticisms of the original loan charge legislation was that the entire charge arose in one tax year, even though the loan might have built up over a number of years. This often had the result that the taxpayer was brought into higher or additional rate tax even though in the years in which the loans had been made he/she was only liable at basic rate. Section 16 addresses this issue by introducing a mechanism to spread the loan charge over three years.

Subsection (1) introduces amendments to F(No 2)A 2017, Sch 11.

Subsection (2) is a minor drafting amendment.

Subsection (3) is the substantive amendment. It introduces a new para 1A to Schedule 11.

New F(No 2A) 2017, Sch 11 para 1A

(1)   The paragraph applies when there is a loan outstanding on 5 April 2019 and a person has made an election for this paragraph to apply. In other words the spreading is not mandatory – it is up to an individual to elect for it to apply.

(2)   Where an election has been made the individual is treated as having taken two further relevant steps in addition to the relevant step which arises on 5 April 2019.

(3)   The first additional step is deemed to occur on the first anniversary of the relevant step.

(4)   The second additional step is deemed to occur on the second anniversary of the relevant step.

(5)   The amount of each of the three steps above is deemed to be one third of the amount of the loan outstanding at the time of the original relevant step. The effect of this is to spread the charge on outstanding loans over three tax years rather than, at present, the whole amount being chargeable in one year.

(6)   This is a drafting amendment to ensure that references to relevant steps elsewhere in the legislation include references to the deemed relevant steps above.

(7)   An election for spreading under this paragraph can be made at any time before 1 October 2020 or at any later time allowed by an officer of HMRC.

(8)   An election cannot be made until a person has complied with his obligation to provide loan charge information under F(No 2)A 2017, Sch 12 para 22.

(9)   Any election once made is irrevocable.

(10)   A person who has made an election under the parallel provisions for trading income provided through loans etc under ITTOIA 2005, ss 23A et seq is treated as also having made an election under this paragraph.

(11)   HMRC may make regulations under sub-para (7) to cover a specified class of persons (ie so as not to require each individual application to be considered separately). This provision was introduced at report stage to cater for continuing problems caused by Covid-19.

(12)   This is a minor drafting amendment.

Section 16(4) introduces amendments relating to loans within ITTOIA 2005, ss 23A et seq (trading income provided by third parties).

Subsection (5) introduces amendments to F(No 2)A 2017, Sch 12.

Subsection (5)(a), (b) provide minor drafting amendments.

Subsection (5)(c) is the substantive amendment. It follows the same pattern as the amendments in 16(3) above by introducing the option of an election to treat the amount of the relevant benefit arising from the outstanding loan as three separate amounts of one third each arising in the tax year of the original benefit and in the two subsequent tax years. Where the individual has ceased to trade before any one of these three dates the relevant benefit is to be treated as a post cessation receipt. The provisions relating to the election for spreading the liability mirror the similar provisions above for employment income.

Subsection (6) introduces Part 2 of Schedule 2, which makes consequential amendments.

17 Loan charge reduced where underlying liability disclosed but unenforceable

(1) In Schedule 11 to F(No.2)A 2017 (employment income provided through third parties: loans etc outstanding on 5 April 2019) after paragraph 1A (as inserted by section 16) insert—

"**1B** (1) This paragraph applies where—

    (a) a person is treated as taking a relevant step within paragraph 1 by reason of making a loan or quasi-loan,

    (b) a reasonable case could have been made that for a qualifying tax year ("the relevant year") A was chargeable to income tax on an amount that was referable to the loan or quasi-loan,

    (c) at a time when an officer of Revenue and Customs had power to recover (from A or any other person) income tax for the relevant year in respect of that amount, a qualifying tax return or two or more qualifying tax returns of the same type taken together contained a reasonable disclosure of the loan or quasi-loan, and

    (d) as at 6 April 2019 an officer of Revenue and Customs had not taken steps to recover (from A or any other person) income tax for the relevant year in respect of that amount.

(2) But this paragraph does not apply if—

    (a) a reasonable case could have been made that for a tax year other than the relevant year ("the alternative year") A was chargeable to income tax on an amount within sub-paragraph (3), and

    (b) it is the case that—

        (i) on or before 5 April 2019 an officer of Revenue and Customs took steps to recover (from A or any other person) income tax for the alternative year in respect of that amount, or

        (ii) the alternative year is not a qualifying tax year.

(3) An amount is within this sub-paragraph if—

    (a) it is the same amount as is mentioned in sub-paragraph (1),

    (b) it is part of the amount mentioned in sub-paragraph (1), or

    (c) it is derived from or represents the whole or part of the amount mentioned in sub-paragraph (1).

(4) Where this paragraph applies, then for the purposes of paragraph 1(4) and 1A(5) the amount of the loan or quasi-loan that is outstanding is to be taken to be reduced (but not below nil) by the amount mentioned in sub-paragraph (1).

(5) For the purposes of sub-paragraph (1)(c) a qualifying tax return, or two or more qualifying tax returns taken together, contained a reasonable disclosure of the loan or quasi-loan if the return or returns taken together—

    (a) identified the loan or quasi-loan,

    (b) identified the person to whom the loan or quasi-loan was made in a case where the loan or quasi-loan was made to a person other than A,

    (c) identified the relevant arrangements in pursuance of which or in connection with which the loan or quasi-loan was made, and

    (d) provided such other information as was sufficient for it to be apparent that a reasonable case could be made that for the relevant year A was chargeable to income tax on an amount that was referable to the loan or quasi-loan.

(6) A reference in sub-paragraph (1)(b), (2) or (5)(d) to A being chargeable to income tax does not include A being chargeable to income tax by reason of section 175 of ITEPA 2003 (benefit of taxable cheap loan treated as earnings).

(7) In this paragraph—

"qualifying tax year" means the tax year 2015–16 and any earlier tax year, and "qualifying tax return" means—

    (a) a return made by A or B under section 8 of TMA 1970 for a qualifying tax year, and any accompanying accounts, statements or documents, or

    (b) a return made by B under paragraph 3 of Schedule 18 to FA 1998 for an accounting period that commenced before 6 April 2016,

and a qualifying tax return is of the same type as another if both fall within the same paragraph of this definition."

(2)   In Schedule 12 to F(No.2)A 2017 (trading income provided through third parties: loans etc outstanding on 5 April 2019) after paragraph 1 insert—

"1A (1)   This paragraph applies where—

    (a)   a loan or quasi-loan is to be treated for the purposes of sections 23A to 23H of ITTOIA 2005 as a relevant benefit by reason of paragraph 1,

    (b)   a reasonable case could have been made that for a qualifying tax year ("the relevant year") T was chargeable to income tax on an amount that was referable to the loan or quasi-loan,

    (c)   at a time when an officer of Revenue and Customs had power to recover (from T or any other person) income tax for the relevant year in respect of that amount, a qualifying tax return or two or more qualifying tax returns taken together contained a reasonable disclosure of the loan or quasi-loan, and

    (d)   as at 6 April 2019 an officer of Revenue and Customs had not taken steps to recover (from T or any other person) income tax for the relevant year in respect of that amount.

(2)   But this paragraph does not apply if—

    (a)   a reasonable case could have been made that for a tax year other than the relevant year ("the alternative year") T was chargeable to income tax on an amount within sub-paragraph (3), and

    (b)   it is the case that—

        (i)   on or before 5 April 2019 an officer of Revenue and Customs took steps to recover (from T or any other person) income tax for the alternative year in respect of that amount, or

        (ii)   the alternative year is not a qualifying tax year.

(3)   An amount is within this sub-paragraph if—

    (a)   it is the same amount as is mentioned in sub-paragraph (1),

    (b)   it is part of the amount mentioned in sub-paragraph (1), or

    (c)   it is derived from or represents the whole or part of the amount mentioned in sub-paragraph (1).

(4)   Where this paragraph applies, then for the purposes of paragraph 1(3)(a) and (3A)(a) the amount of the loan or quasi-loan that is outstanding is to be taken to be reduced (but not below nil) by the amount mentioned in sub-paragraph (1).

(5)   For the purposes of sub-paragraph (1)(c) a qualifying tax return, or two or more qualifying tax returns taken together, contained a reasonable disclosure of the loan or quasi-loan if the return or returns taken together—

    (a)   identified the loan or quasi-loan,

    (b)   identified the person to whom the loan or quasi-loan was made in a case where the loan or quasi-loan was made to a person other than T,

    (c)   identified the relevant arrangements in pursuance of which or in connection with which the loan or quasi-loan was made, and

    (d)   provided such other information as was sufficient for it to be apparent that a reasonable case could be made that for the relevant year T was chargeable to income tax on an amount that was referable to the loan or quasi-loan.

(6)   In this paragraph—

"qualifying tax year" means the tax year 2015–16 and any earlier tax year, and "qualifying tax return" means a return made by T under section 8 of TMA 1970 for a qualifying tax year, and any accompanying accounts, statements or documents."

COMMENTARY ON SECTION 17

Section 17(1) introduces amendments to F(No 2)A 2017, Sch 11 which are designed to limit HMRC's ability to recover amounts due under the loan charge where certain disclosures have been made.

New F(No 2)A 2017, Sch 11, para 1B(1)

This sets out the four qualifying conditions which must be met before relief can be given:

(a)   The person must have taken, or be treated as having taken, a relevant step by virtue of the loan or quasi loan.

(b)   A 'reasonable case' could have been made that for a qualifying tax year that person was chargeable to income tax on an amount which was referable to the loan.

(c)   At a time which was in date for recovery of income tax for the year a qualifying return (or two or more qualifying returns of the same type taken together) contained a reasonable disclosure of the loan or quasi loan. These terms are defined in sub-para (5).

(d)   An officer of HMRC had not taken steps at 6 April 2019 to recover from the person (or any other person) income tax for the year on that amount.

New F(No 2)A 2017, Sch 11, para 1B(2)

This sets out exceptions to the qualifying conditions. Relief is not available where a reasonable case could be made that a person was chargeable to income tax for an alternative year and that either an officer of HMRC took steps to recover income tax for the alternative year, or the alternative year was not a qualifying tax year (ie 2015/16 or any earlier year).

New F(No 2)A 2017, Sch 11, para 1B (3)

This defines the amount on which income was chargeable by reference to the loan or quasi loan. It covers the whole or part of the amount itself or any other amount which is derived from that amount.

New F(No 2)A 2017, Sch 11, para 1B(4)

This gives the relief. Where the conditions are met the amount of the loan outstanding at 5 April 2019 is reduced by the amount given in the previous sub-paragraph. The effect is that no loan charge is due on that net amount. The reduction can only bring the loan charge down to nil – there is no possibility of creating a loss.

New F(No 2)A 2017, Sch 11, para 1B(5)

This defines a reasonable disclosure for the purpose of sub-para (1). There is reasonable disclosure where the return/returns in question identified the loan or quasi loan, identified to whom it was made, identified the relevant arrangements in connection with which the loan was made and provided sufficient information to make it apparent that the person was chargeable on the loan or quasi loan.

New F(No 2)A 2017, Sch 11, para 1B(6)

This is an important exclusion. Entries on a tax return which simply show that a person was taxable on the benefit of a cheap loan are not sufficient for these purposes. The entries must make it apparent that the person was chargeable to income tax on the loan itself – in other words that, in effect, the advance of the loan was earnings.

New F(No 2)A 2017, Sch 11, para 1B(7)

This defines terms for the purpose of this sub-paragraph. A qualifying year is 2015/16 and any earlier tax year, a qualifying return means a return under TMA 1970, s 8 (ie a personal self assessment return), including any accompanying documents, accounts or statements, or under FA 1998, Sch 18, ie a corporation tax return. In other words, a qualifying return can be a return made by the employer or the employee.

New F(No 2)A 2017, Sch 12, para 1A

Section 17(2) introduces a new para 1A into F(No 2)A 2017, Sch 12: this precisely replicates the provisions above in subsection (1) in relation to the parallel provisions for loans in connection with trading income provided by third parties.

The effect of section 17 is thus to remove from charge any loans which would otherwise be caught for tax year 2015/16 or earlier where reasonable disclosure had been made and HMRC had not taken steps to recover the tax by 5 April 2019. Where no reasonable disclosure was made there is no restriction on the charge. For tax years 2016/17 onwards there is no restriction even where reasonable disclosure was made and/or HMRC had not taken steps by 5 April 2019 to recover the tax. Such loans remain within the scope of the charge.

18 Relief from interest on tax payable by a person subject to the loan charge

(1) This section applies where—

(a) a person is chargeable to income tax on any amount by reason of Schedule 11 or 12 to F(No.2)A 2017 or would be so chargeable but for section 15 or 17 of this Act,

(b) before the end of September 2020 the person delivers a return under section 8 of TMA 1970 for the tax year 2018–19, and

(c) at the end of September 2020 the person's self-assessment included in that return is complete and accurate.

(2) If before the end of September 2020 the person discharges their liability to income tax and capital gains tax for the tax year 2018–19—

(a) any amount paid in discharging that liability (other than a payment made on account of income tax for that tax year) is to be taken to not carry interest, and

(b) any amount paid by the person on account of their liability to income tax for the tax year 2019–20 is to be taken to not carry interest.

(3) If before the end of September 2020 the person enters into an agreement with the Commissioners for Her Majesty's Revenue and Customs as to the discharge of their liability to income tax and capital gains tax for the tax year 2018–19—

(a) any amount paid before the end of September 2020 in discharging that liability (other than a payment made on account of income tax for that tax year) is to be taken to not carry interest,

(b) for the purposes of section 101 of FA 2009 the late payment interest start date in respect of any amount paid in accordance with the agreement after the end of September 2020 is 1 October 2020, and

(c) any amount paid by the person on account of their liability to income tax for the tax year 2019–20 is to be taken to not carry interest.

(4) Paragraph (b) of subsection (2) and paragraph (c) of subsection (3) do not apply if at the end of January 2021 the person has neither discharged their liability to income tax and capital gains tax for the tax year 2019–20 nor entered into an agreement with the Commissioners for Her Majesty's Revenue and Customs as to the discharge of that liability.

(5) The Commissioners for Her Majesty's Revenue and Customs may by regulations provide that this section applies to a specified class of persons as if—

(a) the references in this section to the end of September 2020 were to such later time as is specified, and

(b) the reference in subsection (3)(b) to 1 October 2020 were to such later date as is specified.

(6) In subsection (5) "specified" means specified in the regulations.

COMMENTARY ON SECTION 18

Section 18 allows a measure of relief from interest on late payment of tax by individuals subject to the loan charge.

Subsection (1) sets out the first of the qualifying conditions. A person must be chargeable to income tax on any amount by reason of the loan charge (or would be but for the amendments made by this Act); must have delivered a 2018/19 return by 30 September and included in that return a self assessment which is complete and accurate.

Subsection (2) provides that where the above conditions are met and a person makes a payment discharging liability to income tax/capital gains tax for 2018/19 by 30 September 2020 no interest is chargeable on that payment of tax. The same rule applies to payments on account of liability for 2019/20.

Subsection (3) provides a similar rule in cases where a person has not made the payment referred to in subsection (2) above but has reached an agreement on payment terms with HMRC, such as in a time to pay arrangement. Any amount paid by 30 September 2020 under the terms of that agreement is not to carry interest, and for amounts paid after that day late payment interest is to be calculated from 1 October 2020 and not the normal due date.

Subsection (4) provides that if, by 31 January 2021, a person has neither paid the loan charge nor agreed settlement terms with HMRC then the interest abatements in subsections (2) and (3) above do not apply and interest will be calculated on the normal basis. There is thus an incentive for people to bring their affairs up to date by the end of 2021.

Subsection (5) states that HMRC is given the power to introduce regulations to extend the 30 September 2020 deadline by reference to a specified class of persons. This is a similar relaxation to that in section 16(3) above.

19 Minor amendments relating to the loan charge

(1) Schedule 11 to F(No.2)A 2017 (employment income provided through third parties: loans etc outstanding on 5 April 2019) is amended as follows.

(2) In paragraph 35C(2)(b) (date by which loan charge information must be provided) for "1 October 2019" substitute "1 October 2020".

(3) In paragraph 45 (meaning of "A" and "B") after "section 554A(1)(a)" insert "and 554AA(1)(a)".

(4) In Schedule 12 to F(No.2)A 2017 (trading income provided through third parties: loans etc outstanding on 5 April 2019) in paragraph 22(2)(b) (date by which loan charge information must be provided) for "1 October 2019" substitute "1 October 2020".

COMMENTARY ON SECTION 19

Subsection (1) introduces amendments to F(No 2)A 2017, Sch 11.

Subsection (2) states that the date on which loan charge information is to be provided to HMRC is extended from 1 October 2019 to 1 October 2020.

Subsection (3) is a minor drafting amendment.

Subsection (4) similarly extends to 1 October 2020 the date on which information about loans connected to trading income provided by third parties must be provided to HMRC.

20 Repaying sums paid to HMRC under agreements relating to certain loans etc

(1) The Commissioners for Her Majesty's Revenue and Customs ("the Commissioners") must establish a scheme under which they may on an application made to them before 1 October 2021—

  (a) repay the whole or part of a qualifying amount paid or treated as paid to them under a qualifying agreement, or

  (b) waive the payment of the whole or part of a qualifying amount due to be paid to them under a qualifying agreement.

(2) An agreement is a qualifying agreement if—

  (a) it is an agreement with the Commissioners,

  (b) it is made on or after 16 March 2016 and before 11 March 2020, and

  (c) it imposes an obligation on any party to the agreement to pay an amount of income tax that is referable (directly or indirectly) to a qualifying loan or quasi-loan.

(3) An amount paid, treated as paid or due to be paid under a qualifying agreement is a qualifying amount if—

  (a) the amount is referable (directly or indirectly) to a qualifying loan or quasi-loan, and

  (b) the amount is one that an officer of Revenue and Customs had no power to recover at the time the agreement was made.

(4) But an amount that is referable (directly or indirectly) to a qualifying loan or quasi-loan made on or after 9 December 2010 is not a qualifying amount by reason of subsection (3) unless at a time when an officer of Revenue and Customs had power to recover the amount a tax return, or two or more tax returns of the same type taken together, contained a reasonable disclosure of the loan or quasi-loan.

(5) For the purposes of subsection (4), a tax return, or two or more tax returns taken together, contained a reasonable disclosure of the loan or quasi-loan if the return or returns taken together—

  (a) identified the qualifying loan or quasi-loan,

  (b) identified the person to whom the qualifying loan or quasi-loan was made,

(c)   identified any arrangements in pursuance of which, or in connection with which, the qualifying loan or quasi-loan was made, and

(d)   provided such other information as was sufficient for it to be apparent that a reasonable case could have been made that the amount concerned was payable to the Commissioners.

(6)   An amount paid, treated as paid or due to be paid under a qualifying agreement is also a qualifying amount if it is interest on another qualifying amount paid, treated as paid or due to be paid under that agreement.

(7)   A loan or quasi-loan is a qualifying loan or quasi-loan if it is made on or after 6 April 1999 and before 6 April 2016.

(8)   In this section—

"loan" and "quasi-loan" have the meaning they have in Part 1 of Schedule 11 to F(No.2)A 2017 and Schedule 12 to that Act (see paragraph 2 of each of those Schedules),
"tax return" means—

(a)   a return made under section 8 of TMA 1970 and any accompanying accounts, statements or documents, or

(b)   a return made under paragraph 3 of Schedule 18 to FA 1998,

and a tax return is of the same type as another if both fall within the same paragraph of this definition.

(9)   Section 21 makes further provision in connection with the scheme established under this section.

COMMENTARY ON SECTION 20

The amendments to the loan charge legislation in this Act remove all pre-9 December 2010 loans from charge completely and also remove certain loans made later provided that full disclosure was made. However many people will have paid tax by way of agreement with HMRC in relation to such loans. This section provides the power for HMRC to introduce a scheme under which that tax can be repaid.

Subsection (1) sets out the requirement for HMRC to introduce a repayment scheme. Under the scheme application for repayment has to be made to HMRC by 30 September 2021. Where payment of a settlement is due but has not been made (for example where an instalment arrangement has been agreed) the scheme must also allow for HMRC to waive amounts due. The amount to be repaid/waived is known as the qualifying amount.

Subsection (2) sets out the scope of the scheme. It will apply to qualifying agreements, ie agreements made with HMRC between 16 March 2016 and 10 March 2020 which impose an obligation on any party (ie this could include employees, an employer or trustees) to pay an amount of income tax which is attributable to a qualifying loan or quasi loan.

Subsection (3) provides that an amount is a qualifying amount if it is referable, directly or indirectly, to a qualifying loan or quasi loan and the amount is one that an officer of HMRC had no power to recover at the time the agreement was made. At first sight this is an odd provision because it seems counter-intuitive that a person would enter into an agreement to pay tax which HMRC did not have the power to recover. The explanation is that many people will have entered voluntary settlement agreements in advance of tax on the loan charge actually falling due, in order to benefit from the more generous settlement terms which were on offer at the time.

Subsection (4) restricts the availability of relief. An amount attributable to a loan or quasi loan made on or after 9 December 2010 is not a qualifying amount unless at a time when an officer had power to recover an amount of tax a tax return, or two or more returns, contained a reasonable disclosure of the loan or quasi loan. This mirrors the provision in section 17 above, which cancels the loan charge for certain loans made on or after 9 Dec 2010 where adequate disclosure has been made.

Subsection (5) mirrors the definition of reasonable disclosure in section 17(5) above.

Subsection (6) specifies that interest due to be paid under a qualifying agreement is treated as an amount paid under that agreement. In other words where a repayment of tax is made any interest associated with that tax is also repaid.

Subsection (7) provides an important definition. It defines a qualifying loan (or quasi loan) as one made on or after 6 April 1999 and before 6 April 2016. Loans made after that date are not within the terms of the repayment scheme.

Subsection (8) makes minor drafting amendments. Subsection (9) introduces section 21, which makes further provisions in relation to the repayment scheme.

21   Operation of the scheme

(1)   The scheme may make provision—

    (a)   in relation to all qualifying agreements or specified descriptions of qualifying agreements only, and

    (b)   in relation to all qualifying amounts or specified descriptions of qualifying amounts only.

(2)   The scheme may make provision for an amount that is not a qualifying amount by reason only of subsection (4) of section 20 to be treated in certain cases as if it were a qualifying amount.

(3)   The scheme may make provision about the making of applications under the scheme, including—

    (a)   provision as to who is or is not eligible to apply,

    (b)   provision as to the conditions that must be met in order to apply,

    (c)   provision as to the form, manner and content of an application, and

    (d)   provision as to information or evidence to be provided in support of an application.

(4)   The scheme may make provision about the determination of applications under the scheme, including—

    (a)   provision in accordance with which the Commissioners must determine whether to exercise their discretion to repay or waive the payment of a qualifying amount, and

    (b)   provision in accordance with which the Commissioners must determine how much of any qualifying amount to repay or waive.

(5)   The scheme may make provision authorising the Commissioners to make a repayment or waiver conditional—

    (a)   on the applicant or any other person agreeing to the termination or variation of the qualifying agreement concerned,

    (b)   on the applicant or any other person making a new agreement with the Commissioners, or

    (c)   on the satisfaction of such other conditions as may be specified or determined by the Commissioners.

(6)   The scheme may provide that in making any determination under the scheme the Commissioners may or must take account of—

    (a)   the effect the qualifying agreement concerned has had, or may have, on the applicant or any other person (for example, the effect it has had, or may have, on any liability, relief or benefit),

    (b)   the effect any repayment or waiver would have on the applicant or any other person (for example, the effect it would have on any liability, relief or benefit), and

    (c)   such other matters as may be specified.

(7)   The scheme may make provision as to the effect, if any, a repayment or waiver is to have on—

    (a)   the entitlement of the applicant, or any other person, to a payment, benefit or relief under an enactment,

    (b)   the amount or value of such a payment, benefit or relief,

    (c)   any liability the applicant, or any other person, may have under an enactment, or

    (d)   the extent of any such liability.

(8)   The scheme may make provision for or in connection with the recovery by the Commissioners of—

    (a)   any amount repaid under the scheme in circumstances where the Commissioners consider that the repayment should not have been paid, or

(b)   any amount the payment of which has been waived under the scheme in circumstances where the Commissioners consider that the waiver should not have been granted.

(9)   The scheme may make—

(a)   different provision for different purposes or cases,

(b)   provision generally or for specific cases,

(c)   provision subject to exceptions, and

(d)   incidental, supplementary, consequential or transitional provision.

(10)   The scheme may be amended by the Commissioners from time to time.

(11)   An amendment making provision of a kind authorised by subsection (7) may have effect in relation to a repayment paid or waiver granted before the amendment comes into force, but only if the principal effect of the amendment is to benefit persons other than the Commissioners.

(12)   In this section—

"the scheme" means the scheme established under section 20,

"specified" means specified in the scheme, and

"the Commissioners", "qualifying amount" and "qualifying agreement" have the meaning they have in section 20.

COMMENTARY ON SECTION 21

Section 21 sets out the key parameters of the proposed scheme. At the time of writing the rules of the scheme have not been finalised but have been published in draft at: https://assets.publishing.service.gov.uk/government/uploads/system/uploads/attachment_data/file/868925/Draft_scheme_refunding_voluntary_restitution.pdf.

Subsection (1) states that the scheme can make provision for all, or only certain descriptions of, qualifying agreements and for all, or specified descriptions of, qualifying amounts.

Subsection (2) states that the scheme may make provisions for amounts which are not qualifying amounts because of section 20(4) (reasonable disclosure) to be treated as qualifying amounts.

Subsection (3) provides that the scheme may include provisions about the application process including who can apply; what conditions must be met before a person can apply; the form and manner of an application and the information to be provided with an application.

Subsection (4) states that the scheme may make provision about the way applications are determined by HMRC, in particular about how HMRC should exercise its discretion to make repayments or waivers.

Subsection (5) states that the scheme may make provisions for making repayments or waivers conditional on varying or terminating existing agreements, or on the making of a new agreement, or on the satisfaction of any new conditions which HMRC may determine.

Subsection (6) states that the scheme may provide that HMRC must take account of any effect that the previous agreement may have had on any person's liability, relief or benefit and what effect any waiver or repayment may have on a person's liability. The scheme may also provide that HMRC may or must take account of any other matters that may be specified.

Subsection (7) provides that the scheme may make provisions about the effect that a repayment or waiver may have on the entitlement of the claimant or any other person to a payment, benefit or relief, including the amount or value of that payment etc. It may also make provisions about the liability a person may have under any enactment, including its amount or value.

Subsection (8) stipulates that the scheme may make provision for the recovery of any amount repaid under the scheme which should not have been repaid, or the cancellation of any waiver which should not have been made.

Subsection (9) states that the scheme may make different provisions for different purposes or cases, whether general or specific, and may make provisions for exceptional or incidental or supplementary or transitional provisions.

Subsection (10) provides that the scheme may be amended by HMRC from time to time.

Subsection (11) states that an amendment within subsection (7) above may have effect in relation to a repayment etc made before the amendment comes into force, but only in a way which benefits a person other than HMRC.

Subsection (12) defines certain terms for the purpose of the section.

Pensions

22   Annual allowance: tapered reduction

(1)   In Part 4 of FA 2004 (pension schemes), section 228ZA (annual allowance charge: tapered reduction of annual allowance) is amended as follows.

(2)   For subsection (1) substitute—

"(1)   If the individual is a high-income individual for the tax year, the amount of the annual allowance for the tax year in the case of the individual is the amount specified for the tax year by or under section 228 reduced (but not below £4,000) by—

$(AI - £240,000) \times (1 / 2)$

where AI is the individual's adjusted income for the tax year."

(3)   In subsection (3)—

  (a)   in paragraph (a), for "£150,000" substitute "£240,000";
  (b)   in paragraph (b), for "£150,000 minus A" substitute "£240,000 minus the amount specified for the tax year by or under section 228".

(4)   The amendments made by this section have effect for the tax year 2020–21 and subsequent tax years.

COMMENTARY ON SECTION 22

Contributions to a registered pension scheme can be made by or on behalf of an individual every year up to the annual allowance without incurring tax penalties. The annual allowance is set at £40,000 a year, subject to some tapering for high incomes from April 2016.

HM Treasury has reviewed the tapered annual allowance and its impact on the NHS, where senior clinicians were turning down work to avoid paying a pensions tax, as well as on public service delivery more widely.

To support the delivery of public services, particularly in the NHS, section 22 amends the tapered annual allowance legislation in FA 2004, s 228ZA. The two tapered annual allowance thresholds have each been raised by £90,000. This means that from 2020/21 the 'threshold income' will be £200,000, so individuals with income below this level will not be affected by the tapered annual allowance, and the annual allowance will only begin to taper down for individuals who also have an 'adjusted income' (taxable income and pension savings) above £240,000.

For those on the very highest incomes, the minimum level to which the annual allowance can taper down will reduce from £10,000 to £4,000 from 6 April 2020. This reduction will only affect individuals with 'adjusted income' over £300,000.

Chargeable gains

23   Entrepreneurs' relief

Schedule 3 makes provision about relief under Chapter 3 of Part 5 of TCGA 1992.

COMMENTARY ON SECTION 23, SCHEDULE 3

[See Commentary note for Schedule 3]

24   Relief on disposal of private residence

(1)   TCGA 1992 is amended as follows.

(2)   In section 222 (relief on disposal of private residence)—

  (a)   after subsection (5) insert—

"(5A)   But a notice or further notice under subsection (5)(a) determining which of 2 or more residences is an individual's main residence for any period may be given more than 2 years from the beginning of the period if during the period the individual has not held an interest of more than a negligible market value in more than one of the residences.",

    (b)   in subsection (7)(a) (disposal of dwelling-house to a spouse or civil partner)—

        (i)   for "the dwelling-house" substitute "a dwelling-house", and

        (ii)   omit "which is their only or main residence",

    (c)   in subsection (8A) (when living accommodation is job-related for a person) after paragraph (b) insert "; or

        (c)   an armed forces accommodation allowance for or towards costs of the accommodation is paid to, or in respect of, the person or the person's spouse or civil partner", and

    (d)   in subsection (8D) (interpretation) after paragraph (b) insert "; and

        (c)   "armed forces accommodation allowance" means an allowance which is exempt from income tax by reason of section 297D of ITEPA 2003."

(3)   In section 223 (amount of relief)—

    (a)   in subsections (1) and (2)(a) for "18 months" substitute "9 months", and

    (b)   omit subsection (4).

(4)   After section 223 insert—

"223ZA   Amount of relief: individual's residency delayed by certain events

(1)   Subsection (4) below applies where—

    (a)   a gain to which section 222 applies accrues to an individual on the disposal of, or of an interest in, a dwelling-house or part of a dwelling-house,

    (b)   the time at which the dwelling-house or the part of the dwelling-house first became the individual's only or main residence ("the moving-in time") was within the first 24 months of the individual's period of ownership,

    (c)   at no time during the period beginning with the individual's period of ownership and ending with the moving-in time was the dwelling-house or the part of the dwelling-house another person's residence, and

    (d)   during the period beginning with the individual's period of ownership and ending with the moving-in time a qualifying event occurred.

(2)   The following are qualifying events—

    (a)   the completion of the construction, renovation, redecoration or alteration of the dwelling-house or the part of the dwelling-house mentioned in subsection (1);

    (b)   the disposal by the individual of, or of an interest in, any other dwelling-house or part of a dwelling-house that immediately before the disposal was the individual's only or main residence.

(3)   In determining whether and, if so, when a qualifying event within subsection (2)(b) occurred, ignore section 28 (time of disposal where asset disposed of under contract).

(4)   For the purposes of subsections (1) and (2) of section 223, as they have effect in relation to the gain, the dwelling-house or the part of the dwelling-house mentioned in subsection (1) above is to be treated as having been the individual's only or main residence from the beginning of the individual's period of ownership until the moving-in time."

(5)   After section 223A insert—

"223B   Additional relief: part of private residence let out

(1)   Where—

    (a)   a gain to which section 222 applies accrues to an individual on the disposal of, or of an interest in, a dwelling-house or part of a dwelling-house, and

    (b)   at any time in the individual's period of ownership the condition in subsection (2) is met in respect of the dwelling-house, the part of the gain that is within subsection (3) is a chargeable gain only to the extent, if any, to which it exceeds the amount in subsection (4).

(2)   The condition is that—

> (a)   part of the dwelling-house is the individual's only or main residence, and
> (b)   another part of the dwelling-house is being let out by the individual as residential accommodation.

(3)   The part of the gain that is within this subsection is the part that (but for subsection (1)) would be a chargeable gain by reason of the fact that, at the times in the individual's period of ownership when the condition in subsection (2) is met, the individual's only or main residence does not include the part of the dwelling-house that is being let out as residential accommodation.

(4)   The amount is whichever is the lesser of—

> (a)   the amount of the gain that is not a chargeable gain by virtue of section 223, and
> (b)   £40,000.

(5)   Where by reason of section 222(7)(a) the individual's period of ownership mentioned in subsection (1) begins with the beginning of the period of ownership of another person, any question whether the condition in subsection (2) is met at a time that is within both those periods of ownership is to be determined as if the references in subsection (2) to the individual were to that other person."

(6)   In section 224 (amount of relief: further provisions)—

> (a)   in the heading for "Amount of relief" substitute "Relief under sections 223 and 223B",
> (b)   in subsection (1)—
>> (i)   for "the gain", in the first place those words occur, substitute "a gain to which section 222 applies",
>> (ii)   for "section 223" substitute "sections 223 and 223B",
> (c)   in subsection (2) for "section 223" substitute "sections 223 and 223B", and
> (d)   in subsection (3) for "Section 223" substitute "Sections 223 and 223B".

(7)   In section 225E (disposals by disabled persons or persons in care homes etc) in subsection (4) for "18 months" substitute "9 months".

(8)   In section 248E(6) (relief on disposal of joint interests in private residence) for "and 223" substitute ", 223 and 223B".

(9)   The amendment made by subsection (2)(a) has effect in relation to a notice given on or after 6 April 2020.

(10)   The amendments made by subsection (2)(b) have effect in a case where the disposal or death mentioned in subsection (7)(a) of section 222 of TCGA 1992 is made or occurs on or after 6 April 2020.

(11)   The amendments made by subsections (3) to (8) have effect in relation to disposals made on or after 6 April 2020.

COMMENTARY ON SECTION 24

Section 24 makes a number of significant changes to the capital gains tax main residence exemption (aka principal private residence relief, 'PPR relief') which will affect taxpayers who have not occupied the property as their main residence throughout their period of ownership. The two most important changes, the reduction in the final period of exemption from 18 to 9 months and the change to lettings relief, were first announced at the 2018 Budget and were the subject of a consultation in 2019.

Section 24(2) makes three separate changes to the rules in TCGA 1992, s 222. The first change in subsection (2)(a) enacts Extra-statutory Concession ESC D21. The normal rule is that an individual who owns more than one residence can give a notice to HMRC nominating one of them as the main residence for PPR relief within two years of the first point at which they have more than one residence. Further nominations can then be made but can be backdated only for two years. The new rule enables a notice or further notice to be given more than two years after the beginning of the period for which it is to apply if the individual has not held an interest of more than a negligible market value in more than one of the residences during the period. This rule replaces the concession for notices made on or after 6 April 2020 (see subsection (9)).

Although the new rule in effect enacts the concession, it is in fact less restrictive. Under the concession it was a requirement that the individual should have been unaware that a nomination could be made. In such cases the nomination had to be made within a reasonable time of the individual becoming aware of the possibility of so doing, and it was regarded as effective from the date on which the individual first had more than one residence. The concession did not apply to further nominations.

The second change (subsection (2)(b)) amends the rule which applies where there is a transfer between spouses or civil partners of their interest in the main residence, or where the interest passes to the other on death. The other spouse/civil partner inherits the ownership history of the transferor, including their period of ownership and use of the property. For transfers from 6 April 2020 (see subsection (10)), this applies to the transfer of any residence, or interest, whether or not it was the main residence at the time of transfer.

Section 24(2)(c), (d) provide that members of the armed forces who are required to work away from their main residence to fulfil their duties, and who receive an armed forces accommodation allowance instead of being required to live in service accommodation, will be eligible for job-related accommodation relief in respect of their main residence. This provision will apply from the date (still to be fixed) that the relevant regulations bring the income tax exemption for the accommodation allowance into force.

Section 24(3) applies the reduction of the final period of exemption from 18 months to 9 months for disposals on or after 6 April 2020 (subsection (11)). The final period exemption provides relief where the residence is not the main residence during that period but has been at some previous time. The final period remains at 36 months for those who are disabled or in a care home. The Government have stated that they believe a nine-month period exemption strikes the right balance between being long enough to provide relief whilst taxpayers go through the process of selling their home, but not so long that they are able to accrue large amounts of relief on two properties simultaneously, or on homes that are no longer used as their main residence. They cite research that the average time taken to sell a house (ie from listing to sale) is around 4.5 months.

It would seem that the shortened final period of exemption does not generally apply if contracts are exchanged on or before 5 April 2020 and the sale completes later. It is the date of exchange that fixes the date of disposal for capital gains tax (see TCGA 1992, s 28) and there is no anti-forestalling rule in the commencement provisions.

Section 24(4) introduces TCGA 1992, s 232ZA which enacts Extra-statutory Concession D49 for disposals on or after 6 April 2020 (subsection (11)). The new rule allows for a delay in taking up residence because of the completion of construction, renovation, redecoration or alteration of the residence, or because of the continuing occupation of the previous residence while arrangements are made to sell it. In such circumstances, the period of non-occupation between the acquisition and occupation is to be treated as a period of occupation qualifying for relief, provided that period does not exceed two years and no other person has used the property as a residence during that time.

The legislation broadly reproduces the effect of the concession, although the concession allowed for an initial 12-month period, which could be extended to 24 months if a good reason was shown. HMRC considered that if occupation was delayed beyond 24 months from acquisition the concession did not apply, but in *McHugh and another v HMRC* [2018] UKFTT 403 (TC), the First-tier Tribunal held that the concession applied to the 24 months immediately prior to occupation (which in that case was more than 24 months after acquisition). The enacted rule now appears to restore HMRC's original interpretation, as it applies only where occupation begins within the first 24 months of the period of ownership.

The final measure, introduced by section 24(5) (subsections (6) to (11) contain consequential and commencement provisions), is a significant curtailment of the extension of PPR relief to periods during which the residence is let. The new rules are in TCGA 1992, s 223B (replacing the old rules in TCGA 1992, s 223(4)) and apply where PPR relief is only available in part and at some time in the period of ownership there is shared occupancy with a tenant, ie part of the residence is the individual's only or main residence and another part is let out as residential accommodation. The draft legislation published in July 2019 included a requirement that the letting had to be otherwise than in the course of a trade or business, but this requirement is not included in the final legislation. The new rules apply to disposals on or after 6 April 2020 (subsection (11)) and so will apply even where the period of letting began before that date.

The Government has indicated that this change is intended to target PPR relief at owner occupiers. They point out that landlords are able to access other tax benefits not available to owner occupiers such as tax relief on replacing domestic items. The Government does, however, accept that where a lodger does not have exclusive use of any specific area of a residence, their occupation does not affect the owner occupier's claim for full relief and so lettings relief is not in question.

25 Corporate capital losses

Schedule 4 makes provision relating to capital losses made by companies.

COMMENTARY ON SECTION 25, SCHEDULE 4

Section 25 introduces Schedule 4, which extends the corporate loss restriction rules (CTA 2010, Pt 7ZA, introduced by FA 2019) to capital losses. [See Commentary note for Schedule 4]

26 Quarterly instalment payments

(1) The Corporation Tax (Instalment Payments) Regulations 1998 (SI 1998/3175) are amended as follows.

(2) At the end of regulation 3 (large and very large companies) insert—

"(11) A company which—

(a) is chargeable to corporation tax for an accounting period only because of a chargeable gain accruing to the company on the disposal of an asset, and

(b) would, apart from this paragraph, be a very large company by virtue of this regulation in respect of the accounting period,

is to be treated for the purposes of these regulations as if it were a large company by virtue of paragraph (1)."

(3) In regulation 3(10), in the words before paragraph (a), after "12 months" insert "and paragraph (11) does not apply".

(4) The amendments made by this section have effect in relation to accounting periods beginning on or after 11 March 2020.

COMMENTARY ON SECTION 26

Section 26 amends the Corporation Tax (Instalment Payments) Regulations 1998 (SI 1998/3175), which govern the instalment payments of corporation tax by 'large' and 'very large' companies. The amendments will ensure that companies that are only chargeable to corporation tax by virtue of chargeable gains, and which would otherwise not be very large companies for the purposes of these Regulations, will now be treated for the purposes of these Regulations as large companies, rather than as very large companies.

The Regulations require very large companies to pay their tax instalments four months earlier than large companies. The definitions are based on the company's profits, with adjustments for the number of associated companies and the length of the relevant accounting period. So a company that only has chargeable gains might fall into the very large category simply due to having a very short accounting period, perhaps only one day. So the change is to prevent the unfair acceleration of corporation tax payments for these companies.

The amendment applies for accounting periods starting on or after 11 March 2020.

27 Relief from CGT for loans to traders

In section 253(1)(b) of TCGA 1992 (which provides that a loan qualifies for relief only if the borrower is UK resident), at the beginning insert "if the loan is made before 24 January 2019,".

COMMENTARY ON SECTION 27

Section 27 amends the borrower residence condition in TCGA 1992, s 253(1)(b). This allows relief from capital gains tax (or corporation tax, despite the title of section 27) on the capital loss that arises when a loan made to a trader becomes irrecoverable or a payment is made under a guarantee as a result of a trader defaulting on a loan. The change is made as a result of a reasoned opinion issued by the European Commission on 24 January 2019 that the rules breached the EU principle of free movement of capital. The relief breached EU law because the relief was only available where the borrower was UK resident.

For loans made prior to 24 January 2019, the borrower (ie the trader, which may be a sole trader, partner or a company) needed to be UK resident. There was no temporal requirement in TCGA 1992, s 253 as to the residence and so it was assumed that being UK resident at the time the loan was made is sufficient for these purposes.

For loans made on or after 24 January 2019, the residence of the borrower is ignored. In the case of relief where a payment is made under a guarantee, again it is the date that the loan was taken out that is relevant; the loan under which the guarantee payment is made must have been taken out on or after 24 January 2019. Therefore, it may be possible for individuals with irrecoverable loans to non-UK traders or those who have made a payment under a guarantee on behalf of a non-UK trader to claim relief under the loan to trader rules.

The reasoned opinion issued by the European Commission covered relief for loans to traders and share loss relief (see the commentary under section 38).

Reliefs for business

28   Research and development expenditure credit

(1)   In section 104M(3) of CTA 2009 (amount of R&D expenditure credit) for "12%" substitute "13%".

(2)   The amendment made by this section has effect in relation to expenditure incurred on or after 1 April 2020.

COMMENTARY ON SECTION 28

This section amends CTA 2009, Pt 6A to increase the rate of the research and development expenditure credit (RDEC). CTA 2009, s 104M is amended to increase the rate of the RDEC from 12% to 13%. The section provides that the increase in rate relates to expenditure incurred on or after 1 April 2020.

Research and development (R&D) tax credits support the private sector by allowing companies to claim an enhanced corporation tax deduction or payable credit on their R&D costs. Incentivising additional R&D activity is an essential part of the Government's objective to increase productivity and promote growth through innovation within the UK economy.

In order to achieve this objective, the Government has increased the rate of RDEC from 12% to 13%. This increase means that large companies will obtain more financial support from Government when undertaking R&D activities. The ring fence RDEC rate remains at 49%.

In 2018, the rate of RDEC increased from 11% to 12%, which generated a net cashflow benefit of 9.72%. The current increase to 13% will result in a net benefit of 10.53% and may further incentivise the private sector to undertake innovative projects.

Whether or not this increase in RDEC is sufficient to attract multinational company investment into the UK, when compared to other jurisdictions following Brexit, remains to be seen.

29   Structures and buildings allowances: rate of relief

(1)   Part 2A of CAA 2001 (structures and buildings allowances) is amended as follows.

(2)   In section 270AA (application of Part 2A)—

     (a)   in subsection (2) (entitlement to an allowance), at the beginning of paragraph (b) insert "the beginning of", (b)　in subsection (2)(b)(ii), for "50 years" substitute "33 1/3 years", and

(c)　in subsection (5) (basic rule: allowance for a chargeable period of one year), for "2%" substitute "3%".

(3)　In section 270EA (proportionate adjustment in certain cases), in subsection (3)—

(a)　in paragraph (a), for "(b)" substitute "(b)(i)", and

(b)　after paragraph (a) (but before the "or") insert—

"(aa)　the period mentioned in section 270AA(2)(b)(ii) expires part way through the chargeable period,".

(4)　In section 270EB (multiple uses), in subsection (2), for "2%" substitute "3%".

(5)　After section 270GC (but before Chapter 8) insert—

"Chapter 7A

Adjustment for pre-April 2020 allowance

270GD　**Adjustment for pre-April 2020 allowance**

(1)　This section applies if—

(a)　on the relevant date, a person is entitled to an allowance under this Part by reference to qualifying expenditure incurred in relation to a building or structure,

(b)　the person does not dispose of the relevant interest in the building or structure before the end of the period mentioned in section 270AA(2)(b)(ii) (the "allowance period"), and

(c)　at the end of the allowance period, the person is entitled to an allowance under this Part by reference to the qualifying expenditure mentioned in paragraph (a).

(2)　The person is entitled to an additional amount of allowance for the chargeable period in which the allowance period ends.

(3)　The additional amount of the allowance is 1% of the qualifying expenditure multiplied by the following fraction—

$$D/365$$

where D is the number of days during the period beginning with 29 October 2018 and ending with the relevant date in respect of which an allowance under this Part by reference to the qualifying expenditure was made to the person.

(4)　For the purposes of this section "the relevant date" means—

(a)　for income tax purposes, 5 April 2020, or

(b)　for corporation tax purposes, 31 March 2020."

(6)　The amendments made by this section are treated as having come into force—

(a)　for income tax purposes, on 6 April 2020, or

(b)　for corporation tax purposes, on 1 April 2020,

and in subsection (7) references to the commencement date are to be read accordingly.

(7)　For the purposes of subsection (6), in relation to a chargeable period beginning before the commencement date and ending on or after that date, Part 2A of CAA 2001 applies as if—

(a)　the part of the chargeable period falling before the commencement date, and

(b)　the part of the chargeable period falling on or after that date,

were separate chargeable periods.

COMMENTARY ON SECTION 29

A new capital allowance known as the structures and buildings allowance (SBA) was introduced by regulations (SI 2019/1087) under powers conferred by FA 2019, s 30. These regulations inserted a new Part 2A (ss 270AA–270IH) into CAA 2001. This provides relief for qualifying capital expenditure on buildings and structures brought into use for the purposes of a trade, profession, vocation, property business or other qualifying activity. The SBA is available on eligible construction costs incurred on or after 29 October 2018 at an annual rate on a straight-line basis, i e a fixed percentage of the original cost is given as an allowance for each chargeable period. The SBA is available to persons within the charge to either income tax or corporation tax.

The original annual rate at which the SBA was to be given was 2%, so that full relief would be given over a writing-down period of 50 years.

Section 29 increases the annual rate to 3%, and reduces the length of the writing-down period to 33⅓ years. The increase in the annual rate has effect on and after 1 April 2020 for corporation tax (6 April 2020 for income tax), regardless of when the qualifying expenditure was incurred.

For the purpose only of computing the allowance for a chargeable period straddling 1 April (or 6 April) 2020 (the 'commencement date'), that period is split into two separate notional chargeable periods, the second of which begins on the commencement date. It should be noted that there is already provision in the original legislation for the allowance to be proportionately reduced for chargeable periods of less than one year (or if the conditions for entitlement to an SBA are met for only part of a chargeable period). So, for example, for a company accounting period covering the year to 31 December 2020, the allowance for expenditure meeting the entitlement conditions throughout that year will be based on 91 days (1.1.20 to 31.3.20) at 2% and 275 days (1.4.20 to 31.12.20) at 3%.

The reduction from 50 to 33⅓ in the number of years comprised in the writing-down period applies equally to qualifying expenditure which had already attracted an allowance at the old 2% rate before 1 April (6 April) 2020. This is achieved by enabling an additional allowance (equivalent to the shortfall in allowances) to be claimed in the chargeable period in which the writing-down period of 33⅓ years comes to an end. However, this applies only if the person entitled to the allowance on 31 March 2020 for corporation tax (5 April 2020 for income tax) does not dispose of the relevant interest in the building before the end of the writing-down period and continues to be entitled to an allowance in respect of the expenditure at that time. The amount of the additional allowance is 1% of the qualifying expenditure multiplied by the fraction D/365, where D is the number of days, during the period beginning with 29 October 2018 and ending with 31 March (5 April) 2020, for which an SBA was made to the person by reference to that expenditure.

For example, say C Ltd, which has a 31 March accounting date, was entitled with effect from 1 October 2019 to an SBA on qualifying expenditure of £100,000. For the year to 31 March 2020, the available SBA would be £1,000 (£100,000 @ 2% × 183/366). The 33⅓ year writing-down period will end on 30 January 2053. For each accounting period after the first, C will be entitled to an SBA of £3,000 (£100,000 @ 3%). This will continue up to and including the year ending 31 March 2052. By that time, total SBAs of £97,000 will have been available. For the year to 31 March 2053, C will initially be entitled to an SBA of £2,506 (£3,000 × 305/365). But C will also be entitled to an additional SBA of £501 ((£100,000 @ 1%) × 183/365). Total SBAs of £100,007 will now have been available over the writing-down period. In practice, the additional SBA will be restricted to the actual shortfall of £494 so that allowances do not exceed qualifying expenditure. The difference here is due partly to the incidence of leap years and partly to the fact that a 33⅓ year writing-down period does not cover an exact number of days; neither of these helps in the making of precise calculations.

Section 29 also makes a minor technical amendment, of limited practical significance, to allow for the fact that a writing-down period may now end partway through a day. Finally, an amendment is made to clarify that the SBA falls to be proportionately reduced where the writing-down period ends partway through a chargeable period.

30 Structures and buildings allowances: miscellaneous amendments

Schedule 5 makes miscellaneous amendments of CAA 2001 in relation to structures and buildings allowances.

COMMENTARY ON SECTION 30, SCHEDULE 5

[See Commentary note for Schedule 5]

31 Intangible fixed assets: pre-FA 2002 assets etc

(1) Part 8 of CTA 2009 (intangible fixed assets) is amended as follows.

(2) In section 711 (overview of Part 8) in subsection (8) after paragraph (fa) (but before the "and" at the end of that paragraph) insert—

> "(fb) Chapter 16A (debits in respect of assets that were pre-FA 2002 assets etc),
> (fc) Chapter 16B (fungible assets),".

(3) In section 845 (transfer between company and related party treated as at market value) in subsection (4) (exceptions)—

>   (a) omit the "and" at the end of paragraph (d), and
>   (b) at the end of paragraph (e) insert ", and
>
>   (f) sections 900E and 900F (special rules in respect of assets that were pre-FA 2002 assets etc)".

(4) In section 849AB (grant of licence or other right treated as at market value) in subsection (6) (exceptions)—

>   (a) omit the "and" at the end of paragraph (a), and
>   (b) at the end of paragraph (b) insert ", and
>
>   (c) section 900F (special rules in respect of assets that were pre-FA 2002 assets etc)".

(5) Omit section 858 (fungible assets) and the italic heading before that section.

(6) In section 882 (application of Part 8 to assets created or acquired on or after 1 April 2002) for subsection (1) substitute—

> "(1) The general rule is that this Part applies to an intangible fixed asset of a company ("the company") only if one or more of the conditions in subsections (1A) to (1D) is met.
>
> (1A) The condition in this subsection is that the asset is created by the company on or after 1 April 2002.
>
> (1B) The condition in this subsection is that the asset is acquired by the company during the period beginning with 1 April 2002 and ending with 30 June 2020 and either—
>
>>   (a) it is acquired from a person who at the time of the acquisition is not a related party in relation to the company, or
>>   (b) it is acquired in case A (in subsection (3)), case B (in subsection (4)) or case C (in subsection (5)) from a person who at the time of the acquisition is a related party in relation to the company.
>
> (1C) The condition in this subsection is that the asset is acquired by the company on or after 1 July 2020.
>
> (1D) The condition in this subsection is that the asset is held by the company immediately before 1 July 2020 and at that time the company is not within the charge to corporation tax in respect of the asset.
>
> (1E) But the condition in subsection (1D) is to be treated as not met if—
>
>>   (a) at any time during the period beginning with 19 March 2020 and ending with 30 June 2020 the asset is a pre-FA 2002 asset in the hands of any company that is within the charge to corporation tax in respect of the asset, and
>>   (b) after that time but during that period the asset is not acquired by any other company from a person who at the time of the acquisition is not a related party in relation to that other company."

(7) In section 883 (assets treated as created or acquired when expenditure incurred)—

>   (a) after subsection (3) insert—

> "(3A) An intangible asset is treated as acquired on or after 1 July 2020 so far as expenditure on its acquisition is incurred on or after that date.
>
> (3B) An intangible asset is treated as acquired during the period beginning with 1 April 2002 and ending with 30 June 2020 so far as expenditure on its acquisition is incurred during that period.
>
> (3C) An intangible asset is treated as acquired during the period beginning with 19 March 2020 and ending with 30 June 2020 so far as expenditure on its acquisition is incurred during that period.",
>
>   (b) in subsection (4)—

   (i) for "whether" substitute "when", and
   (ii) omit "on or after 1 April 2002", and
 (c) for subsection (5) substitute—

"(5) If by reason of any of subsections (3) to (3C) of this section this Part would apply to an intangible fixed asset of a company to a limited extent only, the asset is to be treated as if it consisted of two separate assets—

   (a) one asset being an asset to which this Part applies, and
   (b) one asset being an asset to which the alternative enactments apply."

(8) Omit section 890 (fungible assets: application of section 858) and the italic heading before that section.

(9) Omit section 891 (realisation and acquisition of fungible assets).

(10) In section 892 (certain assets acquired on transfer of business)—

   (a) in the heading at the end insert "or transfer within a group",
   (b) in subsection (2) omit "and" at the end of paragraph (b),
   (c) in subsection (2) after paragraph (c) insert ", and
    (d) section 171 of that Act (transfers within a group)", and
   (d) after subsection (4) insert—

"(5) If the transfer mentioned in subsection (1) occurred before 1 July 2020, this section applies as if paragraph (d) of subsection (2) were omitted."

(11) In section 893 (assets whose value derives from pre-2002 assets) in subsection (1)(a) for "on or after 1 April 2002" substitute "during the period beginning with 1 April 2002 and ending with 30 June 2020".

(12) In section 895 (assets acquired in connection with disposals of pre-FA 2002 assets) in subsection (1)(b) at the beginning insert "at any time before 1 July 2020".

(13) After Chapter 16 insert—

"Chapter 16A

Debits in respect of assets that were pre-FA 2002 assets etc

Introduction

900A Introduction

(1) This Chapter contains special rules affecting the debits to be brought into account by a company for tax purposes in respect of an intangible fixed asset that is a restricted asset.

(2) Sections 900B to 900D make provision determining when an intangible fixed asset of a company is a restricted asset for the purposes of this Chapter.

(3) Sections 900E and 900F contain the special rules.

(4) The following sections contain supplementary provisions—

   (a) section 900G (meaning of relieving acquisition),
   (b) section 900H (when two persons are related), and
   (c) section 900I (acquisition of asset in pursuance of an unconditional obligation).

When an intangible fixed asset is a restricted asset

900B When an intangible fixed asset is a restricted asset: the first case

(1) An intangible fixed asset of a company is a restricted asset if—

   (a) the company acquired the asset on or after 1 July 2020,
   (b) the company acquired the asset from a person who at the time of the acquisition was a related party in relation to the company, and
   (c) the asset is within subsection (2) or (3).

(2) The asset is within this subsection if—

   (a) the asset was a pre-FA 2002 asset in the hands of any company on 1 July 2020, and
   (b) at no time on or after 1 July 2020 has the asset been the subject of a relieving acquisition.

(3) The asset is within this subsection if—

    (a) the asset was created before 1 April 2002,

    (b) immediately before 1 July 2020 the asset was held by a person other than a company, and

    (c) at no time on or after 1 July 2020 has the asset been the subject of a relieving acquisition.

(4) But the asset is not within subsection (3) if the person mentioned in that subsection ("the intermediary") acquired the asset on or after 1 April 2002 from a person ("the third party") who meets the conditions in subsections (5), (6) and (7).

(5) The third party meets the condition in this subsection if—

    (a) the third party is not a company, or

    (b) the third party is a company in relation to which the intermediary is not a related party at the time of the intermediary's acquisition.

(6) The third party meets the condition in this subsection if at the time of the intermediary's acquisition the third party is not a related party in relation to a company in relation to which the intermediary is a related party.

(7) The third party meets the condition in this subsection if at the time of the acquisition of the asset by the company mentioned in subsection (1) the third party is not a related party in relation to that company.

900C   When an intangible fixed asset is a restricted asset: the second case

(1) An intangible fixed asset of a company ("the asset concerned") is a restricted asset if—

    (a) the company acquired the asset concerned on or after 1 July 2020,

    (b) the company acquired the asset concerned from a person who at the time of the acquisition was a related party in relation to the company, and

    (c) the asset concerned is within subsection (2).

(2) The asset concerned is within this subsection if—

    (a) the asset concerned was created on or after 1 July 2020,

    (b) at no time has the asset concerned been the subject of a relieving acquisition,

    (c) the value of the asset concerned derives in whole or in part from another asset ("the other asset"), and

    (d) the other asset was a pre-FA 2002 asset or a restricted asset in the hands of any company on the date the asset concerned was created.

(3) The condition in subsection (2)(d) is to be treated as met if—

    (a) the other asset was held by a person other than a company on the date the asset concerned was created,

    (b) on the date the asset concerned was created that person was a related party in relation to a company, and

    (c) the other asset would have been a pre-FA 2002 asset or a restricted asset in the hands of that company on the date the asset concerned was created had that company acquired the other asset from that person immediately before that date.

(4) For the purposes of this section the cases in which the value of an asset may be derived from any other asset include any case where—

    (a) assets have been merged or divided,

    (b) assets have changed their nature, or

    (c) rights or interests in or over assets have been created or extinguished.

900D   When an intangible fixed asset is a restricted asset: the third case

(1) An intangible fixed asset of a company ("the asset concerned") is a restricted asset if—

    (a) the company acquired the asset concerned on or after 1 July 2020, and

    (b) the asset concerned is within subsection (2).

(2) The asset concerned is within this subsection if—

    (a) the asset concerned was acquired by any company on or after 1 July 2020 directly or indirectly as a consequence of, or otherwise in connection with, the realisation by another person of an asset ("the other asset"),

    (b)   that company and that other person were related parties at the time of the realisation of the other asset,

    (c)   the other asset was a pre-FA 2002 asset or a restricted asset in the hands of any company at any time during the period beginning with 1 July 2020 and ending with the time of the realisation mentioned in paragraph (a),

    (d)   the other asset was not the subject of a relieving acquisition at any time during the period beginning with 1 July 2020 and ending with the time of the realisation mentioned in paragraph (a), and

    (e)   the asset concerned has not been the subject of a relieving acquisition at any time after the realisation mentioned in paragraph (a).

(3)   The condition in subsection (2)(c) is to be treated as met if—

    (a)   immediately before 1 July 2020 the other asset was held by a person that was not a company,

    (b)   immediately before 1 July 2020 that person was a related party in relation to a company, and

    (c)   the other asset would have been a pre-FA 2002 asset in the hands of that company on 1 July 2020 had that company acquired the asset from that person immediately before that date.

(4)   For the purposes of subsection (2) it does not matter whether—

    (a)   the other asset is the same as the asset concerned,

    (b)   the asset concerned is acquired at the time of the realisation of the other asset, or

    (c)   the asset concerned is acquired by merging assets or otherwise.

The special rules

900E   Special rule: section 900B case

(1)   This section applies in respect of a restricted asset of a company if it is a restricted asset by reason of section 900B.

(2)   If the company was the first company to acquire the asset on or after 1 July 2020, the relevant Chapters of this Part have effect as if the company acquired the asset at no cost.

(3)   If the company was not the first company to acquire the asset on or after 1 July 2020, the relevant Chapters of this Part have effect as if the company acquired the asset for the adjusted amount.

(4)   The adjusted amount is—

$$A - B$$

where—

    A is the amount of consideration—

        (a)   for which the company actually acquired the asset, or

        (b)   if different, for which it would (ignoring this section) be treated for the purposes of the Taxes Acts as having acquired the asset, and

    B is the market value of the asset on the date it was first acquired by a company on or after 1 July 2020.

(5)   Where B is greater than A the adjusted amount is nil.

(6)   In this section—

    "market value", in relation to an asset, means the price the asset might reasonably be expected to fetch on a sale in the open market, and

    "the relevant Chapters of this Part" means—

        (a)   Chapter 3 (debits in respect of intangible fixed assets),

        (b)   Chapter 15 (adjustments on change of accounting policy), and

        (c)   Chapter 5 (calculation of tax written-down value) in so far as it has effect for the purposes of Chapters 3 and 15.

900F   Special rule: section 900C or 900D case

(1)   This section applies in respect of a restricted asset of a company if it is a restricted asset by reason of section 900C or 900D.

(2)   The relevant Chapters of this Part have effect as if the company acquired the asset for the adjusted amount.

(3) The adjusted amount is calculated as follows—

Step 1

Find the amount—

(a) for which the company actually acquired the asset, or

(b) if different, for which it would (ignoring this section) be treated for the purposes of the Taxes Acts as having acquired the asset.

Step 2

Deduct from the amount found at Step 1 such proportion of the notional deduction amount for the relevant other asset or each relevant other asset as is just and reasonable in the circumstances.

(4) Where the deduction at Step 2 results in a negative value the adjusted amount is nil.

(5) In subsection (3)—

"relevant other asset" means an asset by reference to which the conditions in paragraphs (c) and (d) of section 900C(2) or (as the case may be) the conditions in section 900D(2) were met, and

"the notional deduction amount", in relation to a relevant other asset, means—

(a) in a case where section 900E(2) would have applied had the company acquired the relevant other asset instead of the restricted asset, an amount equal to the market value of the relevant other asset at the time the restricted asset was acquired, and

(b) in a case where section 900E(3) would have applied had the company acquired the relevant other asset instead of the restricted asset, an amount equal to the market value of the relevant other asset at the time it was first acquired by a company on or after 1 July 2020, and

(c) in a case where subsection (2) of this section would have applied had the company acquired the relevant other asset instead of the restricted asset, the amount that would have been deducted at step 2 of subsection (3) of this section if the company had acquired the relevant other asset instead of the restricted asset.

(6) In this section "market value" and "the relevant Chapters of this Part" have the same meaning as in section 900E.

Supplementary provisions

900G Meaning of "relieving acquisition"

For the purposes of this Chapter, an asset is the subject of a relieving acquisition if it is acquired by a company from a person who at the time of the acquisition is not a related party in relation to the company.

900H Supplementary provision about when two persons are related

(1) References in this Chapter to one person being a related party in relation to another person are to be read as including references to the participation condition being met as between those persons.

(2) References in subsection (1) to a person include a firm in a case where, for section 1259 purposes, references in this Chapter to a company are read as references to the firm.

(3) In subsection (2) "section 1259 purposes" means the purposes of determining under section 1259 the amount of profits or losses to be allocated to a partner in a firm.

(4) Section 148 of TIOPA 2010 (when the participation condition is met) applies for the purposes of subsection (1) as it applies for the purposes of section 147(1)(b) of TIOPA 2010.

900I Acquisition of asset in pursuance of an unconditional obligation

(1) A company that acquires an intangible fixed asset in pursuance of an unconditional obligation under a contract is to be treated for the purposes of this Chapter as having acquired the asset on the date on which the company became subject to that obligation or (if later) the date on which that obligation became unconditional.

(2) An obligation is unconditional if it may not be varied or extinguished by the exercise of a right (whether under contract or otherwise).

Chapter 16B

Fungible assets

900J   Fungible assets: general

(1) For the purposes of this Part—

(a) fungible assets of the same kind that are held by the same person in the same capacity are treated as indistinguishable parts of a single asset,

(b) that asset is treated as growing as additional assets of the same kind are created or acquired, and

(c) that asset is treated as diminishing as some of the assets are realised.

(2) In this Part "fungible assets" means assets of a nature to be dealt in without identifying the particular assets involved.

900K   Fungible assets: pre-FA 2002 assets and restricted assets

(1) For the purposes of section 900J—

(a) pre-FA 2002 assets,

(b) restricted assets, and

(c) standard intangible fixed assets,

are to be regarded as assets of different kinds.

(2) If section 900J applies (whether or not it is a case where subsection (1) of this section has effect)—

(a) a single asset comprising pre-FA 2002 assets is treated as itself being a pre-FA 2002 asset,

(b) a single asset comprising restricted assets is treated as itself being a restricted asset, and

(c) a single asset comprising standard intangible fixed assets is treated as itself being a standard intangible fixed asset.

900L   Realisation of fungible assets: pre-FA 2002 assets and restricted assets

(1) This section applies if—

(a) a company realises a fungible asset, and

(b) apart from subsection (1) of section 900K, the asset would be treated as part of a single asset comprising more than one of the kinds of asset referred to in that subsection.

(2) The realisation is treated—

(a) as diminishing a single asset of the company comprising pre-FA 2002 assets in priority to diminishing a single asset of the company comprising restricted assets or a single asset of the company comprising standard intangible fixed assets, and

(b) as diminishing a single asset of the company comprising restricted assets in priority to diminishing a single asset of the company comprising standard intangible fixed assets.

900M   Acquisition of fungible assets: pre-FA 2002 assets and restricted assets

(1) Fungible assets acquired by a company that would not otherwise be treated as pre-FA 2002 assets are so treated so far as they are identified, in accordance with the following rules, with pre-FA 2002 assets realised by the company.

(2) Fungible assets acquired by a company that would not otherwise be treated as pre-FA 2002 assets or restricted assets are to be treated as restricted assets so far as they are identified, in accordance with the following rules, with restricted assets realised by the company.

(3) Rule 1 is that assets acquired are identified with pre-FA 2002 assets or restricted assets of the same kind realised by the company within the period beginning 30 days before and ending 30 days after the date of the acquisition.

(4)   The reference in subsection (3) to assets "of the same kind" is to assets that are, or but for section 900K(1) would be, treated as part of a single asset because of section 900J.

(5)   Rule 2 is that assets realised earlier are identified before assets realised later.

(6)   Rule 3 is that assets acquired earlier are identified before assets acquired later.

900N   Debits in respect of a single asset comprising restricted assets

(1)   This section applies in respect of a single asset of a company that comprises restricted assets (and is itself treated as a restricted asset by reason of section 900K(2)(b)).

(2)   The relevant Chapters of this Part have effect as if the company acquired the single asset for the sum of the amounts for which the company would have been treated for the purposes of those Chapters as having acquired each of the restricted assets that comprises the single asset.

(3)   In this section "the relevant Chapter of this Part" has the meaning given by section 900E(6).

900O   Interpretation

In this Chapter—

"restricted asset" has the same meaning as in Chapter 16A, and
"standard intangible fixed asset" means an intangible fixed asset that is neither a pre-FA 2002 asset nor a restricted asset."

(14)   The amendments made by this section have effect in relation to accounting periods beginning on or after 1 July 2020.

(15)   For the purposes of subsection (14), an accounting period beginning before, and ending on or after, 1 July 2020 is to be treated as if so much of the accounting period as falls before that date, and so much of the accounting period as falls on or after that date, were separate accounting periods.

COMMENTARY ON SECTION 31

The principal changes made by section 31 are:
- a limited relaxation of the intangible fixed asset pre-FA 2002 asset rules;
- the introduction of a new class of restricted assets; and
- consequential changes to the fungible asset rules.

Pre-FA 2002 asset changes

Before the changes introduced by section 31 took effect, intangible fixed assets which a company held at 31 March 2002 were excluded from the intangible fixed assets regime and such assets are called pre-FA 2002 assets. This restriction also extended to intangible fixed assets which a company acquired on or after 1 April 2002 from a related party where such assets were pre-FA 2002 assets in the hands of the related party, or where a company acquired an intangible fixed asset which derived its value from a pre-FA 2002 asset held by a related party.

The pre-FA 2002 asset changes introduced by section 31 fall into two categories.

First, intangible fixed assets which were held by a company on 30 June 2020 and in respect of which the company was not within the charge to corporation tax at that time fall within the intangible fixed assets legislation if they are subsequently transferred to a company within the charge to corporation tax (including a related party), or if the company comes within the charge to corporation tax in respect of the assets on or after 1 July 2020. This case covers intangible fixed assets held by a non-UK resident company, or intangible fixed assets held by a non-UK permanent establishment of a UK resident company for which an election under CTA 2009, s 18A has been made (election to exclude profits of a non-UK permanent establishment from the charge to corporation tax). In effect, the measure is an inducement to groups which have previously transferred intangible fixed assets outside the UK tax net to bring such assets back within the UK tax net. See further new CTA 2009, s 882(1D), which is introduced by subsection (6). An anti-forestalling rule applies which excludes an intangible fixed asset from the scope of this relieving provision where the company (acquiring company) acquired the intangible fixed asset on or after 19 March 2020 and before 1 July 2020 and at a time in that period and before the acquiring company acquired the asset it was a pre-FA 2002 asset in the hands of any company and the asset had not been acquired from that company by an unrelated company before it was acquired by the acquiring company (see new CTA 2009, s 882(1E)).

Secondly, there is a partial relaxation of the exclusion for pre-FA 2002 assets where such assets are acquired by a company from a related party on or after 1 July 2020 and such assets are termed 'restricted assets' (see below). There is an important exception to this relaxation, which is that pre-FA 2002 assets that are transferred from one group company to another, and TCGA 1992, s 171 applies to the transfer, continue to be pre-FA 2002 assets in the hands of the transferee (see new CTA 2009, s 892(2)(d), which is introduced by subsection (10)).

(The new CTA 2009, s 882(1A), and (1B) effectively reproduce the former conditions of CTA 2009, s 882(1), save that the new subsection (1B) (rewritten former CTA 2009, s 882(1)(b), (c)) is expressed only to apply to assets acquired before 1 July 2020.)

Restricted assets

Subsection (13) introduces new CTA 2009, Pt 8, Ch 16A, which prescribes the debits to be brought into account in respect of restricted assets. Intangible fixed assets that are acquired by a company (acquiring company) from a related party on or after 1 July 2020 are treated as restricted assets in the following cases:

(1)   where the asset was a pre-FA 2002 asset at 1 July 2020 in the hands of any company and the asset had not been acquired by any company from an unrelated party at any time on or after 1 July 2020 before it was acquired by the acquiring company; or

(2)   where the asset was created before 1 April 2002, at 30 June 2020 the asset was held by a person other than a company and the asset has not been acquired by a company from an unrelated party at any time on or after 1 July 2020 before it was acquired by the acquiring company. An asset will fall outside this condition (and thus the expenditure incurred by the company on acquiring the asset will not be restricted) where, broadly, the person who held the asset at 30 June 2020 acquired the asset from a person that was not related to that person or to the acquiring company. For the detail see CTA 2009, s 900B(4)–(7).

For the above purposes an expanded definition of related party applies and will include cases where the participation condition in TIOPA 2010, s 148 is met in respect of the two persons (including where one of the persons is a partnership) (new CTA 2009, s 900H).

Where the conditions in 1 or 2 are satisfied and the company is the first company to acquire the asset on or after 1 July 2020, the acquiring company is treated as acquiring the intangible fixed asset for nil consideration. On a subsequent acquisition by a related company the asset is treated as being acquired for a consideration equal to the excess of the purchase consideration over the asset's market value at the time that it was first acquired by a company on or after 1 July 2020, or where this amount is negative, for nil consideration.

Similar restrictions apply in the case of:

(1)   an asset that was created on or after 1 July 2020, to the extent that the asset derives its value from a pre-FA 2002 asset or a restricted asset and the asset has not at any time on or after 1 July 2020 been acquired by a company from an unrelated party (new CTA 2009, s 900C); and

(2)   an asset that was acquired by a company from a related party on or after 1 July 2020 where:

     (a)   such asset came into existence directly or indirectly as a result of the realisation by a related party of all or part of an asset (other asset), which was a pre-FA 2002 asset or a restricted asset in the hands of the related party at any time in the period from 1 July 2020 to the time of the realisation;

     (b)   the other asset had not been acquired by a company from an unrelated party at any time on or after 1 July 2020 up to the time of the realisation; and

    (c)   the asset itself had not been acquired by a company from an unrelated party at any time on or after the realisation of the other asset (new CTA 2009, s 900D).

An expanded definition of related party applies and includes cases where the participation condition in TIOPA 2010, s 148 is met in respect of the two persons (including where one of the persons is a partnership) (new CTA 2009, s 900H).

Where the above provisions apply, broadly, the company is only able to obtain relief for the acquisition expenditure on the asset to the extent that such expenditure exceeds what was the market value of the other asset (or relevant proportion in the case of a partial realisation of the other asset). The time at which the market value of the other asset is to be determined is set out in the new CTA 2009, s 900F(5).

Fungible assets

Subsection (13) also introduces new fungible asset rules contained in new CTA 2009, Pt 8, Ch 16B (CTA 2009, ss 900J–900O) as following the FA 2020 changes the transitional provisions dealing with fungible assets (defined as assets that can be dealt in without identifying the particular asset involved – new CTA 2009, s 900J(2)) held at 1 April 2002 need to deal with pre-FA 2002 assets, restricted assets and standard intangible fixed assets (which are fully within the intangible fixed assets legislation). These new sections determine how realisations and acquisitions of fungible assets are to be identified with pre-FA 2002 assets, restricted assets and standard intangible fixed assets and apply broadly in the same way as the former CTA 2009, s 858 (which is repealed with effect for times on or after 1 July 2020 by subsection (5)), save that CTA 2009, s 858 only addressed pre-FA 2002 assets and intangible fixed assets that were fully within the intangible fixed assets legislation.

Consequential amendments

A series of consequential amendments are made as a result of the above amendments. These include:

* modifying CTA 2009, s 883 (assets treated as created or acquired when expenditure incurred) to accommodate the changes introduced by section 31; and
* the modification of CTA 2009, ss 893 and 895 by subsections (11) and (12) so that they only apply to acquisitions before 1 July 2020, as from that date they are replaced by the new CTA 2009, Pt 7, Ch 16A regime for restricted assets that is introduced by subsection (13) and which is considered above.

Miscellaneous measures affecting companies

32   Non-UK resident companies carrying on UK property businesses etc

Schedule 6 makes minor amendments (which arise in consequence of the provision made by Schedule 1 or 5 to FA 2019) in relation to non-UK resident companies that carry on UK property businesses or have other income relating to land in the United Kingdom.

COMMENTARY ON SECTION 32, SCHEDULE 6
[See Commentary note for Schedule 6]

33   Surcharge on banking companies: transferred-in losses

(1)   Chapter 4 of Part 7A of CTA 2010 (surcharge on banking companies) is amended as follows.

(2)   In section 269D (overview of Chapter), after subsection (4) insert—

   "(4A)   Section 269DCA defines "non-banking transferred-in loss relief" for the purposes of calculating a company's surcharge profits."

(3)   In section 269DA (surcharge on banking companies), in subsection (2) (calculation of "surcharge profits")—

     (a)   in the formula, after "NBPLR +" insert "NBTILR +";
     (b)   after the definition of "NBPLR" insert—

      ""NBTILR" is the amount (if any) of non-banking transferred-in loss relief (see section 269DCA);".

(4)   In section 269DC (meaning of "non-banking or pre-2016 loss relief")—

    (a)   in subsection (13) (meaning of "a non-banking or pre-2016 carried-forward capital loss")—

        (i)   in paragraph (a), omit "or as a result of a non-banking loss transfer";

        (ii)   in paragraph (b), for "8(1)(b)" substitute "2A(1)(b)";

    (b)   omit subsections (14) and (15) (meaning of "non-banking loss transfer" and "non-banking company").

(5)   After section 269DC insert—

"269DCA   Meaning of "non-banking transferred-in loss relief"

(1)   In section 269DA(2), "non-banking transferred-in loss relief" means the sum of any amounts that are deducted under section 2A of TCGA 1992 in determining the taxable total profits of the company of the chargeable accounting period in respect of an allowable loss, or any part of an allowable loss, that accrued to the company as a result of a non-banking loss transfer.

(2)   A "non-banking loss transfer" is a transfer to the company of the whole or any part of an allowable loss, by an election under section 171A of TCGA 1992 (reallocation within group), from a non-banking company.

(3)   In this section "non-banking company" means a company that is not a banking company at the time that the allowable loss, or such part of it as the election transfers, is treated as accruing by virtue of the election (see, in particular, section 171B(3) of TCGA 1992)."

(6)   The amendments made by this section have effect in relation to an allowable loss, or any part of an allowable loss, deducted from a chargeable gain accruing on a disposal made on or after 11 March 2020.

COMMENTARY ON SECTION 33

Section 33 (surcharge on banking companies: transferred-in losses) applies to banking companies including building societies (banks) within the charge to UK corporation tax.

The corporation tax surcharge applicable to banks ('bank surcharge') is a charge of 8% on the taxable profits of banking companies, payable in addition to corporation tax. The surcharge was introduced by F(No 2)A 2015, Sch 3, which inserted CTA 2010, Pt 7A, Ch 4. The purpose of the surcharge alongside the earlier bank levy was for banks to make 'a fair contribution in respect of the potential risks they pose to the UK financial system and wider economy'.

The surcharge profits are calculated on the same basis as for corporation tax, but with some reliefs denied. The surcharge legislation, before these latest amendments, had created an anomalous result.

The original legislation operated to prevent a bank to benefit from the transferring in of allowable losses from a non-banking company to reduce future chargeable gains. However, the original legislation failed to prevent the transfers of allowable losses to be used to reduce in-year chargeable gains.

These latest section 33 amendments remove the temporal inconsistency and ensure that banks are not able to reduce their surcharge liability using allowable losses suffered in non-banking parts of their groups, against current and future chargeable gain.

Detailed description of the amendments

Section 33 makes minor amendments to the surcharge on banking companies legislation to introduce a new adjustment to surcharge profits. This adjustment denies relief against the surcharge profits for allowable losses transferred to a banking company from a non-banking company in the same group. The amendment has effect for allowable losses deducted from chargeable gains accruing on or after 11 March 2020. HMRC has published guidance on the bank surcharge impact of transfers between banking and non-banking companies in its Banking Manual at BKM403800.

Subsection (1) introduces amendments to CTA 2010, Pt 7A, Ch 4.

Subsection (2) inserts subsection (4A) into CTA 2010, s 269D ('Overview of Chapter'), which updates the overview to include the newly introduced section 269DCA.

Subsection (3) amends CTA 2010, s 269DA(2). The amendment inserts a new adjustment, 'non-banking transferred-in loss relief', to the formula for calculating 'surcharge profits'. It also introduces the definition of this amendment at the newly introduced CTA 2010, s 269DCA.

Subsection (4) amends CTA 2010, s 269DC to remove references to non-banking loss transfers in s 269DC(13) and removing s 269DC(14) and (15). These provisions are effectively superseded by the new definition for 'non-banking transferred-in loss relief' inserted at CTA 2010, s 269DCA. The amendment updates the reference to TCGA 1992, s 8 to its replacement at TCGA 1992, s 2A.

Subsection (5) inserts section 269DCA into CTA 2010. This section defines 'nonbanking transferred-in loss relief' for the purposes of CTA 2010, s 269DA, which is an allowable loss transferred to a banking company from a non-banking company via an election under TCGA 1992, s 171A. The new section defines a 'nonbanking company' as a company that is not a banking company at the time that the allowable loss arose.

Subsection (6) defines the commencement provisions for the changes. The changes will only apply to allowable losses deducted from chargeable gains arising on disposals made on or after 11 March 2020.

34   CT payment plans for tax on certain transactions with EEA residents

Schedule 7 makes provision for the deferral of the payment of corporation tax arising in connection with certain transactions involving companies resident in an EEA state.

COMMENTARY ON SECTION 34, SCHEDULE 7

Section 34 introduces Schedule 7, which provides for the payment of corporation tax in instalments where the tax arises from certain intra-group transactions to companies resident in EEA member states. [See Commentary note for Schedule 7]

35   Changes to accounting standards affecting leases

(1)   Schedule 14 to FA 2019 (leases: changes to accounting standards etc) is amended as follows.

(2)   In paragraph 13 (cases where asset first recognised for period of account beginning on or after 1 January 2019), for sub-paragraph (1) substitute—

"(1)   This paragraph applies if the first period of account for which the right-of-use asset falls (or would fall) to be recognised for accounting purposes in the accounts of the lessee begins on or after 1 January 2019 (referred to in the following provisions of this paragraph as "the first period of account")."

(3)   For paragraph 14 (cases where asset first recognised for a period of account beginning before 1 January 2019) substitute—

"**14** (1)   This paragraph applies if the first period of account for which the right-of-use asset falls (or would fall) to be recognised for accounting purposes in the accounts of the lessee begins before 1 January 2019.

(2)   The change of basis provisions and this Part of this Schedule have effect—

    (a)   as if there were a change of accounting policy with respect of the accounts of the lessee for the first period of account beginning on or after 1 January 2019, and

    (b)   as if that period of account were the first period of account for which the right-of-use asset falls (or would fall) to be recognised for accounting purposes in the accounts of the lessee."

(4)   Schedule 14 to FA 2019 has effect, and is to be deemed always to have had effect, with the amendments made by this section.

COMMENTARY ON SECTION 35

In January 2016, the International Accounting Standards Board (IASB) issued a new accounting standard ('IFRS 16') for dealing with leases. IFRS 16 is mandatory for all accounts prepared using International Financial Reporting Standards for periods commencing on or after 1 January 2019, with early adoption permitted. In addition, if an entity uses the UK GAAP standard FRS 101, they will also have to adopt IFRS 16 from the effective date. Hereafter references to IFRS 16 will apply to entities using either full IFRS or FRS 101.

Following a wide consultation, it was decided that spreading the tax effect of the transitional adjustment upon the adoption of IFRS 16 provided protection for the Exchequer whilst ensuring fairness for lessees. Schedule 14 to FA 2019 made changes to income tax and corporation tax rules as a result of the introduction of IFRS 16. FA 2019, Sch 14 requires businesses adopting IFRS 16 to spread the tax impact of any transitional lease accounting adjustment over the average remaining lease term.

Section 35 clarifies that FA 2019, Sch 14 spreading rules apply to all lessees adopting IFRS 16 for any period of account. The amendment is treated as always having had effect.

FA 2019, Sch 14, para 13 sets out the transitional adjustments required where a right-of-use asset is first recognised in a period of account beginning on or after 1 January 2019. Paragraph 14 provides for circumstances where a lessee has adopted IFRS 16 for a period of account beginning before 1 January 2019.

This measure confirms that FA 2019, Sch 14 applies to all lessees adopting the new accounting standard, irrespective of when they first adopted IFRS 16.

The practical tax issues relating to the adoption of IRS16 include:

- the calculation of the tax transitional adjustment,
- complexity of the spreading calculation with a separate tax basis for each lease;
- current and deferred tax modelling and forecasting, and
- modelling the interaction with the corporate interest restriction rules.

Detailed description of the measure

Subsection (1) indicates that FA 2019, Sch 14 is amended as detailed below.

Subsection (2) amends FA 2019, Sch 14, para 13(1) to clarify that paragraph 13 applies when a lessee first recognises a right-of-use asset in a period of account beginning on or after 1 January 2019. The amendment clarifies in particular that the paragraph applies in circumstances where the lessee first recognises the right-of-use asset in any period of account beginning on or after 1 January 2019, even if that period is not the first period of account beginning on or after 1 January 2019.

Subsection (3) amends FA 2019, Sch 14, para 14 to clarify that where a lessee has adopted IFRS 16 for a period of account beginning before 1 January 2019, the transitional provisions in paragraph 13 have effect as if IFRS 16 were adopted in the first period of account beginning on or after 1 January 2019.

Subsection (4) provides that the amendments to FA 2019, Sch 14, paras 13 and 14 are treated as always having had effect.

Investments

36   Enterprise investment scheme: approved investment fund as nominee

(1)   Section 251 of ITA 2007 (EIS: approved investment fund as nominee) is amended as follows.

(2)   In subsection (1)—

    (a)   in the opening words, for "Subsection (2) applies" substitute "This section applies",

    (b)   in paragraph (a), for "an approved fund" substitute "an approved knowledge-intensive fund",

    (c)   omit the "and" at the end of paragraph (b),

    (d)   in paragraph (c), for "90%" substitute "50%",

    (e)   after that paragraph insert—

        "(d)   the amounts which the managers have, as nominee for the individual, subscribed for shares issued within 24 months after the closing of the fund represent at least 90% of the individual's investment in the fund,

        (e)   within that 24 month period at least 80% of the individual's investment in the fund is represented by shares in companies which are knowledge-intensive companies at the time the shares are issued, and

(f)   the managers have met such conditions with respect to the provision of information to HMRC Commissioners as the Commissioners consider appropriate for the purposes of this section.", and

(f)   omit the second sentence.

(3)   After that subsection insert—

"(1A) In this section "the managers of an approved knowledge-intensive fund" means the person or persons having the management of an investment fund—

(a)   which is, in the opinion of HMRC Commissioners, a fund established for the purpose of investing wholly, or substantially wholly, in shares in companies which are knowledge-intensive companies at the time the shares are issued, and

(b)   which is, having met such other conditions as HMRC Commissioners consider appropriate for the purposes of this section, approved by them for those purposes."

(4)   In subsection (2), omit "In any case where this subsection applies,".

(5)   After that subsection insert—

"(2A) Accordingly, in a case where section 158 has effect with the modifications in subsection (2), the reference in section 158(4) to the issue of the shares in the preceding tax year is to the issue of the shares in the tax year preceding the tax year in which the fund closes (and references elsewhere in this Part to the issue of shares in a previous tax year are to be read accordingly)."

(6)   In subsection (4), in the opening words, for "an approved fund" substitute "an approved knowledge-intensive fund".

(7)   In subsection (5)(b), for "the Commissioners for Her Majesty's Revenue and Customs" substitute "HMRC Commissioners".

(8)   In subsection (6), for "an approved fund" substitute "an approved knowledge-intensive fund".

(9)   In subsection (7), for "an approved fund" substitute "an approved knowledge-intensive fund".

(10)   After that subsection insert—

"(8) In this section "HMRC Commissioners" means the Commissioners for Her Majesty's Revenue and Customs."

(11)   In the title, for "investment fund" substitute "knowledge-intensive fund".

(12)   The amendments made by this section are treated as having come into force on 6 April 2020 in relation to funds that close on or after that date.

COMMENTARY ON SECTION 36

Following a policy consultation, the Government has acted to reform the Enterprise Investment Scheme (EIS) rules in respect of the operation and structure of approved investment funds.

This section amends the existing rules in ITA 2007, Pt 5 in order to focus investment in knowledge-intensive companies ('KIC's') by approved EIS funds. The amendments also provide additional flexibility in the time period for fund managers to make subscriptions in shares and for investors over the years in which income tax relief is given.

Subsection (2) amends ITA 2007, s 251 and changes 'an approved fund' to 'an approved knowledge-intensive fund', thereby setting out a number of requirements that must be met for investments to be made via an approved knowledge-intensive fund.

The amendments require that the amounts which the managers have subscribed for shares on behalf of the investor within 12 months after the closing of the fund represent at least 50% of the individual's investment in the fund. Furthermore, the amounts which the managers have subscribed for shares on behalf of the investor within 24 months after the closing of the fund must represent at least 90% of the individual's investment in the fund.

As such, there will be increased flexibility for managers, through increasing the time period within which fund capital must be deployed. Approved funds will now have two years within which to deploy capital, with at least 50% of each raise to be invested within the first 12 months of the closing of the fund. The previous rules for approved EIS funds stipulated that 90% of each raise had to be deployed within the first 12 months.

The changes also require that within the 24 month period a minimum of 80% of an individual's investment in the approved knowledge-intensive fund must be invested in KIC's at the time the shares are issued.

ITA 2007, s 251(2A) will also be inserted to amend the tax years in which an individual can claim relief. This new subsection provides that the year in which the fund closes be treated as the year in which the relevant shares were issued, for the purposes of claiming relief in the year preceding that in which the shares were issued. This will allow investors to set their relief against their income tax liabilities in the year before the fund closes, whereas previously this was only permitted in the same year the fund closes. Investors should benefit from this amendment by being able to claim relief earlier through offsetting their relief against income tax liabilities in the year before the fund closes.

Subsection (12) provides for the amendments to apply to approved knowledge-intensive funds that close on or after 6 April 2020.

---

37   Gains from contracts for life insurance etc: top slicing relief

(1)   In Chapter 9 of Part 4 of ITTOIA 2005 (gains from contracts for life insurance etc), sections 535 to 537 (top slicing relief) are amended as follows.

(2)   In section 535 (top slicing relief), at the end insert—

> "(8)   For the purposes of the calculations mentioned in subsection (1)—
>
> > (a)   section 25(2) of ITA 2007 (deductions of reliefs and allowances in most beneficial way for taxpayer) does not apply, and
> >
> > (b)   reliefs and allowances are available for deduction from an amount that, for the purposes of those calculations, is the highest part of the individual's total income for the tax year only so far as they cannot be deducted from other amounts."

(3)   In section 536(1) (top slicing relieved liability: one chargeable event), in paragraph (a) of step 2—

> (a)   omit the "and" at the end of sub-paragraph (i), and
>
> (b)   after the "and" at the end of sub-paragraph (ii) insert—
>
> > "(iii)   in determining the amount of the individual's personal allowance under section 35 of ITA 2007 (but not the amount of any other relief or allowance), it is assumed that the gain from the chargeable event is equal to the amount of the annual equivalent, and".

(4)   In section 537 (top slicing relieved liability: two or more chargeable events), in paragraph (a) of step 2—

> (a)   omit the "and" at the end of sub-paragraph (i), and
>
> (b)   after the "and" at the end of sub-paragraph (ii) insert—
>
> > "(iii)   in determining the amount of the individual's personal allowance under section 35 of ITA 2007 (but not the amount of any other relief or allowance), it is assumed that the total gains from the chargeable events are equal to the amount of the total annual equivalent, and".

(5)   The amendments made by this section have effect in relation to the tax year 2019–20 and subsequent tax years (but see subsection (6) for an exception in the case of the tax years 2019–20 and 2020–21).

(6)   Those amendments do not have effect in relation to the tax year 2019–20 or 2020–21 in the case of an individual who is only liable to tax under Chapter 9 of Part 4 of ITTOIA 2005 for the year in question—

> (a)   on a gain from one chargeable event that occurs before 11 March 2020, or
>
> (b)   on gains from chargeable events each of which occurs before that day.

COMMENTARY ON SECTION 37

Section 37 makes two discrete changes to the computation of top slicing relief in respect of chargeable event gains on life insurance policies, life annuities and capital redemption policies. One change concerns the availability of the personal allowance, and the other is to do with the use of reliefs and allowances generally.

Both changes are effective for 2019/20 onwards, but the legislation provides that they do not apply to a gain from a chargeable event occurring before 11 March 2020 (or to two or more chargeable event gains each occurring before that date). However, in the case of the first change (the availability of the personal allowance), which is beneficial to the taxpayer, HMRC has said that, in practice and by concession, it will apply the new treatment to *all* gains arising in 2019/20 onwards (HMRC Insurance Policyholder Taxation Manual IPTM3820).

Before examining these changes it is worth briefly rehearsing the operation of top slicing relief under ITTOIA 2005, ss 535–537. Three tax calculations are required as follows.

(1)   Calculate the income tax liability, using the steps in ITA 2007, s 23, on all income including the full amount of the chargeable event gain.
(2)   Calculate the income tax liability on the chargeable event gain.
(3)   Calculate the income tax liability on the annual equivalent of the chargeable event gain and multiply it by the number of complete years (N) for which the policy has run before the chargeable event.

Notes

(a)   A chargeable event gain is chargeable only at the excess of higher rate/ additional rate over basic rate, so in (1), (2) and (3) a notional basic rate tax credit is given. In (3) it is given by reference to the annual equivalent and before multiplying the liability by N.
(b)   In calculating liability in (2) and (3), the gain or annual equivalent is treated as the top slice of income.
(c)   The annual equivalent in (3) is found by dividing the gain by N.
(d)   The calculation in (3) is modified if more than one chargeable event gain is taxable in the year.

The difference between (2) and (3) is the amount of top slicing relief due. The relief is then given at step 6 of the calculation in (1).

Availability of the personal allowance

The catalyst for this change was the First-tier Tribunal decision in *Silver v HMRC* [2019] UKFTT 263 (TC). In this case the appellant had a chargeable event gain of just over £110,000 taxable for 2015/16. The policy had been held for 21 years. Her other income amounted to around £31,000. Taking both these into account, her income was too far in excess of £100,000 for her to be entitled to any personal allowance in the calculation in (1) above (see ITA 2007, s 35(2)). The appellant's argument was that once her gain had been divided by 21 in line with (3) above her income was well below £100,000 and she was thus entitled to the full personal allowance in working out the tax payable in (3). In this particular case, once the personal allowance was taken into account in (3), the annual equivalent was within the basic rate band of £32,000; the result of the calculation in (3) was therefore zero, and the taxpayer was entitled to top slicing relief equal to the full amount of the tax calculated at (2). HMRC disagreed, and maintained that if the personal allowance was not due in (1) it was not due in (3) either.

The Tribunal agreed with the appellant, stating that HMRC's interpretation was inconsistent with Parliament's presumed intent. It is known that HMRC is not appealing that decision. Section 37 changes the law in accordance with the Tribunal's decision. That HMRC now agrees with the Tribunal is shown by the following words in the relevant policy paper published at Spring Budget 2020 (see www.gov.uk/ government/publications/changes-to-top-slicing-relief-on-life-insurance-policy-gains- from-11-march-2020):

> 'The original policy intent of [top slicing relief] was to provide relief to taxpayers who have become subject to a higher rate of tax due to a gain being included in their income. The change to the treatment of reduced personal allowances, as set out in this measure, is in line with that original policy intent.'

The amendment to the legislation is that, in the calculation in (3) (including the modified version where there are two or more chargeable event gains taxable in the year), one is to assume, in determining the amount of the individual's personal allowance (but not the amount of any other relief or allowance), that the amount of the chargeable event gain is equal to that of the annual equivalent. The reference to 'any other relief or allowance' would include, for example, qualifying loan interest.

The amendment does not affect a gain from a chargeable event arising in 2018/19 or earlier years, so what is the position now for such gains where open years are concerned? First-tier Tribunal decisions do not set legal precedents, so future tribunals are not obliged to follow the decision in *Silver*. However, that decision taken together with the above policy paper quote must surely be very persuasive.

Use of reliefs and allowances generally

Section 37 also provides that, in the calculations in both (2) and (3) above, deductible reliefs and allowances must be set against other income in priority to the chargeable event gain. This is an exception to the general rule (see ITA 2007, s 25(2)) that reliefs and allowances can be deducted in the way which will result in the greatest reduction in the taxpayer's liability to income tax.

This amendment does not apply to a gain from a chargeable event occurring before 11 March 2020, which begs the question of how to calculate top slicing relief on such gains in tax years that are still open. In this instance there is no case law to assist but it seems clear that the general rule in ITA 2007, s 25(2) must apply, hence the reason it has now been expressly disapplied. Indeed, there does not appear to be any reason why allowances and reliefs should not be set off against different types of income in each of the calculations in (1), (2) and (3) if this gives the best result.

---

38   Losses on disposal of shares: abolition of requirement to be UK business

(1)   The following provisions are repealed—

    (a)   section 134(5) of ITA 2007 (which provides that a company is a qualifying trading company for the purposes of income tax relief under Chapter 6 of Part 4 of that Act only if it carries on its business in the United Kingdom), and

    (b)   section 78(5) of CTA 2010 (which makes corresponding provision for the purposes of corporation tax relief under Chapter 5 of Part 4 of that Act).

(2)   In consequence of the repeals made by subsection (1)—

    (a)   in ITA 2007—

        (i)   in section 134(1), for "D" substitute "C",

        (ii)   in section 147(8), at the end of paragraph (a) insert "or" and omit paragraph (c) together with the "or" before it,

        (iii)   in section 150(1), omit the entry relating to section 134(5)(a), and

        (iv)   in paragraph 38(2) of Schedule 2, in the opening words, for "(2) to (5)" substitute "(2) to (4)", and omit the substituted section 134(5) of ITA 2007, and

    (b)   in CTA 2010—

        (i)   in section 75(8), at the end of paragraph (a) insert "or" and omit paragraph (c) together with the "or" before it,

        (ii)   in section 78(1), for "D" substitute "C",

        (iii)   in section 89(1), omit the entry relating to section 78(5)(a), and

        (iv)   in paragraph 28(4) of Schedule 2, in the opening words, for "(2) to (5)" substitute "(2) to (4)", and omit the substituted section 78(5) of CTA 2010.

(3)   The amendments made by this section have effect in relation to disposals made on or after 24 January 2019.

COMMENTARY ON SECTION 38

Section 38 amends the qualifying trading company conditions in ITA 2007, s 134 and CTA 2010, s 78. These are the share loss relief rules that allow relief from income tax or corporation tax for a capital loss on the disposal of shares in qualifying trading companies. The changes are made as a result of a reasoned opinion issued by the European Commission on 24 January 2019 that the rules breached the EU principle of free movement of capital. The rules breached EU law because relief was only available where the company carried on its business wholly or mainly in the UK.

For disposals of shares prior to 24 January 2019, one of the conditions that needed to be met for the company to be a qualifying trading company was that it carried on its business wholly or mainly in the UK from the later of the two dates below until the date of disposal (ITA 2007, s 134(5); CTA 2010, s 78(5)):

- the date of incorporation, or
- 12 months before the shares were issued

Where the disposal of the shares takes place on or after 24 January 2019, the requirement for the company to carry on its business wholly or mainly in the UK is repealed. Therefore, from this date, as long as the other conditions for relief are met, individuals and companies are able to claim share loss relief on losses arising on shares in non-UK companies.

Note that share loss relief for corporation tax is not often in point, because it only applies where an investment company has a non-controlling interest in a qualifying trading company and then disposes of these shares at a loss (CTA 2010, s 69).

Section 38(1) repeals the condition and section 38(2) makes the necessary consequential amendments to ITA 2007 and CTA 2010. Section 38(3) specifies the operative date.

The reasoned opinion issued by the European Commission covered share loss relief and relief for loans to traders (see the commentary under section 27).

PART 2

DIGITAL SERVICES TAX

Introduction

39   Digital services tax: introduction

(1)   A tax (to be known as "digital services tax") is charged in accordance with this Part on UK digital services revenues arising to a person in an accounting period.

(2)   The Commissioners for Her Majesty's Revenue and Customs (in this Part referred to as "the Commissioners") are responsible for the collection and management of digital services tax.

(3)   In this Part—

    (a)   sections 40 to 45 define "UK digital services revenues" and other key expressions;

    (b)   sections 46 to 51 contain the charge to digital services tax;

    (c)   sections 52 to 56 impose a duty to file returns and other reporting requirements;

    (d)   sections 57 to 60 define groups and related concepts;

    (e)   sections 61 to 64 define accounting periods, the meaning of revenues arising, and other accounts-related concepts;

    (f)   sections 65 to 72 contain supplementary and general provisions.

COMMENTARY ON SECTION 39

Section 39 introduces a new UK tax called digital services tax ('DST'). DST was announced by the Government in the 2018 Budget, to be implemented from April 2020.

For many years now, the concept of a digital services tax has been discussed at a multinational level alongside the numerous ways in which governments across the globe could look to tax digital businesses. The nexus of this debate begins with the release of the first paper related to Base Erosion and Profit Shifting ('BEPS') by the Organisation for Economic Cooperation and Development ('OECD'), titled 'Action 1: Addressing the Tax Challenges of the Digital Economy', released in October 2015. Initially parked in order to address other BEPS action items, the digital tax debate has become much more prevalent in recent years. While the UK Government remains committed to reaching a multinational consensus on the issues presented by the digital economy at OECD level, it was felt that interim unilateral measures were required to take action with a more pressing timetable. In the 2018 Budget, the

Chancellor of the Exchequer said 'Progress is painfully slow. We cannot simply talk forever. So we will introduce a UK Digital Services Tax'.

Legislation introduced in Part 2 of this Act is the product of that unilateral action, consultations and stakeholder discussions.

Digital services revenues, UK digital services revenues etc

40 Meaning of "digital services revenues"

(1) This section applies for the purposes of this Part.

(2) The "digital services revenues" of a group for a period are the total amount of revenues arising to members of the group in that period in connection with any digital services activity of any member of the group.

(3) Where revenues arise in connection with a digital services activity and anything else, the revenues are to be treated as arising in connection with the activity to such extent as is just and reasonable.

COMMENTARY ON SECTION 40

As a new tax, in unchartered territory, many definitions and explanations are required in the legislation. Sections 40–45 seek to define the types of activity and revenues which are within the scope of DST.

Section 40 defines 'digital services revenues' by reference to a group in totality, and in respect of a specific accounting period. Digital services revenues are any revenues, attributed to any group member, provided they arise in connection with a 'digital services activity' by any group member. This is important as it provides the clarification that revenues derived by one group member which arise in connection with a 'digital services activity' performed by another group member are to be 'digital services revenues'. Section 40(3) suggests a just and reasonable approach where revenues derive from multiple activities. 'Digital services activity' is defined at section 43 below.

41 Meaning of "UK digital services revenues"

(1) This section applies for the purposes of this Part.

(2) A group's "UK digital services revenues" for a period are so much of its digital services revenues for that period as are attributable to UK users.

(3) Revenues are attributable to UK users if—

    (a) they are within Case 1, 2 or 3, or

    (b) they are within Case 4 or 5 and, where subsection (9) applies, they are allocated to UK users under that subsection.

This is subject to subsection (10).

(4) Case 1 is where—

    (a) the revenues are online marketplace revenues,

    (b) they arise in connection with a marketplace transaction, and

    (c) a UK user is a party to the transaction.

(5) Case 2 is where—

    (a) the revenues are online marketplace revenues, and

    (b) they arise in connection with particular accommodation or land in the United Kingdom (see section 42).

(6) Case 3 is where—

    (a) the revenues are online marketplace revenues,

    (b) they arise in connection with online advertising for particular services, goods or other property, and

    (c) the advertising is paid for by a UK user.

(7) Case 4 is where—

    (a) the revenues are online advertising revenues,

    (b) they are not within any of Cases 1 to 3, and

    (c) the advertising is viewed or otherwise consumed by UK users.

(8) Case 5 is where—

    (a) the revenues are not within any of Cases 1 to 4, and

(b)   they arise in connection with UK users.

(9)   For the purposes of subsection (3)(b), revenues are to be allocated to UK users to such extent as is just and reasonable where they are—

     (a)   online advertising revenues within Case 4 and the advertising in question is viewed or otherwise consumed by UK users and others;

     (b)   revenues within Case 5 and they arise in connection with UK users and others.

(10)   Online marketplace revenues are treated as not attributable to UK users if—

     (a)   where they arise in connection with a marketplace transaction—

         (i)   they arise in connection with particular accommodation or land outside the United Kingdom (see section 42), and

         (ii)   the only UK user who is a party to the transaction is a provider or seller of the thing to which the transaction relates;

     (b)   in any other case, they arise in connection with particular accommodation or land outside the United Kingdom (see section 42).

(11)   In this section—

"marketplace transaction" means a transaction on the online marketplace between users;

"online advertising revenues" means revenues arising in connection with the provision or facilitation of online advertising;

"online marketplace revenues" means revenues arising in connection with an online marketplace.

(12)   For the purpose of the definition of "marketplace transaction", "transaction on the online marketplace" includes the placing on the marketplace of an order that results in an agreement, even if the agreement between the users is made otherwise than through the marketplace.

COMMENTARY ON SECTION 41

In order to be specifically territorial to the UK, section 41 narrows the scope of 'digital services revenues' to 'UK digital services revenues' by virtue of being attributed to UK users. A group's 'UK digital services revenues' must therefore be (a) digital services revenues by virtue of arising from a digital services activity, and (b) attributable to UK users. Section 41(3)–(10) then describe various Cases to determine whether revenues are attributable to UK users.

Case 1 revenues are revenues from an online marketplace transaction and where a UK user is a party to the transaction. Note that for multi-party transactions between users, only one user must be a UK user for revenues to become Case 1.

Case 2 revenues are revenues from an online marketplace transaction and where the revenues are in connection with accommodation or land in the UK. Per section 42 this means any sale or provision or land or accommodation, related goods or services on the online marketplace. Notably this does not require any user to be a UK user in order for revenues to become Case 2.

Case 3 revenues are revenues from an online marketplace transaction related to advertising, and such advertising is paid for by a UK user. Note that only the user paying for the advertising is relevant here, and not the location of any users viewing that advertising.

Case 4 revenues are any other online advertising revenues where advertising is viewed or consumed by a UK user.

Case 5 revenues are any other revenues arising in connection with UK users.

Businesses must therefore take steps to understand their revenue streams in detail before they can conclude on their UK digital services revenues, including location of user base and consumers of advertising.

Importantly, section 41(9) adds that Case 4 and Case 5 revenues include a just and reasonable override. In Case 4, where advertising is viewed by both UK and non-UK users, a just and reasonable portion of the revenues should be UK digital services revenues. In Case 5, revenues arising in connection with both UK and non-UK users should follow the same process.

As indicated above, there is no such just and reasonable provision as it relates to Case 1, 2 and 3. In those three cases, the definitions must be interpreted as they are written, despite any non-UK user interface leading to such revenues.

The law is worded such that there should be no double counting within the Case buckets, all digital services revenues should be counted once and only once.

It is also important to remember that there is no requirement for UK digital services revenues to have any link to a UK company or UK taxable presence for corporation tax purposes. Only the Cases above, and their link to UK users within the scope of a digital services activity are important. Groups may have Cases of UK digital services revenues despite having no corporation tax presence in the UK at all.

In order to successfully interpret these Cases, one must however understand the defined terms used. Digital services activity is defined at section 43 and UK user at section 44.

42   UK digital services revenues: accommodation and land

(1)   This section, which supplements section 41 (meaning of a group's UK digital services revenues), applies for the purpose of determining when online marketplace revenues arise in connection with accommodation or land.

(2)   The revenues are treated as arising in connection with accommodation if they arise in connection with—

    (a)   the provision of accommodation, or

    (b)   the provision of services, goods or other property in relation to accommodation, in connection with the provision of the accommodation on the online marketplace.

(3)   The revenues are treated as arising in connection with land if they arise in connection with—

    (a)   the sale of an estate, interest or right in or over land, or

    (b)   the provision of services, goods or other property in relation to land, in connection with the sale of an estate, interest or right in or over the land on the online marketplace.

(4)   In this section—

    (a)   any reference to providing or selling anything includes offering to provide or sell it;

    (b)   any reference to providing goods or other property includes providing it temporarily;

    (c)   "online marketplace revenues" means revenues arising in connection with an online marketplace.

COMMENTARY ON SECTION 42

Section 42 contains a particular exclusion from UK digital services revenues as it relates to Case 1 (and 3) for online marketplace revenues in connection with land or accommodation outside the UK, and where the only UK user is the seller/provider of the land or accommodation. Online marketplace revenues where there is UK user involvement on the buy/demand side of such a transaction are not excluded.

Other digital services revenues which are not in respect of an online marketplace transaction and relate to land or accommodation outside the UK are also excluded from the definition of UK digital services revenues. This could for example exclude associated online advertising revenues relating to overseas land or accommodation.

43   Meaning of "digital services activity" etc

(1)   This section applies for the purposes of this Part.

(2)   "Digital services activity" means providing—

    (a)   a social media service,

    (b)   an internet search engine, or

    (c)   an online marketplace.

(3)   "Social media service" means an online service that meets the following conditions—

    (a)   the main purpose, or one of the main purposes, of the service is to promote interaction between users (including interaction between users and user-generated content), and

    (b)   making content generated by users available to other users is a significant feature of the service.

(4) "Internet search engine" does not include a facility on a website that merely enables a person to search—

    (a)   the material on that website, or

    (b)   the material on that website and on closely related websites.

(5) "Online marketplace" means an online service that meets the following conditions—

    (a)   the main purpose, or one of the main purposes, of the service is to facilitate the sale by users of particular things, and

    (b)   the service enables users to sell particular things to other users, or to advertise or otherwise offer particular things for sale to other users.

(6) In subsection (5)—

    (a)   "thing" means any services, goods or other property;

    (b)   any reference to the sale of a thing includes hiring it.

(7) Any reference to providing a social media service, internet search engine or online marketplace includes carrying on an associated online advertising service; and any reference to a social media service, internet search engine or online marketplace is to be read accordingly.

(8) In this section "associated online advertising service" means an online service that—

    (a)   facilitates online advertising, and

    (b)   derives significant benefit from its association with the social media service, internet search engine or online marketplace.

(9) Where an associated online advertising service derives significant benefit from its association with more than one type of digital services activity, revenues arising from the service are to be treated as attributable to each of the types of digital services activity in question to such extent as is just and reasonable.

(10) See also section 45 (exclusion for online financial marketplaces).

COMMENTARY ON SECTION 43

Section 43 describes the three kinds of activity which meet the required definition of a digital services activity. Each of a business's online activities will need to be separately considered as to whether they are a digital services activity; and businesses may have multiple digital services activities.

It is noteworthy that the UK has chosen three specific business models where they see the most need for an alteration in the way that large businesses are taxed. While to some extent, 'all businesses are digital', the Government have been careful not to target any and every online business, but those models where they see the contribution of a user base located in the UK as a key value driver which is not currently recognised in traditional transfer pricing models.

While the activities listed are intentionally targeted in scope, it is of course difficult to define in law what exactly a 'social media service', an 'internet search engine' and an 'online marketplace' are.

Social media services are defined by virtue of a main purpose to promote social interaction between users and user-generated content, and where making the user-generated content available to others is a significant feature of the service.

Internet search engine is not defined. However, search functions which search for data on that website or closely related sites are excluded.

Online marketplaces are defined by virtue of a main purpose to facilitate sales between users of goods, services or other property.

Where a business has an online advertising service which benefits from the association with the service itself, these associated online advertising services are taken to be included in the definitions. Provision of online advertising on a standalone basis is not a digital services activity.

It is a gating condition of a digital services activity that the activity is provided to users. Internal services are therefore not a digital services activity. Digital services activities should be defined prior to any consideration of revenues attached to those services. HMRC has issued detailed guidance to consider various examples of online services and whether they (a) meet the definition of a digital services activity, and (b) whether they should be viewed as a combined activity or separately identifiable activities.

44   Meaning of "user" and "UK user"

(1)   This section applies for the purposes of this Part.

(2)   Any reference to a user, in relation to a digital services activity of a person (the "provider"), does not include—

    (a)   the provider or a member of the same group as the provider, or

    (b)   an employee of a person within paragraph (a), acting in the course of that person's business.

(3)   "UK user" means any user who it is reasonable to assume—

    (a)   in the case of an individual, is normally in the United Kingdom;

    (b)   in any other case, is established in the United Kingdom.

COMMENTARY ON SECTION 44

The definition of a user and a UK user are addressed in section 44. Users excludes group companies and employees acting in the course of the group's business. Thinking of users as then independent individuals or businesses utilising the service, a UK user is then defined as where it is reasonable to assume that they are normally in the UK (for an individual) or established in the UK (for a business).

There could be one or multiple users related to any online transaction, and user is purposefully not defined with respect to a 'buyer' or 'seller' – all parties to an online marketplace transaction are deemed to be users. HMRC guidance discusses the potential difficulty in identifying a user when considering long value chains and large groups with multiple potential beneficiaries of a goods or service provided online.

It is noteworthy that the definition of a UK user includes what is 'reasonable to assume', as this infers that a business can use judgement to ascertain whether an individual user is normally in the UK, or a business is established in the UK. Factors such as IP address, payment details, billing or delivery address may be useful indicators. A business should collect and retain evidence of their judgement. Feedback from a number of large businesses indicates that tracing the ultimate users of their services can be somewhat difficult, and this data may not be readily available.

Now that we have defined a UK user and the various digital services activities, we can revisit section 41 to determine a group's UK digital services revenues. UK digital services revenues must again relate to one of the digital services activities and be attributed to a UK user. The latter is determined by the five Cases described in section 41.

---

45   Exclusion for online financial marketplaces

(1)   In this Part any reference to an online marketplace excludes one that is for the time being an online financial marketplace.

(2)   An online marketplace is an "online financial marketplace" for a relevant accounting period if more than half of the revenues arising to the provider in the accounting period in connection with the online marketplace arise in connection with the provider's facilitation of the trading of financial instruments, commodities or foreign exchange.

(3)   In subsection (2)—

    (a)   the reference to the trading of financial instruments includes the creation of such instruments;

    (b)   the reference to the trading of commodities is to the kind of commodities, and the kind of trading, occurring on a commodities exchange.

(4)   In this section—

"financial instrument" means—

    (a)   a financial instrument within the meaning of the applicable accounting standards (see section 64), or

    (b)   a contract of insurance as defined by section 64 of FA 2012;

"provider" means the person providing the online marketplace;

"relevant accounting period" means an accounting period of the group of which the provider is a member.

COMMENTARY ON SECTION 45

As it relates to online marketplaces, section 45 specifically excludes an online financial marketplace, defined as a marketplace which derives more than half of its revenues from facilitation of trading financial instruments, commodities or foreign exchange.

Other exclusions from the definition of a digital services activity must be inferred, for example businesses providing online content, selling hardware or software online, TV and broadcasting services. Such business models have been quoted as not intentionally within the scope of DST in the past. Individual groups must of course consider the legislation on its merits, alongside HMRC guidance, to determine whether they have a digital services activity.

Charge to tax

46   Meaning of "the threshold conditions"

(1)   For the purposes of this Part "the threshold conditions", in relation to a group, for an accounting period are—

>   (a)   that the total amount of digital services revenues arising in that period to members of the group exceeds £500 million, and
>   (b)   that the total amount of UK digital services revenues arising in that period to members of the group exceeds £25 million.

(2)   But if the duration of the accounting period is less than a year, the amounts mentioned in subsection (1)(a) and (b) are proportionately reduced.

COMMENTARY ON SECTION 46

Section 46 contains the threshold conditions which limit those businesses impacted by DST to only those with the largest revenue base from digital activities. In a 12 month accounting period a group must have both digital services revenues of over £500m and UK digital services revenues of over £25m to breach the DST thresholds – both thresholds must be breached. We must also remember that these thresholds are group wide and so all digital services revenues of all group members must be summed. The threshold conditions are proportionately reduced for shorter accounting periods.

It is notable that the threshold conditions are by reference to digital services revenues and not all revenues. Large businesses with only certain business areas falling to be treated as digital services may therefore escape the charge – only the very largest businesses with also a very large revenue base from digital activities will breach the conditions.

The threshold conditions do therefore provide that businesses with global revenues of over £500m and some potentially in-scope activity will need to consider the conditions. An understanding of which revenues are in scope, and the volume of in-scope activities related to UK users is therefore necessary before concluding whether DST applies. There may be considerable work for businesses here (in each and every accounting period no less) in order to conclude that they do not breach the thresholds.

Where a business does breach the thresholds then DST is potentially chargeable and DST returns required. This is the case even if no DST is ultimately payable due to the alternative basis of charge or relief for cross-border transactions (which are discussed below) as these require claim / election within the DST return. It is plausible therefore that DST nil returns could be filed.

47   Charge to DST

(1)   This section applies where the threshold conditions are met in relation to a group for an accounting period.

(2)   Each person who was a member of the group in the accounting period (a "relevant person") is liable to digital services tax in respect of UK digital services revenues arising in that period.

(3)   To find the liability of a relevant person to digital services tax in respect of the accounting period, take the following steps.

Step 1

Take the total amount of UK digital services revenues arising to members of the group in the accounting period.

Step 2

Deduct £25million from the amount found under step 1.

Step 3

Calculate 2% of the amount calculated under step 2.

The result is "the group amount".

Step 4

The relevant person's liability to digital services tax in respect of the accounting period is the appropriate proportion of the group amount.

(4) In this section "the appropriate proportion" means such proportion of the total amount of UK digital services revenues arising to members of the group in the accounting period as is attributable to the relevant person.

(5) If the duration of the accounting period is less than a year, the sum mentioned in step 2 of subsection (3) is proportionately reduced.

(6) This section is subject to section 48 (alternative basis of charge).

COMMENTARY ON SECTION 47

Section 47 provides the steps to calculate a DST charge which is then applied to any member of a group which breached the threshold conditions in that period. In line with the threshold conditions, an annual allowance of the first £25m of revenues is provided, such that DST is only charged on UK digital services revenues above this threshold. The £25m threshold is sensibly reduced for short accounting periods.

While the DST liability falls to every group member separately, it is calculated on a group wide basis. A rate of 2% is applied to [total UK digital services revenues of the group less £25m] to provide the group wide charge, which is then allocated to group members based on the proportion of revenues they contributed to the calculation, such that each group member may have its own liability. Most importantly to note at this stage is that, after the first exempt £25m, the 2% tax is applied to gross revenues, and not profits.

---

48 Alternative basis of charge

(1) This section applies if a valid election under this section in respect of an accounting period has been made in the group's DST return for that period (whether as originally made or by amendment).

(2) An election under this section is valid if it specifies the categories of revenues in relation to which it applies (or specifies that it applies in relation to all categories).

(3) For this purpose, the categories of revenues are—

    (a) revenues arising in connection with any social media service;
    (b) revenues arising in connection with any internet search engine;
    (c) revenues arising in connection with any online marketplace.

(4) To find the liability of a relevant person to digital services tax in respect of the accounting period, take the following steps (instead of the steps set out in section 47(3)).

Step 1

Take the total amount of UK digital services revenues arising to members of the group in the accounting period.

Step 2

Apportion the total amount found under step 1 between the three categories of revenues.

Step 3

For each category of revenues, the "net revenues" is the amount by which the amount of revenues apportioned under step 2 exceeds the relevant proportion of £25million.

"The relevant proportion" is—

    R / TR
    where—

        (a) R is the amount of revenues apportioned under step 2 to the category, and
        (b) TR is the total amount found under step 1.

Step 4

For each specified category of revenues, calculate the operating margin.

"The operating margin" is—

$R - (E / R)$

where—

    (a)   R has the same meaning as in step 3, and

    (b)   E is the amount of relevant operating expenses of the group that are recognised in the accounting period (as to which, see section 48).

If R does not exceed E, the operating margin is nil.

Step 5

For each specified category of revenues, the taxable amount is 0.8 x the operating margin x the net revenues.

For any other category of revenues, the taxable amount is 2% of the net revenues.

Step 6

Add together the taxable amounts calculated under step 5.

The result is "the group amount".

Step 7

The relevant person's liability to digital services tax in respect of the accounting period is the appropriate proportion of the group amount.

(5)   If the duration of the accounting period is less than a year, the sum mentioned in step 3 of subsection (4) is proportionately reduced.

(6)   In this section—

     "the appropriate proportion" has the meaning given by section 47;

     "relevant person" has the same meaning as in section 47;

     "specified", in relation to a category of revenues, means a category of revenues specified in the election.

COMMENTARY ON SECTION 48

Sections 48 and 49 describe an alternative basis of charge which may be elected to be used for either all categories of digital services revenues, or specifically against one category. The categories are listed as revenues from the three types of digital business. Importantly, this means that the alternative basis of charge could be used across the board of specifically for some revenues but not others.

The alternative basis of charge may be used to apply a reduced rate of DST to a category of revenues with a low operating margin. The result of the alternative basis of charge is that no DST is due on a loss-making category, and a reduced rate may apply to a category with an operating margin of less than 2.5%.

The calculation of the alternative basis of charge spreads the £25m threshold amount proportionately between UK digital services revenue categories, before applying a rate of [0.8 x the operating margin] to that category. The rate of 2% would apply to non-elected categories. As explained above, this means a UK digital services category with an operating margin above 2.5% would be better to not elect for the alternative basis of charge but those with a lower operating margin would benefit from the election.

---

49   Section 48: meaning of "relevant operating expenses"

(1)   This section supplements section 48.

(2)   The "relevant operating expenses" of a group, in relation to a specified category of revenues, means any expenses of a member of the group attributable to the earning of UK digital services revenues within the specified category, except excluded expenses.

(3)   "Excluded expenses" means any expenses—

    (a)   in respect of interest (or anything equivalent, from a commercial perspective, to interest),

    (b)   attributable to the acquisition of a business or part of a business,

    (c)   occurring otherwise than in the normal course of business,

    (d)   resulting from a change in the valuation of any tangible or intangible asset, or

    (e)   in respect of any tax (arising under the law of any territory).

(4)   Where expenses are attributable to—

(a)   the earning of UK digital services revenues within the specified category, and

(b)   anything else,

the expenses are to be treated as relevant operating expenses to such extent as is just and reasonable.

(5)   In this section "specified" has the meaning given by section 48.

COMMENTARY ON SECTION 49

The operating margin is calculated by reference to the UK digital services revenues in the relevant category and the relevant UK operating expenses of the group with respect of that same category. Expenses should be allocated between the category and other categories on a just and reasonable basis. Certain expenses must be excluded from the calculation as listed at section 49(3). The operating margin is nil where the calculation produces a negative number, meaning the DST liability will be nil for any loss-making category. Assessing which group expenses may be included, and further how to allocate those expenses between the DST activity categories is likely to be a time intensive task for many businesses.

While the alternative basis of charge election will be welcome for groups with loss making categories of revenues, those operating a revenue category on a low margin basis will suffer the most under either basis of calculation. As DST is a gross revenues tax, with limited link to profitability, it is of course most burdensome for those with a high revenue and a high cost base. Feedback from some large volume but low margin businesses already demonstrates that gross revenue taxes could drastically impact margins, and ultimately, business viability. Gross revenue taxes are generally criticised for this reason, as the burden they place on different business models can vary dramatically.

50   Relief for certain cross-border transactions

(1)   This section applies if a claim under this section in respect of an accounting period has been included in the group's DST return for that period (whether as originally made or by amendment).

(2)   For the purposes of step 1 in section 47(3) or 48(4), disregard 50% of any UK digital services revenues arising to a member of the group in the accounting period in connection with a relevant cross-border transaction.

(3)   For the purposes of step 4 in section 48(4), disregard 50% of any relevant operating expenses of a member of the group recognised in the accounting period that result from a relevant cross-border transaction.

(4)   "Relevant cross-border transaction" means a marketplace transaction where—

(a)   the online marketplace is provided by a member of the group,

(b)   a foreign user is a party to the transaction, and

(c)   all or part of any revenues arising to a member of the group in connection with the transaction are (or would be) subject to a foreign DST charge.

(5)   In this section—

"foreign user" means a user who it is reasonable to assume—

(a)   in the case of an individual, is normally in a territory outside the United Kingdom;

(b)   in any other case, is established in a territory outside the United Kingdom,

and a reference to the foreign user's "territory" is to be read accordingly;

"foreign DST charge" means a charge (known by any name) under the law of the foreign user's territory which is similar to digital services tax;

"marketplace transaction" has the meaning given by section 41;

"relevant operating expenses" has the meaning given by section 49.

COMMENTARY ON SECTION 50

Section 50 describes the ability to include a claim in a group's DST return for relief from DST where the same revenues are also subject to an overseas DST charge. Where an online marketplace transaction includes a foreign user, and as a result of such, revenues derived from that transaction are (or would be) subject to a foreign DST charge, then 50% of such revenues can be disregarded in the DST liability calculations. If applying the alternative basis of charge the attributable expenses should also be reduced by 50% in the operating margin calculation. The inclusion of language ('or would be') is to reflect that foreign DSTs may be calculated in different ways, with some calculations not specifically tracing on a revenues basis. Revenues which have contributed toward increasing a foreign DST charge should be included here, as well as those which can directly trace a DST charge to the same revenues.

An overseas DST charge must be similar to UK DST to ensure a valid claim for cross-border relief. HMRC guidance indicates that they would look for similarities in overall objective, a gross revenue basis and a user contribution link in assessing similarity – and will look to include a list at a later date.

Section 50 looks to avoid multiple charges to DST on the same revenues as several other taxing jurisdictions have introduced or look to introduce digital taxes under similar pretences. It does so however by only reducing the revenue base of a multi-national transaction by 50%, meaning that a second overseas territory would need to do the same to eliminate double taxation. There may be instances where double (or even triple) taxation under DSTs remain. What will be welcomed by taxpayers here is the unilateral and mechanical nature of the claim – this relief may be claimed without a bi-lateral review process which could be costly and time consuming.

Critics may also point out that section 50 does not eliminate double taxation, as a gross revenue tax is already a double tax (given that global profits are assumed to already be taxed in the appropriate jurisdiction under traditional transfer pricing principles). The same benefit outlined above of a unilateral review process is also a detriment of the tax as a whole: as a gross revenue based tax, DST is outside the scope of the UK's double tax treaty network and therefore cannot be challenged on a bi-lateral basis in the way that other instances of double taxation might be.

51   When DST is due and payable

Digital services tax in respect of an accounting period is due and payable on the day following the end of 9 months from the end of the accounting period.

COMMENTARY ON SECTION 51

Section 51 instructs that DST payment must be made within nine months and one day from the end of each accounting period. DST returns, compliance and administration are dealt with in later sections and in Schedule 8.

Duty to submit returns etc

52   Meaning of "the responsible member"

(1)   In this Part any reference to "the responsible member" of a group, at any time, is a reference to the following person—

    (a)   if at that time a nomination under subsection (2) is in force, the person nominated;

    (b)   otherwise, the parent of the group.

(2)   The parent of a group may nominate a person to be "the responsible member" of the group if—

    (a)   the person is a member of the group,

    (b)   the person is a company, and

    (c)   the parent agrees in writing to provide the person with everything the person may reasonably require in order to comply with—

        (i)   any obligation imposed by or under this Part, or

        (ii)   any other obligation imposed on the person in connection with any digital services tax liability of any member of the group.

(3)   A nomination is in force from the time it is made until any of the following events occurs—

    (a)   the parent nominates another person;

    (b)   the person nominated ceases to be a member of the group or ceases to be a company;

    (c)   an officer of Revenue and Customs or the parent revokes the nomination.

(4) An officer of Revenue and Customs may revoke a nomination only if the officer has reason to believe that the person nominated—

    (a)   is not being provided with something the person reasonably requires in order to comply with an obligation of a kind mentioned in subsection (2)(c), or

    (b)   is not complying with any such obligation.

(5) An officer of Revenue and Customs revokes a nomination by notifying the parent and the nominated person of the revocation.

The revocation has effect when the notification is issued.

(6) Any nomination, or revocation of a nomination, must be in writing.

COMMENTARY ON SECTION 52

DST is calculated by reference to the activities and revenues at the group level, but the technical liability to DST falls on any impacted company. To simplify matters, the legislation provides for the compliance and administration of DST to be the responsibility of a single company in the group. Section 52 starts the instructions on DST administration by defining a responsible member of a group. It does so by defining the parent company of a group as the responsible member for group affairs, unless a nomination is made. A nomination can be made by the parent company for any other group company to be the responsible member provided they do so in writing, and with agreement that they will make all information available for that member to comply with the DST responsibilities of the group. A non-UK parented group may wish to appoint a UK tax resident company as the responsible member to utilise an already existing HMRC relationship at that level.

Such a nomination applies from that date until either a future nomination, the responsible member no longer being a group company, or HMRC revocation (which may only be in a case where the responsible member is not or cannot comply with its obligations as stated). Guidance suggests that HMRC will not revoke a nomination on the basis of simple administrative errors but only where necessary information is not being provided which could lead to a risk of loss of tax.

There is no need to submit the nomination to HMRC alongside registration, but it must be available on request.

53   Continuity of obligations etc where change in the responsible member

(1) This section applies if at any time ("the relevant time") a person ("the new responsible member") becomes the responsible member of a group in place of another person ("the old responsible member").

(2) The relevant obligations and liabilities of the new responsible member include any relevant obligations and liabilities of the old responsible member as respects the group.

(3) Anything done as respects the group by or in relation to the old responsible member, before the relevant time, is treated as having been done by or in relation to the new responsible member.

(4) Accordingly, a penalty may be imposed on the new responsible member in respect of anything done before the relevant time if, at that time, a penalty could have been imposed on the old responsible member in respect of the thing done.

(5) Anything done by HMRC in relation to the old responsible member as respects the group, before the end of the day the change is notified, is treated for all relevant purposes as done by or in relation to the new responsible member.

(6) Anything (including any proceedings) relating to the group that, at any time during the period beginning with the relevant time and ending with the day the change is notified, is in the process of being done in relation to the old responsible member may be continued in relation to the new responsible member.

(7) Accordingly, any reference in an enactment or other instrument to the responsible member of the group is to be read, so far as necessary for the purposes of giving effect to any of subsections (2) to (6), as being or including a reference to the new responsible member.

(8) In this section—

    (a)   any reference to an act includes an omission;

    (b)   any reference to the day the change is notified is to the day on which an officer of Revenue and Customs receives notification, in accordance with section 55, that the new responsible member has become the responsible member of the group;

(c) "relevant obligations and liabilities" means any obligations or other liabilities relating to digital services tax;

(d) "relevant purposes" means any purposes relating to digital services tax.

(9) Nothing in this section—

(a) prevents HMRC or anyone else, after the relevant time, from imposing a penalty, exercising any other power, or doing anything else, in relation to the old responsible member in respect of anything done before the relevant time, or

(b) affects the validity of anything done before the relevant time.

COMMENTARY ON SECTION 53

Section 53 contains detailed wording concerning the continuity of the group's DST obligations passing between responsible members in the event of a change. Simply put, the group's DST affairs are the responsibility of any appointed responsible member, and any change in this party includes a transfer of all past liabilities, responsibilities, actions taken by the group or HMRC, legislative impact etc all as if the new responsible member was a continuing person from the old responsible member. That is not to say that the departing responsible member was never responsible for their actions, merely that there is continuity of responsibility to avoid changing responsible members as a way of limiting exposure for any past matters.

The responsible member of the group must provide certain information to HMRC when the threshold conditions are breached by the group. There is a requirement for a group to assess both its worldwide revenues and UK revenues to determine whether the two pronged threshold conditions have been breached. The responsible member therefore assumes responsibility for regular testing of these threshold conditions.

54 Duty to notify HMRC when threshold conditions are met

(1) This section applies—

(a) in relation to the first accounting period of a group in respect of which the threshold conditions are met, and

(b) where a direction under section 56 has been given in respect of a group, in relation to the first relevant accounting period in respect of which the threshold conditions are met.

In paragraph (b) "relevant accounting period" means the accounting period specified in the direction or any subsequent accounting period.

(2) The responsible member must provide specified information to HMRC.

(3) The information must be provided in the specified way.

(4) The information must be provided before the end of the period of 90 days from the end of the accounting period.

(5) In subsections (2) and (3) "specified" means specified in a notice published by HMRC.

COMMENTARY ON SECTION 54

Section 54 instructs the responsible member to provide a notification to HMRC within 90 days from the end of the accounting period in which the DST threshold conditions are breached. This could therefore be required as early as 29 July 2020 for groups with an April year end. The potential size of this task, and the short time frame available to conclude, should not be underestimated. Penalties for failure to notify may be levied where the notification deadline is missed without a reasonable excuse.

Legislation provides that the notification must be in a specified way with specified information per HMRC notice. Guidance goes further to describe the information that should be included in a notification. It must be submitted via the DST portal on the GOV.UK website and includes Government Gateway details, name and address of the ultimate parent, details of the responsible member, start and end dates of the first DST accounting period, and an individual's contact details.

55   Duty to notify HMRC of change in relevant information

(1)   This section applies where section 54 applies or has applied in relation to a group.

(2)   If at any relevant time there is a change in relevant information relating to the group, the responsible member must notify HMRC of that change.

(3)   The notification must be given in the specified way.

(4)   The notification must be given before the end of the period of 90 days beginning with the day on which the change occurs.

(5)   In subsection (3) "specified" means specified in a notice published by HMRC.

(6)   In this section—

"relevant information" means information of a kind specified under section 54(2);

"relevant time" means any time—

(a)   after the time when the information is provided under section 54 or (if earlier) the last time by which the information may be provided in accordance with that section, and

(b)   before the giving of a direction under section 56 in relation to the group.

COMMENTARY ON SECTION 55

Section 55 states that HMRC must be told of any changes to such information by the responsible member within a 90 day time limit also. Changes that HMRC expects to be notified about include any contact details, changes in the responsible member via nomination, and changes in the accounting period end date. There is no need to notify HMRC of a company joining or leaving the group as part of this process.

56   Duty to file returns

(1)   This section applies where the threshold conditions are met in relation to a group for an accounting period.

(2)   The responsible member must deliver a DST return—

(a)   for the accounting period, and

(b)   for each subsequent accounting period, subject to subsection (3).

(3)   An officer of Revenue and Customs may, on the application of the responsible member, direct that the duty to deliver a DST return does not apply in relation to an accounting period specified in the direction or subsequent accounting periods.

(4)   Such a direction may be given only if it appears to the officer that the threshold conditions will not be met in relation to the group for any accounting period beginning with the specified accounting period.

(5)   Nothing in a direction under subsection (3) prevents the further application of this section to the group, in any subsequent accounting period in which the threshold conditions are met.

(6)   Schedule 8 contains provision about DST returns, enquiries, assessments etc.

COMMENTARY ON SECTION 56

The responsible member also assumes the responsibility of preparing DST returns for the group per section 56. A DST return must be provided for all accounting periods starting with the period in which the notification was made in respect of. Details of the returns, enquiries and assessments process are included in Schedule 8 and are discussed separately.

HMRC may direct that DST returns are no longer required at their discretion, should the responsible member apply for consideration that the threshold conditions are not met. This could occur for instance where a protective registration is submitted before a group has had sufficient time to conclude on the specifics of the threshold conditions in the first accounting period of relevance, where it is later discovered that the conditions are not (and are not likely to be) breached.

Groups, parents and members

57   Meaning of "group", "parent" etc

(1)   In this Part "group" means—

(a)   any entity which—

   (i) is a relevant entity (see section 58), and

   (ii) meets condition A or B (see subsections (2) and (3)), and

 (b) each subsidiary (if any) of the entity mentioned in paragraph (a).

(2) Condition A is that the entity—

 (a) is a member of a GAAP group, and

 (b) is not a subsidiary of an entity that—

   (i) is a relevant entity, and

   (ii) itself meets condition A.

(3) Condition B is that the entity is not a member of a GAAP group.

(4) In this Part—

 (a) references to the "parent" of a group are to the entity mentioned in subsection (1)(a);

 (b) references to a "member" of a group are to an entity mentioned in subsection (1)(a) or (b);

 (c) "subsidiary" has the meaning given by the applicable accounting standards.

(5) In this section "GAAP group" means a group within the meaning of the applicable accounting standards.

(6) For the meaning of "the applicable accounting standards" see section 64.

COMMENTARY ON SECTION 57

As DST relies on activities and revenues of a group in totality, and the members of that group, specific definitions of those terms are required at sections 57 and 58.

Section 57 then tells us that such relevant entities could be a 'parent' if they meet the definition of subsection (1)(a), or a 'subsidiary' if they meet the definition of subsection (1)(b), and that both parent and subsidiary are part of the 'group' for the purposes of this Part. These definitions refer to the accounting definitions of a GAAP group for these purposes, but also include relevant entities which are not part of a GAAP group as a potential parent entity. This ensures that individual relevant entities which are not part of any accounting group with other entities are still a 'group' for the purposes of this Part (ie a single member group is still a 'group').

---

58 Section 57: meaning of "relevant entity"

(1) In section 57 "relevant entity" means—

 (a) a company, or

 (b) an entity the shares or other interests in which are listed on a recognised stock exchange and are sufficiently widely held.

(2) Shares or other interests in an entity are "sufficiently widely held" if no participator in the entity holds more than 10% by value of all the shares or other interests in the entity.

(3) The following are not relevant entities—

 (a) the Crown;

 (b) a Minister of the Crown;

 (c) a government department;

 (d) a Northern Ireland department;

 (e) a foreign sovereign power.

(4) In this section—

 (a) "participator" has the meaning given by section 454 of CTA 2010;

 (b) "recognised stock exchange" has the meaning given by section 1137 of CTA 2010;

 (c) the reference to shares or other interests being listed on a recognised stock exchange is to be read in accordance with section 1137 of CTA 2010.

(5) For the meaning of "company" see section 72.

COMMENTARY ON SECTION 58

Section 58 instructs that a relevant entity is any company, or another kind of entity which has interests listed on a registered stock exchange and with sufficiently widely held interests. Certain Government and Crown interests are specifically excluded at subsection (3). Other terms take their general definition from other areas of the Taxes Acts.

59   Continuity of a group over time

(1)   In this Part, this section applies for the purpose of determining whether a group at any time (Time 2) is the same group as a group at any earlier time (Time 1).

(2)   The group at Time 2 is the same group as the group at Time 1 if and only if the entity that is the parent of the group at Time 2—

(a)   was the parent of the group at Time 1, and

(b)   was the parent of a group at all times between Time 1 and Time 2.

COMMENTARY ON SECTION 59

Section 59 states that for a group to have continuity, the parent entity must be the same through all passage of time. Under this definition, any break for a mere moment in the parent of a group constitutes a new group.

60   Treatment of stapled entities

(1)   This section applies where two or more entities—

(a)   would, apart from this section, be the parent of a group, and

(b)   are stapled to each other.

(2)   This Part applies as if—

(a)   the entities were subsidiaries of another entity (the "deemed parent"), and

(b)   the deemed parent were within section 57(1)(a) (conditions for being the parent of a group).

(3)   For the purpose of this section, an entity (A) is "stapled" to another entity (B) if, in consequence of the nature of the rights attaching to the shares or other interests in A (including any terms or conditions attaching to the right to transfer the interests), it is necessary or advantageous for a person who has, disposes of or acquires shares or other interests in A also to have, dispose of or acquire shares or other interests in B.

COMMENTARY ON SECTION 60

Section 60 applies a deemed parent definition to bring two otherwise separate groups but where parents are stapled together as one group. This tackles any potential avoidance of the threshold conditions by manipulating the group definition.

Accounting periods, accounts etc

61   Accounting periods and meaning of "a group's accounts"

(1)   This section applies for the purposes of this Part.

(2)   A group's first accounting period—

(a)   begins with 1 April 2020, and

(b)   ends with the first accounting reference date to occur after that date or, if earlier, with 31 March 2021.

This is subject to subsection (4) (rule for groups coming into existence after 1 April 2020).

(3)   Any other accounting period of a group—

(a)   begins immediately after the end of the previous accounting period, and

(b)   ends with the first accounting reference date to occur after it begins or, if earlier, one year after it begins.

(4)   In the case of a group formed after 1 April 2020, its first accounting period—

(a)   begins with the date on which it is formed, and

(b)   ends with the first accounting reference date to occur after that date or, if earlier, one year after it begins.

(5)   In this section "accounting reference date" means the date to which the group's accounts are made up.

(6)   Any reference to a group's accounts is to—

(a)   the consolidated accounts of the group's parent and its subsidiaries, or

(b) the parent's accounts (if the parent is the only member of the group throughout the period in question).

COMMENTARY ON SECTION 61

DST is calculated and reported by reference to accounting periods. However, section 61 informs that DST is to take effect from 1 April 2020. It does so by defining the first accounting period to begin with 1 April 2020 and run to the group accounting reference date, with a backstop of 31 March 2021 to ensure each period is 12 months or less. DST accounting periods are then defined to run to each 12 month period, or a group accounting reference date change, whichever is the earlier. For the most part this should ensure that DST periods match group consolidated accounting periods.

62 Apportionment of revenues or expenses to accounting period

(1) This section applies if a group's period of account does not coincide with an accounting period.

(2) The revenues or expenses of a period of account may be apportioned to the parts of that period falling within different accounting periods.

(3) The apportionment must be made by reference to the number of days in the periods concerned.

COMMENTARY ON SECTION 62

As stated, accounting dates are defined by reference to the group's consolidated accounts or the parent's accounts in a solus entity situation. The 12 month backstop may mean that in an exceptional case the DST accounting period does not match group consolidated accounting reference dates. Section 62 instructs that where this is the case, a daily apportionment of revenues and expenses is required to compare data to that required for DST.

There may also be discrepancies between DST periods and UK tax periods if accounts of subsidiary UK companies do not have a matching reference date to group accounts.

63 Meaning of revenues arising, or expenses recognised, in a period

(1) In this Part any reference to revenues arising to members of a group in a period, or to expenses of members of a group recognised in a period, is to be interpreted as follows.

(2) For any period of account of the group for which the group's accounts are produced in accordance with the applicable accounting standards, the reference is to—

(a) revenues (however described) or expenses recognised in the income statement (or in profit and loss) for that period, or

(b) if any consolidation exemption applies, to revenues (however described) or expenses that would be recognised in the income statement (or in profit and loss) for that period if no consolidation exemption were applicable.

(3) For any period of account of the group not falling within subsection (2), the reference is to revenues or expenses that would be recognised in the income statement (or in profit and loss) in the group's accounts produced in accordance with IAS for the period if such accounts were produced (and no consolidation exemption was applicable).

(4) If the group does not produce accounts for any period ("the relevant period") in an accounting period, the reference is to revenues or expenses that would be recognised in the income statement (or in profit and loss) in the group's accounts produced in accordance with IAS for the relevant period if such accounts were produced (and no consolidation exemption was applicable).

(5) In this section "consolidation exemption" means any exemption in the applicable accounting standards from a requirement to consolidate revenues.

COMMENTARY ON SECTION 63

For DST purposes more broadly, revenues and expenses that are recognised in any period should be calculated by reference to accounting standards. There is some further detail here in sections 63 and 64 on how to use accounting data for the purposes of this Part. There is a requirement when assimilating data to use an applicable accounting standard as used at group level.

64 Meaning of "the applicable accounting standards" etc

(1) This section applies for the purposes of this Part.

(2) "The applicable accounting standards", in relation to a group, means—

    (a) for any period for which the group's accounts are produced in accordance with UK GAAP, UK GAAP;

    (b) for any period for which the group's accounts are produced in accordance with acceptable overseas GAAP, acceptable overseas GAAP;

    (c) for any period for which the group's accounts are produced in accordance with a specified standard, that standard;

    (d) otherwise, IAS.

(3) "UK GAAP"—

    (a) means generally accepted accounting practice in relation to accounts of UK companies (other than accounts prepared in accordance with IAS) that are intended to give a true and fair view, and

    (b) has the same meaning in relation to persons other than companies, and companies that are not UK companies, as it has in relation to UK companies.

"UK companies" here means companies incorporated or formed under the law of a part of the United Kingdom.

(4) "Acceptable overseas GAAP" means the generally accepted accounting practice and principles of any of the following—

Canada;
China;
Japan;
South Korea;
the United States of America.

(5) "IAS" means—

    (a) International Accounting Standards,

    (b) International Financial Reporting Standards, and

    (c) related interpretations,

issued or adopted, from time to time, by the International Accounting Standards Board.

(6) In subsection (2)(c), "specified" means specified in a notice published by HMRC.

COMMENTARY ON SECTION 64

Continuing from section 63, presently the legislation allows use of UK GAAP, or the overseas GAAP of the five stated jurisdictions. Where a different GAAP is being used in group accounts, IAS / IFRS data must be used.

This of course means that any group preparing consolidated financial statements under an overseas GAAP not listed must prepare full IAS consolidated financial statements for this purpose.

Supplementary

65 Anti-avoidance

(1) Any tax advantage that would (apart from this section) arise from relevant avoidance arrangements is to be counteracted by the making of such adjustments as are just and reasonable.

(2) The adjustments (whether or not made by an officer of Revenue and Customs) may be made by way of an assessment, the modification of an assessment, amendment or disallowance of a claim, or otherwise.

(3) Arrangements are "relevant avoidance arrangements" if their main purpose, or one of their main purposes, is to enable a person to obtain a tax advantage.

(4) But arrangements are not "relevant avoidance arrangements" if the obtaining of any tax advantage that would (apart from this section) arise from them can reasonably be regarded as consistent with—

(a)   any principles on which the provisions of this Part that are relevant to the arrangements are based (whether express or implied), and

(b)   the policy objectives of those provisions.

(5)   In this section—

"arrangements" include any agreement, understanding, scheme, transaction or series of transactions (whether or not legally enforceable);

"tax" means digital services tax (and "tax advantage" is to be construed accordingly);

"tax advantage" includes—

(a)   avoidance or reduction of a charge to tax or an assessment to tax,

(b)   repayment or increased repayment of tax,

(c)   avoidance of a possible assessment to tax, and

(d)   deferral of a payment of tax or advancement of a repayment of tax.

COMMENTARY ON SECTION 65

A targeted anti-avoidance measure for DST is included at section 65, drafted similarly to other recent anti-avoidance, for example in the anti-hybrid provisions in TIOPA 2010, Pt 6A. Any arrangement entered into by a taxpayer with a main purpose of obtaining a tax advantage may be counteracted by a just and reasonable adjustment. Tax is specifically defined as DST here. The drafting is intentionally broad and allows any such adjustment to be made to give a just and reasonable outcome, including assessments or otherwise, by HMRC or the taxpayer. One exception to any anti-avoidance application is where the arrangements and the associated tax advantage are consistent with the principles of the legislation and the policy objectives therein. This is included to ensure that sensible tax planning decisions (for example, claiming to apply the alternative basis of charge where it would produce a reduced liability) are not counteracted by the anti-avoidance, given they are within the policy intent of the provisions.

66   Notice requiring payment from other group members

(1)   This section applies where any DST liability relating to a group for an accounting period is unpaid at the end of the period of 3 months after the relevant date.

(2)   A designated officer may give a notice (a "payment notice") to a relevant person requiring that person, within 30 days of the giving of the notice, to pay all unpaid DST liabilities relating to the group for the accounting period.

(3)   A payment notice must state—

(a)   the amount of any digital services tax or penalty that remains unpaid,

(b)   the date any digital services tax or penalty first became payable, and

(c)   the relevant person's right of appeal.

(4)   A payment notice may not be given more than 3 years and 6 months after the relevant date.

(5)   If the DST liability arose because of a determination under Part 5 of Schedule 8, the relevant date is the date on which the notice of determination is issued.

(6)   If the DST liability arose because of a self-assessment, the relevant date is the later of—

(a)   the date on which the tax becomes due and payable;

(b)   in a case where the DST return is delivered after the filing date, the date on which the return is delivered;

(c)   if notice of enquiry is given, the date on which the enquiry is completed;

(d)   if more than one notice of enquiry is given, the date on which the last notice is given;

(e)   if as a result of such an enquiry the DST return is amended, the date on which the notice of the amendment is issued;

(f)   if there is an appeal against such an amendment, the date on which the appeal is finally determined.

(7)   If the DST liability arose because of an assessment under Part 6 or 7 of Schedule 8, the relevant date is—

(a)   if there is no appeal against the assessment, the date on which the notice of assessment is issued, or

(b)   if there is such an appeal, the date on which the appeal is finally determined.

(8)   If the DST liability arose because of a penalty, the relevant date is the date on which the notice of the penalty is issued.

(9)   A payment notice may be given anywhere in the world, to any relevant person (whether or not resident in the United Kingdom).

(10)   Schedule 9 makes further provision about payment notices.

(11)   In this section—

"designated officer" means an officer of Revenue and Customs who has been designated by the Commissioners for the purposes of this Part;

"DST liability", in relation to a group for an accounting period, means—

(a)   a liability of a relevant person to digital services tax in respect of that period, or

(b)   a liability of a person to a penalty for anything done (or not done) in respect of the accounting period;

"the filing date" has the same meaning as in Schedule 8 (see paragraph 1(1));

"relevant person" means any person who was a member of the group in the accounting period.

(12)   The reference in subsection (6) to a self-assessment includes a reference to a self-assessment that supersedes a determination (see paragraph 18 of Schedule 8).

(13)   In this section references to "digital services tax" include references to interest on digital services tax.

COMMENTARY ON SECTION 66

Section 66 contains provisions which allow HMRC to issue a payment notice to collect DST from any group member where it remains unpaid by the responsible member after three months. This joint and several liability therefore means that where the responsible member has not paid their DST, any member of the group (whether UK company or otherwise) could be liable for the group's full charge.

The timeframe for HMRC to issue a payment notice is from three months after the 'relevant date' to three years and six months after the 'relevant date'. Broadly, the relevant date is defined as the final date when the DST liability was due to be paid by the responsible member. This is of course a complex definition taking into account not only the usual payment deadline but considering self-assessment, enquiries, assessments, and determinations. The detail of these measures are included in Schedule 8 and 9 of the Act.

67   Interest on overdue DST

(1)   Digital services tax carries interest at the applicable rate from the date when the tax becomes due and payable until payment.

(2)   This applies even if the date when the tax becomes due and payable is—

(a)   a Saturday or Sunday,

(b)   Good Friday, Christmas day, a bank holiday or other public holiday, or

(c)   a day specified in an order made under section 2 of the Banking and Financial Dealings Act 1971 (power to suspend financial dealings).

(3)   In this section "the applicable rate" means the rate applicable under section 178 of FA 1989.

COMMENTARY ON SECTION 67

Sections 67 and 68 concern interest on underpaid or overpaid DST. Where DST is unpaid or overdue, HMRC will charge late payment interest per current established rates from due date to payment date. Do note that the rate of late payment interest changed on 7 April 2020.

68   Interest on overpaid DST etc

(1)   Where a payment in respect of a person's digital services tax liability for an accounting period is made before the due date, the payment carries interest at the applicable rate from the later of—

(a)   the date the payment is made, and

(b)   6 months and 13 days from the start of the accounting period, until the due date.

(2) Where a repayment of digital services tax paid by a person for an accounting period falls to be made, the repayment carries interest at the applicable rate—

(a) from the due date or, if later, the date the digital services tax was paid, and

(b) until the order for repayment is issued.

(3) Where a repayment of digital services tax is a repayment of tax paid by a person on different dates, it is to be treated so far as possible as a repayment of tax paid on a later (rather than an earlier) date among those dates.

(4) Where—

(a) interest has been paid to a person under this section,

(b) there is a change in the person's assessed liability,

(c) the change does not correct (wholly or in part) an error made by an officer of Revenue and Customs, and

(d) as a result of the change (and in particular not as a result of an error in the calculation of interest) it appears to an officer of Revenue and Customs that some or all of the interest ought not to have been paid,

the interest that ought not to have been paid may be recovered from the person.

(5) For the purposes of subsection (4)(b) there is a change in a person's assessed liability if (and only if)—

(a) an assessment, or an amendment of an assessment, of the amount of digital services tax payable by the person for the accounting period in question is made, or

(b) an HMRC determination of that amount is made,

whether or not any previous assessment or determination has been made.

(6) In this section—

"the applicable rate" has the same meaning as in section 67;

"the due date", in relation to an accounting period, means the date digital services tax for the accounting period becomes due and payable;

"error" includes—

(a) any computational error, and

(b) the allowance of a claim that ought not to have been allowed;

"HMRC determination" means a determination under Part 5 of Schedule 8.

COMMENTARY ON SECTION 68

Where DST is overpaid or paid early, HMRC will award repayment interest per current rates. The dates to which repayment interest applies are more complex, as they must consider filing and payment due dates, as well as set offs against other taxes paid by different persons.

69 Recovery of DST liability

(1) Any amount due by way of DST liability is recoverable as a debt due to the Crown.

(2) In this section "DST liability" has the same meaning as in section 66.

COMMENTARY ON SECTION 69

Section 69 explicitly states that DST is a debt due to the Crown and thus recoverable in the same manner as other established taxes.

70 Minor and consequential amendments

Schedule 10 contains minor and consequential amendments.

71 Review of DST

(1) The Treasury must, before the end of 2025, conduct a review of digital services tax and prepare a report of the review.

(2) The Treasury must lay a copy of the report before Parliament.

COMMENTARY ON SECTION 71

The promised 'sunset clause' is included at section 71 of this Part. Section 71 requires the Treasury to conduct a review of the DST measures and prepare a report, to be laid before Parliament. This report must be prepared before the end of 2025. This clause sets a backstop date by which Treasury must consider the merits of DST and its long-term prospects. The Government have stated their commitment to reaching a multilateral solution to the taxation of the digital economy as part of the OECD Inclusive Framework's measures to replace the UK unilateral DST in due course. Should the OECD be successful in reaching such a consensus, we may see section 71 applied much earlier than 2025 to remove DST altogether, to be replaced with the OECD solution. There remains debate and cynicism as to whether the OECD Inclusive Framework members can reach the required consensus to establish such a multilateral solution. If no such solution is reached, we may find that the outcome of the sunset clause report is merely that the UK's unilateral solution remains necessary and for the long term. A similar conversation regarding the temporary nature of the UK's unilateral taxing measures was previously held at the introduction of the diverted profits tax ('DPT'), with many commentators seeing DPT as a temporary measure while international conversations on the Base Erosion and Profit Shifting ('BEPS') measures continued to take place. DPT remains in UK law five years later with no sign of repeal.

International comparisons and US position

As part of understanding the UK's position with respect to its DST it is important to be aware of the international climate regarding such taxes. The OECD discussions to form a multilateral consensus position on digital tax continue, and with impetus there is hope that such a consensus could be reached by early 2021. Outside of the OECD position, unilateral digital taxes continue to be introduced around the world in the absence of a joint solution. Even in Europe, at the time of writing different unilateral digital taxes have been implemented in Turkey, Austria, Italy, France and Hungary. Many more proposals exist and are gaining traction. The taxes being introduced are targeted at further alignment of digital activity and tax base; but vary widely in definitions of in-scope activities and revenues, as well as including different thresholds for the size of business that will be impacted. Large multinationals in the digital space therefore have quite the task on their hands in the current climate to understand these taxes and gather the required data to be compliant with them.

It goes without saying that many US headquartered technology businesses will bear the greatest overall DST burden. In 2019 the US investigated France for its digital services tax plans, threatening to introduce greater tariffs on France's wine imports if the tax were to go ahead. After some detailed exchanges, a temporary pause on collection of the tax was deemed sufficient to manage the position, however the US unease with European digital taxes has not gone away. The Trump administration continues to express distain at DSTs around the world, vocal in their position that such taxes unfairly target US headquartered groups. Further investigations and heated international debates are likely to take place in the coming months.

Deductibility of DST for corporation tax purposes

Questions have been raised regarding the interaction of DST with corporation tax, particularly in whether DST could be credited against UK corporation tax or deducted in the calculation of taxable profits as an expense.

No provision for credit relief exists, so a liability to DST certainly cannot be credited against corporation tax payable. DST is certainly intended to be a further tax levied, and as discussed above, is outside the realm of the bi-lateral double tax treaty network to alleviate double taxation.

The question of whether the UK DST may be deductible when calculating taxable profits for corporation tax purposes is an interesting one, and there are no provisions within the DST legislation discussing this matter. HMRC guidance suggests that this is a first principles question for any UK tax resident entity calculating its taxable profits: it must determine whether its costs incurred are wholly and exclusively for the purposes of its trade. Any liability to DST technically arises to each individual company, and therefore a UK tax resident entity with a liability to DST must answer this question. HMRC guidance is promising in this area, the paragraph below indicating that in most circumstances, having recognised a DST liability in individual entity accounts, HMRC would expect to see the cost as a deductible expense for corporation tax purposes.

'The availability of any deduction will depend on the particular facts and circumstances of the business. However, it should be noted that a company's DST expense is directly related to the earning of its revenues and is a legal obligation of performing that trade. Therefore, in most cases it is likely the expense will have been incurred wholly and exclusively for the purposes of the trade.'

We must remember that the UK DST liability falls to each entity with UK digital services revenues, which may or may not be a UK corporation taxpayer. Overseas tax resident companies with UK digital services revenues must therefore apply their own corporate tax principles in their home jurisdiction to determine if they may deduct UK DST in calculating their taxable profits for foreign corporation tax purposes. Similarly, a UK corporation tax payer who suffers an overseas DST liability will need to apply UK corporation tax principles to that question; in a similar way to assessing whether UK DST is incurred wholly and exclusively for the purposes of its trade.

General

72 Interpretation of Part

In this Part—

"accounting period" has the meaning given by section 61;
"the applicable accounting standards" has the meaning given by section 64;
"the Commissioners" has the meaning given by section 39;
"company" has the meaning given by section 1121(1) of CTA 2010;
"digital services activity" has the meaning given by section 43;
"digital services revenues" has the meaning given by section 40;
"group" has the meaning given by section 57;
"group's accounts" has the meaning given by section 61;
"HMRC" means Her Majesty's Revenue and Customs;
"IAS" has the meaning given by section 64;
"member" has the meaning given by section 57;
"parent" has the meaning given by section 57;
"the responsible member" has the meaning given by section 52;
"subsidiary" has the meaning given by section 57;
"the threshold conditions" has the meaning given by section 46;
"UK digital services revenues" has the meaning given by section 41;
"UK user" has the meaning given by section 44;
"user" has the meaning given by section 44.

PART 3
OTHER TAXES
Inheritance tax

73 Excluded property etc

(1) IHTA 1984 is amended as follows.

(2) In section 48 (excluded property)—

    (a)   in subsection (3)(a), for "settlement was made" substitute "property became comprised in the settlement (but see also subsection (3F))",

    (b)   in subsection (3A)(a), for "settlement was made" substitute "property became comprised in the settlement (but see also subsection (3F))",

    (c)   in subsection (3E), for "settlement is made" substitute "property became comprised in the settlement (but see also subsection (3F))", and

    (d)   after subsection (3E) insert—

"(3F) If—

    (a)   an amount is payable in respect of property ("the existing property") comprised in a settlement, and

    (b)   the amount represents an accumulation of income which (once accumulated) becomes comprised in the settlement, subsections (3)(a), (3A)(a) and (3E) have effect, in the case of the amount, as if any reference to the time it became comprised in the settlement were to the time the existing property became comprised in the settlement."

(3) After section 48 insert—

"48A Commencement of settlement

In this Act any reference to the commencement of a settlement is to the time when property first becomes comprised in it."

(4) Omit section 60 (meaning of commencement of settlement for purposes of Chapter).

(5) In section 64 (charge at ten-year anniversary)—

 (a) in subsection (1B)—
  (i) after "settlor of" insert "property comprised in",
  (ii) for "settlement was made" substitute "property became comprised in the settlement (but see also subsection (1BA))", and
  (iii) after "income of the settlement" insert "that arose (directly or indirectly) from the property", and

 (b) after that subsection insert—

"(1BA) If—
 (a) an amount is payable in respect of property ("the existing property") comprised in a settlement, and
 (b) the amount represents an accumulation of income which (once accumulated) becomes comprised in the settlement,

subsection (1B) has effect, in the case of the amount, as if any reference to the time it became comprised in the settlement were to the time the existing property became comprised in the settlement."

(6) In section 65 (charge at other times)—

 (a) in subsection (7A), for "settlement made" substitute "property became comprised in settlement",
 (b) in subsection (8)—
  (i) after "settlor of" insert "property comprised in",
  (ii) for "settlement was made" substitute "property became comprised in the settlement (but see also subsection (8A))", and
  (iii) for "property comprised in the settlement" substitute "the property", and

 (c) after that subsection insert—

"(8A) If—
 (a) an amount is payable in respect of property ("the existing property") comprised in a settlement, and
 (b) the amount represents an accumulation of income which (once accumulated) becomes comprised in the settlement,

subsection (8) has effect, in the case of the amount, as if any reference to the time it became comprised in the settlement were to the time the existing property became comprised in the settlement."

(7) In section 74A (arrangements involving acquisition of interest in settled property etc)—

 (a) in subsection (2)(a), for "settlement was made" substitute "relevant settled property became comprised in the settlement", and
 (b) in subsection (3)(a), for "settlement was made" substitute "relevant settled property became comprised in the settlement".

(8) In section 157(3) (non-residents' bank accounts), for "he made" substitute "the settled property became comprised in".

(9) In section 237(1)(b) (imposition of charge), for "the chargeable transfer is made by the making of a settlement or" substitute "property becomes comprised in a settlement by virtue of the chargeable transfer or the chargeable transfer".

(10) In section 272 (general interpretation)—

(a)   before the definition of "conditionally exempt transfer" insert—

""commencement" of a settlement has the meaning given by section 48A;", and

(b)   in the definition of "foreign-owned", in paragraph (b)(ii), at the end insert "(and section 64(1BA) applies for the purposes of this sub-paragraph as it applies for the purposes of section 64(1B))".

(11)   In relation to any chargeable transfer made on or after the day on which this Act is passed, the amendments made by this section are treated as always having been in force. Section 2(3) of IHTA 1984 applies for the purposes of this subsection.

COMMENTARY ON SECTION 73

Section 73, which will have effect for every chargeable transfer made on or after Royal Assent (22 July 2020) (with the amendments treated as always having been in force), puts beyond doubt an interpretation which HMRC and the profession have been arguing over for many years.

It amends the wording of IHTA 1984, ss 48, 65 and 74A (governing excluded property, charges on exits and arrangements involving acquisitions of interests in settled property) so that the words 'settlement was made' are replaced by 'property became comprised in the settlement', ensuring that additions of assets by UK domiciled (or formerly domiciled resident) individuals to trusts made when they were non-domiciled cannot be excluded property and will therefore be within the scope of inheritance tax.

IHTA 1984, s 48 governs whether excluded property treatment is applied to property comprised in a settlement. The settlor's domicile at the time the settlement was made is fundamental in determining whether settled property is excluded property. IHTA 1984, s 48 basically provides that (along with certain reversionary interests and other exempt assets), any foreign property comprised in a settlement will be excluded property unless the settlor was UK domiciled (or, from 2017, a formerly domiciled resident) at the time the settlement was made.

A formerly domiciled resident is an individual with a UK domicile of origin, subsequently displaced with a foreign domicile of choice, who is UK resident for the tax year in question and was also UK resident for at least one of the two preceding tax years.

The amendments to IHTA 1984, s 48 mean that the settlor must have not only been non-UK domiciled (and not a formerly domiciled resident) when the settlement was made (defined as when property was first added to it), but must also have had that status at the time of any additions to the settlement, for excluded property treatment to apply to those additions.

Consequential amendments have also been made to IHTA 1984, ss 157, 237 and the definitions in IHTA 1984, s 272 to substitute the same wording.

New IHTA 1984, ss 48(3F) and 65(8A) make clear that amounts representing accumulations of income arising from existing trust property which become comprised in the settlement are to be treated as though references to the time they became comprised in the settlement were to the time the existing property became comprised in the settlement, for these purposes, ie the settlor's domicile at the time the income-bearing property was added will govern whether or not it is excluded property.

New IHTA 1984, s 48A (applying to the entirety of the settled property section of IHTA 1984) replaces s 60 (which applied for the purposes of Chapter III only) to state that: 'in this Act any reference to the commencement of a settlement is to the time when property first becomes comprised in it.'

---

74   Transfers between settlements etc

(1)   IHTA 1984 is amended as follows.

(2)   After section 81A insert—

"81B   Excluded property: property to which section 80 applies

(1)   This section applies to property to which section 80 (initial interest of settlor etc) applies.

(2)   If the property would apart from this section be excluded property by virtue of section 48(3)(a) or (3A)(a), the property is at any time in a tax year to be regarded as excluded property for the purposes of this Chapter, except sections 78 and 79, only if Conditions A and B are met.

(3)   Section 65(8) has effect in relation to the property only if Condition A is met (in addition to any condition mentioned in that provision).

(4)   Condition A is that the actual settlor was not domiciled in the United Kingdom at the time of the occasion first referred to in section 80(1).

(5)   Condition B is that the actual settlor is not a formerly domiciled resident for the tax year.

(6)   In this section "the actual settlor" means the person who is the settlor of the property in relation to the settlement first mentioned in section 80(1).

(7)   Where the occasion first referred to in section 80(1) occurred before the day on which the Finance Act 2020 was passed, this section has effect as if, in subsection (2), "or (3A)(a)" were omitted."

(3)   In section 82 (excluded property)—

   (a)   in subsection (1), omit "80 or",
   (b)   in subsection (2)—

      (i)   omit "80 or", and
      (ii) for "settlement was made" substitute "property became comprised in the settlement",

   (c)   in subsection (3), omit paragraph (a),
   (d)   in subsection (4), omit paragraph (a),
   (e)   after that subsection insert—

"(5)   This section does not apply in relation to a case to which section 82A applies.", and

   (f)   in the heading at the end insert ": property to which section 81 applies (old cases)".

(4)   After section 82 insert—

"82A   Excluded property: property to which section 81 applies (new cases)

(1)   This section—

   (a)   applies where, at any time on or after the day on which the Finance Act 2020 is passed, property ceases to be comprised in a settlement ("the first settlement") but is treated as a result of section 81 as remaining comprised in that settlement for the purposes of this Chapter, and
   (b)   applies whether or not at any subsequent time the property is comprised in the first settlement without regard to that section.

(2)   If the property would apart from this section be excluded property by virtue of section 48(3)(a) or (3A)(a), the property is to be regarded as excluded property for the purposes of this Chapter, except sections 78 and 79, at any time only if the non-domicile condition is met in relation to each qualifying transfer occurring on or before that time.

(3)   Section 65(8) has effect in relation to the property at any time only if (in addition to the condition mentioned there) the non-domicile condition is met in relation to each qualifying transfer occurring on or before that time; but, for the purposes of this subsection, the non-domicile condition has effect with the omission of subsection (6)(a)(ii).

(4)   For the purposes of this section each of the following is a "qualifying transfer"—

   (a)   the occasion on which section 81 applies to the property; and
   (b)   any subsequent occasion on which the property would, if the effect of section 81 were ignored, become comprised in a settlement to which this Chapter applies (including the first settlement).

(5)   But a qualifying transfer does not occur as a result of—

   (a)   an assignment by a beneficiary of an interest in a settlement, or
   (b)   an exercise of a general power of appointment,

unless the time of the assignment or exercise of the power falls on or after the day on which the Finance Act 2020 is passed.

(6) For the purposes of this section "the non-domicile condition" is—

    (a) in a case where a qualifying transfer occurs as a result of an assignment by a beneficiary of an interest in a settlement or an exercise of a general power of appointment, that the beneficiary or the person exercising the power—

        (i) was not domiciled in the United Kingdom at the time of the assignment or exercise of the power, and

        (ii) is not a formerly domiciled resident for the tax year in which the time mentioned in subsection (2) falls;

    (b) in a case in which section 81 applies which is not within paragraph (a), that the person who was the settlor of the property in relation to the first settlement was not domiciled in the United Kingdom immediately before the time when the property ceased to be comprised in the first settlement;

    (c) in any other case, that the person who was the settlor of the property in relation to the first settlement was not domiciled in the United Kingdom immediately before the time of the subsequent occasion.

(7) If—

    (a) the settlor mentioned in subsection (6)(b) or (c) has died before the time mentioned there, and

    (b) the death does not give rise to a qualifying transfer,

the non-domicile condition is treated as met.

(8) In this section any reference to a qualifying transfer occurring as a result of—

    (a) an assignment by a beneficiary of an interest in a settlement, or

    (b) an exercise of a general power of appointment,

includes the transfer occurring partly as a result of the assignment or exercise of the power.

(9) In this section any reference to an assignment includes an assignation."

(5) In relation to any chargeable transfer made on or after the day on which this Act is passed, the amendments made by subsections (2) and (3) are treated as always having been in force.

Section 2(3) of IHTA 1984 applies for the purposes of this subsection.

COMMENTARY ON SECTION 74

Section 74 imports the same 'property became comprised in the settlement' wording into the already somewhat complex area governed by IHTA 1984, ss 80–82. These sections apply further tests which must be met for excluded property status to apply where property is initially subject to interests in possession for spouses in succession, and where property moves between settlements to make clear that excluded property status will depend on the current domicile of the settlor (or other person) that causes the property to move to another trust.

IHTA 1984, s 80 provides that where property becomes comprised in a settlement where the settlor, his or her spouse, civil partner, widower or widow, is beneficially entitled to an interest in possession (IIP) in that property, a special rule applies if the property or any part of it subsequently becomes held on relevant property trusts such that neither spouse or civil partner is beneficially entitled to an IIP (from 22 March 2006 the only 'qualifying' new IIPs for these purposes are disabled persons' interests (DPIs) and immediate post-death interests (IPDIs). Transitional serial interests do not qualify).

In these circumstances, property is treated for the purposes of the relevant property charging provisions (apart from determining the ten-year anniversaries of the settlement), as not having become comprised in the settlement when it was made; instead, the property is treated as having become comprised in a separate settlement at the time when the last of the settlor, his or her spouse, civil partner, widower or widow ceased to be beneficially entitled to either a pre-22 March 2006 (qualifying) IIP, or a DPI or IPDI in it.

This applies regardless of the trusts on which it then becomes held. When the spouse or civil partner with the succeeding interest ceases to have an IIP in all or part of the property, then that part is treated as becoming comprised in a separate settlement at that time. The separate settlement is treated as having been made by the spouse or civil partner whose interest has ceased.

IHTA 1984, s 81 provides that, generally, where property ceases to be comprised in one settlement and becomes comprised in another then, unless in the meantime any person becomes beneficially entitled to the property (and not merely to an IIP in it), it is treated as remaining comprised in the first settlement.

Section 74 inserts new IHTA 1984, ss 81B and 82A and amends s 82 which now deals only with events arising before Royal Assent (22 July 2020).

New IHTA 1984, s 81B states that for the purposes of s 80, property will only be excluded property for a tax year if both conditions A and B are met:

- condition A is that the original settlor was not domiciled in the UK at the time the property first became comprised in the settlement
- condition B is that the original settlor is not a formerly domiciled resident for the tax year

IHTA 1984, s 82 (excluded property to which s 81 applies) provides that, where s 80 or s 81 applies, an extra requirement must be satisfied if property which would otherwise be excluded property is to be treated as such.

The effect of IHTA 1984, ss 80 and 82 together is that for excluded property status to be maintained, not only must the settlor of the original settlement not have been domiciled in the UK when he made the original settlement but the settlor of the new settlement (ie the last of the settlor, the settlor's spouse, civil partner or widow or widower to have a pre-22 March 2006 IIP, a DPI or an IPDI) must not have been domiciled in the UK (or a formerly domiciled resident) at the time of the transfer.

New IHTA 1984, s 82A adds to this by stating that trust property will only be regarded as excluded property for the purposes of the relevant property provisions, if the non-domicile condition is met in relation to each 'qualifying transfer' occurring on or before that time, ie excluded property treatment will depend on the current domicile of the settlor (or other person) that caused the property to move to the other trust.

'Qualifying transfers' include any occasions on which IHTA 1984, s 81 applies to the property or any later transfer of the same property between settlements to which the relevant property provisions apply (even if that is a transfer back to the original settlement).

Following Royal Assent (22 July 2020), 'qualifying transfers' for the purposes of IHTA 1984, s 82A will also include assignments by a beneficiary of an interest in a settlement, or an exercise of a general power of appointment.

IHTA 1984, s 82A provides that where a 'qualifying transfer' occurs as a result of an assignment by a beneficiary of an interest in a settlement or an exercise of a general power of appointment, excluded property treatment will only apply if the beneficiary or the person exercising the power was not domiciled in the UK (nor a formerly domiciled resident) at the time of the assignment or exercise of the power.

Where an assignment or exercise of a general power is not involved, for excluded property treatment to apply, the person who was the settlor of the property in the first settlement must not have been domiciled in the UK immediately before the property ceased to be comprised in that settlement.

However, the non-domicile condition will be treated as met in cases where the 'qualifying transfer' occurs after the death of the settlor (and does not occur as a result of an assignment or exercise of a general power of appointment).

75   Relief for payments to victims of persecution during Second World War era

(1)   IHTA 1984 is amended as follows.

(2)   In section 153ZA (inheritance tax relief for payments to victims of persecution during Second World War era: qualifying payments) after subsection (8) insert—

"(8A)   Regulations under this section may have effect in relation to deaths occurring before the regulations are made."

(3)   In Schedule 5A (inheritance tax relief for payments to victims of persecution during Second World War era), in Part 1 (compensation payments), after paragraph 9 insert—

"**10** A one-off payment of a fixed amount from the Kindertransport Fund established by the Government of the Federal Republic of Germany".

(4) The amendment made by subsection (3) has effect in relation to deaths occurring on or after 1 January 2019.

COMMENTARY ON SECTION 75

Section 75, as promised, inserts a new sub-section (8A) into IHTA 1984, s 153ZA (qualifying payments to victims of persecution during the Second World War era) stating that regulations made under that section may have effect for deaths occurring before those regulations are made.

The section also inserts a new category into IHTA 1984, Sch 5A, Pt 1 (compensation payments) to include one-off payments of fixed amounts from the Kindertransport Fund established by the Government of the Federal Republic of Germany (this amendment has effect in relation to deaths occurring on or after 1 January 2019).

Stamp duty land tax

76 Exceptional circumstances preventing disposal of interest in three year period

(1) In FA 2003, Schedule 4ZA (stamp duty land tax: higher rates for additional dwellings etc) is amended as follows.

(2) In paragraph 3 (single dwelling transactions)—

    (a)   in sub-paragraph (7)(b) for "the period of three years beginning with the day after the effective date of the transaction concerned" substitute "a permitted period";

    (b)   after sub-paragraph (7) insert—

"(7A)   For the purposes of sub-paragraph (7)(b), the permitted periods are—

    (a)   the period of three years beginning with the day after the effective date of the transaction concerned, or

    (b)   if HMRC are satisfied that the purchaser or the purchaser's spouse or civil partner would have disposed of the major interest in the sold dwelling within that three year period but was prevented from doing so by exceptional circumstances that could not reasonably have been foreseen, such longer period as HMRC may allow in response to an application made in accordance with sub-paragraph (7B).

(7B)   An application for the purposes of sub-paragraph (7A)(b) must—

    (a)   be made within the period of 12 months beginning with the effective date of the transaction disposing of the major interest in the sold dwelling, and

    (b)   be made in such form and manner, and contain such information, as may be specified by HMRC.

(7C)   Schedule 11A (claims not included in returns) does not apply in relation to an application made in accordance with sub-paragraph (7B)."

(3) In paragraph 8 (further provision in connection with paragraph 3(6) and (7))—

    (a)   in sub-paragraph (3), after "paragraph 3(7)" insert "by virtue of paragraph 3(7A)(a)";

    (b)   in sub-paragraph (4), after "paragraph 3(7)" insert "by virtue of paragraph 3(7A)(a)";

    (c)   after sub-paragraph (4) insert—

"(5)   Where HMRC grant an application made in accordance with paragraph 3(7B)—

    (a)   the land transaction return in respect of the transaction concerned is treated as having been amended to take account of the application of paragraph 3(7) by virtue of paragraph 3(7A)(b), and

    (b)   HMRC must notify the purchaser accordingly."

(4) The amendments made by this section have effect in a case where the effective date of the transaction concerned is on or after 1 January 2017.

COMMENTARY ON SECTION 76

This section amends FA 2003, Sch 4ZA, relating to stamp duty land tax (SDLT) rates on the purchase by individuals of second residential properties in England and Wales. Ordinarily an additional rate of 3% SDLT applies on top of the standard rates for SDLT for purchases of residential homes by individuals or companies who already own another residential property ('Additional Property SDLT Charge'). However there is a relief for this extra 3% charge if an individual hasn't sold his or her previous main residence after purchasing a replacement main residence, but sells the previous main residence within three years of purchasing the replacement main residence. The original provisions allow an individual to claim a refund of the Additional Property SDLT Charge if the previous main residence is sold within three years of purchasing the replacement main residence. The claim must be made within 12 months of the sale of the previous main residence or 12 months of the filing date of the land transaction return whichever is later.

Section 76 inserts a provision whereby the three-year period may be extended to a longer period if:

'HMRC are satisfied that the purchaser or the purchaser's spouse or civil partner would have disposed of the major interest in the sold dwelling within that three year period but was prevented from doing so by exceptional circumstances that could not reasonably have been foreseen ...'.

The changes come into force where the effective date of the transaction concerned, namely the date of the purchase of the replacement main residence, is on or after 1 January 2017 and where the three-year time limit to sell the previous main residence ended on or after 1 January 2020.

The measures were triggered by COVID-19 but HMRC states the following regarding exceptional circumstances:

'Exceptional circumstances are by their nature difficult to anticipate, but would include, for example prevention of the sale as a result of a restriction imposed by a public authority (eg the government restrictions placed on the housing market as a result of the COVID-19 pandemic).'

HMRC confirms that exceptional circumstances will not include the following:

- fluctuations in the housing market which deter owners from selling within the three-year time limit at market values applying at that time, or
- the ordinary and 'everyday' events that occur in the buying and selling of property, such as prospective purchasers changing their mind and dropping out of the transaction.

Stamp duty and stamp duty reserve tax

77 Stamp duty: transfers of unlisted securities and connected persons

After section 47 of FA 2019 insert—

"47A Stamp duty: transfers of unlisted securities and connected persons

(1) This section applies if—

 (a) an instrument transfers unlisted securities to a company or a company's nominee for consideration,

 (b) the person transferring the securities is connected with the company or is the nominee of a person connected with the company, and

 (c) some or all of the consideration consists of the issue of shares.

(2) In this section "unlisted securities" means stock or marketable securities that are not listed securities within the meaning of section 47 (stamp duty: transfers of listed securities and connected persons).

(3) For the purposes of the enactments relating to stamp duty the amount or value of the consideration is to be treated as being equal to—

 (a) the amount or value of the consideration for the transfer, or

 (b) if higher, the value of the unlisted securities.

(4) For the purposes of subsection (3) "the enactments relating to stamp duty" means the Stamp Act 1891 and any enactment amending that Act or that is to be construed as one with that Act.

(5) For the purposes of this section—

    (a)   the value of unlisted securities is to be taken to be the market value of the securities at the date the instrument is executed;

    (b)   "market value" has the same meaning as in TCGA 1992 and is to be determined in accordance with sections 272 and 273 of that Act (valuation).

(6) Section 1122 of CTA 2010 (connected persons) has effect for the purposes of this section.

(7) This section is to be construed as one with the Stamp Act 1891.

(8) This section has effect in relation to instruments executed on or after the date on which FA 2020 is passed."

COMMENTARY ON SECTION 77

Sections 77 and 78 relate to stamp duty (which is chargeable on instruments of transfer of UK stock and marketable securities) and stamp duty reserve tax (SDRT) (which is chargeable on any agreement to transfer UK chargeable securities and essentially applies to electronic share transfers). Together the two taxes are referred to as stamp taxes. The rate of tax is 0.5% except when the transfer is into clearance services or in respect of the issue of depositary receipts, in which case the rate is 1.5%.

Anti-avoidance provisions were introduced in the Finance Act 2019 with new targeted market value rules. The rules apply where either money is paid, there is nil consideration or where the consideration is other than money and are targeted at contrived arrangements involving the transfer of listed shares to connected companies in a way to minimise stamp taxes on the acquisition of high-value share portfolios. FA 2019, ss 47 and 48 provide that in respect of such transfers stamp taxes will be chargeable on the higher of the amount or value of the consideration, and the market value of the securities (the market value rule).

At the same time as introducing these provisions the Government announced a consultation on the consideration rules for stamp taxes on shares, including extending the new provisions in FA 2019, ss 47 and 48 to unlisted securities. The consultation closed on 30 January 2019, with the summary of responses published on 11 July 2019, coinciding with draft legislation extending the market value rule to the transfer of unlisted shares to connected companies. Therefore the extension of these anti-avoidance rules has been expected well in advance of implementation, effective from 22 July 2020, being the date of Royal Assent of the Finance Act 2020.

The Government has not published how common are such tax avoidance arrangements involving 'contrived arrangements' and the acquisition of high-value share portfolios, but the new legislation will fill any loop-hole which may have existed involving unlisted securities.

New FA 2019, s 47A

Section 77 inserts a new section 47A into FA 2019, with effect for instruments executed on or after 22 July 2020 extending the market value rule to unlisted securities in circumstances where there is a transfer of such securities to a connected company and the consideration is by way of issue of securities.

FA 2019, s 47A(1)(a)–(c) requires three conditions to be met for the market value rule to apply for stamp duty, namely:

- there is an instrument which transfers unlisted securities to a company or its nominee for consideration;
- the person transferring the securities is connected with the company or is the nominee connected with that company; and
- some or all of the consideration for the transfer consists of the issue of shares.

The first condition will cover any stock transfer forms and any other type of documentation which effectively transfers any interest in such securities. Unlisted securities, defined in FA 2019, s 47A(2), are any securities which are not defined as listed securities in FA 2019, s 47, namely stock or marketable securities which are regularly traded on (a) a regulated market; (b) a multilateral trading facility, or (c) recognised foreign exchanges. The usual concept of unlisted securities are, essentially, shares in private companies, for which there are no markets on which the shares can be traded, and which change hands subject to the company's Articles of Association. The FA 2019 provisions are more specific and have a wider definition being as follows:

- A regulated market is a multilateral system operated by a market operator where the securities traded (shares, bonds etc) are admitted in accordance with a defined procedure, and in the UK must be authorised and supervised by the Financial Conduct Authority (FCA). The FCA and HMRC websites list these markets.
- A multilateral trading facility (MTF) is a multilateral system which can be operated either by a regulated market or an investment firm. MTFs provide similar services to regulated markets but do not have the same level of obligations or regulation as regulated markets. They must also be authorised and regulated by the FCA. AIM, the Alternative Investment Market operated by the LSE, is an MTF.
- A recognised foreign exchange is one which falls within ITA 2007, s 1005 – HMRC provides a list of recognised foreign exchanges at www.gov.uk/guidance/recognised-stock-exchanges.

When the three conditions in FA 2019, s 47A apply, the amount or value of the consideration for the transfer will be deemed to be the greater of that amount or the 'value' of the unlisted securities for stamp taxes purposes. Such 'value' is defined as having the same meaning in TCGA 1992, ss 272, 273, where market value means the price which those assets might reasonably be expected to fetch on a sale in the open market and for unquoted shares and securities means, that in determining the open market value it should be assumed that: (a) the purchaser has all the information reasonably required for the purchase, (b) there is a willing vendor by private treaty, and (c) it is an arm's length transaction. Market value for stamp duty is to be calculated at the date the instrument is executed.

Connected person is the definition used in CTA 2010, s 1122. Essentially any person making the transfer will be connected with the company in the following circumstances:

- If the transferor is a company they will be connected if:
  - the same person has control of both companies;
  - a person has control of one company and persons connected with that person have control of the other company; or
  - a group of two or more persons has control of both companies and the groups either consist of the same persons or could be so regarded if (in one or more cases) a member of either group were replaced by a person with whom the member is connected.
- If the transferor is an individual he or she will be connected with a company if the individual has control of the company or together with other persons connected with that individual has control of the company.

---

78   SDRT: unlisted securities and connected persons

After section 48 of FA 2019—

"48A   SDRT: unlisted securities and connected persons

(1)   This section applies if a person is connected with a company and—

     (a)   the person or the person's nominee—

         (i)   agrees to transfer unlisted securities to the company or the company's nominee for consideration in money or money's worth, or

         (ii)   transfers such securities to the company or the company's nominee for consideration in money or money's worth, and

     (b)   some or all of the consideration consists of the issue of shares.

(2)   In this section "unlisted securities" means chargeable securities that are not listed securities within the meaning of section 48 (SDRT: listed securities and connected persons).

(3)   For the purposes of stamp duty reserve tax chargeable under section 87 of FA 1986 (the principal charge), the amount or value of the consideration is to be treated as being equal to—

     (a)   the amount or value of the consideration for the transfer, or

(b)   if higher, the market value of the unlisted securities at the time the agreement is made.

(4)   Subsection (5) has effect for the purposes of stamp duty reserve tax chargeable under section 93 of FA 1986 (depositary receipts) or section 96 of that Act (clearance services).

(5)   If the amount or value of the consideration for any transfer of unlisted securities is less than the value of those securities at the time they are transferred, the transfer is to be treated as being for an amount of consideration in money equal to that value.

(6)   For the purposes of this section—

     (a)   the value of unlisted securities is to be taken to be their market value;

     (b)   "market value" has the same meaning as in TCGA 1992 and is to be determined in accordance with sections 272 and 273 of that Act (valuation).

(7)   Section 1122 of CTA 2010 (connected persons) has effect for the purposes of this section.

(8)   This section is to be construed as one with Part 4 of FA 1986.

(9)   This section has effect—

     (a)   in relation to the charge to tax under section 87 of FA 1986 where—

         (i)   the agreement to transfer securities is conditional and the condition is satisfied on or after the relevant date, or

         (ii)   in any other case, the agreement is made on or after that date;

     (b)   in relation to the charge to tax under section 93 or 96 of that Act, where the transfer is on or after the relevant date (whenever the arrangement was made).

     In this subsection "the relevant date" is the day on which FA 2020 is passed."

COMMENTARY ON SECTION 78

Section 78 inserts a new section 48A into FA 2019 mirroring the extension of FA 2019, s 47A by virtue of section 75, relating to unlisted securities transferred to connected companies, and where there is an issue of shares by way of consideration. The provisions are construed as being within FA 1986, Pt 4, the primary legislation covering SDRT.

The new FA 2019, s 48A requires two conditions for the stamp taxes market value provisions to apply, namely:

- a person is connected with a company and that person or its nominee agrees to transfer or transfers unlisted securities to the company/its nominee for consideration in money or money's worth; and
- some or all of the consideration consists of the issue of shares.

Under these provisions if the amount or value of the consideration for any such transfer is less than their value at that time, the transfer will be treated as being made for consideration in money equal to their value. The definition of unlisted securities is identical to that in new section FA 2019, s 47A as discussed above, as are the definitions of value, namely under TCGA 1992; and as is the definition of connected persons, under CTA 2010, s 1122. Furthermore, the provisions become effective as from 22 July 2020, being the day of Royal Assent of FA 2020, in respect of any conditional agreement for which the condition is satisfied and in any other case in respect of any agreement or any transfer made on or after that date.

79   Stamp duty: acquisition of target company's share capital

(1)   Section 77A of FA 1986 (disqualifying arrangements) is amended as follows.

(2)   In subsection (2), after paragraph (b) insert—

"but a person who has held at least 25% of the issued share capital of the target company at all times during the relevant period is not within paragraph (a) or (b)."

(3)   After that subsection insert—

"(2A)   For the purposes of subsection (2) the "relevant period" is the period of 3 years ending immediately before the time at which the shares in the acquiring company are issued (or first issued) as consideration for the acquisition."

(4)   In subsection (3) omit "But".

(5)   After subsection (5) insert—

"(5A)   The Treasury may by regulations amend subsection (2) or (2A) so as to alter the percentage or length of the period for the time being specified there.

(5B)   The power to make regulations under subsection (5A) is exercisable by statutory instrument subject to annulment in pursuance of a resolution of the House of Commons."

(6)   The amendments made by this section have effect in relation to instruments executed on or after the day on which this Act is passed.

COMMENTARY ON SECTION 79

Section 79 amends the rules so that share for share reorganisations which represent partition demerger arrangements should be capable of falling within the provisions for stamp duty relief.

By way of background, UK tax legislation provides for demergers to be done on a tax neutral basis, subject to strict conditions but including in respect of stamp duty as discussed below. In a demerger, essentially the holdings of shareholders in the company prior to any reorganisation are mirrored in their new shareholdings immediately following the reorganisation. However when there is a partition demerger, namely when a company transfers the trade and assets of two of its businesses (or shares in 75% subsidiaries) to its shareholders, but with the ultimate share ownership being maintained, a charge to stamp duty would arise. Section 79 now provides that partition demergers will be capable of falling within stamp duty relief by ensuring that the arrangements do not fall within the disqualifying provisions for the relief which are themselves contained in FA 1986, s 77A.

Stamp duty is not chargeable on certain transfers involved in corporate reorganisations, by virtue of FA 1986, s 77, namely on share for share exchanges. The conditions for the relief, subject to there being no disqualifying arrangements at the time of transfer, are as follows:

●   the arrangements involve the acquisition of the whole of the issued share capital of the target company ('Target') by the acquiring company, and are for bona fide commercial reasons, and do not form any scheme or arrangement to avoid stamp duty, stamp duty reserve tax, income tax, corporation tax or capital gains tax;

●   the consideration for the acquisition of Target consists only of the issue of shares in the acquiring company to the shareholders of Target;

●   after the acquisition of Target, each of its shareholders is a shareholder in the acquiring company;

●   the shares in the acquiring company are the same classes as were the shares in Target immediately before the acquisition and the number of shares of any particular class in the acquiring company are in the same proportion (or nearly so) as the number of shares of that class in Target's share capital immediately before the acquisition; and

●   the proportion of shares in any particular class in the acquiring company held by any shareholder is the same (or nearly so) as held by that shareholder in Target immediately before the acquisition.

The disqualifying arrangements under FA 1986, s 77A are that it is reasonable to assume that a purpose of the arrangements is for a particular person or persons to obtain control of the acquiring company. Section 79 amends these provisions for transactions effected on or after 22 July 2020 (the date of Royal Assent) so that the 'change of control' disqualifying arrangements will not apply to any person who has held at least 25% of the issue share capital of Target during the period of three years ending immediately before the time when the shares in the acquiring company are issued as consideration for Target's acquisition.

Value added tax

80   Call-off stock arrangements

(1)   VATA 1994 is amended as follows.

(2)   After section 14 insert—

"Goods supplied between the UK and member States under call-off stock arrangements

14A   Call-off stock arrangements

Schedule 4B (call-off stock arrangements) has effect."

(3)   In section 69 (breaches of regulatory provisions)—

   (a)   in subsection (1)(a) for "or paragraph 5 of Schedule 3A" substitute ", paragraph 5 of Schedule 3A or paragraph 9(1) or (2)(a) of Schedule 4B", and

   (b)   in subsection (2) after "under" insert "paragraph 8 or 9(2)(b) of Schedule 4B or".

(4)   In Schedule 4 (matters to be treated as a supply of goods or services) in paragraph 6, after sub-paragraph (2) insert—

"(3)   Sub-paragraph (1) above is subject to paragraph 2 of Schedule 4B (call-off stock arrangements)."

(5)   After Schedule 4A insert—

"SCHEDULE 4B

CALL-OFF STOCK ARRANGEMENTS

Section 14A

Where this Schedule applies

1 (1)   This Schedule applies where—

   (a)   on or after 1 January 2020 goods forming part of the assets of any business are removed—

      (i)   from the United Kingdom for the purpose of being taken to a place in a member State, or

      (ii)   from a member State for the purpose of being taken to a place in the United Kingdom,

   (b)   the goods are removed in the course or furtherance of that business by or under the directions of the person carrying on that business ("the supplier"),

   (c)   the goods are removed with a view to their being supplied in the destination State, at a later stage and after their arrival there, to another person ("the customer"),

   (d)   at the time of the removal the customer is entitled to take ownership of the goods in accordance with an agreement existing between the customer and the supplier,

   (e)   at the time of the removal the supplier does not have a business establishment or other fixed establishment in the destination State,

   (f)   at the time of the removal the customer is identified for the purposes of VAT in accordance with the law of the destination State and both the identity of the customer and the number assigned to the customer for the purposes of VAT by the destination State are known to the supplier,

   (g)   as soon as reasonably practicable after the removal the supplier records the removal in the register provided for in Article 243(3) of Council Directive 2006/112/EC of 28 November 2006 on the common system of value added tax, and

   (h)   the supplier includes the number mentioned in paragraph (f) in the recapitulative statement provided for in Article 262(2) of Council Directive 2006/112/EC.

(2)   In this Schedule—

"the destination State" means—

      (a)   in a case within paragraph (i) of sub-paragraph (1)(a), the member State concerned, and

      (b)   in a case within paragraph (ii) of sub-paragraph (1)(a), the United Kingdom, and

"the origin State" means—

  (a) in a case within paragraph (i) of sub-paragraph (1)(a), the United
     Kingdom, and
  (b) in a case within paragraph (ii) of sub-paragraph (1)(a), the member
     State concerned.

Removal of the goods not to be treated as a supply

2 The removal of the goods from the origin State is not to be treated by reason of
paragraph 6(1) of Schedule 4 as a supply of goods by the supplier.

Goods transferred to the customer within 12 months of arrival

3 (1) The rules in sub-paragraph (2) apply if—

  (a) during the period of 12 months beginning with the day the goods arrive in
     the destination State the supplier transfers the whole property in the
     goods to the customer, and
  (b) during the period beginning with the day the goods arrive in the destina-
     tion State and ending immediately before the time of that transfer no
     relevant event occurs.

(2) The rules are that—

  (a) a supply of the goods in the origin State is deemed to be made by the
     supplier,
  (b) the deemed supply is deemed to involve the removal of the goods from the
     origin State at the time of the transfer mentioned in sub-paragraph (1),
  (c) the consideration given by the customer for the transfer mentioned in
     sub-paragraph (1) is deemed to have been given for the deemed supply,
     and
  (d) an acquisition of the goods by the customer in pursuance of the deemed
     supply is deemed to take place in the destination State.

(3) For the meaning of a "relevant event", see paragraph 7.

Relevant event occurs within 12 months of arrival

4 (1) The rules in sub-paragraph (2) apply (subject to paragraph 6) if—

  (a) during the period of 12 months beginning with the day the goods arrive in
     the destination State a relevant event occurs, and
  (b) during the period beginning with the day the goods arrive in the destina-
     tion State and ending immediately before the time that relevant event
     occurs the supplier does not transfer the whole property in the goods to
     the customer.

(2) The rules are that—

  (a) a supply of the goods in the origin State is deemed to be made by the
     supplier,
  (b) the deemed supply is deemed to involve the removal of the goods from the
     origin State at the time the relevant event occurs, and
  (c) an acquisition of the goods by the supplier in pursuance of the deemed
     supply is deemed to take place in the destination State.

(3) For the meaning of a "relevant event", see paragraph 7.

Goods not transferred and no relevant event occurs within 12 months of arrival

5 (1) The rules in sub-paragraph (2) apply (subject to paragraph 6) if during the
period of 12 months beginning with the day the goods arrive in the destination State
the supplier does not transfer the whole property in the goods to the customer and no
relevant event occurs.

(2) The rules are that—

  (a) a supply of the goods in the origin State is deemed to be made by the
     supplier,
  (b) the deemed supply is deemed to involve the removal of the goods from the
     origin State at the beginning of the day following the expiry of the period
     of 12 months mentioned in sub-paragraph (1), and
  (c) an acquisition of the goods by the supplier in pursuance of the deemed
     supply is deemed to take place in the destination State.

(3) For the meaning of a "relevant event", see paragraph 7.

Exception to paragraphs 4 and 5: goods returned to origin State

6 The rules in paragraphs 4(2) and 5(2) do not apply if during the period of 12
months beginning with the day the goods arrive in the destination State—

(a)   the goods are returned to the origin State by or under the direction of the supplier, and

(b)   the supplier records the return of the goods in the register provided for in Article 243(3) of Council Directive 2006/112/EC.

Meaning of "relevant event"

7 (1)   For the purposes of this Schedule each of the following events is a relevant event—

(a)   the supplier forms an intention not to supply the goods to the customer (but see sub-paragraph (2)),

(b)   the supplier forms an intention to supply the goods to the customer otherwise than in the destination State,

(c)   the supplier establishes a business establishment or other fixed establishment in the destination State,

(d)   the customer ceases to be identified for the purposes of VAT in accordance with the law of the destination State,

(e)   the goods are removed from the destination State by or under the directions of the supplier otherwise than for the purpose of being returned to the origin State, or

(f)   the goods are destroyed, lost or stolen.

(2)   But the event mentioned in paragraph (a) of sub-paragraph (1) is not a relevant event for the purposes of this Schedule if—

(a)   at the time that the event occurs the supplier forms an intention to supply the goods to another person ("the substitute customer"),

(b)   at that time the substitute customer is identified for the purposes of VAT in accordance with the law of the destination State,

(c)   the supplier includes the number assigned to the substitute customer for the purposes of VAT by the destination State in the recapitulative statement provided for in Article 262(2) of Council Directive 2006/112/EC, and

(d)   as soon as reasonably practicable after forming the intention to supply the goods to the substitute customer the supplier records that intention in the register provided for in Article 243(3) of Council Directive 2006/112/EC.

(3)   In a case where sub-paragraph (2) applies, references in this Schedule to the customer are to be then read as references to the substitute customer.

(4)   In a case where the goods are destroyed, lost or stolen but it is not possible to determine the date on which that occurred, the goods are to be treated for the purposes of this Schedule as having been destroyed, lost or stolen on the date on which they were found to be destroyed or missing.

Record keeping by the supplier

8 In a case where the origin State is the United Kingdom, any record made by the supplier in pursuance of paragraph 1(1)(g), 6(b) or 7(2)(d) must be preserved for such period not exceeding 6 years as the Commissioners may specify in writing.

Record keeping by the customer

9 (1)   In a case where the destination State is the United Kingdom, the customer must as soon as is reasonably practicable make a record of the information relating to the goods that is specified in Article 54A(2) of Council Implementing Regulation (EU) No. 282/2011 of 15 March 2011 laying down implementing measures for Directive 2006/112/EC on the common system of value added tax.

(2)   A record made under this paragraph must—

(a)   be made in a register kept by the customer for the purposes of this paragraph, and

(b)   be preserved for such period not exceeding 6 years as the Commissioners may specify in writing."

(6)   In Schedule 6 (valuation of supplies: special cases) in paragraph 6(1) in paragraph (c) after "that Schedule" insert "; or

    "(d)   paragraph 4(2)(a) or 5(2)(a) of Schedule 4B".

(7)   The Value Added Tax Regulations 1995 (S.I. 1995/2518) are amended as follows.

(8)   In regulation 21 (interpretation of Part 4)—

(a)   the existing text becomes paragraph (1), and

(b) after that paragraph insert—

"(2) For the purposes of this Part—

    (a) goods are removed from the United Kingdom under call-off stock arrangements if they are removed from the United Kingdom in circumstances where the conditions in paragraphs (a) to (g) of paragraph 1(1) of Schedule 4B to the Act are met,

    (b) references to "the customer" or "the destination State", in relation to goods removed from the United Kingdom under call-off stock arrangements, are to be construed in accordance with paragraph 1 of Schedule 4B to the Act, and

    (c) "call-off stock goods", in relation to a taxable person, means goods that have been removed from the United Kingdom under call-off stock arrangements by or under the directions of the taxable person."

(9) After regulation 22 insert—

"**22ZA** (1) A taxable person must submit a statement to the Commissioners if any of the following events occurs—

    (a) goods are removed from the United Kingdom under call-off stock arrangements by or under the directions of the taxable person;

    (b) call-off stock goods are returned to the United Kingdom by or under the directions of the taxable person at any time during the period of 12 months beginning with their arrival in the destination State;

    (c) the taxable person forms an intention to supply call-off stock goods to a person ("the substitute") other than the customer in circumstances where—

        (i) the taxable person forms that intention during the period of 12 months beginning with the arrival of the goods in the destination State, and

        (ii) the substitute is identified for VAT purposes in accordance with the law of the destination State.

(2) The statement must—

    (a) be made in the form specified in a notice published by the Commissioners,

    (b) contain, in respect of each event mentioned in paragraph (1) which has occurred within the period in respect of which the statement is made, such information as may from time to time be specified in a notice published by the Commissioners, and

    (c) contain a declaration that the information provided in the statement is true and complete.

(3) Paragraphs (3), (4) and (6) of regulation 22 have effect for the purpose of determining the period in respect of which the statement must be made, but as if—

    (a) in paragraph (3)(a) of regulation 22, for "paragraphs (4) to (6)" there were substituted "paragraphs (4) and (6)",

    (b) in paragraph (3)(a) of regulation 22, for "the EU supply of goods is made" there were substituted "the event occurs",

    (c) in paragraph (4)(a) of regulation 22, for "the supply is made" there were substituted "the event occurs", and

    (d) in paragraph (6) of regulation 22, the reference to paragraph (1) of that regulation were a reference to paragraph (1) of this regulation.

(4) In determining the period in respect of which the statement must be made, the time at which an event mentioned in paragraph (1)(a) of this regulation is to be taken to occur is the time the goods concerned are removed from the United Kingdom (rather than the time the condition mentioned in paragraph (g) of paragraph 1(1) to Schedule 4B to the Act is met in respect of the removal)."

(10) In regulation 22B (EC sales statements: supplementary)—

    (a) in paragraph (1) for the words from "statements", in the first place it occurs, to "and" substitute "more than one statement is to be submitted under regulations 22 to",

    (b) in paragraph (2) after "22" insert ", 22ZA", and

    (c) in paragraph (3), in the words before paragraph (a), after "22" insert ", 22ZA".

(11) Regulation 22ZA of the Value Added Tax Regulations 1995 (as inserted by subsection (9)) is to be treated for the purposes of sections 65 and 66 of VATA 1994 as having been made under paragraph 2(3) of Schedule 11 to that Act.

COMMENTARY ON SECTION 80

'Call-off stock' refers to goods which are removed from one EU Member State to another with a view to their subsequently being supplied to a customer in the destination Member State. EU legislation came into force with effect from 1 January 2020 to simplify and harmonise the VAT treatment of call-off stock across all Member States (including, until the end of the Brexit transitional period, the UK). The amendments made by section 78 will therefore apply retrospectively from that date.

The UK legislation takes the form of a new VATA 1994, s 14A and Sch 4B, with consequential amendments to VATA 1994, s 69 (penalties for breach of regulatory provisions), Sch 4 (matters to be treated as a supply of goods or services), Sch 6 (valuation of supplies) and SI 1995/2518, Pts 4 and 4A (sales statements).

VATA 1994, Sch 4B provides that the movements of call-off stock between the UK and EU Member States (and vice versa), which would otherwise be regarded as a supply for acquisition in the country of departure and an acquisition by the supplier in the country of destination, are not so regarded until the customer 'calls-off' the stock, ie the whole property in the goods is transferred to the customer. The advantage of this arrangement is that the initial movement of the goods is not regarded as the transfer of own goods by the supplier, with the result that the supplier is not required to register for VAT in the destination country.

The call-off stock rules contain a number of conditions, principal among which are:

- there must be an agreement between the supplier and the customer
- the supplier must not be established in the destination country
- the customer must be registered for VAT in the destination country, and must provide the supplier with that number
- the supplier must maintain a call-off stock register and complete the necessary sales statements
- the customer must also maintain a call-off stock register
- transfer of ownership of the goods must take place within 12 months of the original removal

A 'relevant event' may be triggered if the conditions are not complied with, with the consequence that the supplier will be regarded as having made a supply for acquisition at the time of the relevant event, and will be required to register for VAT in the country of destination, and to account for VAT on the acquisition in that country and any subsequent supplies in that country.

The legislation also contains provisions for the goods to be returned to the country of despatch, and for substitution of the customer.

Brexit implications

Unless any agreement to the contrary is reached during the transition period, the call-off stock simplification will no longer apply to the UK, or at least will need substantial modification, at the end of that period. UK businesses involved in such transactions may wish to consider alternatives, such as registering for VAT in a single EU Member State, holding a stock of goods there and applying the simplification to stock supplied on a call-off basis to the other 26 Member States.

Alcohol liquor duties

81   Post-duty point dilution of wine or made-wine

(1) After section 55 of ALDA 1979 insert—

> **"55ZA   Post-duty point dilution of wine or made-wine**
>
> (1) This section applies if—
>
> > (a)   wine or made-wine is imported into the United Kingdom or produced in the United Kingdom for sale,
> >
> > (b)   excise duty is chargeable on the wine or made-wine as a result of section 54 or 55,
> >
> > (c)   after the excise duty point in relation to that charge, a person mixes or

otherwise adds, at any place in the United Kingdom, water or any other substance to the wine or made-wine in a case where what results ("the new product") is intended for sale, and

(d) if the addition had taken place immediately before that duty point, the amount of the excise duty would have been greater than the amount actually payable.

(2) The addition attracts a penalty under section 9 of the Finance Act 1994 (civil penalties), and the new product is liable to forfeiture.

(3) This section has effect, despite section 8 of the Isle of Man Act 1979, as if a removal of wine or made-wine to the United Kingdom from the Isle of Man constituted its importation into the United Kingdom (and references to the charge to excise duty as a result of section 54 or 55 and to the excise duty point are to be read accordingly)."

(2) The amendment made by this section has effect in relation to any addition of water or any other substance on or after 1 April 2020.

COMMENTARY ON SECTION 81

Section 81 amends the Alcoholic Liquor Duties Act 1979 (ALDA) to bring in sanctions for post duty point dilution of wine or made-wine which would have resulted in a higher amount of duty being payable if dilution had been carried out before the duty point.

Section 81(1) inserts ALDA 1979, s 55ZA. ALDA 1979, s 55ZA provides the framework for penalties and forfeiture when water or any other substance is mixed with or added to wine or made-wine after the excise duty point, in circumstances where the excise duty would have been greater if the addition had occurred in advance of the duty point.

Section 81(2) provides that the change is introduced with effect from 1 April 2020.

Tobacco products duty

82   Rates of tobacco products duty

(1) In Schedule 1 to TPDA 1979 (table of rates of tobacco products duty), for the Table substitute—

"TABLE

1 Cigarettes	An amount equal to the higher of— (a)16.5% of the retail price plus £237.34 per thousand cigarettes, or (b)£305.23 per thousand cigarettes.
2 Cigars	£296.04 per kilogram
3 Hand-rolling tobacco	£253.33 per kilogram
4 Other smoking tobacco and chewing tobacco	£130.16 per kilogram
5 Tobacco for heating	£243.95 per kilogram"

(2) The amendment made by this section is treated as having come into force at 6pm on 11 March 2020.

COMMENTARY ON SECTION 82

Section 82 deals with changes to the rates of tobacco products duty and the level of Minimum Excise Tax (MET) on cigarettes. This duty is payable if a person makes or imports certain tobacco products. The Government announced at Spring Budget 2020 that the duty rate on all tobacco products will increase by 2% above the Retail Price Index inflation. Hand-rolling tobacco will rise by an additional 4%, to 6% above Retail Price Index inflation.

Schedule 1 to Tobacco Products Duty Act 1979 (table of rates of tobacco products duty) is amended to reflect the rates of duty which came into force from 6pm on 11 March 2020.

Vehicle taxes

83   Rates for light passenger or light goods vehicles, motorcycles etc

(1)   Schedule 1 to VERA 1994 (annual rates of vehicle excise duty) is amended as follows.

(2)   In paragraph 1 (general rate)—

> (a)   in sub-paragraph (2) (vehicle not covered elsewhere in Schedule with engine cylinder capacity exceeding 1,549cc), for "£265" substitute "£270", and
>
> (b)   in sub-paragraph (2A) (vehicle not covered elsewhere in Schedule with engine cylinder capacity not exceeding 1,549cc), for "£160" substitute "£165".

(3)   In paragraph 1B (graduated rates for light passenger vehicles registered before 1 April 2017), for the Table substitute—

"CO_2 emissions figure		Rate	
(1)	(2)	(3)	(4)
Exceeding	Not exceeding	Reduced rate	Standard rate
g/km	g/km	£	£
100	110	10	20
110	120	20	30
120	130	115	125
130	140	140	150
140	150	155	165
150	165	195	205
165	175	230	240
175	185	255	265
185	200	295	305
200	225	320	330
225	255	555	565
255	—	570	580".

(4)   In the sentence immediately following the Table in that paragraph, for paragraphs (a) and (b) substitute—

> "(a)   in column (3), in the last two rows, "320" were substituted for "555" and "570", and
>
> (b)   in column (4), in the last two rows, "330" were substituted for "565" and "580"."

(5)   In paragraph 1GC (graduated rates for first licence for light passenger vehicles registered on or after 1 April 2017), for Table 1 (vehicles other than higher rate diesel vehicles) substitute—

"CO_2 emissions figure		Rate	
(1)	(2)	(3)	(4)
Exceeding	Not exceeding	Reduced rate	Standard rate
g/km	g/km	£	£
0	50	0	10
50	75	15	25
75	90	100	110

90	100	125	135
100	110	145	155
110	130	165	175
130	150	205	215
150	170	530	540
170	190	860	870
190	225	1295	1305
225	255	1840	1850
255	—	2165	2175".

(6) In that paragraph, for Table 2 (higher rate diesel vehicles) substitute—

"CO_2 emissions figure		Rate
(1)	(2)	(3)
Exceeding	Not exceeding	Rate
g/km	g/km	£
0	50	25
50	75	110
75	90	135
90	100	155
100	110	175
110	130	215
130	150	540
150	170	870
170	190	1305
190	225	1850
225	255	2175
255	—	2175".

(7) In paragraph 1GD(1) (rates for any other licence for light passenger vehicles registered on or after 1 April 2017)—

    (a)   in paragraph (a) (reduced rate), for "£135" substitute "£140", and
    (b)   in paragraph (b) (standard rate), for "£145" substitute "£150".

(8) In paragraph 1GE(2) (rates for light passenger vehicles registered on or after 1 April 2017 with a price exceeding £40,000)—

    (a)   in paragraph (a), for "£440" substitute "£465", and
    (b)   in paragraph (b), for "£450" substitute "£475".

(9) In paragraph 1J(a) (rates for light goods vehicles that are not pre-2007 or post-2008 lower emission vans), for "£260" substitute "£265".

(10)   In paragraph 2(1) (rates for motorcycles)—

    (a)   in paragraph (b) (motorbicycles with engine cylinder capacity exceeding 150cc but not exceeding 400cc), for "£43" substitute "£44",

    (b)   in paragraph (c) (motorbicycles with engine cylinder capacity exceeding 400cc but not exceeding 600cc), for "£66" substitute "£67", and

    (c)   in paragraph (d) (other cases), for "£91" substitute "£93".

(11)   The amendments made by this section have effect in relation to licences taken out on or after 1 April 2020.

COMMENTARY ON SECTION 83

Section 83 makes amendments to a number of rates of vehicle excise duty (VED) in the Vehicle Excise and Registration Act 1994 (VERA), Sch 1.

VERA 1994, Sch 1, Pt I: General

Section 83(2) increases the general rate, ie the annual rate for vehicles in respect of which no other annual rate is specified, to:

- £165 for vehicles with an engine cylinder capacity not exceeding 1549cc
- £270 for vehicles with an engine cylinder capacity exceeding 1549cc

VERA 1994, Sch 1, Pt IA: Light passenger vehicles registered before 1 April 2017

Section 83(3) and (4) substitute new VED rates for light passenger vehicles registered before 1 April 2017 in VERA 1994, Sch 1 para 1B. The reduced rate applies to alternatively fuelled light passenger vehicles, including those powered by bioethanol and liquid petroleum gas and hybrids.

VERA 1994, Sch 1, Pt 1AA: Light passenger vehicles registered on or after 1 April 2017

Section 83(5) and (6) amend VED rates on the first vehicle licence for light passenger vehicles first registered on or after 1 April 2017 by substituting Table 1 and Table 2 in VERA 1994, Sch 1, Pt 1AA, para 1GC. Table 1 includes the standard rate and reduced rate. Table 2 includes the rates for higher rate diesel vehicles, applying to light passenger vehicles which are propelled by diesel and do not meet the Euro 6d emissions standard.

Section 83(7) increases the rate of duty applicable to light passenger vehicles first registered on or after 1 April 2017 from the second vehicle licence onwards in VERA 1994, Sch 1, Pt 1AA, para 1GD. The reduced rate of duty is increased from £135 to £140 per annum. The standard rate of duty is increased from £145 to £150 per annum.

Section 83(8) increases the rate of duty applicable to light passenger vehicles with a price exceeding £40,000, registered less than six years before the licence commencement date, as follows:

- reduced rate: from £440 to £465
- standard rate: from £450 to £475

in VERA 1994, Sch 1, Pt 1AA, para 1GE(2).

VERA 1994, Sch 1, Pt IB: Light goods vehicles

Section 83(9) increases VED rates on some light goods vehicles first registered on or after March 2001 from £260 to £265 in VERA 1994, Sch 1, Pt IB, para 1J(a).

VERA 1994, Sch 1, Pt II: Motorcycles

Section 83(10) increases VED rates on motorcycles (VERA 1994, Sch 1, Pt II, para 2(1)) weighing no more than 450 kilograms unladen. The rate of duty increases as follows:

- from £43 to £44 for motorcycles with an engine size of over 150cc but not more than 400cc
- from £66 to £67 for motorcycles with an engine size of over 400cc but not more than 600cc
- from £91 to £93 in any other case

Section 83(11) provides for the changes in rates to take effect in relation to vehicle licenses taken out on or after 1 April 2020.

84   Applicable CO_2 emissions figure determined using WLTP values

(1)   In Schedule 1 to VERA 1994 (annual rates of duty) in paragraph 1GA(5) (meaning of "the applicable CO_2 emissions figure")—

    (a)   omit "and" at the end of paragraph (a),

    (b)   in paragraph (b)—

        (i)   after "figure" insert "of a vehicle first registered before 1 April 2020",

        (ii)   for "light-duty" substitute "light", and

        (iii)   after "EU certificate of conformity" insert "or UK approval certificate", and

    (c)   at the end of paragraph (b) insert ", and

        (c)   for the purpose of determining the applicable CO_2 emissions figure of a vehicle first registered on or after 1 April 2020, ignore any values specified in an EU certificate of conformity or UK approval certificate that are not WLTP (worldwide harmonised light vehicle test procedures) values".

(2)   The amendments made by this section have effect in relation to licences taken out on or after 1 April 2020.

COMMENTARY ON SECTION 84

Section 84 makes several amendments to VERA 1994, to facilitate the implementation of a new regime for calculating the CO2 emissions of cars known as the worldwide harmonised light vehicles test procedure (WLTP).

Section 84(1) amends several paragraphs of VERA 1994, Sch 1 in relation to CO2 emissions figures and WLTP.

Section 84(2) provides that the changes have effect in relation to licences taken out on or after 1 April 2020.

85   Electric vehicles: extension of exemption

(1)   VERA 1994 is amended as follows.

(2)   In paragraph 25 of Schedule 2 (exempt vehicles: light passenger vehicles with low CO2 emissions) omit sub-paragraphs (5) and (6) (no exemption if vehicle price exceeds £40,000 etc).

(3)   As a consequence, Part 1AA of Schedule 1 (annual rates of duty: light passenger vehicles registered on or after 1 April 2017) is amended as follows.

(4)   In paragraph 1GB (exemption from paying duty on first vehicle licence for certain vehicles)—

    (a)   in sub-paragraph (1) omit "(2) or", and

    (b)   omit sub-paragraph (2).

(5)   In paragraph 1GD (rates of duty payable on any other vehicle licence for vehicle), in sub-paragraph (2) omit "or (4)".

(6)   In paragraph 1GE (higher rates of duty: vehicles with a price exceeding £40,000)—

    (a)   omit sub-paragraphs (3) and (4), and

    (b)   in sub-paragraph (5) for "sub-paragraphs (2) and (4) do" substitute "Sub-paragraph (2) does".

(7)   In paragraph 1GF (calculating the price of a vehicle), in sub-paragraph (1) omit "and (3)(a)".

(8)   The amendments made by this section come into force on 1 April 2020 but do not apply in relation to licences in force immediately before that date.

COMMENTARY ON SECTION 85

Section 85 deals with the extension of the exemption for electric vehicles. The Government announced at Spring Budget 2020 that legislation will be introduced so that zero-emission light passenger vehicles registered until 31 March 2025 will be exempted from the additional supplement (expensive car supplement) for those vehicles with a price list exceeding £40,000.

This section will amend the Vehicle Excise and Registration Act 1994 (VERA) to exempt all registered zero-emission light passenger vehicles registered from 1 April 2017 from the vehicle excise duty (VED) supplement for light passenger vehicles with a list price exceeding £40,000, when their licence is renewed on or after 1 April 2020. These changes do not apply in relation to licences in force immediately before that date.

The Vehicle Excise and Registration Act 1994, Sch 2, para 25 is amended to remove the relevant sub-paras that prevent vehicles priced over £40,000 from benefitting from the exemption.

The measure means that electric vehicles costing more than £40,000 will not be required to pay the £320 additional supplement. As this was the only road tax that electric cars were subject to, this means all fully electric cars are now VED exempt.

86 Motor caravans

(1) In VERA 1994, in Part 1AA of Schedule 1 (annual rates of duty: light passenger vehicles registered on or after 1 April 2017), paragraph 1GA is amended as follows.

(2) After sub-paragraph (1) insert—

"(1A) But this Part of this Schedule does not apply to a motor caravan which is first registered, under this Act or under the law of a country or territory outside the United Kingdom, on or after 12 March 2020."

(3) After sub-paragraph (2) insert—

"(2A) For the purposes of sub-paragraph (1A) a vehicle is a "motor caravan" if the certificate mentioned in sub-paragraph (1)(b) identifies the vehicle as a motor caravan within the meaning of Annex II to Directive 2007/46/EC."

COMMENTARY ON SECTION 86

Section 86 provides that type approved M1SA motorhomes first registered from 12 March 2020 will no longer fall within the light passenger vehicles class (VERA 1994, Sch 1, Pt 1AA) for vehicle excise duty (VED). They will instead be taxed, for the most part, at the rate for the Private/Light Goods class. From 1 April 2021, VED for new motorhomes will be aligned with the Light Goods Vehicles class.

87 Exemption in respect of medical courier vehicles

(1) Schedule 2 to VERA 1994 (exempt vehicles) is amended as follows.

(2) In the heading before paragraph 6, after "Ambulances" insert ", medical courier vehicles".

(3) After paragraph 6 insert

"6A (1) A vehicle is an exempt vehicle if—

    (a)   it is used primarily for the transportation of medical items,

    (b)   it is readily identifiable as a vehicle used for the transportation of medical items by being marked "Blood" on both sides, and

    (c)   it is registered under this Act in the name of a charity whose main purpose is to provide services for the transportation of medical items.

(2) In this paragraph—

"charity" means a charity as defined by paragraph 1 of Schedule 6 to the Finance Act 2010;

"medical items" means items intended for use for medical purposes, including in particular—

    (a)   blood;

    (b)   medicines and other medical supplies;

    (c)   items relating to people who are undergoing medical treatment;

"item" includes any substance."

(4) The amendments made by this section come into force on 1 April 2020.

COMMENTARY ON SECTION 87

Section 87 provides for exemption from vehicle excise duty (VED) for purpose-built vehicles used by medical courier charities (commonly referred to as 'blood bikes').

Section 87(2) makes changes to VERA 1994, Sch 2 (which deals with those vehicles which are exempt from VED).

Section 87(3) sets out the criteria which must be met for a vehicle to qualify for exemption, namely:

- the vehicle is primarily used for the transportation of medical items
- the vehicle is readily identifiable as a vehicle used for the transportation of medical items by being marked with the word 'blood' on both sides
- the vehicle is registered to a charity whose main purpose is to provide transportation for medical items

Section 87(4) provides that this exemption is in force from 1 April 2020.

88   HGV road user levy

(1) Section 5(2) of the HGV Road User Levy Act 2013 (HGV road user levy charged for all periods for which a UK heavy goods vehicle is charged to vehicle excise duty) does not apply where the period for which a UK heavy goods vehicle is charged to vehicle excise duty is a period that begins in the exempt period.

(2) Section 6(2) of the 2013 Act (HGV road user levy charged in respect of non-UK heavy goods vehicle for each day on which the vehicle is used or kept on a road to which the Act applies) does not apply in respect of any day in the exempt period.

(3) The exempt period is the period of 12 months beginning with 1 August 2020.

(4) Section 7 of the 2013 Act (rebate of levy) has effect as if, after subsection (2A), there were inserted—

"(2B) A rebate entitlement also arises where HGV road user levy has been paid in respect of a non-UK heavy goods vehicle in accordance with section 6(2) in respect of any part of the exempt period within the meaning of section 88(3) of the Finance Act 2020."

COMMENTARY ON SECTION 88

Section 88 suspends both the charging and collection of the HGV road user levy for a period of 12 months. The 12-month period runs from 1 August 2020 to 31 July 2021. Where the levy has been paid in respect of a non-UK heavy goods vehicle in relation to this 12-month exempt period, a rebate will be available.

Section 88(1) provides for exemption for UK heavy goods vehicles whilst section 88(2) provides for exemption for non-UK heavy goods vehicles.

Section 88(3) sets the timeframe for the exempt period (ie between 1 August 2020 and 31 July 2021).

Section 88(4) inserts a new HGV Road Levy User Act 2013, s 7(2B) which provides the basis for the rebate for non-UK heavy goods vehicles. There is no similar provision for UK heavy goods vehicles as these will benefit from a full 12-month suspension when their vehicle excise duty licence is renewed.

Hydrocarbon oil duties

89   Rebated fuel: private pleasure craft

Schedule 11 makes provision about the use of rebated fuel in private pleasure craft.

COMMENTARY ON SECTION 89, SCHEDULE 11

[See Commentary note for Schedule 11]

Air passenger duty

90   Rates of air passenger duty from 1 April 2021

(1) In section 30(4A) of FA 1994 (air passenger duty: long haul rates)—

    (a) in paragraph (a), for "£80" substitute "£82", and

    (b) in paragraph (b), for "£176" substitute "£180".

(2) The amendments made by this section have effect in relation to the carriage of passengers beginning on or after 1 April 2021.

COMMENTARY ON SECTION 90

Section 90 increases the rates of APD for long-haul flights (ie over 2000 miles) by £2 (standard class) and £4 (any other class) with effect from 1 April 2021. The rates for short-haul flights remain unchanged. Advance notice of the change is given to provide the industry with sufficient time to adapt to the new rates.

Gaming duty

91 Amounts of gross gaming yield charged to gaming duty

(1) In section 11(2) of FA 1997 (rates of gaming duty), for the table substitute—

"TABLE

Part of gross gaming yield	Rate
The first £2,471,000	15%
The next £1,703,500	20%
The next £2,983,000	30%
The next £6,296,500	40%
The remainder	50%".

(2) The amendment made by this section has effect in relation to accounting periods beginning on or after 1 April 2020.

COMMENTARY ON SECTION 91

Section 91 increases the gross gaming yield (GGY) bands for gaming duty so that they rise in line with the retail price index. No changes are made to the rate of duty. Section 91(1) makes the changes to the bands in FA 1997, s 11(2) whilst section 91(2) provides that these changes come into force for accounting periods beginning on or after 1 April 2020.

Environmental taxes

92 Rates of climate change levy until 1 April 2021

(1) Paragraph 42 of Schedule 6 to FA 2000 (climate change levy: amount payable by way of levy) is amended as follows.

(2) In sub-paragraph (1), for the table substitute—

"TABLE

Taxable commodity supplied	Rate at which levy payable if supply is not a reduced-rate supply
Electricity	£0.00811 per kilowatt hour
Gas supplied by a gas utility or any gas supplied in a gaseous state that is of a kind supplied by a gas utility	£0.00406 per kilowatt hour
Any petroleum gas, or other gaseous hydrocarbon, supplied in a liquid state	£0.02175 per kilogram
Any other taxable commodity	£0.03174 per kilogram".

(3) In sub-paragraph (1)—

    (a)   in paragraph (ba) (reduced-rate supplies of electricity), for "7" substitute "8",

    (b)   after that paragraph insert—

        "(bb) if the supply is a reduced-rate of supply of any petroleum gas, or other gaseous hydrocarbon, supplied in a liquid state, 23 per cent of the amount that would be payable if the supply were a supply to which paragraph (a) applies;", and

(c)   in paragraph (c) (other reduced-rate supplies), for "22" substitute "19".

(4)   In consequence of the amendment made by subsection (3), in the Notes to paragraph 2 of Schedule 1 to the Climate Change Levy (General) Regulations 2001, for the definition of "r" substitute—

"r = 0.92 in the case of electricity; 0.77 in the case of any petroleum gas, or other gaseous hydrocarbon, supplied in a liquid state; and 0.81 in any other case."

(5)   The amendments made by this section have effect in relation to supplies treated as taking place on or after 1 April 2020.

COMMENTARY ON SECTION 92

Section 92 amends the main rates of climate change levy (CCL) for 2020 to 2021, implementing the rates announced at Budget 2018. Early announcement was made to give those affected as much time as possible to prepare. This measure also amends the reduced rates of CCL for qualifying businesses in the Climate Change Agreements scheme.

The changes to the main rates are in line with the Government's commitment to continue to rebalance the electricity to gas ratio announced at Budget 2016. The electricity rate will be lowered and the gas rate will increase, so that the gas rate reaches 60% of the electricity rate in 2021 to 2022.

The changes to the reduced rates seek to limit the impact on Climate Change Agreements scheme participants to a Retail Prices Index increase only.

This section amends the CCL main rates and the reduced rates in FA 2000, Sch 6, Pt IV, para 42.

The amendments made by this section have effect in relation to supplies treated as taking place on or after 1 April 2020.

---

93   Rates of climate change levy from 1 April 2021

(1)   Paragraph 42 of Schedule 6 to FA 2000 (climate change levy: amount payable by way of levy) is amended as follows.

(2)   In sub-paragraph (1), for the table substitute—

"TABLE

Taxable commodity supplied	*Rate at which levy payable if supply is not a reduced-rate supply*
Electricity	£0.00775 per kilowatt hour
Gas supplied by a gas utility or any gas supplied in a gaseous state that is of a kind supplied by a gas utility	£0.00465 per kilowatt hour
Any petroleum gas, or other gaseous hydrocarbon, supplied in a liquid state	£0.02175 per kilogram
Any other taxable commodity	£0.03640 per kilogram".

(3)   In sub-paragraph (1)(c), as amended by section 92(3)(c), for "19" substitute "17".

(4)   In consequence of the amendment made by subsection (3), in the definition of "r" in the Notes to paragraph 2 of Schedule 1 to the Climate Change Levy (General) Regulations 2001, as amended by section 92(4), for "0.81" substitute "0.83".

(5)   The amendments made by this section have effect in relation to supplies treated as taking place on or after 1 April 2021.

COMMENTARY ON SECTION 93

Section 93 amends the main rates of climate change levy (CCL) for 2021 to 2022, implementing the rates announced at Budget 2018.

The changes to the main rates are in line with the Government's commitment to continue to rebalance the electricity to gas ratio announced at Budget 2016. The electricity rate will be lowered and the gas rate will increase, so that the gas rate reaches 60% of the electricity rate in 2021 to 2022.

This section amends the CCL main rates and the reduced rates in FA 2000, Sch 6, Pt IV, para 42.

The amendments made by this section have effect in relation to supplies treated as taking place on or after 1 April 2021.

94   Rates of landfill tax

(1)   Section 42 of FA 1996 (amount of landfill tax) is amended as follows.

(2)   In subsection (1)(a) (standard rate), for "£91.35" substitute "£94.15".

(3)   In subsection (2) (reduced rate for certain disposals), in the words after paragraph (b)—

    (a)   for "£91.35" substitute "£94.15", and

    (b)   for "£2.90" substitute "£3".

(4)   The amendments made by this section have effect in relation to disposals made (or treated as made) on or after 1 April 2020.

COMMENTARY ON SECTION 94

Section 94 increases the rates of landfill tax with effect in relation to disposals made or treated as made on or after 1 April 2020 as follows:

- where the full rate applies, to £94.15
- in the case of qualifying (ie less polluting) material or fines, to £3

95   Carbon emissions tax

Schedule 12 makes provision about carbon emissions tax.

COMMENTARY ON SECTION 95, SCHEDULE 12

[See Commentary note for Schedule 12]

96   Charge for allocating allowances under emissions reduction trading scheme

(1)   The Treasury may impose charges by providing in regulations for emissions allowances to be allocated in return for payment.

(2)   Regulations under subsection (1) may in particular include provision—

    (a)   for persons other than persons to whom a trading scheme applies to be allocated emissions allowances in return for payment;

    (b)   as to the imposition of fees and the making and forfeiting of deposits;

    (c)   as to the person by whom allocations in return for payment are to be conducted;

    (d)   for allocations in return for payment to be overseen by an independent person appointed by the Treasury;

    (e)   for the imposition of penalties for failure to comply with the terms of the regulations or of a scheme under subsection (3);

    (f)   for the imposition of interest in respect of any charges, fees or penalties due under the regulations;

    (g)   for and in connection with the recovery of any charges, fees, penalties or interest due under the regulations;

    (h)   conferring rights of appeal against decisions made in allocations in return for payment, the forfeiting of deposits and the imposition of penalties (including specifying the person, court or tribunal to hear and determine appeals).

(3)   The Treasury may make schemes about the conduct and terms of allocations of emissions allowances in return for payment (the schemes having effect subject to any regulations under this section).

(4)   Schemes under subsection (3) may in particular include provision about—

    (a)   who may participate in allocations in return for payment,

    (b)   the allowances to be allocated in return for payment, and

    (c)   where and when allocations in return for payment are to take place.

(5)   Regulations under this section are to be made by statutory instrument.

(6)   A statutory instrument containing the first regulations under this section may not be made unless a draft of the instrument has been laid before, and approved by a resolution of, the House of Commons.

(7)   Any other statutory instrument containing regulations under this section is subject to annulment in pursuance of a resolution of the House of Commons (unless a draft of the instrument has been laid before, and approved by a resolution of, that House).

(8)   In this section—

    "emissions allowance" means an allowance under paragraph 5 of Schedule 2 to the Climate Change Act 2008 relating to a trading scheme;

    "trading scheme" means a trading scheme dealt with under Part 1 of that Schedule (schemes limiting activities relating to emissions of greenhouse gas).

COMMENTARY ON SECTION 96

Currently, section 44(1) of the Climate Change Act 2008 (CCA 2008) provides the power for the relevant national authorities to make provisions by regulations for trading schemes relating to greenhouse gas emissions. However, CCA 2008, Sch 2, para 5(4) imposes a prohibition on the exchange of allowances in return for consideration.

Section 96 allows the Treasury to make regulations which provide for the allocation of emissions allowances in return for payment under an emissions reduction trading scheme (UK ETS), as defined by CCA 2008. The relevant regulations will be made by statutory instrument.

'Emissions allowance' means an allowance under CCA 2008, Sch 2, Pt 1, para 5 relating to a trading scheme.

'Trading scheme' means a trading scheme dealt with under CCA 2008, Sch 2, Pt 1 (schemes limiting activities relating to emissions of greenhouse gas).

Regulations to be introduced may include provisions:

- defining the type of person who can be allocated emissions allowances in return for payment, what allowances may be allocated and where allocations can take place
- Defining what are 'emissions allowances' and 'trading schemes'
- imposing fees and the making and forfeiting of deposits
- the appointment of an independent person by the Treasury to oversee allocations made in return for payment
- imposing penalties for failure to comply with the terms of the regulations or of a scheme
- imposing interest in respect of any charges, fees or penalties due under the regulations; for and in connection with the recovery of any charges, fees, penalties or interest due under the regulations
- conferring rights of appeal against decisions made under the regulations

Import duty

97   International trade disputes

In section 15(1)(b) of TCTA 2018 (import duty: international disputes etc), for "is authorised under international law" substitute "considers that (having regard to the matters set out in section 28 and any other relevant matters) it is appropriate".

COMMENTARY ON SECTION 97

Section 97 amends the Taxation (Cross-border Trade) Act 2018, s 15 to enable the Secretary of State to vary the rate of import duty when a dispute or other issue has arisen between the UK Government and the government of another country after the UK Government has had regard to its international arrangements and considers it appropriate to do so. This is in connection with the UK's departure from the EU.

The Taxation (Cross-border Trade) Act 2018, s 15 is amended so that the requirement for 'authorisation' (in the context of varying duty in international disputes) is removed and instead there is a requirement for the Government to consider it appropriate, after having regard to the requirements of the Taxation (Cross-border Trade) Act 2018, s 28 and any other relevant matters.

PART 4

MISCELLANEOUS AND FINAL

Insolvency

98   HMRC debts: priority on insolvency

(1)   In section 386 of the Insolvency Act 1986 (preferential debts)—

    (a)   in subsection (1) after "other deposits" insert "; certain HMRC debts";

    (b)   in subsection (1B) for "or 15BB" substitute ", 15BB or 15D".

(2)   In Schedule 6 to that Act (preferential debts) after paragraph 15C insert—

"Category 9: Certain HMRC debts

15D (1)   Any amount owed at the relevant date by the debtor to the Commissioners in respect of—

    (a)   value added tax, or

    (b)   a relevant deduction.

(2)   In sub-paragraph (1), the reference to "any amount" is subject to any regulations under section 99(1) of the Finance Act 2020.

(3)   For the purposes of sub-paragraph (1)(b) a deduction is "relevant" if—

    (a)   the debtor is required, by virtue of an enactment, to make the deduction from a payment made to another person and to pay an amount to the Commissioners on account of the deduction,

    (b)   the payment to the Commissioners is credited against any liabilities of the other person, and

    (c)   the deduction is of a kind specified in regulations under section 99(3) of the Finance Act 2020.

(4)   In this paragraph "the Commissioners" means the Commissioners for Her Majesty's Revenue and Customs."

(3)   In section 129(2) of the Bankruptcy (Scotland) Act 2016 (asp 21) (priority in distribution: meaning of certain expressions) in the definition of "secondary preferred debt" for "paragraph 7 or 8" substitute "any of paragraphs 7 to 8A".

(4)   In Part 1 of Schedule 3 to that Act (list of preferred debts) after paragraph 8 insert—

"Certain HMRC debts

8A (1)   Any amount owed at the relevant date by the debtor to the Commissioners in respect of—

    (a)   value added tax, or

    (b)   a relevant deduction.

(2)   In sub-paragraph (1), the reference to "any amount" is subject to any regulations under section 99(1) of the Finance Act 2020.

(3)   For the purposes of sub-paragraph (1)(b) a deduction is "relevant" if—

    (a)   the debtor is required, by virtue of an enactment, to make the deduction from a payment made to another person and to pay an amount to the Commissioners on account of the deduction,

    (b)   the payment to the Commissioners is credited against any liabilities of the other person, and

    (c)   the deduction is of a kind specified in regulations under section 99(3) of the Finance Act 2020.

(4)   In this paragraph "the Commissioners" means the Commissioners for Her Majesty's Revenue and Customs."

(5)   In Article 346 of the Insolvency (Northern Ireland) Order 1989 (SI 1989/2405 (NI 19)) (preferential debts)—

    (a)   in paragraph (1) after "other deposits" insert "; certain HMRC debts";

    (b)   in paragraph (1B) for "or 20" substitute ", 20 or 22".

(6)   In Schedule 4 to that Order (preferential debts) after paragraph 21 insert—

"Category 9: Certain HMRC debts

22 (1)   Any amount owed at the relevant date by the debtor to the Commissioners in respect of—

   (a)   value added tax, or
   (b)   a relevant deduction.

(2)   In sub-paragraph (1), the reference to "any amount" is subject to any regulations under section 99(1) of the Finance Act 2020.

(3)   For the purposes of sub-paragraph (1)(b) a deduction is "relevant" if—

   (a)   the debtor is required, by virtue of an enactment, to make the deduction from a payment made to another person and to pay an amount to the Commissioners on account of the deduction,
   (b)   the payment to the Commissioners is credited against any liabilities of the other person, and
   (c)   the deduction is of a kind specified in regulations under section 99(3) of the Finance Act 2020.

(4)   In this paragraph "the Commissioners" means the Commissioners for Her Majesty's Revenue and Customs."

(7)   The amendments made by this section do not apply in relation to any case where the relevant date is before 1 December 2020.

COMMENTARY ON SECTION 98

This section amends section 386 of, and Schedule 6 to, the Insolvency Act 1986 (preferential debts) by making certain Crown debts rank ahead of floating charge holders and unsecured creditors.

The rationale behind the introduction is that certain amounts are collected by the debtor company on behalf of others, eg VAT and PAYE, and that these should therefore be accounted for separately because in HMRC's view they do not form part of the insolvent company's assets (albeit there is no trust created when the amounts are collected).

The provision has caused some controversy. When the insolvency regime was reformed by the Enterprise Act 2002 HMRC gave up their preferential status in exchange for the creation of 'the prescribed part' an amount of up to £800,000 which is deducted from amounts owing to floating charge holders to create a fund payable to unsecured creditors. This section reverses that and further erodes the amounts available to floating charge holders (often asset-based lenders). Furthermore, the old preference was limited to, for example, PAYE arrears for the 12 months prior to the date of insolvency (the relevant date). The new provision appears to have no such limitation. Although there is a power to proscribe a period by regulation.

Section 98(1) inserts into Insolvency Act 1986, s 386 a new category in the list of preferential debts comprising 'certain HMRC debts'.

Section 98(2) inserts into Insolvency Act 1986, Sch 6 'Category 9: Certain HMRC Debts'. These are amounts owed at the relevant date in respect of VAT and relevant deductions.

These are amounts which are proscribed by regulations made under section 99 (see below).

Basically, a deduction is a 'relevant deduction' if, first, the debtor is obliged to deduct an amount from a payment to another and account for it to HMRC; secondly, when the payment is made it is credited against liabilities of that other person; and thirdly, the deduction is specified under regulations made under section 99 (see below).

The Insolvency Act 1986 applies to corporate insolvency in England, Wales and Scotland (albeit that the insolvency rules made under the Act differ between England and Wales, and Scotland). Scotland has a different personal bankruptcy regime so section 98(3) and (4) amend the Bankruptcy (Scotland) Act 2016, s 129(2) in a similar way.

Northern Ireland has its own insolvency regime so section 98(5) and (6) amend the Insolvency (Northern Ireland) Order 1989, art 346, Sch 4 in a similar way.

Section 98(7) provides for the amendments made by section 98 not to apply to any case where the relevant date, basically the date when the company or person went into an insolvency process, is before the 1 December 2020. There appears to be no limitation on the time when the deduction was made prior to the relevant date albeit that regulations made under section 99 (see below) provide for a time limit to be specified.

99 HMRC debts: regulations

(1) The Treasury may by regulations provide that only the following amounts are secondary preferential debts (or, in relation to Scotland, secondary preferred debts) for the purpose of a relevant provision—

(a) in the case of amounts owed in respect of value added tax, amounts referable to such period as is specified in the regulations;

(b) in the case of amounts owed in respect of a relevant deduction, amounts owed in respect of a deduction from a payment made during such period as is specified in the regulations.

(2) In subsection (1) "relevant provision" means—

(a) paragraph 15D(1) of Schedule 6 to the Insolvency Act 1986 (preferential debts: certain HMRC debts);

(b) paragraph 8A(1) of Schedule 3 to the Bankruptcy (Scotland) Act 2016 (asp 21) (list of preferred debts: certain HMRC debts);

(c) paragraph 22(1) of Schedule 4 to the Insolvency (Northern Ireland) Order 1989 (SI 1989/2405 (NI 19)) (preferential debts: certain HMRC debts).

(3) The Treasury may by regulations specify kinds of deductions for the purposes of—

(a) paragraph 15D(3)(c) of Schedule 6 to the Insolvency Act 1986;

(b) paragraph 8A(3)(c) of Schedule 3 to the Bankruptcy (Scotland) Act 2016 (asp 21);

(c) paragraph 22(3)(c) of Schedule 4 to the Insolvency (Northern Ireland) Order 1989 (SI 1989/2405 (NI 19)).

(4) Regulations under this section may contain transitional or supplementary provision.

(5) Regulations under this section—

(a) are to be made by statutory instrument;

(b) are subject to annulment in pursuance of a resolution of the House of Commons.

COMMENTARY ON SECTION 99

Section 99 provides authority for the Treasury to make the regulations for the purposes of section 98.

Section 99(1) and (2) provides for the Treasury to make regulations that provide that only amounts for specified periods can be included. For VAT it is the amounts owed for such period as is specified in the regulations. For amounts in respect of relevant deductions it is for amounts owed in respect of a relevant deduction from a payment made during such period as is specified.

Section 99(3) provides for the Treasury to make regulations that specify the kinds of deductions that section 98 applies to.

Draft regulations have been drafted for the purposes of section 99(3): 'The Insolvency Act 1986 (HMRC Debts: Priority on Insolvency) Regulations 2020'. The deductions specified are those under:

(a) Finance Act 2004, s 61;

(b) Social Security (contributions) Regulations 2001, Sch 4, para 6(1)(b);

(c) Income Tax (PAYE) Regulations 2003, reg 21; and

(d) Education (Student Loans) (Repayment) Regulations 2009, reg 50.

At the time of writing the regulations are still in draft form and there is no SI number.

At the time of writing no draft regulations have been produced for the purposes of section 99(1) and (2) which can specify the length of the period prior to the relevant date to which the preference applies.

Joint and several liability

100   Joint and several liability of company directors etc

(1) Schedule 13 makes provision for individuals to be jointly and severally liable, in certain circumstances involving insolvency or potential insolvency, for amounts payable to the Commissioners for Her Majesty's Revenue and Customs by bodies corporate or unincorporate.

(2) A reference in Schedule 13 to a tax liability of a company does not include—

(a) any tax liability that relates to a period ending before the day on which this Act is passed;

(b) any tax liability (other than one that relates to a period) arising from an event or default occurring before that day.

(3) For the purposes of subsection (2), a tax liability relates to a period if—

(a) the liability arises in respect of a particular tax year, accounting period or other period, or

(b) the amount of the liability is calculated by reference to a particular period.

(4) A reference in paragraph 5 of Schedule 13 to a penalty does not include any penalty in respect of which the determination to impose the penalty, or (as the case may be) the commencement of proceedings before the tribunal for the penalty to be imposed, occurs before the day on which this Act is passed.

COMMENTARY ON SECTION 100

Section 100(1) introduces Schedule 13 which makes provision for certain individuals to be jointly and severally liable for debts of bodies corporate or unincorporate which are owed to HMRC in circumstances where the bodies corporate or unincorporate are insolvent or potentially insolvent.

Joint and several liability allows the creditor, in this case HMRC, to recover against any of those that are jointly and severally liable without having to join the others. In this case, once an individual has been made jointly and severally liable, HMRC can recover the whole of the amount against that individual. The person against whom recovery is made then has a right of recovery against the other parties that were jointly and severally liable. Where a director is made jointly and severally liable with the company, HMRC will be able to recover against the director leaving the director to recover against the company. If the company is insolvent this means the director will in effect be subrogated to the rights that HMRC had against the company. This might be seen as HMRC gaining a preference over other creditors. Again, the provisions are controversial in that in the case of companies they are seen as 'piercing the veil of incorporation'. Many considered that HMRC already had sufficient tools to collect these debts.

The reference to bodies unincorporate brings in limited liability partnerships (but not 1907 limited partnerships or 1890 partnerships see further Schedule 13 paragraph 1(3)).

Section 100(2) and (3) effectively restrict the commencement of the application of Schedule 13 by stating that it does not apply to any tax liability which relates to an accounting period which ends before the 22 July 2020 or, where the liability arises as a result of an event or default, it does not apply to any event or default which arises before the 22 July 2020.

Likewise, section 100(4) provides that any reference to a penalty in paragraph 5 of Schedule 13 only applies to a penalty imposed after 22 July 2020 or where the proceedings before a tribunal to impose a penalty were commenced after 22 July 2020.

General anti-abuse rule

101   Amendments relating to the operation of the GAAR

Schedule 14 makes—

(a) provision about the procedural requirements and time limits for the making of adjustments by virtue of section 209 of FA 2013, and

(b) provision amending paragraph 5 of Schedule 43C to that Act.

COMMENTARY ON SECTION 101, SCHEDULE 14

[See Commentary note for Schedule 14]

Compensation schemes etc

102   Tax relief for scheme payments etc

Schedule 15 makes provision for tax relief in respect of—

(a)   payments made under or otherwise referable to the Windrush Compensation Scheme,

(b)   payments under the Troubles Permanent Disablement Payment Scheme, and

(c)   other compensation payments made by or on behalf of a government, public authority or local authority.

COMMENTARY ON SECTION 102, SCHEDULE 15

Section 102 and Schedule 15 introduce income tax and capital gains tax exemptions, and an inheritance tax relief, for payments made under the Windrush Compensation Scheme launched in April 2019 and the Troubles Permanent Disablement Payment Scheme launched in May 2020.

Home Office guidance on eligibility for compensation under the Windrush Compensation Scheme, established for those who suffered 'direct impact or loss' because they could not demonstrate their lawful right to live in the UK, is available via https://tinyurl.com/yedaw45v.

The Troubles Permanent Disablement Payment Scheme was established, under the law of Northern Ireland, by The Victims' Payments Regulations, SI 2020/103 (https://tinyurl.com/ybpf3efd). It provides for payments to be made to people living with permanent disablement because of injury sustained in a Troubles-related incident.

Schedule 15 also introduces a retrospective power enabling HM Treasury to make regulations providing similar exemptions and reliefs for payments under other compensation schemes.

Administration

103   HMRC: exercise of officer functions

(1)   Anything capable of being done by an officer of Revenue and Customs by virtue of a function conferred by or under an enactment relating to taxation may be done by HMRC (whether by means involving the use of a computer or otherwise).

(2)   Accordingly, it follows that HMRC may (among other things)—

(a)   give a notice under section 8, 8A or 12AA of TMA 1970 (notice to file personal, trustee or partnership return);

(b)   amend a return under section 9ZB of that Act (correction of personal or trustee return);

(c)   make an assessment to tax in accordance with section 30A of that Act (assessing procedure);

(d)   make a determination under section 100 of that Act (determination of penalties);

(e)   give a notice under paragraph 3 of Schedule 18 to FA 1998 (notice to file company tax return);

(f)   make a determination under paragraph 2 or 3 of Schedule 14 to FA 2003 (SDLT: determination of penalties).

(3)   Anything done by HMRC in accordance with subsection (1) has the same effect as it would have if done by an officer of Revenue and Customs (or, where the function is conferred on an officer of a particular kind, an officer of that kind).

(4)   In this section—

"HMRC" means Her Majesty's Revenue and Customs;

references to an officer of Revenue and Customs include an officer of a particular kind, such as an officer authorised for the purposes of an enactment.

(5)   This section is treated as always having been in force.

(6)   However, this section does not apply in relation to anything mentioned in subsection (1) done by HMRC if—

(a)   before 11 March 2020, a court or tribunal determined that the relevant act was of no effect because it was not done by an officer of Revenue and Customs (or an officer of a particular kind), and

(b)   at the beginning of 11 March 2020, the order of the court or tribunal giving effect to that determination had not been set aside or overturned on appeal.

COMMENTARY ON SECTION 103

Section 103 provides that functions assigned to an HMRC officer in relation to taxation may be done by HMRC by means of an automated process or otherwise, and have the same legal effect as it would have if done by the officer. The provision affirms 'long standing and widely accepted operational practice' and means that action following the issue of automated notices can 'take place without ambiguity', HMRC said in its explanatory note.

Subsection (2) lists some of the tasks to which this measure applies. They include giving a notice under TMA 1970, s 8, 8A or 12AA to file a tax return, amending a return under TMA 1970, s 9ZB, and making an assessment in accordance with TMA 1970, s 30A.

Subsection (5) provides that the measure is treated as always having been in force. But subsection (6) disapplies it in a case where a court or tribunal determined before 11 March 2020 that the relevant act was ineffective, because it was not done by an HMRC officer, and that decision was not set aside or overturned before that date.

104   Returns relating to LLP not carrying on business etc with view to profit

(1)   In TMA 1970 after section 12ABZA insert—

"12ABZAA   Returns relating to LLP not carrying on business etc with view to profit

(1)   This section applies where—

(a)   a person delivers a purported partnership return ("the relevant return") in respect of a period ("the relevant period"),

(b)   the relevant return—

(i)   is made on the basis that the activities of a limited liability partnership ("the LLP") are treated, under section 863 of ITTOIA 2005 or section 1273 of CTA 2009, as carried on in partnership by its members ("the purported partnership"), and

(ii)   relates to the purported partnership, but

(c)   the LLP does not carry on a business with a view to profit in the relevant period (and, accordingly, its activities are not treated as mentioned in paragraph (b)(i)).

(2)   For the purposes of the relevant enactments, treat the relevant return as a partnership return (and, accordingly, anything done under a relevant enactment in connection with the relevant return has the same effect as it would have if done in connection with a partnership return in a corresponding partnership case).

(3)   "Relevant enactment" means—

(a)   any of the following—

(i)   sections 12AC and 28B (enquiries into partnership returns),

(ii)   Part 4 of FA 2014 (follower notices and accelerated payment notices), and

(b)   any enactment relating to, or applying for the purposes of, an enactment within paragraph (a).

(4)   In relation to the relevant return, the relevant enactments apply with the necessary modifications, including in particular the following—

(a)   "partner" includes purported partner, and

(b)   "partnership" includes the purported partnership.

(5)   In this section—

"business" includes trade or profession;

"corresponding partnership case" means a corresponding case in which the limited liability partnership in question carries on a business with a view to profit in the relevant period;

"purported partner" means any person who was a member of the LLP in the relevant period;

"purported partnership return" means anything that—

(a)   purports to be a partnership return, and

(b)   is in a form, and is delivered in a way, that a partnership return could have been made and delivered in a corresponding partnership case."

(2)   The amendment made by subsection (1) is treated as always having been in force.

(3)   However, that amendment does not apply in relation to a purported partnership return if—

(a)   before 11 March 2020, a court or tribunal determined, in proceedings to which a limited liability partnership was a party, that the purported partnership return was not a return under section 12AA of TMA 1970, and

(b)   at the beginning of 11 March 2020, the order of the court or tribunal giving effect to that determination had not been set aside or overturned on appeal.

(4)   In Part 1 of Schedule 14 to F(No.2)A 2017 (digital reporting and record-keeping for income tax etc: amendments of TMA 1970), after paragraph 10B insert—

"**10BA** (1)   Section 12ABZAA (returns relating to LLP not carrying on business etc with view to profit) is amended as follows.

(2)   For subsection (2) substitute—

"(2)   For the purposes of the relevant enactments—

(a)   where the relevant return purports to be a section 12AA partnership return, treat it as a section 12AA partnership return;

(b)   where the relevant return purports to be a Schedule A1 partnership return, treat it as a Schedule A1 partnership return,

(and, accordingly, anything done under a relevant enactment in connection with the relevant return has the same effect as it would have if done in connection with a section 12AA or Schedule A1 partnership return (as the case may be) in a corresponding partnership case)."

(3)   In subsection (5), in the definition of "purported partnership return"—

(a)   in paragraph (a), for "partnership return" substitute "section 12AA or Schedule A1 partnership return";

(b)   in paragraph (b), for "partnership return" substitute "section 12AA or Schedule A1 partnership return (as the case may be)"."

(5)   The reference in section 61(6) of F(No 2)A 2017 (commencement) to Schedule 14 to that Act is to be read as a reference to that Schedule as amended by subsection (4) of this section.

COMMENTARY ON SECTION 104

Section 104 inserts new TMA 1970, s 12ABZAA, which treats as a partnership return any 'purported partnership return' made by a limited liability partnership (LLP) that is not carrying on business with a view to profit. The effect of the measure is that HMRC can amend the LLP's return and its members' returns on the conclusion of an enquiry.

Subsection (2) provides that the measure is retrospective. But subsection (3) disapplies it in a case where a court or tribunal determined before 11 March 2020 that the purported partnership return was not a return under TMA 1970, s 12AA, and that decision was not set aside or overturned before that date.

New TMA 1970, s 12ABZAA provides that the return is treated as a partnership return for the purposes of 'relevant enactments'. These are TMA 1970, ss 12AC and 28B (notice of enquiry and completion of enquiry into partnership return); FA 2014, Pt 4 (follower notices and accelerated payments); and any enactment relating to, or applying for the purposes of, those enactments.

---

105   Interest on unpaid tax in case of disaster etc of national significance

(1)   Section 135 of FA 2008 (interest on unpaid tax in case of disaster etc of national significance) is amended as follows.

(2)   In subsection (2), for the words from "arising" to the end substitute "that—

  (a) arises under or by virtue of an enactment or a contract settlement, and

  (b) is of a description (if any) specified in the order."

(3) In subsection (4)—

  (a) after "relief period" insert ", in relation to a deferred amount,";

  (b) in paragraph (b), after "revoked" insert "or amended so that it ceases to have effect in relation to the deferred amount".

(4) In subsection (10)—

  (a) at the end of paragraph (a), omit "and";

  (b) at the end of paragraph (b) insert ", and

   (c) may specify different dates in relation to liabilities of different descriptions."

(5) The amendments made by this section have effect from 20 March 2020.

COMMENTARY ON SECTION 105

Section 105 amends FA 2008, s 135 (interest on unpaid tax in case of disaster etc of national significance) with effect from 20 March 2020, to enable HM Treasury to specify in an order which payments of tax, deferred by agreement during a period of national emergency or disaster, will not attract interest or surcharges during the deferral period.

Section 105 was introduced at the report stage of the Finance Bill. FA 2008, s 135 did not previously enable implementation of the Government's policy of deferring specific liabilities due to HMRC for specific periods in response to the COVID-19 pandemic and 'ensuring that no interest or surcharge apply to those targeted deferrals', HM Treasury said in an explanatory note.

The Chancellor of the Exchequer announced on 20 March that traders would have the option to defer VAT payments due for the next quarter until 31 March 2021, and that self-assessment taxpayers would have the option to defer their second payment on account for 2019/20 until 31 January 2021.

Coronavirus

106 Taxation of coronavirus support payments

(1) Schedule 16 makes provision about the taxation of coronavirus support payments.

(2) In this section, and in that Schedule, "coronavirus support payment" means a payment made (whether before or after the passing of this Act) under any of the following schemes—

  (a) the coronavirus job retention scheme;

  (b) the self-employment income support scheme;

  (c) any other scheme that is the subject of a direction given under section 76 of the Coronavirus Act 2020 (functions of Her Majesty's Revenue and Customs in relation to coronavirus or coronavirus disease);

  (d) the coronavirus statutory sick pay rebate scheme;

  (e) a coronavirus business support grant scheme;

  (f) any scheme specified or described in regulations made under this section by the Treasury.

(3) The Treasury may by regulations make provision about the application of Schedule 16 to a scheme falling within subsection (2)(c) to (f) (including provision modifying paragraph 8 of that Schedule so that it applies to payments made under a coronavirus business support grant scheme).

(4) Regulations under this section may make provision about coronavirus support payments made before (as well as after) the making of the regulations.

(5) In this section, and in that Schedule—

  "coronavirus" and "coronavirus disease" have the meaning they have in the Coronavirus Act 2020 (see section 1 of that Act);

  "coronavirus business support grant scheme" means any scheme (whether announced or operating before or after the passing of this Act), other than a scheme within subsection (2)(a) to (d), under which a public authority makes grants to businesses with the object of providing support to those businesses in connection with any effect or anticipated effect (direct or indirect) of coronavirus or coronavirus disease;

"the coronavirus job retention scheme" means the scheme (as it has effect from time to time) that is the subject of the direction given by the Treasury on 15 April 2020 under section 76 of the Coronavirus Act 2020;

"the coronavirus statutory sick pay rebate scheme" means the scheme (as it has effect from time to time) given effect to by the Statutory Sick Pay (Coronavirus) (Funding of Employers' Liabilities) Regulations 2020 (SI 2020/512);

"employment-related scheme" means the coronavirus job retention scheme or the coronavirus statutory sick pay rebate scheme;

"the self-employment income support scheme" means the scheme (as it has effect from time to time) that is the subject of the direction given by the Treasury on 30 April 2020 under section 76 of the Coronavirus Act 2020.

(6)   Examples of coronavirus business support grant schemes as at 24 June 2020 include—

(a)   the small business grant fund that is the subject of the guidance about that scheme and the retail, hospitality and leisure grant fund published by the Department for Business, Energy & Industrial Strategy on 1 April 2020;

(b)   the retail, hospitality and leisure grant fund that is the subject of that guidance;

(c)   the local authority discretionary grants fund that is the subject of the guidance about that scheme published by the Department for Business, Energy & Industrial Strategy on 13 May 2020;

(d)   the schemes corresponding to the small business grant fund, retail and hospitality grant fund and local authority discretionary grants fund in Scotland, Wales and Northern Ireland."

COMMENTARY ON SECTION 106, SCHEDULE 16

Section 106 and Schedule 16 were introduced at the report stage of the Finance Bill and approved on 2 July 2020. They provide for the taxation of coronavirus support payments paid to employers and businesses, and set out compliance and enforcement powers enabling HMRC to recover overpayments. See the commentary note under Schedule 16 regarding the legal framework and HMRC guidance relating to the coronavirus support schemes.

The Government published an explanatory note (https://tinyurl.com/y9ymo7cl) and a tax information and impact note (TIIN) (https://tinyurl.com/yd28s9nd).

The TIIN said the rationale for the tax charge was that the payments were 'supplanting' people's income. The measure also provides for 'an income tax charge on the recipient of a SEISS or CJRS payment to which they are not entitled or where a CJRS payment has not been used to pay furloughed employee costs,' the TIIN noted.

HMRC is given the power to raise income tax assessments to recover such amounts, and will be able to charge a penalty in cases of deliberate non-compliance. Financial Secretary to the Treasury Jesse Norman told the House of Commons on 2 July 2020:

'HMRC has given a clear undertaking that these powers will not be used to penalise taxpayers who may be going through difficult times but make honest mistakes in their applications. As previously stated, the powers are designed to be proportionate, and they balance the fact that we are in unprecedented and uncertain times with the need to ensure that HMRC has sufficient powers to enforce the schemes according to eligibility criteria set out and to protect the Exchequer.'

Responding on 12 June 2020 to a technical consultation on draft legislation, the Chartered Institute of Taxation had said:

'We urge HMRC to take a reasonable approach to enforcement in cases where recipients of CSPs were not entitled to the amount they received. As noted above, there will be cases where people have made inadvertent errors in claims which may not come to light for some time. There will be cases where the person just did not know of the requirement to notify an overpayment. It is imperative that HMRC obtain a full understanding of the facts in every case and take a proportionate and targeted approach in their compliance activity in the months ahead.'

The CIOT also pointed out that guidance published at GOV.UK about the CJRS and SEISS schemes had been 'constantly evolving', making it difficult for people to keep up-to-date with changes:

> 'Some of what is being added to the guidance may well impact on claims that have already been made ... It is possible that a person who has already received a payment on the understanding that they were eligible at the time they made their claim may subsequently feel they should not have claimed on the basis of HMRC's updated guidance.'

Section 106(2) provides that a coronavirus support payment (CSP) for this purpose is a payment made under:

- the coronavirus job retention scheme (CJRS);
- the self-employment income support scheme (SEISS);
- any other scheme that is the subject of a direction under Coronavirus Act 2020, s 76;
- the coronavirus statutory sick pay rebate scheme (CSSPRS, see the Statutory Sick Pay (Coronavirus) (Funding of Employers' Liabilities) Regulations, SI 2020/512);
- a coronavirus business support grant scheme as defined in s 106(5), (6);
- any other scheme specified in regulations made under s 106.

107   Enterprise management incentives: disqualifying events

(1)   The modifications made by this section apply for the purposes of determining whether a disqualifying event occurs or is treated as occurring in relation to an employee in accordance with section 535 of ITEPA 2003 (enterprise management incentives: disqualifying events relating to employee).

(2)   Paragraph 26 of Schedule 5 to ITEPA 2003 (requirement as to commitment of working time) has effect as if, in sub-paragraph (3)—

   (a)   the "or" at the end of paragraph (c) were omitted, and
   (b)   at the end of paragraph (d), there were inserted ", or

      (e)   not being required to work for reasons connected with coronavirus disease (within the meaning given by section 1(1) of the Coronavirus Act 2020)."

(3)   Paragraph 27 of that Schedule (meaning of "working time") has effect as if, in sub-paragraph (1)(b), for "(d)" there were substituted "(e)".

(4)   Section 535 of ITEPA 2003 has effect as if, in the closing words of subsection (3), for "(d)" there were substituted "(e)".

(5)   The modifications made by this section have effect in relation to the period—

   (a)   beginning with 19 March 2020, and
   (b)   ending with 5 April 2021.

(6)   The Treasury may by regulations made in the tax year 2020–21 amend subsection (5)(b) by replacing "2021" with "2022".

COMMENTARY ON SECTION 107

The COVID-19 pandemic has impacted the operation of the various tax-favoured employee share plans in the UK. HMRC has previously published a bulletin to address some of these issues. However, that bulletin left a number of queries in relation to Enterprise Management Incentive (EMI) options unanswered (in particular in relation to the implications of COVID-19 in the context of the 'working time requirement') under the EMI legislation. On 26 June 2020, the Government tabled a new clause for the Finance Bill 2020 in relation to the 'working time requirement' in the context of COVID-19.

By way of background, ITEPA 2003, Sch 5, paras 26 and 27 set out the details of the 'working time requirement' and provide that an employee can only be granted an EMI option and benefit from the associated tax advantages if they work for the relevant company for an average of at least 25 hours per week or, if less, 75% of their overall 'working time'. If the employee does not meet this requirement throughout the time they hold the EMI option, the option will be subject to a 'disqualifying event' (as defined in ITEPA 2003, s 535) and will therefore lose the beneficial EMI tax treatment if not exercised within 90 days of such a disqualifying event. It was therefore likely that there were a number of employees who hold EMI options and who would have technically ceased to meet this requirement as a result of being furloughed (or otherwise reducing their working hours) due to COVID-19.

New section 107 provides for a new paragraph (e) at the end of ITEPA 2003, Sch 5, para 26(3) which, in effect provides a time limited exception that there will be no 'disqualifying event' resulting from an EMI option holder not being required to work for reasons connected with coronavirus disease (as defined in the Coronavirus Act 2020, s 1(1)). The explanatory notes state that this includes circumstances where the individual has had to take leave, is furloughed or reduces their working hours because of COVID-19. This section will have effect from 19 March 2020 to 5 April 2021 (although there is provision for HM Treasury to extend the exception for a further twelve months by regulations if the COVID-19 pandemic has not ended by April 2021).

This is a welcome development. Given it is stated to apply from 19 March 2020, it appears that, even where an employee was furloughed (or otherwise ceased to meet the 'working time requirement' due to COVID-19) more than 90 days ago (and therefore their options would otherwise have been subject to a 'disqualifying event'), their option will not be treated as having been subject to a 'disqualifying event' (although this would require the amendment to be given retrospective effect, and it is not entirely clear how this is achieved). Furthermore, it is helpful that section 107 provides for an extension to the 2021/22 tax year, if required (for example, if there is a 'second wave' of COVID-19 which requires similar measures in the coming months).

One point to note is that section 107 does *not* provide for the *grant* of new EMI options to employees who would otherwise meet the 'working time requirement' in the EMI legislation but are not being required to work due to coronavirus. That said, draft legislation published on 21 July 2020 for the next Finance Bill does provide that such employees will be eligible to be granted an EMI option, notwithstanding they will not meet the 'working time requirement' at the time of grant. In its Employment Related Securities Bulletin 36 (July 2020), HMRC confirms that if an employee is unable to meet the 'working time requirement' due to the COVID-19 pandemic (ie being furloughed, working reduced hours or taking unpaid leave), the time which they would have spent on the business of the company will count towards their working time. This new provision will also have retrospective effect from 19 March 2020 and will apply until 5 April 2021 (and again, there is provision for this relaxation to be extended to 5 April 2022, if required).

108   Protected pension age of members re-employed as a result of coronavirus

(1) In FA 2004, in Schedule 36 (pension schemes etc), paragraph 22 (rights to take benefit before normal minimum pension age) is amended as follows.

(2) In sub-paragraph (7F), at the end of paragraph (b) insert ", and

> (c)   that the member is or was employed as mentioned in sub-paragraph (7B)(a) where—
>> (i)   the employment began at any time during the coronavirus period, and
>> (ii)   the only or main reason that the member was taken into employment was to help the employer to respond to the public health, social, economic or other effects of coronavirus."

(3) After sub-paragraph (7J) insert—

"(7K)   In sub-paragraph (7F)(c)—

> "coronavirus" has the same meaning as in the Coronavirus Act 2020 (see section 1(1) of that Act);
> "the coronavirus period" means the period beginning with 1 March 2020 and ending with 1 November 2020.

(7L)   The Treasury may by regulations amend the definition of "the coronavirus period" in sub-paragraph (7K) so as to replace the later of the dates specified in it with another date falling before 6 April 2021.

(7M)   The power in sub-paragraph (7L) may be exercised on more than one occasion."

(4)   The amendments made by this section are treated as having come into force on 1 March 2020.

COMMENTARY ON SECTION 108

Some individuals who were members of pension schemes before 6 April 2006, including some police, firefighters and other uniformed service personnel, have protected pension ages in respect of those schemes, meaning they are able to receive pension benefits at an age below the current normal minimum pension age of 55.

Under current legislation, those individuals with a protected pension age in the range 50 to 54 would lose the benefit of their protected pension age and become liable to unauthorised payment tax charges if they access their pension benefits and either (i) continue to work without a break in service, or (ii) return immediately to service without a break of at least one month.

The Government has temporarily suspended these rules if such individuals returned to work as part of the Government's response to coronavirus (COVID-19).

Section 108 amends FA 2004, Sch 36, para 22 so individuals who took their pension benefits before age 55 in reliance on a protected pension age will not lose the benefit of their protected pension age if they were re-employed in relation to coronavirus. Individuals will retain their protected pension age regardless of whether there is a requirement in the individual's scheme that their pension must be abated due to their re-employment.

This easement covers the period from 1 March to 1 November 2020, at which time it will be reviewed.

109   Modifications of the statutory residence test in connection with coronavirus

(1)   This section applies for the purposes of determining—

    (a)   whether an individual was or was not resident in the United Kingdom for the tax year 2019–20 for the purposes of relevant tax, and

    (b)   if an individual was not so resident in the United Kingdom for the tax year 2019–20 (including as a result of this section), whether the individual was or was not resident in the United Kingdom for the tax year 2020–21 for the purposes of relevant tax.

"Relevant tax" has the meaning given by paragraph 1(4) of Schedule 45 to FA 2013 (statutory residence test).

(2)   That Schedule is modified in accordance with subsections (3) to (13).

(3)   Paragraph 8 (second automatic UK test: days at overseas homes) has effect as if after sub-paragraph (5) there were inserted—

"(5A)   For the purposes of sub-paragraphs (1)(b) and (4), a day does not count as a day when P is present at a home of P's in the UK if it is a day that would fall within the third case in paragraph 22(7) (if P were present in the UK at the end of it)."

(4)   Paragraph 22 (key concepts: days spent) has effect as if—

    (a)   in sub-paragraph (2), for "two cases" there were substituted "three cases";

    (b)   after sub-paragraph (6) there were inserted—

"(7)   The third case is where—

    (a)   that day falls within the period beginning with 1 March 2020 and ending with 1 June 2020,

    (b)   on that day P is present in the UK for an applicable reason related to coronavirus disease, and

    (c)   in the tax year in question, P is resident in a territory outside the UK ("the overseas territory").

(8)   The following are applicable reasons related to coronavirus disease—

    (a)   that P is present in the UK as a medical or healthcare professional for purposes connected with the detection, treatment or prevention of coronavirus disease;

    (b)   that P is present in the UK for purposes connected with the development or production of medicinal products (including vaccines), devices, equipment or facilities related to the detection, treatment or prevention of coronavirus disease.

(9)   For the purposes of paragraph (7)(c), P is resident in an overseas territory in the tax year in question if P is considered for tax purposes to be a resident of that territory in accordance with the laws of that territory.

(10)   The Treasury may by regulations made by statutory instrument—

   (a)   amend sub-paragraph (7)(a) so as to replace the later of the dates specified in it with another date falling before 6 April 2021;

   (b)   amend this paragraph so as to add one or more applicable reasons related to coronavirus disease.

(11)   The powers under sub-paragraph (10) may be exercised on more than one occasion.

(12)   A statutory instrument containing regulations under sub-paragraph (10) is subject to annulment in pursuance of a resolution of the House of Commons."

(5)   Paragraph 23 (key concepts: days spent and the deeming rule) has effect as if after sub-paragraph (5) there were inserted—

"(5A)   For the purposes of sub-paragraph (3)(b) and (4), a day does not count as a qualifying day if it is a day that would fall within the third case in paragraph 22(7) (if P were present in the UK at the end of it)."

(6)   Paragraph 28(2) (rules for calculating the reference period) has effect as if—

   (a)   in paragraph (b) the "and" at the end were omitted;

   (b)   after paragraph (b) there were inserted—

   "(ba)   absences from work at times during the period specified in an emergency volunteering certificate issued to P under Schedule 7 to the Coronavirus Act 2020 (emergency volunteering leave), and";

   (c)   in paragraph (c), for "or (b)" there were substituted ", (b) or (ba)".

(7)   Paragraph 29 (significant breaks from UK or overseas work) has effect as if in sub-paragraphs (1)(b) and (2)(b), for "or parenting leave" there were substituted ", parenting leave or emergency volunteering leave under Schedule 7 to the Coronavirus Act 2020".

(8)   Paragraph 32 (family tie) has effect as if after sub-paragraph (4) there were inserted—

"(4A)   But a day does not count as a day on which P sees the child if the day on which P sees the child would be a day falling within the third case in paragraph 22(7) (if P were present in the UK at the end of it)."

(9)   Paragraph 34 (accommodation tie) has effect as if after sub-paragraph (1) there were inserted—

"(1A)   For the purposes of sub-paragraph (1)—

   (a)   if the place is available to P on a day that would fall within the third case in paragraph 22(7) (if P were present in the UK at the end of that day), that day is to be disregarded for the purposes of sub-paragraph (b), and

   (b)   a night spent by P at the place immediately before or after a day that would fall within the third case in paragraph 22(7) (if P were present in the UK at the end of that day) is to be disregarded for the purposes of sub-paragraph (c)."

(10)   Paragraph 35 (work tie) has effect as if after sub-paragraph (2) there were inserted—

"(3)   But a day that would fall within the third case in paragraph 22(7) (if P were present in the UK at the end of it) does not count as a day on which P works in the UK."

(11)   Paragraph 37 (90-day tie) has effect as if—

   (a)   the existing text were sub-paragraph (1);

   (b)   after that sub-paragraph, there were inserted—

"(2)   For the purposes of sub-paragraph (1), a day that would fall within the third case in paragraph 22(7) (if P were present in the UK at the end of it) does not count as a day P has spent in the UK in the year in question."

(12)   Paragraph 38 (country tie) has effect as if after sub-paragraph (3) there were inserted—

"(4)   For the purposes of sub-paragraph (3), P is to be treated as not being present in the UK at the end of a day that would fall within the third case in paragraph 22(7) (if P were present in the UK at the end of that day)."

(13)   Paragraph 145 (interpretation) has effect as if at the appropriate place there were inserted—

""coronavirus disease" has the same meaning as in the Coronavirus Act 2020 (see section 1(1) of that Act);".

COMMENTARY ON SECTION 109

Section 109 amends the statutory residence test rules for certain days spent working in the UK for reasons related to coronavirus or days spent volunteering in health or social care. The statutory residence test is used to determine the UK residence status of individuals for the purposes of income tax, capital gains tax, inheritance tax and corporation tax, to the extent that the residence status of individuals is applicable to the latter two taxes (FA 2013, Sch 45, Pt 1, para 1(4)). The statutory residence test is made up of three parts: the automatic UK tests, the automatic overseas tests and the sufficient ties tests (FA 2013, Sch 45, Pt 1).

An individual is UK resident for the tax year if they meet any of the automatic UK tests and none of the automatic overseas tests or they meet none of the automatic UK tests, none of the automatic overseas tests and meet the sufficient ties test (FA 2013, Sch 45, Pt 1, paras 3, 5). An individual is UK non-resident for the tax year if they meet any of the automatic overseas tests or they meet none of the automatic UK tests, none of the automatic overseas tests and do not meet the sufficient ties test (FA 2013, Sch 45, Pt 1, paras 3, 4).

Where the individual arrives in the UK or leaves the UK in the tax year, if they are UK resident under the statutory residence test it may be possible to split the tax year into periods of UK residence and non-residence for the purposes of the taxation of income and gains if any of the Cases in FA 2013, Sch 45, Pt 3, paras 44–51 apply.

Tax years to which the changes apply

Section 109(1) states that the changes made to the statutory residence test apply for the purposes of determining the individual's residence status for the 2019/20 tax year. The changes apply to the determination of the individual's residence status for the 2020/21 tax year only if the individual was non-resident in the UK in the 2019/20 tax year. This means that if the individual was UK resident in 2019/20, the provisions in section 109 do not apply when determining residence status in 2020/21. This is a key point and when reading the commentary below, it is important to bear this in mind.

Day-counting

Section 109(4) needs to be considered first, as most of the other changes in this section refer to the amendments introduced by this subsection.

This amends the day-counting provisions in FA 2013, Sch 45, Pt 2, para 22 and adds a new exception to the general day-counting rule. These exceptions are known as 'cases' in the legislation. The general rule is that a UK day is one in which the individual is present in the UK at the end of the day (ie midnight).

A day in which the individual is present in the UK at midnight is not counted as a UK day if (FA 2013, Sch 45, Pt 2, para 22(7)):

(a)   it falls within the period beginning with 1 March 2020 and ending with 1 June 2020 (although bear in mind 'Tax years to which the changes apply' above)

(b)   the individual is in the UK on that day for an applicable reason related to coronavirus disease, and

(c)   the individual is tax resident in another territory in that tax year under the rules of that territory

Medical or healthcare professionals are in the UK for an applicable reason related to coronavirus disease if they are here for purposes connected with detection, treatment or prevention of coronavirus disease. Other people (which may include medical or healthcare professionals) are in the UK for an applicable reason related to coronavirus disease if they are here for purposes connected with the development or production of medicinal products (the legislation mentions vaccines, but this might include drug treatments), devices, equipment or facilities related to the detection, treatment or prevention of coronavirus disease. 'Coronavirus disease' is defined as COVID-19 (FA 2020, s 109(13); Coronavirus Act 2020, s 1(1)).

Both the end date in (a) above and the definition of applicable reason related to coronavirus disease can be amended by statutory instrument.

Note that where the individual is present in the UK due to coronavirus but the conditions listed above are not met, this may not count as a UK day if it falls within the exceptional circumstances rule in FA 2013, Sch 45, Pt 2, para 22(4)–(6). The legislation has not been amended as this can be dealt with through guidance. HMRC accepts that certain circumstances related to coronavirus may amount to exceptional circumstances, e g the individual is advised to self-isolate in the UK or is unable to leave the UK due to travel restrictions. See RDRM11005 for full details. The days that can be ignored for UK day-counting due to exceptional circumstances are limited to 60 days in the tax year. Once that limit is reached, any additional days are counted as UK days.

Section 109(5) amends the anti-avoidance deeming rule for day-counting in FA 2013, Sch 45, Pt 2, para 23. The deeming rule applies if the individual is in the UK for part of the day but not at midnight at the end of the day (a 'qualifying day') for more than 30 days in the tax year. Once this threshold is reached, every additional day in which the individual is present in the UK at any point is counted as a UK day. The deeming rule is amended so that days which fall into the exception in FA 2013, Sch 45, Pt 2, para 22(7) (see above) do not count as a 'qualifying day' for the purposes of the 30-day total and nor are they counted as a UK day if the individual's 'qualifying days' exceed 30.

Second automatic UK test (home in the UK)

Section 109(3) amends the second automatic UK test (the home in the UK test) in FA 2013, Sch 45, Pt 1, para 8. One of the conditions that must be met for that test is that the individual has a home in the UK at which they are present for at least part of the day (no matter how short) on at least 30 days in the tax year. If the individual is present at their UK home at any time on a day that falls into the exception in FA 2013, Sch 45, Pt 2, para 22(7) (see 'Day-counting' above), this does not count as a day of presence for the 30-day condition.

Whether the individual works full-time for the purposes of the third automatic UK test, third automatic overseas test and split year Cases 1, 5 and 6

Section 109(6) amends the rules for calculating the reference period for the purposes of FA 2013, Sch 45, Pt 1, paras 9(2), 14(3). These are the complicated calculations that must be performed to determine if the individual works at least an average of 35 hours per week (ie 'sufficient hours') in the UK or abroad (as appropriate). This is important for the full-time working in the UK test (third automatic UK test) and the full-time working abroad test (third automatic overseas test), but also for split year Cases 1 (starting full-time work overseas), 5 (starting full-time work in the UK) and 6 (ceasing full-time work overseas), which apply the calculations.

When calculating whether the individual has worked 'sufficient hours' in the UK or abroad, at Step 3 of the calculation it is possible to deduct days of leave as listed in FA 2013, Sch 45, Pt 2, para 28. It is important that such days are deducted as otherwise the individual would have to work much greater hours than 35 hours per week during their working days in order to compensate for days of leave and still average over 35 hours' work per week.

Deductible days of leave under FA 2013, Sch 45, Pt 2, para 28 include reasonable amounts of annual leave and parental leave as well as sick leave. This paragraph is amended to include days of absence from work during a period of emergency volunteering leave. This is leave specified in an emergency volunteering certificate issued to the individual under Coronavirus Act 2020, Sch 7. Such certificates cover an absence of two, three or four consecutive weeks in a 16-week volunteering period and allow the individual to volunteer in the health or social care sector. Given this is UK-based leave, it is more likely to be in point when calculating whether the individual works full-time in the UK.

The rules regarding embedded non-working days in FA 2013, Sch 45, Pt 2, para 28(2)(c), (5), (6) include emergency volunteering leave. Non-working days (eg weekends and bank holidays) can only be deducted if there are at least three days of leave prior to the non-working day(s) and at least three days of leave after the non-working day(s).

Section 109(7) amends the definition of 'significant break' in FA 2013, Sch 45, Pt 2, para 29. The full-time working in the UK test, the full-time working abroad test and split year Cases 1 (starting full-time work overseas), 5 (starting full-time work in the UK) and 6 (ceasing full-time work overseas) all include a condition that the individual must not have had a 'significant break' from work during the relevant period for those tests/Cases.

The individual has a 'significant break' from work if there is a period of 31 days or more during which there is no day in which the individual:

- does at least three hours' work in the UK (full-time working in the UK test and Case 5) or abroad (full-time working abroad test, Case 1 and Case 6).
- would have done at least three hours' work in the UK/abroad had they not been on annual leave, sick leave, parental leave or emergency volunteering leave under Coronavirus Act 2020, Sch 7 (as discussed above)

When considering the amendments made by section 109(6), (7), bear in mind 'Tax years to which the changes apply' above.

Sufficient ties test

All the UK ties for the sufficient ties test have been amended by section 109. As mentioned at the beginning of this commentary, the sufficient ties test is important where the individual does not meet any of the automatic tests. The sufficient ties test looks at the connections the individual has with the UK in the tax year, the days the individual has spent in the UK in the tax year (see 'Day-counting' above) and whether the individual was UK resident in any of the previous three tax years (FA 2013, Sch 45, Pt 1, paras 17–20). The more UK ties the individual has, the fewer days they can spend in the UK in the tax year before they meet the sufficient ties test.

When considering the commentary below, bear in mind 'Tax years to which the changes apply' above.

Section 109(8) amends the family tie in FA 2013, Sch 45, Pt 2, para 32. The individual has a family tie if they have a UK resident spouse/civil partner (or common law equivalent) or minor child. There is an exception where the individual sees the child for fewer than 61 days in the tax year or part of the tax year up to the child's 18th birthday. If the individual sees the child for any part of a day, this counts as a day for these purposes unless the day falls into the exception in FA 2013, Sch 45, Pt 2, para 22(7) (see 'Day-counting' above).

Section 109(9) amends the accommodation tie in FA 2013, Sch 45, Pt 2, para 34. The individual has an accommodation tie if they have a place to live in the UK which is available to them for a continuous period of at least 91 days in the tax year and they actually spend one night there. However, the UK accommodation is not counted as available for the purposes of the 91-day condition, nor is a night spent there counted as a night, if it falls into the exception in FA 2013, Sch 45, Pt 2, para 22(7) (see 'Day-counting' above).

Section 109(10) amends the work tie in FA 2013, Sch 45, Pt 2, para 35. The individual has a work tie if they work in the UK for 40 days or more in the tax year. A day of work is one in which more than three hours' work is performed in the UK. However, the day is not counted for the purposes of the 40-day condition if it falls into the exception in FA 2013, Sch 45, Pt 2, para 22(7) (see 'Day-counting' above).

Section 109(11) amends the 90-day tie in FA 2013, Sch 45, Pt 2, para 37. The individual has a 90-day tie if they spent more than 90 days in the UK in either of the two previous tax years. A day is excluded for the 90-day condition if it falls into the exception in FA 2013, Sch 45, Pt 2, para 22(7) (see 'Day-counting' above).

Section 109(12) amends the country tie in FA 2013, Sch 45, Pt 2, para 38. The country tie is considered only where the individual was UK resident for one or more of the three previous tax years. The individual has a country tie if they spend more midnights in the UK than in any other country in the tax year. Midnights in the UK are not counted where they fall into the exception in FA 2013, Sch 45, Pt 2, para 22(7) (see 'Day-counting' above).

110   Future Fund: EIS and SEIS relief

(1) This section applies if an individual to whom shares in a company have been issued—

> (a)   enters into a convertible loan agreement with the company under the Future Fund on or after 20 May 2020, and
> (b)   subsequently receives value from the company under the terms of the agreement.

(2) If, as a result of the receipt of value, any EIS relief attributable to shares issued before the relevant time would (apart from this subsection) be withdrawn or reduced under section 213 of ITA 2007, the value received is to be ignored for the purposes of that section.

(3) If, as a result of the receipt of value, any SEIS relief attributable to shares issued before the relevant time would (apart from this subsection) be withdrawn or reduced under section 257FE of ITA 2007, the value received is to be ignored for the purposes of that section.

(4) If, as a result of the receipt of value, shares issued before the relevant time would (apart from this subsection) cease to be eligible shares by reason of paragraph 13(1)(b) of Schedule 5B to TCGA 1992, the value received is to be ignored for the purposes of that paragraph.

(5) In this section—

> "the Future Fund" means the scheme of that name operated from 20 May 2020 by the British Business Bank plc on behalf of the Secretary of State;
> "the relevant time" means the time when the individual enters into the convertible loan agreement.

COMMENTARY ON SECTION 110

This section amends the current rules for the Seed Enterprise Investment Scheme (SEIS) and Enterprise Investment Scheme (EIS) as a result of the Government's introduction of the Future Fund.

The Future Fund was set up to assist businesses adversely impacted by the coronavirus outbreak who may have been unable to access other Government-funded support programmes. Government investment under the Future Fund is subject to matched funding of at least an equivalent amount provided by private investors. Investment must be provided through a convertible loan note and therefore the investment itself will not qualify for SEIS or EIS relief.

The amendments have been introduced to ensure that SEIS or EIS investors in a company who also support the company using a Future Fund convertible loan note will not lose relief on previous SEIS or EIS qualifying investments when the loan is redeemed, repaid or converted. This was identified as a potential discouragement for existing qualifying investors who may have otherwise lost their relief depending on how and when the convertible loan ended.

Under the existing rules, such events would have represented a return of value from the company to the investor. If this event took place within the relevant three-year holding period there would have been a clawback of tax relief previously claimed, depending on the original amount of tax relief and the value received by the investor.

Subsection (1) defines the circumstances in which the section applies, including that the qualifying shares must have been issued to the relevant investor prior to them investing in the company under a Future Fund convertible loan note on or after 20 May 2020.

Subsections (2), (3) and (4) provide that the amount of value received in respect of the Future Fund loan note through its repayment, redemption or conversion, should be ignored for the purposes of SEIS and EIS relief. There should therefore be no reduction or withdrawal of EIS relief (subsection (2)) or SEIS relief (subsection (3)), and there should be no impact on the eligibility of the shares for EIS capital gains tax reinvestment relief (subsection (4)), due to additional investment as part of the Future Fund.

Preparing for new tax

111 Preparing for a new tax in respect of certain plastic packaging

The Commissioners for Her Majesty's Revenue and Customs may make preparations for the introduction of a new tax to be charged in respect of certain plastic packaging.

COMMENTARY ON SECTION 111

Section 111 authorises HMRC to make preparations for the introduction of a new tax to be charged in respect of certain plastic packaging.

Budget 2020 announced that, following a consultation in 2019, the Government will introduce a plastic packaging tax from April 2022. The tax will be applied at the rate of £200 per tonne to plastic packaging, manufactured in or imported into the UK, that contains less than 30% recycled plastic. The stated aim is to 'incentivise the use of recycled plastic in packaging and help tackle the scourge of plastic in the natural environment'.

An HMRC consultation, published on 11 March 2020 and extended to 20 August 2020, (https://tinyurl.com/r6uc4tz) invites comments on the design, implementation and administration of the tax.

Local loans

112 Limits on local loans

(1)   In section 4(1) of the National Loans Act 1968 (which sets a limit on local loans made in pursuance of section 3 of that Act)—

    (a)   for "£85 billion" substitute "£115 billion", and

    (b)   for "£95 billion" substitute "£135 billion".

(2)   The Local Loans (Increase of Limit) Order 2019 (SI 2019/1317) is revoked.

(3)   This section comes into force on such day as the Treasury may by regulations made by statutory instrument appoint.

COMMENTARY ON SECTION 112

Section 112 gives HM Treasury the power to increase, by means of a statutory instrument, limits on loans to local authorities from the Public Works Loan Board, which is managed by the UK Debt Management Office. The limits are set out in National Loans Act 1968, s 4(1).

Other

113 Interpretation

In this Act the following abbreviations are references to the following Acts—

ALDA 1979	Alcoholic Liquor Duties Act 1979
CAA 2001	Capital Allowances Act 2001
CTA 2009	Corporation Tax Act 2009
CTA 2010	Corporation Tax Act 2010
FA, followed by a year	Finance Act of that year
F(No.2)A, followed by a year	Finance (No.2) Act of that year
HODA 1979	Hydrocarbon Oil Duties Act 1979
IHTA 1984	Inheritance Tax Act 1984
ITA 2007	Income Tax Act 2007
ITEPA 2003	Income Tax (Earnings and Pensions) Act 2003
ITTOIA 2005	Income Tax (Trading and Other Income) Act 2005
TCGA 1992	Taxation of Chargeable Gains Act 1992
TCTA 2018	Taxation (Cross-border Trade) Act 2018
TMA 1970	Taxes Management Act 1970

TPDA 1979	Tobacco Products Duty Act 1979
VATA 1994	Value Added Tax Act 1994
VERA 1994	Vehicle Excise and Registration Act 1994

114   Short title

This Act may be cited as the Finance Act 2020.

SCHEDULE 1

WORKERS' SERVICES PROVIDED THROUGH INTERMEDIARIES

Section 7

PART 1

AMENDMENTS TO CHAPTER 8 OF PART 2 OF ITEPA 2003

1 Chapter 8 of Part 2 of ITEPA 2003 (application of provisions to workers under arrangements made by intermediaries) is amended as follows.

2 For the heading of the Chapter substitute "Workers' services provided through intermediaries to small clients".

3 (1)   Section 48 (scope of Chapter) is amended as follows.

(2)   In subsection (1) for the words from ", but" to the end substitute "in a case where the services are provided to a person who is not a public authority and who either—

    (a)   qualifies as small for a tax year, or

    (b)   does not have a UK connection for a tax year."

(3)   After subsection (3) insert—

"(4)   For provisions determining when a person qualifies as small for a tax year, see sections 60A to 60G.

(5)   For provision determining when a person has a UK connection for a tax year, see section 60I."

4 (1)   Section 50 (worker treated as receiving earnings from employment) is amended as follows.

(2)   In subsection (1) before paragraph (a) insert—

"(za)   the client qualifies as small or does not have a UK connection,".

(3)   After subsection (4) insert—

"(5)   The condition in paragraph (za) of subsection (1) is to be ignored if—

    (a)   the client concerned is an individual, and

    (b)   the services concerned are performed otherwise than for the purposes of the client's business.

(6)   For the purposes of paragraph (za) of subsection (1) the client is to be treated as not qualifying as small for the tax year concerned if the client is treated as medium or large for that tax year by reason of section 61TA(3)(a)."

5 After section 60 insert—

"When a person qualifies as small for a tax year

60A   When a company qualifies as small for a tax year

(1)   For the purposes of this Chapter, a company qualifies as small for a tax year if one of the following conditions is met (but this is subject to section 60C).

(2)   The first condition is that the company's first financial year is not relevant to the tax year.

(3)   The second condition is that the small companies regime applies to the company for its last financial year that is relevant to the tax year.

(4)   For the purposes of this section, a financial year of a company is "relevant to" a tax year if the period for filing the company's accounts and reports for the financial year ends before the beginning of the tax year.

(5)   Expressions used in this section and in the Companies Act 2006 have the same meaning in this section as in that Act.

60B   When a company qualifies as small for a tax year: joint ventures

(1)   This section applies when determining for the purposes of section 60A(3) whether the small companies regime applies to a company for a financial year in a case where—

    (a)   at the end of the financial year the company is jointly controlled by two or more other persons, and

    (b)   one or more of those other persons are undertakings ("the joint venturer undertakings").

(2)   If the company is a parent company, the joint venturer undertakings are to be treated as members of the group headed by the company.

(3)   If the company is not a parent company, the company and the joint venturer undertakings are to be treated as constituting a group of which the company is the parent company.

(4)   In this section the expression "jointly controlled" is to be read in accordance with those provisions of international accounting standards which relate to joint ventures.

(5)   Expressions used in this section and in the Companies Act 2006 have the same meaning in this section as in that Act.

60C   When a company qualifies as small for a tax year: subsidiaries

(1)   A company does not qualify as small for a tax year by reason of the condition in section 60A(3) being met if—

    (a)   the company is a member of a group at the end of its last financial year that is relevant to the tax year,

    (b)   the company is not the parent undertaking of that group at the end of that financial year, and

    (c)   the undertaking that is the parent undertaking of that group at that time does not qualify as small in relation to its last financial year that is relevant to the tax year.

(2)   Where the parent undertaking mentioned in subsection (1)(c) is not a company, sections 382 and 383 of the Companies Act 2006 have effect for determining whether the parent undertaking qualifies as small in relation to its last financial year that is relevant to the tax year as if references in those sections to a company and a parent company included references to an undertaking and a parent undertaking.

(3)   For the purposes of subsections (1)(c) and (2) a financial year of an undertaking that is not a company is "relevant to" a tax year if it ends at least 9 months before the beginning of the tax year.

(4)   For the purposes of this section, a financial year of a company is "relevant to" a tax year if the period for filing the company's accounts and reports for the financial year ends before the beginning of the tax year.

(5)   Expressions used in this section and in the Companies Act 2006 have the same meaning in this section as in that Act.

60D   When a relevant undertaking qualifies as small for a tax year

(1)   Sections 60A to 60C apply in relation to a relevant undertaking as they apply in relation to a company, subject to any necessary modifications.

(2)   In this section "relevant undertaking" means an undertaking in respect of which regulations have effect under—

    (a)   section 15(a) of the Limited Liability Partnerships Act 2000,

    (b)   section 1043 of the Companies Act 2006 (unregistered companies), or

    (c)   section 1049 of the Companies Act 2006 (overseas companies).

(3)   Expressions used in this section and in the Companies Act 2006 have the same meaning in this section as in that Act.

60E   When other undertakings qualify as small for a tax year

(1)   An undertaking that is not a company or a relevant undertaking qualifies as small for a tax year if one of the following conditions is met.

(2)   The first condition is that the undertaking's first financial year is not relevant to the tax year.

(3)   The second condition is that the undertaking's turnover for its last financial year that is relevant to the tax year is not more than the amount for the time being specified in the second column of item 1 of the Table in section 382(3) of the Companies Act 2006.

(4)   For the purposes of this section a financial year of an undertaking is "relevant to" a tax year if it ends at least 9 months before the beginning of the tax year.

(5)   In this section—

"relevant undertaking" has the meaning given by section 60D, and

"turnover", in relation to an undertaking, means the amounts derived from the provision of goods or services after the deduction of trade discounts, value added tax and any other taxes based on the amounts so derived.

(6)   Expressions used in this section and in the Companies Act 2006 have the same meaning in this section as in that Act.

60F   When other persons qualify as small for a tax year

(1)   For the purposes of this Chapter, a person who is not a company, relevant undertaking or other undertaking qualifies as small for a tax year if the person's turnover for the last calendar year before the tax year is not more than the amount for the time being specified in the second column of item 1 of the Table in section 382(3) of the Companies Act 2006.

(2)   In this section—

"company" and "undertaking" have the same meaning as in the Companies Act 2006,

"relevant undertaking" has the meaning given by section 60D, and

"turnover", in relation to a person, means the amounts derived from the provision of goods or services after the deduction of trade discounts, value added tax and any other taxes based on the amounts so derived.

60G   Sections 60A to 60F: connected persons

(1)   This section applies where—

     (a)   it is necessary for the purposes of determining whether a person qualifies as small for a tax year ("the tax year concerned") to first determine the person's turnover for a financial year or calendar year ("the assessment year"), and

     (b)   at the end of the assessment year the person is connected with one or more other persons ("the connected persons").

(2)   For the purposes of determining whether the person qualifies as small for the tax year concerned the person's turnover for the assessment year is to be taken to be the sum of—

     (a)   the person's turnover for the assessment year, and

     (b)   the relevant turnover of each of the connected persons.

(3)   In subsection (2)(b) "the relevant turnover" of a connected person means—

     (a)   in a case where the connected person is a company, relevant undertaking or other undertaking, its turnover for its last financial year that is relevant to the tax year concerned, and

     (b)   in a case where the connected person is not a company, relevant undertaking or other undertaking, the turnover of the connected person for the last calendar year ending before the tax year concerned.

(4)   For the purposes of subsection (3)(a)—

     (a)   a financial year of a company or relevant undertaking is relevant to the tax year concerned if the period for filing accounts and reports for the financial year ends before the beginning of the tax year concerned, and

     (b)   a financial year of any other undertaking is relevant to the tax year concerned if it ends more than 9 months before the beginning of the tax year concerned.

(5)   In a case where—

     (a)   the person mentioned in subsection (1)(a) is a company or relevant undertaking, and

     (b)   at the end of the assessment period the person is a member of a group,

the person is to be treated for the purposes of this section as not being connected with any person that is a member of that group.

(6)   In this section—

"turnover", in relation to a person, means the amounts derived from the provision of goods or services after the deduction of trade discounts, value added tax and any other taxes based on the amounts so derived, and

"relevant undertaking" has the meaning given by section 60D.

(7) For provision determining whether one person is connected with another, see section 718 (connected persons).

(8) Expressions used in this section and in the Companies Act 2006 have the same meaning in this section as in that Act.

60H Duty on client to state whether it qualifies as small for a tax year

(1) This section applies if, in the case of an engagement that meets conditions (a) to (b) in section 49(1), the client receives from the client's agent or the worker a request to state whether in the client's opinion the client qualifies as small for a tax year specified in the request.

(2) The client must provide to the person who made the request a statement as to whether in the client's opinion the client qualifies as small for the tax year specified in the request.

(3) If the client fails to provide the statement by the time mentioned in subsection (4) the duty to do so is enforceable by an injunction or, in Scotland, by an order for specific performance under section 45 of the Court of Session Act 1988.

(4) The time is whichever is the later of—

    (a) the end of the period of 45 days beginning with the date the client receives the request, and

    (b) the beginning of the period of 45 days ending with the start of the tax year specified in the request.

(5) In this section "the client's agent" means a person with whom the client entered into a contract as part of the arrangements mentioned in paragraph (b) of section 49(1).

When a person has a UK connection

60I When a person has a UK connection for a tax year

(1) For the purposes of this Chapter, a person has a UK connection for a tax year if (and only if) immediately before the beginning of that tax year the person—

    (a) is resident in the United Kingdom, or

    (b) has a permanent establishment in the United Kingdom.

(2) In this section "permanent establishment"—

    (a) in relation to a company, is to be read (by virtue of section 1007A of ITA 2007) in accordance with Chapter 2 of Part 24 of CTA 2010, and

    (b) in relation to any other person, is to be read in accordance with that Chapter but as if references in that Chapter to a company were references to that person.

Interpretation"

6 In section 61(1) (interpretation), in the definition of company, before "means" insert "(except in sections 60A to 60G)".

PART 2

AMENDMENTS TO CHAPTER 10 OF PART 2 OF ITEPA 2003

7 Chapter 10 of Part 2 of ITEPA 2003 (workers' services provided to public sector through intermediaries) is amended as follows.

8 For the heading of the Chapter substitute "Workers' services provided through intermediaries to public authorities or medium or large clients".

9 (1) Section 61K (scope of Chapter) is amended as follows.

(2) In subsection (1) for the words "to a public authority through an intermediary" substitute "through an intermediary in a case where the services are provided to a person who—

    (a) is a public authority, or

    (b) qualifies as medium or large and has a UK connection for a tax year".

(3) After subsection (2) insert—

"(3)   For the purposes of this Chapter a person qualifies as medium or large for a tax year if the person does not qualify as small for the tax year for the purposes of Chapter 8 of this Part (see sections 60A to 60G).

(4)   Section 60I (when a person has a UK connection for a tax year) applies for the purposes of this Chapter."

10 In section 61L (meaning of "public authority") in subsection (1)—

    (a)   after paragraph (a) insert—

        "(aa) a body specified in section 23(3) of the Freedom of Information Act 2000,",

    (b)   omit the "or" at the end of paragraph (e), and

    (c)   after paragraph (f) insert ", or

        (g)   a company connected with any person mentioned in paragraphs (a) to (f)".

11 (1)   Section 61M (engagements to which the Chapter applies) is amended as follows.

(2)   In subsection (1)—

    (a)   omit paragraph (b),

    (b)   omit the "and" at the end of paragraph (c), and

    (c)   after paragraph (c) insert—

    "(ca) the client—

        (i)   is a public authority, or

        (ii)   is a person who qualifies as medium or large and has a UK connection for one or more tax years during which the arrangements mentioned in paragraph (c) have effect, and".

(3)   After subsection (1) insert—

"(1A)   But sections 61N to 61R do not apply if—

    (a)   the client is an individual, and

    (b)   the services are provided otherwise than for the purposes of the client's trade or business."

12 (1)   Section 61N (worker treated as receiving earnings from employment) is amended as follows.

(2)   In subsection (3)—

    (a)   after "subsections (5) to (7)" insert "and (8A)", and

    (b)   after "61T" insert ", 61TA".

(3)   For subsection (5) substitute—

"(5)   Unless and until the client gives a status determination statement to the worker (see section 61NA), subsections (3) and (4) have effect as if for any reference to the fee-payer there were substituted a reference to the client; but this is subject to section 61V.

(5A)   Subsections (6) and (7) apply, subject to sections 61T, 61TA and 61V, if—

    (a)   the client has given a status determination statement to the worker,

    (b)   the client is not the fee-payer, and

    (c)   the fee-payer is not a qualifying person."

(4)   In subsection (8) (meaning of "qualifying person") before paragraph (a) insert—

    "(za) has been given by the person immediately above them in the chain the status determination statement given by the client to the worker,".

(5)   After subsection (8) insert—

"(8A)   If the client is not a public authority, a person is to be treated by subsection (3) as making a deemed direct payment to the worker only if the chain payment made by the person is made in a tax year for which the client qualifies as medium or large and has a UK connection."

13 After section 61N insert—

"61NA   Meaning of status determination statement

(1)   For the purposes of section 61N "status determination statement" means a statement by the client that—

(a) states that the client has concluded that the condition in section 61M(1)(d) is met in the case of the engagement and explains the reasons for that conclusion, or

(b) states (albeit incorrectly) that the client has concluded that the condition in section 61M(1)(d) is not met in the case of the engagement and explains the reasons for that conclusion.

(2) But a statement is not a status determination statement if the client fails to take reasonable care in coming to the conclusion mentioned in it.

(3) For further provisions concerning status determination statements, see section 61T (client-led status disagreement process) and section 61TA (duty for client to withdraw status determination statement if it ceases to be medium or large)."

14 In section 61O(1) (conditions where intermediary is a company) for paragraph (b) substitute—

"(b) it is the case that—

(i) the worker has a material interest in the intermediary,

(ii) the worker has received a chain payment from the intermediary, or

(iii) the worker has rights which entitle, or which in any circumstances would entitle, the worker to receive a chain payment from the intermediary."

15 In section 61R (application of Income Tax Acts in relation to deemed employment) omit subsection (7).

16 For section 61T substitute—

"61T   Client-led status disagreement process

(1) This section applies if, before the final chain payment is made in the case of an engagement to which this Chapter applies, the worker or the deemed employer makes representations to the client that the conclusion contained in a status determination statement is incorrect.

(2) The client must either—

(a) give a statement to the worker or (as the case may be) the deemed employer that—

(i) states that the client has considered the representations and has decided that the conclusion contained in the status determination statement is correct, and

(ii) states the reasons for that decision, or

(b) give a new status determination statement to the worker and the deemed employer that—

(i) contains a different conclusion from the conclusion contained in the previous status determination statement,

(ii) states the date from which the client considers that the conclusion contained in the new status determination statement became correct, and

(iii) states that the previous status determination statement is withdrawn.

(3) If the client fails to comply with the duty in subsection (2) before the end of the period of 45 days beginning with the date the client receives the representations, section 61N(3) and (4) has effect from the end of that period until the duty is complied with as if for any reference to the fee-payer there were substituted a reference to the client; but this is subject to section 61V.

(4) A new status determination statement given to the deemed employer under subsection (2)(b) is to be treated for the purposes of section 61N(8)(za) as having been given to the deemed employer by the person immediately above the deemed employer in the chain.

(5) In this section—

"the deemed employer" means the person who, assuming one of conditions A to C in section 61N were met, would be treated as making a deemed direct payment to the worker under section 61N(3) on the making of a chain payment;

"status determination statement" has the meaning given by section 61NA.

61TA   Duty for client to withdraw status determination statement if it ceases to be medium or large

(1)   This section applies if in the case of an engagement to which this Chapter applies—

    (a)   the client is not a public authority,

    (b)   the client gives a status determination statement to the worker, the client's agent or both, and

    (c)   the client does not (but for this section) qualify as medium or large for a tax year beginning after the status determination statement is given.

(2)   Before the beginning of the tax year the client must give a statement to the relevant person, or (as the case may be) to both of the relevant persons, stating—

    (a)   that the client does not qualify as medium or large for the tax year, and

    (b)   that the status determination statement is withdrawn with effect from the beginning of the tax year.

(3)   If the client fails to comply with that duty the following rules apply in relation to the engagement for the tax year—

    (a)   the client is to be treated as medium or large for the tax year, and

    (b)   section 61N(3) and (4) have effect as if for any reference to the fee-payer there were substituted a reference to the client.

(4)   For the purposes of subsection (2)—

    (a)   the worker is a relevant person if the status determination statement was given to the worker, and

    (b)   the deemed employer is a relevant person if the status determination statement was given to the client's agent.

(5)   In this section—

"client's agent" means a person with whom the client entered into a contract as part of the arrangements mentioned in section 61M(1)(c);

"the deemed employer" means the person who, assuming one of conditions A to C in section 61N were met, would be treated as making a deemed direct payment to the worker under section 61N(3) on the making of a chain payment;

"status determination statement" has the meaning given by section 61NA."

17 (1)   Section 61W (prevention of double charge to tax and allowance of certain deductions) is amended as follows.

(2)   In subsection (1)—

    (a)   in paragraph (b) for "a public authority" substitute "another person ("the client")", and

    (b)   in paragraph (d) for "that public authority" substitute "the client".

(3)   In subsection (2)(b) for "public authority" substitute "client".

PART 3

CONSEQUENTIAL AND MISCELLANEOUS AMENDMENTS

18 In section 61D of ITEPA 2003 (managed service companies: worker treated as receiving earnings from employment) for subsection (4A) substitute—

"(4A)   This section does not apply where the provision of the relevant services gives rise (directly or indirectly) to an engagement to which Chapter 10 applies and either—

    (a)   the client for the purposes of section 61M(1) is a public authority, or

    (b)   the client for the purposes of section 61M(1)—

        (i)   qualifies as medium or large for the tax year in which the payment or benefit mentioned in subsection (1)(b) is received, and

        (ii)   has a UK connection for the tax year in which the payment or benefit mentioned in subsection (1)(b) is received.

(4B)   Sections 60I (when a person has a UK connection for a tax year), 61K(3) (when a person qualifies as medium or large for a tax year) and 61L (meaning of public authority) apply for the purposes of subsection (4A).

(4C)   It does not matter for the purposes of subsection (4A) whether the client for the purposes of this Chapter is also "the client" for the purposes of section 61M(1)."

19 After section 688A of ITEPA 2003 insert—

"688AA   Workers' services provided through intermediaries: recovery of PAYE

(1)   PAYE Regulations may make provision for, or in connection with, the recovery of a deemed employer PAYE debt from a relevant person.

(2)   "A deemed employer PAYE debt" means an amount—

(a)   that a person ("the deemed employer") is liable to pay under PAYE regulations in consequence of being treated under section 61N(3) as having made a deemed direct payment to a worker, and

(b)   that an officer of Revenue and Customs considers there is no realistic prospect of recovering from the deemed employer within a reasonable period.

(3)   "Relevant person", in relation to a deemed employer PAYE debt, means a person who is not the deemed employer and who—

(a)   is the highest person in the chain identified under section 61N(1) in determining that the deemed employer is to be treated as having made the deemed direct payment, or

(b)   is the second highest person in that chain and is a qualifying person (within the meaning given by section 61N(8)) at the time the deemed employer is treated as having made that deemed direct payment."

20 In section 60 of FA 2004 (construction industry scheme: meaning of contract payments) after subsection (3) insert—

"(3A)   This exception applies in so far as—

(a)   the payment can reasonably be taken to be for the services of an individual, and

(b)   the provision of those services gives rise to an engagement to which Chapter 10 of Part 2 of ITEPA 2003 applies (workers' services provided through intermediaries to public authorities or medium or large clients).

(3B)   But the exception in subsection (3A) does not apply if, in the case of the engagement mentioned in paragraph (b) of that subsection, the client for the purposes of section 61M(1) of ITEPA 2003—

(a)   is not a public authority, and

(b)   either—

(i)   does not qualify as medium or large for the tax year in which the payment concerned is made, or

(ii)   does not have a UK connection for the tax year in which the payment concerned is made.

(3C)   Sections 60I (when a person has a UK connection for a tax year), 61K(3) (when a person qualifies as medium or large for a tax year) and 61L (meaning of public authority) of ITEPA 2003 apply for the purposes of subsection (3B)."

21 For the italic heading before section 141A of CTA 2009 substitute "Worker's services provided through intermediary to public authority or medium or large client".

22 In the heading of section 141A of CTA 2009 for "public sector" substitute "public authority or medium or large client".

23 (1)   Part 13 of CTA 2009 (additional relief for expenditure on research and development) is amended as follows.

(2)   In section 1129 (qualifying expenditure on externally provided workers: connected persons) after subsection (4) insert—

"(4A)   In subsection (2) the reference to the staff provision payment is to that payment before any deduction is made from the payment under—

(a)   section 61S of ITEPA 2003,

(b)   regulation 19 of the Social Security Contributions (Intermediaries) Regulations 2000, or

(c)   regulation 19 of the Social Security Contributions (Intermediaries) (Northern Ireland) Regulations 2000."

(3)   In section 1131 (qualifying expenditure on externally provided workers: other cases) after subsection (2) insert—

"(3)   In subsection (2) the reference to the staff provision payment is to that payment before any deduction is made from the payment under—

(a)   section 61S of ITEPA 2003,

(b)   regulation 19 of the Social Security Contributions (Intermediaries) Regulations 2000, or

(c)   regulation 19 of the Social Security Contributions (Intermediaries) (Northern Ireland) Regulations 2000."

(4)   After section 1131 insert—

"1131A   Sections 1129 and 1131: secondary Class 1 NICS paid by company

(1)   This section applies if—

(a)   a company makes a staff provision payment,

(b)   the company is treated as making a payment of deemed direct earnings the amount of which is calculated by reference to the amount of the staff provision payment, and

(c)   the company pays a secondary Class 1 national insurance contribution in respect of the payment of deemed direct earnings.

(2)   In determining the company's qualifying expenditure on externally provided workers in accordance with section 1129(2) or section 1131(2) the amount of the staff payment provision is to be treated as increased by the amount of the contribution.

(3)   In determining the company's qualifying expenditure on externally provided workers in accordance with section 1129(2) the aggregate of the relevant expenditure of each staff controller is to be treated as increased by the amount of the contribution.

(4)   But subsection (2) does not apply to the extent that the expenditure incurred by the company in paying the contribution is met directly or indirectly by a staff controller.

(5)   "A payment of deemed direct earning" means a payment the company is treated as making by reason of regulation 14 of the Social Security Contributions (Intermediaries) Regulations 2000 or regulation 14 of the Social Security Contributions (Intermediaries) (Northern Ireland) Regulations 2000."

PART 4

COMMENCEMENT AND TRANSITIONAL PROVISIONS

Commencement

24 The amendments made by Part 1 of this Schedule have effect for the tax year 2021–22 and subsequent tax years.

25 The amendments made by Part 2 of this Schedule have effect in relation to deemed direct payments treated as made on or after 6 April 2021.

26 The amendment made by paragraph 18 of this Schedule has effect for the purposes of determining whether section 61D of ITEPA 2003 applies in a case where the payment or benefit mentioned in subsection (1)(b) of that section is received on or after 6 April 2021.

27 The amendment made by paragraph 20 of this Schedule has effect in relation to payments made under a construction contract on or after 6 April 2021.

28 The amendments made by paragraph 23 of this Schedule have effect in relation to expenditure incurred on or after 6 April 2021.

29 Sections 101 to 103 of FA 2009 (interest) come into force on 6 April 2021 in relation to amounts payable or paid to Her Majesty's Revenue and Customs under regulations made by virtue of section 688AA of ITEPA 2003 (as inserted by paragraph 19 of this Schedule).

Transitional provisions

30 (1)   This paragraph applies where—

(a)   the client in the case of an engagement to which Chapter 10 of Part 2 of ITEPA 2003 applies is not a public authority within the meaning given by section 61L of ITEPA 2003 (as that section had effect before the amendments made by paragraph 10 of this Schedule), and

(b)   a chain payment is made on or after 6 April 2021 that can reasonably be taken to be for services performed by the worker before 6 April 2021.

(2) The chain payment is to be disregarded for the purposes of Chapter 10 of Part 2 of ITEPA 2003.

31 (1) This paragraph applies where—

    (a)   the client in the case of an engagement to which Chapter 10 of Part 2 of ITEPA 2003 applies is not a public authority within the meaning given by section 61L of ITEPA 2003 (as that section had effect before the amendments made by paragraph 10 of this Schedule), and

    (b)   one or more qualifying chain payments are made in the tax year 2021–22 or a subsequent tax year ("the tax year concerned") to the intermediary.

(2) A chain payment made to the intermediary is a qualifying chain payment if it can reasonably be taken to be for services performed by the worker before 6 April 2021.

(3) A chain payment made to the intermediary is also a qualifying chain payment if—

    (a)   another chain payment ("the earlier payment") was made before 6 April 2021 to a person other than the intermediary,

    (b)   the earlier payment can reasonably be taken to be for the same services as the chain payment made to the intermediary, and

    (c)   the person who made the earlier payment would, but for paragraph 25 of this Schedule, have been treated by section 61N(3) and (4) of ITEPA 2003 as making a deemed direct payment to the worker at the same time as they made the earlier payment.

(4) Chapter 8 of Part 2 of ITEPA 2003 applies in relation to the engagement for the tax year concerned (in addition to Chapter 10 of Part 2 of ITEPA 2003), but as if—

    (a)   the amendments made by Part 1 of this Schedule had not been made, and

    (b)   the qualifying chain payments received by the intermediary in the tax year concerned are the only payments and benefits received by the intermediary in that year in respect of the engagement.

32 (1) This paragraph applies for the purposes of paragraphs 30 and 31 where a chain payment ("the actual payment") is made that can reasonably be taken to be for services of the worker performed during a period that begins before and ends on or after 6 April 2021.

(2) The actual payment is to be treated as two separate chain payments—

    (a)   one consisting of so much of the amount or value of the actual payment as can on a just and reasonable apportionment be taken to be for services performed before 6 April 2021, and

    (b)   another consisting of so much of the amount or value of the actual payment as can on a just and reasonable apportionment be taken to be for services performed on or after 6 April 2021.

33 For the purposes of section 61N(5), (5A)(a) and (8)(za) of ITEPA 2003 it does not matter whether the status determination statement concerned is given before 6 April 2021 or on or after that date.

34 For the purposes of section 61T of ITEPA 2003—

    (a)   it does not matter whether the representations to the client mentioned in subsection (1) of that section were made before 6 April 2021 or on or after that date, but

    (b)   in a case where the representations were made before 6 April 2021 that section has effect as if the reference in subsection (3) to the date the client receives the representations were to 6 April 2021.

COMMENTARY ON SCHEDULE 1

Schedule 1 amends the intermediaries' legislation (commonly referred to as 'IR35') in ITEPA 2003, Pt 2 Chs 8 and 10. It extends the regime which has applied to public sector organisations engaging workers via intermediaries since April 2017, to all engagers other than those defined as small.

IR35, named after the Inland Revenue press release which announced the measures in March 1999, came into force in April 2000. Despite a review by the Office of Tax Simplification in 2011 and various calls for reform, the regime remained unchanged until April 2017. Following 2015 Summer Budget, the Government released a discussion document seeking views on how to make IR35 more effective in protecting the Exchequer, raising concerns about the levels of non-compliance with the legislation and the corresponding loss of tax and National Insurance revenues. This was followed by an announcement on Budget Day 2016 that IR35 would be reformed for public sector organisations from April 2017 with a view to considering the private sector in due course. At the October 2018 Budget the Government announced that the public sector rules would be extended to all engagers other than those defined as small. The extension was due to take effect in April 2020 but has been deferred to April 2021 due to the COVID-19 outbreak.

Schedule 1, Part 1

Part 1 amends ITEPA 2003, ss 48–61 (Pt 2, Ch 8): Workers' services provided through intermediaries.

Paragraph 3

Paragraph 3 provides for the current rules in ITEPA 2003, ss 48–61 (Pt 2, Ch 8) to continue to apply to clients who are not public sector organisations and who are either small or do not have a UK connection in a tax year. Further detail on these criteria are set out in paragraph 5. This provision applies on a tax year by tax year basis such that clients will be best advised to keep their circumstances under review.

Where Chapter 8 applies, the intermediary providing the worker's services will be responsible for assessing employment status for IR35 purposes and for accounting for any PAYE and NIC due.

Paragraph 4

Where a client is an individual and is small, or does not have a UK connection, paragraph 4 ensures that ITEPA 2003, Pt 2, Ch 8 does not apply where the services provided by the intermediary are for private purposes rather than for the purposes of the client's business.

Paragraph 5

Paragraph 5 inserts new ITEPA 2003, ss 60A–60H to Chapter 8 which detail the conditions under which the client will qualify as small or not having a UK connection in a tax year.

ITEPA 2003, ss 60A–60G: When a person qualifies as small for a tax year

Companies

Where the client is a company, the qualifying criteria for being 'small' are as per the small companies' regime set out in Companies Act 2006, ss 382, 383. A company is small if it meets at least two of the following criteria for two consecutive financial years:

- turnover not exceeding £10.2m
- a balance sheet total (assets) not exceeding £5.1m
- an average of no more than 50 employees

A company is always small in its first financial year, unless it is excluded from the small companies' regime. Companies Act 2006, s 384 excludes public companies and certain companies in the financial services industry, together with members of groups containing traded companies, entities with securities traded on a regulated market in the EEA and certain financial services entities.

In assessing whether the IR35 rules in ITEPA 2003, ss 48–61 (Pt 2, Ch 8) apply to a specific tax year, a company will be small if the small companies' regime applies to the last financial year that is relevant to the tax year and also to the preceding financial year. A financial year is relevant to a tax year if the period for filing the company's accounts and reports for that financial year ends before the beginning of the tax year.

Example

The company's financial year ended on 30 September 2019. The accounts and reports for this year were due to be filed with Companies House by 30 June 2020 – in 2020/21. Unless there is a change in accounting date, the year ended 30 September 2019 is the last financial year for which the filing period ends before the tax year 2021/22. Hence the financial year to 30 September 2019 is relevant to 2021/22.

If a company ceases to meet the qualifying criteria for being small, it must apply the IR35 rules in ITEPA 2003, ss 61K–61X (Pt 2, Ch 10) from the start of the tax year following the filing date for the second financial year in which it ceases to meet the criteria. So in the above example, if the company met the qualifying criteria for being small for the year ended 30 September 2017, but failed to meet the criteria for each of the financial years to 30 September 2018 and 2019, it will have to apply the rules in ITEPA 2003, ss 61K–61X for 2021/22.

Joint ventures

A company that participates in a joint venture cannot be small if any of the other parties in the joint venture do not qualify as small.

Groups

A subsidiary company cannot be small where the group's parent does not qualify as small in relation to its last financial year that is relevant to the tax year concerned. A parent company can only qualify as small if the entire group qualifies as small.

The rules relating to companies in new ITEPA 2003, ss 60A–60C will also apply to limited liability partnerships.

Unincorporated businesses

Unincorporated businesses will only need to consider the turnover test to establish whether they are small. The test will be by reference to the last financial year ending at least nine months before the start of the tax year. As with companies, an unincorporated business will always be treated as small in its first financial year.

Similar rules apply to sole traders, but the test is based on the calendar year ending before the start of the tax year.

Connected persons

Turnover for the purposes of assessing whether an entity qualifies as small must include the turnover of each connected person (excluding group companies which are dealt with separately under the provisions for group companies). Connected persons are as defined in ITA 2007, s 993.

New ITEPA 2003, s 60H: Duty on client to state whether it qualifies as small for a tax year

Where an engagement is 'within IR35' such that the intermediary would be obliged to operate PAYE and NIC under ITEPA 2003, ss 48–61 (Pt 2, Ch 8), new section 60H provides for the worker or the client's agent to ask the client to confirm that they qualify as small for the tax year in question. The tax year must be specified in the request. This provision allows the worker and the agent to confirm that the obligation to operate PAYE and NIC does sit with the intermediary. On receipt of a request, the client must provide a statement that it qualifies as small for the tax year by the later of:

* 45 days after receipt of the request, and
* 45 days from the beginning of the tax year in question.

New ITEPA 2003, s 60I: When a person has a UK connection for a tax year

Clients that do not have a UK connection remain within the ITEPA 2003, ss 48–61 (Pt 2, Ch 8) rules such that the intermediary providing the worker's services will be responsible for assessing employment status for IR35 purposes and for accounting for any PAYE and NIC due. New ITEPA 2003, s 60I specifies that a client will be regarded as having a UK connection for a tax year if immediately before the beginning of the tax year it is UK tax resident or has a permanent establishment in the UK.

Schedule 1, Part 2

Part 2 amends ITEPA 2003, ss 61K–61X (Pt 2, Ch 10): Workers' services provided to public sector through intermediaries. Chapter 10 places the obligation for assessing the employment status of engagements for IR35 purposes on the client rather than the intermediary. The entity paying the intermediary is required to operate PAYE and NIC where an engagement is 'inside IR35.'

Paragraphs 9–11

Paragraph 9 extends the application of ITEPA 2003, Pt 2, Ch 10 beyond public authorities to include clients outside of the public sector who qualify as medium or large and have a UK connection for a tax year. Medium or large means not qualifying as small as set out in new ITEPA 2003, ss 60A–60G (as explained above). Having a UK connection is set out in section 60I (as explained above).

As with Chapter 8, Chapter 10 will not apply where the services provided by the intermediary are for private purposes rather than for the purposes of the client's business.

Paragraph 12

Under the existing legislation the client is only obliged to notify the party that they contract with (eg an employment agency) of whether they have assessed an engagement as 'inside' or 'outside' of IR35. There are no obligations on any party to inform the worker of the assessment, or for the status assessment to be communicated down the supply chain, for example where there are multiple agencies. This has resulted in a lack of visibility and clarity around obligations to operate PAYE and NIC where required and how to resolve disputes where parties in the supply chain do not agree with the client's status assessment.

Under the new rules, paragraph 12 provides that the client must provide a status determination statement (now defined in new ITEPA 2003, s 61NA – see below) both to the worker as well as to the party they contract with. Unless and until the client meets its obligations to provide the status determination statement to both parties, the client will be the fee-payer.

Where there is a longer contractual chain (eg multiple agencies) each recipient of the status determination statement is responsible for passing it down the contractual chain until it reaches the fee-payer. Failure to pass on the status determination statement will result in the entity at fault becoming the fee-payer.

Paragraph 13

Paragraph 13 introduces a new ITEPA 2003, s 61NA which defines a status determination statement.

The status determination statement is made by the client and must state in relation to the engagement that either:

- the client has concluded that the condition in ITEPA 2003, s 61M(1)(d) is met (ie that the engagement is 'inside' IR35) and the reasons for that conclusion, or
- the client has concluded that the condition in ITEPA 2003, s 61M(1)(d) is not met (ie that the engagement is 'outside' IR35) and the reasons for that conclusion.

The client must take reasonable care in reaching its conclusions. If it does not, any statement will not be a valid status determination statement, such that the client will not have met their obligations under the legislation, and they will be the fee-payer. Reasonable care, as established by case law, is the behaviour which is that of a prudent and reasonable person in the position of the person in question. In its guidance, HMRC acknowledges that the circumstances of clients completing status determination statements will vary greatly and that what is necessary for each client to discharge that responsibility should be viewed in the light of their abilities, experience, and circumstances. It is clearly important for clients to ensure that they have robust policies and processes in place in relation to status determinations and that they retain adequate records to demonstrate that they are taking reasonable care. HMRC's draft guidance can be found at ESM10014.

Paragraph 14

This paragraph amends ITEPA 2003, s 61O(1) which sets out the conditions that need to be met for ITEPA 2003, ss 61K–61X (Pt 2, Ch 10) to apply where the intermediary is a company. Under existing legislation, the individual worker must have a material interest in the company for Chapter 10 to apply. This amendment extends s 61O(1) to include situations where the worker not having a material interest has either received a chain payment from the intermediary, or the worker has rights which either entitle, or which in any circumstances would entitle, the worker to receive a chain payment from the intermediary.

Paragraph 15

This paragraph removes ITEPA 2003, s 61R(7). Section 61R(7) applies where the worker is UK resident and performs services in the UK, but where the client is non-resident and does not have a permanent establishment in the UK. Where the client pays the UK worker's intermediary directly (as opposed to via an agency or other intermediary) ITEPA 2003, s 61R(7) treats the non-resident client as UK tax resident for the purposes of ITEPA 2003, Pt 2, Ch 10. This section is largely irrelevant for public sector organisations but is more likely to apply to private sector organisations when the regime is extended to them. It has been criticised as a difficult provision to enforce given that the client has no UK tax presence and hence it will be removed. ITEPA 2003, ss 48–61 (Pt 2, Ch 8) will therefore apply to UK intermediaries paid directly by clients who are not UK resident and who do not have a permanent establishment in the UK. This is consistent with ITEPA 2003, s 60I per commentary on Part 1 above.

Paragraph 16

Paragraph 16 inserts new ITEPA 2003, ss 61T and 61TA into Chapter 10. Section 61T introduces the new client-led status disagreement process. Section 61TA imposes a duty on a client to withdraw a status determination statement if it ceases to be medium or large.

ITEPA 2003, s 61T: Client-led status disagreement process

The worker or their deemed employer can make representations to the client that a status determination statement is incorrect at any time during the engagement and prior to the final payment that is made in relation to the engagement. The end client is not obliged to respond to representations made outside of this timeframe.

The deemed employer will usually be the same person as the fee-payer, but it may be another person in the contractual chain if the fee-payer is not a qualifying person for example because the worker controls the fee-payer.

Within 45 days of receiving the representations, the client must provide to the worker or deemed employer either:

- a statement that the representations have been considered, it has been concluded that the status determination statement is correct and the reasons for the conclusions reached; or
- a new status determination statement with a different determination and the dates from which the new status determination applies and the previous determination is withdrawn.

Failure to meet these obligations will result in the client being the fee-payer.

ITEPA 2003, s 61TA: Duty for client to withdraw status determination statement if it ceases to be medium or large

Where a client that has provided a status determination statement no longer qualifies as medium or large for the next tax year, it must provide a statement to the worker and deemed employer (where applicable) stating that it no longer qualifies as medium or large and confirming that the status determination statement is withdrawn from the beginning of the next tax year. This statement must be provided before the beginning of the tax year in which the client ceases to qualify as medium or large. Failure to meet this obligation will result in the client continuing to be treated as medium or large for the tax year concerned.

Schedule 1, Part 3

Paragraph 19 amends the PAYE provisions in ITEPA 2003 by inserting new section 688AA. It allows for the PAYE regulations to be amended to provide for the recovery of a PAYE debt from the client or from the first agency in the contractual chain (if that agency is not the deemed employer), where HMRC have no realistic prospect of recovering the PAYE debt from the deemed employer within a reasonable period.

Schedule 1, Part 4

These provisions take effect for 2021/22 and subsequent tax years and will apply to payments made to intermediaries on or after 6 April 2021. For private sector organisations, there is an exclusion for payments which can reasonably be taken to relate to services performed by the worker before 6 April 2021 with provision for apportionment where the payment covers services performed before 6 April 2021 and on or after 6 April 2021.

SCHEDULE 2

THE LOAN CHARGE: CONSEQUENTIAL AMENDMENTS

Sections 15 and 16

PART 1

AMENDMENTS TO F(NO 2)A 2017 IN CONSEQUENCE OF SECTION 15

1 Schedule 11 to F(No.2)A 2017 (employment income provided through third parties: loans etc outstanding on 5 April 2019) is amended as follows.

2 In paragraph 1 (application of Part 7A of ITEPA 2003: relevant step) in sub-paragraph (2) for the words from "before" to the end substitute "before the end of 5 April 2019."

3 For the italic heading before paragraph 2 substitute "Meaning of "loan" and "quasi loan"".

4 In paragraph 2 (meaning of "loan", "quasi-loan" and "approved repayment date") omit sub-paragraph (6).

5 (1) Paragraph 4 (when an amount of a loan is outstanding: certain repayments to be disregarded) is amended as follows.

(2) In sub-paragraph (1)(b)(ii) for "the relevant date" substitute "5 April 2019".

(3) In sub-paragraph (2) for "the relevant date" substitute "5 April 2019".

(4) Omit sub-paragraph (4).

6 In paragraph 5 (meaning of "outstanding": loans where A or B acquires a right to payment of the loan) in sub-paragraph (1)(b) for "6 April 1999" substitute "9 December 2010".

7 In paragraph 13 (meaning of "outstanding": quasi-loans where A or B acquires a right to the payment or transfer of assets) in sub-paragraph (1)(b) for "6 April 1999" substitute "9 December 2010".

8 Omit paragraph 19 (meaning of "approved fixed term loan") and the italic heading before that paragraph.

9 For the heading of Part 2 substitute "Accelerated payments".

10 Omit paragraphs 20 to 22 and the italic headings before each of those paragraphs.

11 Omit the italic heading before paragraph 23.

12 (1) Paragraph 23 (accelerated payments) is amended as follows.

(2) In sub-paragraph (1)—

    (a) in paragraph (d) for "the relevant date" substitute "5 April 2019", and
    (b) in paragraph (e) for "the relevant date" substitute "5 April 2019".

(3) Omit sub-paragraph (4).

13 (1) Paragraph 35A (when the duty to provide loan charge information arises) is amended as follows.

(2) Omit sub-paragraph (3).

(3) In sub-paragraph (4) in the words before paragraph (a) for "third" substitute "second".

(4) In sub-paragraph (5)—

    (a) in the words before paragraph (a) for "fourth" substitute "third",
    (b) in paragraph (a) for the words from the beginning to "conditions" substitute "neither the first nor the second condition", and
    (c) in paragraph (b)—

        (i) for "and (2)(b)" substitute "and (2)", and
        (ii) omit the words from "(and if paragraph" to "omitted)".

(5) In sub-paragraph (6) in the words before paragraph (a) for "fourth" substitute "third".

(6) In sub-paragraph (7) omit paragraph (b).

14 In paragraph 35B (duty of appropriate third party to provide information to A) in sub-paragraph (1) omit "Q,".

15 (1)   Paragraph 35D (meaning of "loan charge information") is amended as follows.

(2)   In sub-paragraph (1)—

(a)   in paragraph (e) omit ", or the loan mentioned in paragraph 35A(3)(a),",

(b)   in paragraph (j) omit ", Q", and

(c)   in paragraph (k) omit ", or in a case within paragraph 35A(3)(a),".

(3)   In sub-paragraph (2) omit paragraph (a).

16 (1)   Paragraph 36 (duty to provide loan charge information to B) is amended as follows.

(2)   In sub-paragraph (1)(b) for "6 April 1999" substitute "9 December 2010".

(3)   In sub-paragraph (2) for the words from "the period" to the end substitute "15 April 2019".

(4)   Omit sub-paragraph (4).

17 Schedule 12 to F(No.2)A 2017 (trading income provided through third parties: loans etc outstanding on 5 April 2019) is amended as follows.

18 For the italic heading before paragraph 2 substitute "Meaning of "loan" and "quasi loan"".

19 In paragraph 2 (meaning of "loan", "quasi-loan" and "approved repayment date") omit sub-paragraph (6).

20 Omit paragraphs 15 to 18 and the italic heading before each of those paragraphs.

21 (1)   Paragraph 19 (accelerated payments: application of paragraph 20) is amended as follows.

(2)   In sub-paragraph (1)—

(a)   in paragraph (e) for "the relevant date" substitute "5 April 2019", and

(b)   in paragraph (f) for "the relevant date" substitute "5 April 2019".

(3)   Omit sub-paragraph (3).

22 In paragraph 23 (meaning of "loan charge information") in sub-paragraph (2) omit paragraph (a).

PART 2
AMENDMENTS IN CONSEQUENCE OF SECTION 16
ITEPA 2003

23 ITEPA 2003 is amended as follows.

24 (1)   Section 554A (application of Chapter 2 of Part 7A: the main case) is amended as follows.

(2)   In subsection (2) after "paragraph 1" insert "or 1A".

(3)   For subsection (4) substitute—

"(4)   Chapter 2 does not apply by reason of—

(a)   a relevant step taken on or after A's death if—

(i)   the relevant step is within section 554B, or

(ii)   the relevant step is within section 554C by virtue of subsection (1)(ab) of that section,

(b)   a relevant step within paragraph 1 of Schedule 11 to F(No.2)A 2017 which is treated as being taken on or after A's death, or

(c)   a relevant step within paragraph 1A of Schedule 11 to F(No.2)A 2017 in a case where the initial step (within the meaning given by sub-paragraph (1)(a) of that paragraph) is treated as being taken on or after A's death."

25 In section 554Z (interpretation: general) in subsection (10)(d) after "paragraph 1" insert "or 1A".

F(No.2)A 2017

26 Schedule 11 to F(No.2)A 2017 (employment income provided through third parties: loans etc outstanding on 5 April 2019) is amended as follows.

27 In paragraph 2 (meaning of "loan", "quasi-loan" and "approved repayment date")—

(a)   in sub-paragraph (2), in the words before paragraph (a), for "paragraph 1" substitute "paragraphs 1 and 1A",

(b)   in sub-paragraph (4) for "paragraph 1" substitute "paragraphs 1 and 1A", and

(c)   in sub-paragraph (5) for "paragraph 1" substitute "paragraphs 1 and 1A".

28 In paragraph 3(1) (meaning of "outstanding": loans) for "paragraph 1" substitute "paragraphs 1 and 1A".

29 In paragraph 4 (when an amount of a loan is outstanding: certain repayments to be disregarded) in sub-paragraph (6) for "the relevant step treated as taken by paragraph 1" substitute "a relevant step treated as taken by paragraph 1 or 1A".

30 In paragraph 5 (meaning of "outstanding": loans where A or B acquires a right to payment of the loan) in sub-paragraph (2)(b) for "paragraph 1(4)" substitute "paragraphs 1(4) and 1A(5)".

31 In paragraph 7 (meaning of "outstanding": loans in currencies other than stirling) in sub-paragraph (3) after "relevant step" insert "within paragraph 1".

32 In paragraph 10 (meaning of "outstanding": loans made in a depreciating currency) in sub-paragraph (1)(b) after "relevant step" insert "within paragraph 1".

33 In paragraph 11(1) (meaning of "outstanding": quasi-loans) for "paragraph 1" substitute "paragraphs 1 and 1A".

34 In paragraph 12 (certain payments or transfers to be disregarded for the purposes of paragraph 11) in sub-paragraph (5) for "the relevant step treated as taken by paragraph 1" substitute "a relevant step treated as taken by paragraph 1 or 1A".

35 In paragraph 13 (meaning of "outstanding": quasi-loans where A or B acquires a right to the payment or transfer of assets) in sub-paragraph (2)(b) for "paragraph 1(4)" substitute "paragraphs 1(4) and 1A(5)".

36 In paragraph 15 (meaning of "outstanding": quasi-loans in currencies other than sterling) in sub-paragraph (3) after "relevant step" insert "within paragraph 1".

37 In paragraph 18 (meaning of "outstanding": quasi-loans made in a depreciating currency) in sub-paragraph (1)(b) after "relevant step" insert "within paragraph 1".

38 After paragraph 35 insert—

"Exclusion for relevant step within paragraph 1A where initial step excluded

35ZA Chapter 2 of Part 7A of ITEPA 2003 does not apply by reason of a relevant step within paragraph 1A if that Chapter does not apply by reason of the initial step (within the meaning given by sub-paragraph (1)(a) of paragraph 1A)."

Social Security (Contributions) Regulations 2001

39 (1)   The Social Security (Contributions) Regulations 2001 (S.I. 2001/1004) are amended as follows.

(2)   In regulation 22B (amounts to be treated as earnings: Part 7A of ITEPA 2003) in paragraph (3A)(a) after "paragraph 1" insert "or 1A".

(3)   In regulation 22C (amounts to be treated as earnings paid to or for the benefit of the earner: Schedule 11 to F(No.2)A 2017) in paragraph (1)—

(a)   after "paragraph 1" insert "or 1A", and

(b)   after "paragraph 1(2)" insert "or 1A(3) or (4)".

COMMENTARY ON SCHEDULE 2

Schedule 2 provides consequential drafting amendments relating to sections 15 and 16 and contains nothing of substance. [See Commentary note for sections 15 and 16]

SCHEDULE 3
ENTREPRENEURS' RELIEF

Section 23

PART 1
REDUCTION IN LIFETIME LIMIT

Reduction in lifetime limit

1 In section 169N of TCGA 1992 (entrepreneurs' relief: amount of relief)—

    (a)   in subsection (4), for "£10 million" substitute "£1 million";

    (b)   in subsection (4A), for "£10 million" substitute "£1 million".

Commencement

2 The amendments made by paragraph 1 have effect in relation to disposals made on or after 11 March 2020.

Anti-forestalling: unconditional contracts

3 (1)   This paragraph applies where an asset is conveyed or transferred on or after 11 March 2020 under a contract made before that date that is not conditional.

(2)   Despite section 28(1) of TCGA 1992 (disposal under unconditional contract made at time of contract and not at time of later conveyance or transfer), the disposal is to be treated for the purposes of paragraph 2 as taking place at the time the asset is conveyed or transferred, and not at the time the contract is made, unless the condition in sub-paragraph (3) or (4) is met.

(3)   The condition in this sub-paragraph is that—

    (a)   the parties to the contract are not connected persons,

    (b)   no purpose of entering into the contract was obtaining an advantage by reason of the application of section 28(1) of TCGA 1992, and

    (c)   the person making the conveyance or transfer makes a claim which includes a statement that the condition in paragraph (b) is met.

(4)   The condition in this sub-paragraph is that—

    (a)   the parties to the contract are connected persons,

    (b)   the contract was entered into wholly for commercial reasons,

    (c)   no purpose of entering into the contract was obtaining an advantage by reason of the application of section 28(1) of TCGA 1992, and

    (d)   the person making the conveyance or transfer makes a claim which includes a statement that the conditions in paragraphs (b) and (c) are met.

(5)   Section 169M(2) and (3) of TCGA 1992 apply to a claim under sub-paragraph (3)(c) or (4)(d) as if it were a claim under that section.

Anti-forestalling: reorganisations of share capital

4 (1)   This paragraph applies where—

    (a)   on or after 6 April 2019 but before 11 March 2020, there is a reorganisation, and

    (b)   on 11 March 2020—

        (i)   the company is the relevant individual's personal company and is either a trading company or the holding company of a trading group, and

        (ii)   the relevant individual is an officer or employee of the company or (if the company is a member of a trading group) of one or more companies which are members of the trading group.

(2)   In sub-paragraph (1) "the relevant individual" means—

    (a)   where a claim under section 169M of TCGA 1992 is made jointly by the trustees of a settlement and a qualifying beneficiary, the qualifying beneficiary;

    (b)   where a claim under that section is made by an individual, the individual.

(3)   Where an election in respect of the reorganisation is made under section 169Q of TCGA 1992 (reorganisations: disapplication of section 127) on or after 11 March 2020,

the disposal of the original shares is to be treated for the purposes of paragraph 2 as taking place at the time of the election and not at the time of the reorganisation.

(4) References in this paragraph to a reorganisation do not include an exchange of shares or securities which is treated as a reorganisation by virtue of section 135 or 136 of TCGA 1992 (but see paragraph 5).

Anti-forestalling: exchanges of securities etc

5 (1) This paragraph applies where—

  (a) on or after 6 April 2019 but before 11 March 2020, there is an exchange of shares or securities within section 135(1) of TCGA 1992, and

  (b) the condition in sub-paragraph (2) or (3) is met.

(2) The condition in this sub-paragraph is that—

  (a) the persons who hold shares or securities in company B immediately after the exchange are substantially the same as those who held shares or securities in company A immediately before the exchange, or

  (b) the persons who have control of company B immediately after the exchange are substantially the same as those who had control of company A immediately before the exchange.

(3) The condition in this sub-paragraph is that—

  (a) the relevant shareholders, taken together, hold a greater percentage of the ordinary share capital in company B immediately after the exchange than they held in company A immediately before the exchange, and

  (b) on 11 March 2020—

    (i) company B is the relevant individual's personal company and is either a trading company or the holding company of a trading group, and

    (ii) the relevant individual is an officer or employee of company B or (if company B is a member of a trading group) of one or more companies which are members of the trading group.

(4) In sub-paragraph (3)—

"the relevant individual" means—

  (a) where a claim under section 169M of TCGA 1992 is made jointly by the trustees of a settlement and a qualifying beneficiary, the qualifying beneficiary;

  (b) where a claim under that section is made by an individual, the individual;

"the relevant shareholders" means the persons who—

  (a) immediately after the exchange, hold shares or securities in company B, and

  (b) immediately before the exchange, also held shares or securities in company A.

(5) For the purposes of sub-paragraph (2)(a), connected persons are to be treated as the same person.

(6) Where an election in respect of the exchange is made under section 169Q of TCGA 1992 (reorganisations: disapplication of section 127) on or after 11 March 2020, the disposal of the original shares is to be treated for the purposes of paragraph 2 as taking place at the time of the election and not at the time of the exchange.

(7) Where, before the exchange, the Commissioners for Her Majesty's Revenue and Customs have issued a notification in respect of it under section 138(1) of TCGA 1992 (advance clearance procedure)—

  (a) sections 127 to 131 of that Act apply with the necessary adaptations as if—

    (i) company A and company B were the same company, and

    (ii) the exchange were a reorganisation;

  (b) section 169Q of that Act applies as if the exchange were treated as a reorganisation by virtue of section 135 of that Act.

Interpretation

6 (1) Paragraphs 2 to 5 are to be construed as if they were contained in Chapter 3 of Part 5 of TCGA 1992, subject to sub-paragraph (2).

(2) In those paragraphs—

"company A" and "company B" have the same meanings as in section 135 of TCGA 1992;

"original shares" has the meaning given by section 126 of TCGA 1992;

"reorganisation" has the meaning given by that section;

"trading company" and "trading group" have the meanings given by paragraph 1 of Schedule 7ZA to TCGA 1992.

PART 2

RE-NAMING THE RELIEF

7 (1) In section 169H(1) of TCGA 1992 (relief under Chapter 3 of Part 5: introduction), for "to be known as "entrepreneurs' relief"" substitute "to be known as "business asset disposal relief"".

(2) In consequence of that amendment—

    (a)   in the rest of TCGA 1992, for "entrepreneurs' relief", wherever occurring, substitute "business asset disposal relief";

    (b)   in section 169V of TCGA 1992 (operation of deferred entrepreneurs' relief), for "ER purposes", wherever occurring, substitute "relevant purposes".

(3) Nothing in this paragraph affects the operation of Chapter 3 of Part 5 of TCGA 1992.

8 This Part of this Schedule has effect for the tax year 2020–21 and subsequent tax years.

COMMENTARY ON SCHEDULE 3

Part 1 of Schedule 3 reduces the lifetime limit for capital gains tax entrepreneurs' relief from £10 million to £1 million for disposals on or after Budget Day, 11 March 2020.

The relief provides for a reduced rate of CGT of 10% to apply to gains on disposals by individuals of all or part of their business or of shares in their personal company, and disposals by trustees of business assets. Relief is only available to a particular taxpayer up to a maximum amount of gains over the lifetime of the taxpayer (so that it might be used up entirely by a single disposal or spread over two or more disposals relating to different businesses). The lifetime limit has been increased several times but this is the first reduction. There is no clawback of relief previously given in consequence of the reduction.

Although there was no consultation or other pre-announcement of this measure, following criticisms levelled at the relief there was some anticipation that changes to the relief could be made or even that the relief would be abolished. In October 2019, for example, the Institute for Fiscal Studies (IFS) commented that 'if one of the aims of reduced capital gains tax rates on business assets is to incentivise individuals to invest more in their business, [the] evidence suggests they are not working'. The IFS estimated that entrepreneurs' relief cost the Government £2.4 billion a year.

There are no transitional rules in Schedule 3. The £1 million limit will therefore apply to cases where negotiations for sale were underway before 11 March 2020 but no contract had been entered into or where the business ceased before 11 March 2020 but the disposal is on or after that date. It will also apply to associated disposals (TCGA 1992, s 169K) where the disposal of business assets was before 11 March 2020 and to deferred gains coming back into charge as a result of a chargeable event (TCGA 1992, ss 169T–169V) occurring on or after that date.

Following the speculation about changes to the relief it is perhaps unsurprising that some taxpayers took action in the run up to Budget Day with the intention of securing their entitlement to the £10 million lifetime limit. As a result, paragraphs 3–5 of Schedule 3 contain rules ('anti-forestalling rules') to counter three types of arrangements of which HMRC was aware, as follows.

- Arrangements which seek to exploit the rule in TCGA 1992, s 28(1) which fixes the time of disposal for CGT purposes as the date of an unconditional contract rather than the date when the contract is completed (by conveyance etc). The arrangements seen by HMRC typically consist of a sale before 11 March 2020 to a specially created company or other vehicle where the buyer 'stands on contract' (ie does not complete the contract) until a further purchaser is found. The normal effect would be for the disposal to be treated as before 11 March 2020 and therefore for the £10 million limit to apply. The anti-forestalling rule treats the disposal as taking place on completion, so that if completion is on or after 11 March 2020, the £1 million limit applies. This treatment is only for the purpose of applying the change in the lifetime limit and does not affect the disposal date for other CGT purposes (such as determining the tax year of disposal). Note that the exceptions to this rule for commercial transactions do not apply if there is any purpose of obtaining a tax advantage as a result of s 28(1). There is no exception where such a purpose is insignificant.

- The second rule applies to arrangements seeking to exploit the rule in TCGA 1992, s 169Q, which allows an election to be made to disapply the reorganisation of share capital rules in TCGA 1992, s 126 so that there is a disposal of the old shares which can qualify for entrepreneurs' relief. The rule is aimed at cases where the same person owns affected shares before and after the reorganisation and could have made a claim for entrepreneurs' relief on a disposal of the new shares on 11 March 2020. The rule is limited to reorganisations between 6 April 2019 and 11 March 2020 but there is no motive test or exception for wholly commercial transactions.

- The third rule is similar to the second but applies only to share exchanges within TCGA 1992, s 135(1) (such exchanges being specifically excluded from the second rule). It applies to two types of case and HMRC has given examples of where each would apply. The first case (para 5(2)) would include a situation where three equal shareholders in company A (each holding one third of the shares) have different holdings in company B (say, 20%, 20% and 60%) following the exchange. The second case (para 5(3)) would include a situation where before the exchange there are three equal shareholders in company A (each holding one third of the shares) and after the exchange, and the exit or retirement of one of the shareholders, the remaining two original shareholders each have a 50% share in company B. Paragraph 5(7) is difficult to follow, but it applies where HMRC has given advance clearance (under TCGA 1992, s 138) in respect of a share exchange to which the anti-forestalling rule applies. In effect, in such circumstances, the anti-avoidance rule in TCGA 1992, s 137 is disapplied so that it is not possible for the taxpayer to claim that the anti-avoidance rule should in fact apply. If such a claim were made, the consequence would otherwise be that the share exchange rules would not apply and there would be a disposal of the shares or securities in company A at the time of the exchange (ie before 11 March 2020).

HMRC has indicated that published guidance will include worked examples of when the anti-forestalling rules will apply.

There are no anti-forestalling rules relating to schemes of reconstruction within TCGA 1992, s 136 or to elections under TCGA 1992, s 169R (where qualifying corporate bonds are acquired in a reorganisation).

Anyone who is uncertain whether the anti-forestalling rules apply to a particular case can seek advice from HMRC using the Non-Statutory Clearance Service, subject to the normal conditions. The Service will be available for this purpose from the date of Royal Assent.

Part 2 of Schedule 3 changes the name of entrepreneurs' relief to 'business asset disposal relief' for 2020/21 onwards. The change was unexpected and unexplained.

SCHEDULE 4

CORPORATE CAPITAL LOSSES

Section 25

PART 1

CORPORATE CAPITAL LOSS RESTRICTION

Restriction on deduction from chargeable gains: main provisions

1 Part 7ZA of CTA 2010 (restrictions on obtaining certain deductions) is amended as follows.

2 After section 269ZB insert—

"269ZBA   Restriction on deductions from chargeable gains

(1) This section has effect for determining the taxable total profits of a company for an accounting period.

(2) The sum of any deductions made by the company for the accounting period under section 2A(1)(b) of TCGA 1992 (allowable losses accruing in earlier accounting periods) may not exceed the relevant maximum.

But this is subject to subsection (7).

(3) In this section the "relevant maximum" means the sum of—

    (a)   50% of the company's relevant chargeable gains for the accounting period, and

    (b)   the amount of the company's chargeable gains deductions allowance for the accounting period.

(4) Section 269ZF contains provision for determining a company's relevant chargeable gains for an accounting period.

(5) A company's "chargeable gains deductions allowance" for an accounting period—

    (a)   is so much of the company's deductions allowance for the period as is specified in the company's tax return as its chargeable gains deductions allowance for the period, and

    (b)   accordingly, is nil if no amount of the company's deductions allowance for the period is so specified.

(6) An amount specified under subsection (5)(a) as a company's chargeable gains deductions allowance for an accounting period may not exceed the difference between—

    (a)   the amount of the company's deductions allowance for the period, and

    (b)   the total of any amounts specified for the period under—

        (i)   section 269ZB(7)(a) (trading profits deductions allowance),

        (ii)   section 269ZC(5)(a) (non-trading income profits deductions allowance), and

        (iii)   in the case of an insurance company, section 269ZFC(5)(a) (BLAGAB deductions allowance).

(7) Subsection (2) does not apply in relation to a company for an accounting period where, in determining the company's qualifying chargeable gains for the period, the amount given by step 1 in section 269ZF(3) is not greater than nil."

3 (1) Section 269ZC (restriction on deductions from non-trading profits) is amended in accordance with this paragraph.

(2) In subsection (2), for "the relevant maximum" substitute "the difference between—

    (a)   the relevant maximum, and

    (b)   the amount of any deductions made by the company for the accounting period under section 2A(1)(b) of TCGA 1992 (allowable losses accruing in earlier accounting periods)."

(3) For subsection (3) substitute—

    "(3) In this section the "relevant maximum" means the sum of—

        (a)   50% of the company's total relevant non-trading profits for the accounting period, and

(b)   the amount of the company's total non-trading profits deductions allowance for the accounting period.

(3A)   A company's "total non-trading profits deductions allowance" for the accounting period is the sum of—

(a)   the company's non-trading income profits deductions allowance (see subsection (5)), and

(b)   the company's chargeable gains deductions allowance (see section 269ZBA(5))."

(4)   In subsection (4), for "relevant non-trading profits" substitute "total relevant non-trading profits".

(5)   In subsection (5) for ""non-trading profits deductions allowance"", in both places it occurs, substitute ""non-trading income profits deductions allowance"".

(6)   In subsection (6)—

(a)   in the words before paragraph (a), for ""non-trading profits deductions allowance"" substitute ""non-trading income profits deductions allowance"", and

(b)   for paragraph (b) substitute—

"(b)   the total of any amounts specified for the period under—

(i)   section 269ZB(7)(a) (trading profits deductions allowance),

(ii)   section 269ZBA(5)(a) (chargeable gains deductions allowance), and

(iii)   in the case of an insurance company, section 269ZFC(5)(a) (BLAGAB deductions allowance)."

(7)   In subsection (8), for "relevant non-trading profits" substitute "qualifying non-trading income profits and qualifying chargeable gains".

4 In section 269ZD (restriction on deductions from total profits), in subsection (2)(b), after sub-paragraph (i) (before the "and") insert—

"(ia)   any deductions made by the company for the accounting period under section 2A(1)(b) of TCGA 1992 (allowable losses accruing in earlier accounting periods),".

5 In section 269ZF (relevant profits), after subsection (2) insert—

"(2A)   A company's "relevant chargeable gains" for an accounting period are—

(a)   the company's qualifying chargeable gains for the accounting period (see subsection (3)), less

(b)   the company's chargeable gains deductions allowance for the accounting period (see section 269ZBA(5)).

But if the allowance mentioned in paragraph (b) exceeds the qualifying chargeable gains mentioned in paragraph (a), the company's "relevant chargeable gains" for the accounting period are nil.

(2B)   A company's "total relevant non-trading profits" for an accounting period are—

(a)   the sum of—

(i)   the company's qualifying non-trading income profits for the period, and

(ii)   the company's qualifying chargeable gains for the period, less

(b)   the company's total non-trading profits deductions allowance for the period (see section 269ZC(3A))."

6 In section 269ZF, in subsection (3), for steps 3 to 5 substitute—

"Step 3—trading profits, non-trading income profits and chargeable gains

Divide the company's total profits for the accounting period (as modified under step 1(2)) into—

(a)   profits of a trade of the company (the company's "trading profits"),

(b)   profits, other than chargeable gains, that are not profits of a trade of the company (the company's "non-trading income profits"), and

(c)   chargeable gains included in the total profits (the company's "chargeable gains").

Step 4—apportionment of the step 2 amount

(1)   Allocate the whole of the step 2 amount to one of, or between two or all of, the following—

  (a)   the company's trading profits,
  (b)   the company's non-trading income profits, and
  (c)   the company's chargeable gains.

(2)   Reduce, but not below nil, each of the company's trading profits, non-trading income profits and chargeable gains by the amount (if any) allocated to it under paragraph (1).

Step 5—amount of qualifying trading profits, qualifying non-trading income profits and qualifying chargeable gains

The amounts resulting from step 3, after any reduction under step 4, are—

  (a)   in the case of the amount in step 3(a), the company's qualifying trading profits,
  (b)   in the case of the amount in step 3(b), the company's qualifying non-trading income profits, and
  (c)   in the case of the amount in step 3(c), the company's qualifying chargeable gains."

7 In section 269ZF(4) (calculation of modified total profits)—

  (a)   omit "and" at the end of paragraph (f), and
  (b)   after paragraph (g) insert "; and

  (h)   make no deductions under section 2A(1)(b) of TCGA 1992 (allowable losses accruing in earlier accounting periods)."

Insolvent companies

8 After section 269ZW insert—

"269ZWA   Increase of deductions allowance for insolvent companies

(1)   This section applies in relation to a company if—

  (a)   the company has gone into insolvent liquidation (see subsection (4)), or
  (b)   a corresponding situation exists in relation to the company in a country or territory outside the United Kingdom.

(2)   The company's deductions allowance for a winding up accounting period (as determined in accordance with section 269ZR or 269ZW) is to be treated (for all purposes) as increased by—

  (a)   the amount of chargeable gains accruing to the company in the accounting period after deducting any allowable losses accruing to the company in the period, or
  (b)   if lower, the amount of any allowable losses previously accruing to the company, so far as not previously deducted under section 2A(1) of TCGA 1992.

(3)   In determining the amount of chargeable gains accruing to the company in a winding up accounting period for the purposes of subsection (2), ignore—

  (a)   any chargeable gains (but not any allowable losses) accruing to the company on the disposal of an asset if—

    (i)   section 171(1) of TCGA 1992 (transfers within a group: no gain no loss) applied in relation to the disposal by which the company acquired the asset (the "no gain/no loss disposal"),
    (ii)   the asset was acquired by the company, by virtue of the no gain/no loss disposal, in a winding up accounting period, and
    (iii)   the company making the no gain/no loss disposal has not, at that time, gone into insolvent liquidation, and

  (b)   any chargeable gains (but not any allowable losses) transferred to the company in accordance with an election made under section 171A of TCGA 1992 (election to reallocate gain or loss to another member of the group) if—

    (i)   the election is made in a winding up accounting period, and

  (ii) the company from which the chargeable gain is transferred has not, at the time the election is made, gone into insolvent liquidation.

(4) For the purposes of this section, a company has gone into insolvent liquidation if—

  (a) it has gone into liquidation, within the meaning of section 247(2) of the Insolvency Act 1986 or article 6(2) of the Insolvency (Northern Ireland) Order 1989 (SI 1989/2405 (NI 19), and

  (b) at the time it goes into liquidation, its assets are insufficient for the payment of its debts and other liabilities and the expenses of the winding up.

(5) In this section a "winding up accounting period" means—

  (a) the accounting period of the company that begins when the winding up starts (within the meaning of section 12(7) of CTA 2009), and

  (b) each subsequent accounting period."

9 In section 269ZZ (company tax return to specify amount of deductions allowance), in subsection (1), after paragraph (a) (but before the "and") insert—

  "(aa) if section 269ZWA (increase of deductions allowance for insolvent companies) applies, what that amount would be without the increase provided for by subsection (2) of that section,".

Companies without a source of chargeable income

10 After section 269ZY of CTA 2010 insert—

"269ZYA Deductions allowance for company without a source of chargeable income

(1) This section applies in relation to a company and a financial year ("the relevant financial year") if—

  (a) the company has no source of chargeable income (see subsection (2)) throughout the relevant financial year, and

  (b) if the company is a member of a group (see section 269ZZB) at any time during the relevant financial year, each other company that is, at any time during the relevant financial year, a member of the group has no source of chargeable income throughout the relevant financial year.

(2) For the purposes of this section and section 269ZYB, a company "has no source of chargeable income" if the company is either—

  (a) not within the charge to corporation tax, or

  (b) chargeable to corporation tax only because of a chargeable gain accruing to the company on the disposal of an asset.

(3) A company may make a claim under this section in respect of an accounting period if—

  (a) the accounting period falls wholly within the relevant financial year, and

  (b) the company is chargeable to corporation tax for the accounting period only because of a chargeable gain accruing to the company on the disposal of an asset.

(4) If a claim is made by a company under this section in respect of an accounting period (a "claim AP"), the company's deductions allowance for the claim AP is the lower of—

  (a) the available deductions allowance amount (see subsection (9)),

  (b) the total amount of allowable losses accruing to the company in any previous accounting period, so far as not previously deducted under section 2A(1)(a) or (b) of TCGA 1992, and

  (c) the chargeable gains accruing to the company in the claim AP.

(5) A claim under this section in respect of an accounting period—

  (a) must be made within the period of two years after the end of the accounting period, but

  (b) may not be made before the end of the relevant financial year.

(6) Sections 269ZR to 269ZY (deductions allowances) do not apply to a claim AP.

(7) Subsection (8) applies if—

  (a) there is at least one claim AP falling wholly within the relevant financial year, and

    (b)   there is at least one accounting period falling wholly within the relevant financial year in respect of which no claim is made under this section (an "alternative AP").

(8)   The company's deductions allowance for an alternative AP is the lower of—

    (a)   the deductions allowance that would be available, ignoring the effect of this section (see sections 269ZR to 269ZY), and

    (b)   the available deductions allowance amount (see subsection (9)).

(9)   For the purposes of this section, the "available deductions allowance amount" is—

    (a)   £5,000,000, less

    (b)   the total of the deductions allowance amounts (if any) already claimed by—

        (i)   the company, and

        (ii)   if the company is a member of a group at any time during the relevant financial year, each other company that is, at any time during the relevant financial year, a member of the group,

    in respect of each claim AP and alternative AP that falls wholly within the relevant financial year.

(10)   In this section, references to the deductions allowance amounts claimed by a company in respect of an accounting period—

    (a)   for a claim AP, are references to any deductions allowance claimed by the company under this section in respect of the period, and

    (b)   for an alternative AP, are references to any other amount specified in the company's tax return as its chargeable gains deductions allowance for the period.

(11)   For the purposes of subsection (9)(b), in the cases listed in the first column of the table below, the rules in the second column apply to determine the order in which deductions allowance amounts are to be treated as claimed in respect of the accounting periods—

Case	Rule
1 There is a claim AP and another claim AP starting on the same day or a different day.	The order in which the claims under this section are made.
2 There is an alternative AP ("AP1") and another alternative AP ("AP2") starting on a later day.	AP1 before AP2.
3 There is an alternative AP and another alternative AP starting on the same day.	The order in which the tax returns for the alternative APs are delivered.
4 There is a claim AP and an alternative AP starting on the same day, an earlier day or a later day.	The claim AP before the alternative AP.

269ZYB   **Provisional application of section 269ZYA**

(1)   This section applies in relation to a company and an accounting period if—

    (a)   the conditions in section 269ZYA(3)(a) and (b) are met in relation to the accounting period, and

    (b)   the company's tax return for the accounting period is delivered before the end of the financial year in which the accounting period falls ("the relevant financial year").

(2)   The company may make a declaration in the return for the accounting period that—

    (a)   at all earlier times in the relevant financial year—

        (i)   the company had no source of chargeable income (see section 269ZYA(2)), and

       (ii)   if the company is a member of a group, each other member of the group had no source of chargeable income, and

    (b)   the person intends to make a claim under section 269ZYA(3) in respect of the accounting period.

(3)   Until the declaration ceases to have effect, section 269ZYA has effect as if the company had made a claim under that section.

(4)   The declaration ceases to have effect if—

    (a)   it is withdrawn,

    (b)   it is superseded by a claim made under section 269ZYA, or

    (c)   the company or, if the company is a member of a group, another member of the group, acquires a source of chargeable income before the end of the relevant financial year.

(5)   So far as not previously ceasing to have effect under subsection (4), the declaration ceases to have effect two years after the end of the accounting period in respect of which it is made.

(6)   If the declaration ceases to have effect, all necessary adjustments must be made, by assessment, amendment of returns or otherwise.

(7)   Subsection (6) applies despite any limitation on the time within which assessments or amendments may be made."

Offshore collective investment vehicles

11 In section 269ZZB of CTA 2010 (meaning of "group"), at the end insert—

"(9)   For the purposes of the application of this Part in relation to a collective investment vehicle to which paragraph 4 of Schedule 5AAA to TCGA 1992 applies, the reference in paragraph 4(2) of that Schedule to "relevant purposes" is to be treated as including a reference to the purposes of this section."

Insurance companies: ring fence

12 (1)   Section 210A of TCGA 1992 (insurance: ring-fencing of losses) is amended as follows.

(2)   In subsection (2), after "to the company", in the first place it occurs, insert "as permitted by subsection (2A)".

(3)   After subsection (2) insert—

"(2A)   The following deductions may be made from the shareholders' share of the BLAGAB chargeable gains accruing to the company in an accounting period—

    (a)   any available non-BLAGAB allowable losses accruing to the company in the period may be deducted under section 2A(1)(a), and

    (b)   after making any deductions within paragraph (a), any available non-BLAGAB allowable losses previously accruing to the company, which have not been allowed as a deduction from chargeable gains accruing in the period or in any previous accounting period, may (subject to section 269ZFC of CTA 2010) be deducted under section 2A(1)(b).

(2B)   But those deductions may not reduce the shareholders' share of BLAGAB chargeable gains below nil.

(2C)   The amount of "available non-BLAGAB allowable losses" accruing to a company in an accounting period is the amount by which the non-BLAGAB allowable losses accruing to the company in the accounting period exceed the non-BLAGAB chargeable gains so accruing."

(4)   In subsection (6)(a)—

    (a)   omit "amount by which", and

    (b)   omit "exceeds the shareholders' share of BLAGAB chargeable gains so accruing".

(5)   In subsection (8), in the words before paragraph (a)—

    (a)   for "If the" substitute "If there are", and

    (b)   omit "exceed the BLAGAB allowable losses so accruing".

(6)   In subsection (8)(b), after "deduction" insert ", under step 2 of section 75(1) of FA 2012,".

(7)   For subsection (9) substitute—

"(9)   If there are BLAGAB allowable losses accruing to the company in the subsequent accounting period, the amount arrived at under subsection (7)(a) is increased by the shareholders' share of the amount of those allowable losses."

(8)   In subsection (13)—

    (a)   in the definition of "BLAGAB allowable losses", at the end insert "but excluding any allowable losses deducted under step 2 of section 75(1) of FA 2012 in determining the BLAGAB chargeable gains of the company for an accounting period,";

    (b)   in the definition of "BLAGAB chargeable gains", after "means chargeable gains" insert "(as adjusted for allowable losses in accordance with section 75 of FA 2012)".

13 After section 269ZFB of CTA 2010 insert—

"269ZFC   Restriction on deductions of non-BLAGAB allowable losses from BLAGAB chargeable gains

(1)   This section has effect for determining the taxable total profits of an insurance company for an accounting period.

(2)   The sum of any deductions of non-BLAGAB allowable losses from the shareholders' share of BLAGAB chargeable gains made by an insurance company for an accounting period under section 2A(1)(b) of TCGA 1992, as permitted by section 210A(2A)(b) of that Act, may not exceed the relevant maximum.

(3)   In this section, the "relevant maximum" means the sum of—

    (a)   50% of the company's relevant BLAGAB chargeable gains for the accounting period, and

    (b)   the amount of the company's BLAGAB deductions allowance for the accounting period.

(4)   A company's "relevant BLAGAB chargeable gains" for an accounting period are—

    (a)   the shareholders' share of the BLAGAB chargeable gains for the accounting period, after any reduction under section 210A(2A)(a) of TCGA 1992, less

    (b)   the amount of the company's BLAGAB deductions allowance for the accounting period.

But if the allowance mentioned in paragraph (b) exceeds the shareholders' share of the BLAGAB chargeable gains mentioned in paragraph (a), the company's "relevant BLAGAB chargeable gains" for the accounting period are nil.

(5)   A company's "BLAGAB deductions allowance" for an accounting period—

    (a)   is so much of the company's deductions allowance for the period as is specified in the company's tax return as its BLAGAB deductions allowance for the period, and

    (b)   accordingly, is nil if no amount of the company's deductions allowance for the period is so specified.

(6)   An amount specified under subsection (5)(a) as the company's BLAGAB deductions allowance for an accounting period may not exceed the difference between—

    (a)   the amount of the company's deductions allowance for the period, and

    (b)   the total of any amounts specified for the period under section 269ZB(7)(a) (trading profits deductions allowance), section 269ZBA(5)(a) (chargeable gains deductions allowance) and section 269ZC(5)(a) (non-trading income profits deductions allowance).

(7)   In this section, "BLAGAB chargeable gains", "insurance company" and "the shareholders' share of BLAGAB chargeable gains" have the same meaning as in section 210A of TCGA 1992."

14 (1)   Part 7ZA of CTA 2010 is amended in accordance with this paragraph.

(2)   In section 269ZD(2)(b)—

    (a)   omit the "and" after sub-paragraph (ia) (inserted by paragraph 4 of this Schedule), and

    (b)   after sub-paragraph (ii) insert "and

> (iia)   any deductions of non-BLAGAB allowable losses from the share-holders' share of BLAGAB chargeable gains made for the accounting period under section 2A(1)(b) of TCGA 1992, as permitted by section 210A(2A)(b) of that Act."

(3)   In section 269ZFB(2), at the end of paragraph (b) insert "and provided that no deductions of non-BLAGAB allowable losses from the shareholders' share of BLAGAB chargeable gains are to be made under section 2A(1)(b) of TCGA 1992, as permitted by section 210A(2A)(b) of that Act."

15 In section 95 of FA 2012 (use of non-BLAGAB allowable losses to reduce I-E profit) for "in accordance with section 210A(2) of TCGA 1992" substitute "under section 2A(1) of TCGA 1992, as permitted by section 210A(2) and (2A) of that Act,".

Oil activities: ring fence

16 In section 197 of TCGA 1992 (disposals of interests in oil fields etc: ring fence provisions), after subsection (4) insert—

> "(4A)   A deduction in respect of an aggregate loss accruing in a chargeable period that is (in accordance with subsection (4)(b) and (c)) allowable as a deduction against an aggregate gain treated as accruing in a later period is to be ignored for the purposes of section 269ZBA of CTA 2010 (corporate capital loss restriction: restriction on deductions from chargeable gains)."

Clogged losses

17 In section 18 of TCGA 1992 (transactions between connected persons) at the end insert—

> "(9)   If deductible clogged losses have accrued to a company, the company may make a claim in respect of an accounting period for—
>
> (a)   an amount of the deductible clogged losses to be treated, for the purposes of section 2A(1)(a), as allowable losses accruing in the accounting period, and
>
> (b)   the same amount of allowable losses accruing to the company in the period to be treated, for the purposes of section 2A(1)(b), as allowable losses previously accruing to the company while it was within the charge to corporation tax.
>
> (10)   The amount in respect of which the claim is made may not exceed the total amount of any allowable losses accruing to the company in the accounting period for which the claim is made.
>
> (11)   In subsection (9), "deductible clogged losses" means losses which would, apart from Part 7ZA of CTA 2010, be deductible under subsection (3) from chargeable gains accruing to the company in an accounting period.
>
> (12)   A claim under subsection (9) must be made by being included in the company's tax return for the accounting period for which the claim is made."

Pre-entry losses

18 (1)   Schedule 7A of TCGA 1992 (restriction on set-off of pre-entry losses) is amended in accordance with this paragraph.

(2)   In paragraph 6(1)(b), after "from that gain" insert "(subject to sub-paragraphs (1A) to (1C))".

(3)   In paragraph 6(1)(c), after "section 2A(1)" insert "(subject to sub-paragraphs (1A) to (1C))".

(4)   After sub-paragraph (1) insert—

> "(1A)   Sub-paragraph (1B) applies, in respect of an accounting period, if the amount of chargeable gains accruing to the company in the period exceeds the total of—
>
> (a)   the amount of pre-entry losses accruing to the company in the period that are deductible under sub-paragraph (1)(a), and
>
> (b)   the amount of allowable losses, other than pre-entry losses, accruing to the company in the period.
>
> (1B)   Where this sub-paragraph applies in respect of an accounting period—

   (a)   the sum of any deductions under sub-paragraph (1)(b) may not exceed the total of—

      (i)   the amount of pre-entry losses that, on the assumption in sub-paragraph (1C), would be deductible under sub-paragraph (1)(b), and

      (ii)   the amount of allowable losses (other than pre-entry losses) that, on the assumption in sub-paragraph (1C), would be deductible under section 2A(1), and

   (b)   for the purposes of sub-paragraph (1)(c), the deductions made under section 2A(1) may not exceed the difference between—

      (i)   the total of the amounts mentioned in paragraph (a)(i) and (ii), and

      (ii)   the amount of pre-entry losses deducted under sub-paragraph (1)(b).

(1C)   The assumption is that deductions under sub-paragraph (1)(b) are treated for the purposes of Part 7ZA of CTA 2010 (restrictions on obtaining certain deductions) as if they were made under section 2A(1)(b) of this Act."

Real estate investment trusts

19 Part 12 of CTA 2010 (real estate investment trusts) is amended as follows.

20 In section 535B (use of pre-April 2019 residual business losses or deficits) at the end insert—

"(4)   In determining, for the purposes of subsection (2)(a), the amount of allowable losses accruing on disposals made before 6 April 2019 which would otherwise have been deducted from gains accruing to residual business of the company, section 269ZBA (restriction on deductions) is to be ignored."

21 In section 550 (attribution of distributions) at the end insert—

"(4)   In determining the amount of relevant non-chargeable gains for the purposes of this section, section 269ZBA (restriction on deductions) is to be ignored."

22 In section 556 (disposal of assets) in subsection (7), for "and 535A" substitute ", 535A and 535B".

Counteraction of avoidance arrangements

23 (1)   Section 19 of F(No.2)A 2017 (losses: counteraction of avoidance arrangements) is amended in accordance with this paragraph.

(2)   In subsection (8), before paragraph (a) insert—

"(za)   section 2A(1) of TCGA 1992 (allowable capital losses);".

(3)   At the end insert—

"(13)   In the case of a tax advantage as a result of a deduction (or increased deduction) under section 2A(1) of TCGA 1992, subsections (10) and (11) have effect as if the references to 1 April 2017 were to 1 April 2020."

Minor and consequential amendments to Part 7ZA of CTA 2010

24 Part 7ZA of CTA 2010 is amended as follows.

25 (1)   Section 269ZB (restriction on deductions from trading profits) is amended in accordance with this paragraph.

(2)   In subsection (8), for paragraph (b) substitute—

"(b)   the total of—

      (i)   the amount of the company's total non-trading profits deductions allowance for the period (see section 269ZC(3A)), and

      (ii)   in the case of an insurance company, any amount specified for the period under section 269ZFC(5)(a) (BLAGAB deductions allowance)."

(3)   Omit subsection (9) (meaning of a company's "deductions allowance").

26 In section 269ZC (restriction on deductions from non-trading profits) omit subsection (7) (meaning of a company's "deductions allowance").

27 In section 269ZD (restriction on deductions from total profits) omit subsection (6) (meaning of a company's "deductions allowance").

28 After section 269ZD insert—

"269ZDA References to a company's "deductions allowance"

(1) This section applies for the purposes of sections 269ZB to 269ZD and 269ZFC.

(2) A company's "deductions allowance" for an accounting period is to be determined in accordance with section 269ZR where, at any time in that period—

    (a) the company is a member of a group (see section 269ZZB), and

    (b) one or more other companies within the charge to corporation tax are members of that group.

(3) Otherwise, a company's "deductions allowance" for an accounting period is to be determined in accordance with section 269ZW.

(4) But subsections (2) and (3) are subject to section 269ZYA (deductions allowance for company without a source of chargeable income)."

29 (1) Section 269ZF ("relevant trading profits" and "relevant non-trading profits") is amended in accordance with this paragraph.

(2) In subsection (2)—

    (a) for ""relevant non-trading profits"", in both places it occurs, substitute ""relevant non-trading income profits"",

    (b) in paragraph (a), for "qualifying non-trading profits" substitute "qualifying non-trading income profits", and

    (c) in paragraph (b) for "non-trading profits deductions allowance" substitute "non-trading income profits deductions allowance".

(3) In subsection (3), in the words before step 1, for "and qualifying non-trading profits" substitute ", qualifying non-trading income profits and qualifying chargeable gains".

(4) In subsection (3), in paragraph (3) of step 1—

    (a) for "and relevant non-trading profits" substitute ", qualifying non-trading income profits and qualifying chargeable gains", and

    (b) for "both" substitute "each".

(5) In subsection (3), in paragraph (3) of step 2—

    (a) for "and the qualifying non-trading profits" substitute ", qualifying non-trading income profits and qualifying chargeable gains", and

    (b) for "both" substitute "each".

(6) In the heading, for "and "relevant non-trading profits"" substitute ", "total relevant non-trading profits" etc".

30 (1) Section 269ZFA ("relevant profits") is amended as follows.

(2) In subsection (1)(b), for "section 269ZD(6)" substitute "section 269ZDA".

(3) In subsection (2)—

    (a) in paragraph (a), for "qualifying trading profits and qualifying non-trading profits" substitute "modified total profits", and

    (b) in paragraph (b), for "in determining" substitute "which could be relieved against".

31 In section 269ZG (general insurance companies: excluded accounting periods), in subsection (1), for "269ZE" substitute "269ZD".

32 In section 269ZR (deductions allowance for company in a group), at the end insert—

"(5) See section 269ZYA for further provision about the deductions allowance for a company without a source of chargeable income which is a member of a group."

33 In section 269ZW (deductions allowance for company not in a group), at the end insert—

"(4) See section 269ZYA for further provision about the deductions allowance for a company without a source of chargeable income."

34 In section 269ZZ (company tax return to specify amount of deductions allowance), in subsection (2)—

    (a) after "section 269ZB(2)," insert "269ZBA(2),", and

(b)   for "or 269ZD(2) or section 124D(1) of FA 2012" substitute ", 269ZD(2) or 269ZFC(2)".

35 (1)   Section 269ZZA(1) (excessive specification of deductions allowance: application of section) is amended in accordance with this paragraph.

(2)   After paragraph (b) insert—

"(ba) the company's chargeable gains deductions allowance for the period,".

(3)   In paragraph (c) for "non-trading profits deductions allowance" substitute "non-trading income profits deductions allowance".

(4)   After paragraph (d) insert—

"(da) the company's BLAGAB deductions allowance for the period."

(5)   Omit paragraph (e).

Minor and consequential amendments to Part 7A of CTA 2010

36 Part 7A of CTA 2010 (banking companies: restrictions on obtaining certain deductions) is amended as follows.

37 (1)   Section 269CB (restriction on deductions for non-trading deficits from loan relationships) is amended as follows.

(2)   In subsection (2)—

(a)   for "relevant non-trading profits", in both places it occurs, substitute "total relevant non-trading profits", and

(b)   for "subsection (2)" substitute "subsection (2B)".

(3)   In subsection (3), for "relevant non-trading profits", in both places it occurs, substitute "total relevant non-trading profits".

38 In section 269CN (definitions)—

(a)   omit the definition of "relevant non-trading profits", and

(b)   at the end insert—

""total relevant non-trading profits", in relation to a company, has the meaning given by section 269ZF(2B)."

COMMENTARY ON SCHEDULE 4, PART 1

Part 1 amends Part 7ZA of CTA 2010 to include carried forward allowable losses within the regime for restricting the set off of carried forward losses for corporation tax purposes.

General rule

Very broadly, CTA 2010, Pt 7ZA provides that companies can only set off carried forward losses equivalent to 50% of their chargeable profits for a period, to the extent that those profits exceed £5 million. That limit is reduced by reference to the number of group companies and the length of the accounting period.

The amendments now provide that the 50% limit also applies to the setting off of carried forward allowable losses against chargeable gains of the company.

The main provision is CTA 2010, s 269ZBA, which tells us that a company will have to state a 'chargeable gains deductions allowance' in a tax return for the relevant period. If it does not do so, there will be no chargeable gains deductions allowance and the set off of carried forward allowable losses will be restricted to 50% of all chargeable gains of the period.

The chargeable gains deductions allowance cannot exceed the difference between the company's general deductions allowance and the sum of its trading profits deductions allowance, its non-trading income profits deductions allowance and the BLAGAB deductions allowance in the case of an insurance company.

Much of the rest of Part 1 comprises amendments to CTA 2010, Pt 7ZA consequential on bringing allowable losses into the general loss restriction regime.

Companies with no chargeable income

There are special rules in CTA 2010, s 269ZYA for companies which only have chargeable gains and no income chargeable to corporation tax. This provision applies to companies which are not within the charge to corporation tax or are only chargeable to corporation tax because of a chargeable gain on disposing of an asset.

If the company makes a claim, the deductions allowance for the 'claim AP' is the lower of:

- The 'available deductions allowance amount' (see below)
- The total amount of carried forward allowable losses, and
- The chargeable gains arising to the company in the claim AP.

The general principle is that, where a company only has chargeable gains, it will only have a one-day accounting period, which would otherwise reduce the £5 million deductions allowance to something under £14,000. This provision would allow the company to nevertheless have the benefit of a full deductions allowance, to use the whole of its allowable losses or to shelter the whole of the gain in these circumstances.

It is possible for a company to have more than one such short accounting period in the same financial year, so the 'available deductions allowance amount', referred to above, is restricted by reference to any deductions allowance given in respect of other accounting periods within the same financial year. Similarly, there is a provision to ensure that, where there is an accounting period in the same financial year in which no claim is made under this provision (an 'alternative AP'), restrictions are made in respect of the deductions allowance given under the normal provisions.

Broadly the deductions allowances for multiple APs within the same financial year are given in the order in which they are claimed, not in chronological order of the accounting periods. The relevant rules are set out in a table in the legislation.

Insolvent companies

New CTA 2010, s 269ZWA gives companies in insolvent liquidation an additional deductions allowance. The new provision applies to a company in liquidation, as defined by Insolvency Act 1986, s 247(2) or the Insolvency (Northern Ireland) Order 1989, art 6(2) (SI 1989/2405 (NI 19)), where the assets are insufficient for the payment of its debts and other liabilities. It also applies to non-UK companies which have gone into a corresponding form of insolvent liquidation.

If CTA 2010, s 269ZWA applies, the deductions allowance is increased by the lower of the company's net chargeable gains in the winding up accounting period or its carried forward allowable capital losses. In order to prevent avoidance, however, this does not take into account gains arising on intra-group transfers into the company, to which TCGA 1992, s 171 apply, or to chargeable gains transferred into the company under TCGA 1992, s 171A.

This provision appears to be intended to relax the restriction on the use of carried forward losses in cases where gains arise as part of the winding up process.

Clogged losses

TCGA 1992, s 18 is amended for companies that have allowable losses carried forward arising from connected person transactions, as well as allowable losses arising in an accounting period. The carried forward losses are restricted to set off against gains arising on disposals to the same connected person, whereas the losses arising in the period may not be. However, the current year losses are set off against current year gains, leaving only an aggregate gain to be sheltered by carried forward losses.

Under the new rule, if the company makes a claim, and if the use of the carried forward loss would be restricted by CTA 2020, Pt 7ZA, the 'clogged losses' can be used to shelter the current year gains and the same amount of current year allowable losses will be carried forward.

This provision does not, however, affect the requirement that the clogged losses can only be used against gains arising on disposals to the same connected person.

Pre-entry losses

Pre-entry losses (TCGA 1992, Sch 7A) are part of a separate regime for carrying forward surplus losses. The rules are amended so that the allowable loss restriction rules apply to carried forward pre-entry losses, too.

Other provisions in Part 1

The rules for the counteraction of avoidance arrangements relating to losses (F(No 2)A 2017, s 19) are amended to bring capital losses within their scope.

There are also specific rules for offshore collective investment vehicles, insurance companies, real estate investment trusts (REITs) and oil companies.

PART 2

CORPORATE CAPITAL LOSS DEDUCTIONS: MISCELLANEOUS PROVISION

Companies without a source of chargeable income: carry back of losses

39 In section 2A of TCGA 1992 (company's total profits to include chargeable gains), after subsection (2) insert—

"(3) Subsection (4) applies if—

(a) a company has two or more accounting periods that fall wholly within the same financial year,

(b) the company is chargeable to corporation tax for each of those accounting periods only because of a chargeable gain accruing to the company on the disposal of asset, and

(c) in the period (if any) between each of those accounting periods, the company is not within the charge to corporation tax.

(4) For the purposes of determining the amount of chargeable gains to be included in the company's total profits for each of the accounting periods by reference to which this subsection applies, subsection (1) has effect as if after paragraph (a) (before the "and") there were inserted—

"(aa) so far as not otherwise deducted under this section, any allowable losses accruing to the company in another accounting period that falls wholly within the same financial year as the period mentioned in paragraph (a),"."

Insurance companies: minor amendments to TCGA 1992 and FA 2012

40 In section 210A of TCGA 1992, in subsection (10C), for the words from "In determining" to "an accounting period" substitute "For the purposes of subsections (10A) and (10B)".

41 In section 93 of FA 2012 (minimum profits test), at the end insert—

"(6) For the purposes of this section, assume that non-BLAGAB allowable losses cannot be deducted to any extent from BLAGAB chargeable gains (and, accordingly, assume that section 95 is not included in this Act)."

COMMENTARY ON SCHEDULE 4 PART 2

The general capital gains rules for setting off allowable losses against chargeable gains – TCGA 1992, s 2A – are amended for companies that have more than one very short accounting period where the company is only within the charge to corporation tax because of chargeable gains during a financial year. In such situations, the company can set off allowable losses against any chargeable gains accruing in the same financial year, even if this is effectively a carry back of the losses, and without any restriction under the corporate loss restriction regime.

There is also a clarification of the general rules relating to life insurance companies, so that non-BLAGAB allowable losses are assumed not to have been deducted from BLAGAB chargeable gains.

PART 3

COMMENCEMENT AND ANTI-FORESTALLING PROVISION

Commencement

42 The amendments made by this Schedule have effect in relation to accounting periods beginning on or after 1 April 2020.

43 (1) Paragraph 44 applies where a company has an accounting period beginning before 1 April 2020 and ending on or after that date (the "straddling period").

(2) For the purposes of paragraph 44—

  (a) the "pre-commencement period" means the part of the straddling period falling before 1 April 2020, and

  (b) the "post-commencement period" means the part of the straddling period falling on or after that date.

44 (1) The amount of chargeable gains to be included in the company's total profits for the straddling period is the total of—

  (a) the chargeable gains accruing to the company in the pre-commencement period, after making any deductions under section 2A(1) of TCGA 1992, and

  (b) the chargeable gains accruing to the company in the post-commencement period, after making any deductions under that section.

(2) For the purposes of sub-paragraph (1)(a) and (b), section 2A of TCGA 1992 applies as if the pre-commencement period and the post-commencement period were separate accounting periods, subject to the modification in sub-paragraph (3).

(3) For the purposes of determining the amount to be included in the company's total profits in respect of chargeable gains for a period, the reference in section 2A(1)(a) of TCGA 1992 to any allowable losses accruing to the company in the period is to be treated as including—

  (a) for the purposes of the pre-commencement period, a reference to any allowable losses accruing to the company in the post-commencement period so far as they exceed the chargeable gains accruing to the company in the post-commencement period, and

  (b) for the purposes of the post-commencement period, a reference to any available allowable losses accruing to the company in the pre-commencement period so far as they exceed the chargeable gains accruing to the company in the pre-commencement period.

(4) For the purposes of applying Part 7ZA of CTA 2010 in relation to the straddling period—

  (a) section 269ZBA of that Act applies in relation to the post-commencement period as if it were a separate accounting period,

  (b) the reference in section 269ZF(4)(h) to deductions under section 2A(1)(b) of TCGA 1992 is to be treated as if it were a reference only to deductions under that provision from the chargeable gains of the post-commencement period, and

  (c) the reference in step 3(c) of section 269ZF to the chargeable gains included in the company's total profits is to be treated as if it were a reference to the total of—

    (i) the chargeable gains accruing to the company in the pre-commencement period, after making any deductions under section 2A(1)(a) or (b) of TCGA 1992, and

    (ii) the chargeable gains accruing to the company in the post-commencement period, after making any deductions under section 2A(1)(a) of that Act.

45 (1) This paragraph applies in relation to a non-UK resident company which carries on a UK property business or has other UK property income—

  (a) if the conditions in sub-paragraph (2) are met, and

  (b) unless the company has elected that this paragraph is not to apply.

(2) The conditions are met if the company—

  (a) is within the charge to income tax for the tax year 2019–20,

  (b) is chargeable to corporation tax for an accounting period falling wholly within the period beginning with 1 April 2020 and ending with 5 April 2020 because of a chargeable gain accruing to the company on the disposal of an asset, and

  (c) is within the charge to corporation tax on income for an accounting period beginning on 6 April 2020.

(3) For the purposes of determining the amount to be included in the company's total profits in respect of chargeable gains for an accounting period mentioned in sub-paragraph (2)(b) or (2)(c), the reference in section 2A(1)(a) of TCGA 1992 to any allowable losses accruing to the company in the period is to be treated as including—

  (a) for the purposes of an accounting period mentioned in sub-paragraph (2)(b), a reference to any allowable losses accruing to the company in the accounting period mentioned in sub-paragraph (2)(c) (so far as those losses are not otherwise deducted under section 2A(1) of TCGA 1992), and

(b)   for the purposes of the accounting period mentioned in sub-paragraph (2)(c), a reference to any allowable losses accruing to the company in an accounting period mentioned in sub-paragraph (2)(b) (so far as those losses are not otherwise deducted under section 2A(1) of TCGA 1992).

(4)   For the purposes of the application of Part 7ZA of CTA 2010 in relation to the accounting periods mentioned in sub-paragraphs (2)(b) and (2)(c)—

(a)   section 269ZYA of CTA 2010 (deductions allowance for company without a source of chargeable income) applies as if the company had made a claim under that section in respect of each accounting period mentioned in sub-paragraph (2)(b), and

(b)   the company's deductions allowance for the accounting period mentioned in sub-paragraph (2)(c) is treated as being reduced by the amount of the company's deductions allowance for each accounting period mentioned in sub-paragraph (2)(b).

Anti-forestalling provision

46 (1)   This sub-paragraph applies if—

(a)   a company has an accounting period ending before 1 April 2020,

(b)   the company would, apart from this paragraph, obtain a tax advantage as a result of a deduction, or an increased deduction, under section 2A(1)(b) of TCGA 1992,

(c)   the tax advantage arises as a result of arrangements entered into on or after 29 October 2018, and

(d)   the main purpose, or one of the main purposes, of the arrangements is to secure a tax advantage as a result of the fact that section 269ZBA of CTA 2010, inserted by this Schedule, is not to have effect for the accounting period for which the deduction would be made.

(2)   If sub-paragraph (1) applies, the deductions made by the company for the accounting period under section 2A(1)(b) of TCGA 1992 may not exceed 50% of the company's qualifying chargeable gains for the period.

(3)   So far as necessary for the purposes of this paragraph, Part 7ZA of CTA 2010 is treated as having come into force on the same day as this paragraph.

(4)   This paragraph is treated as having come into force on 29 October 2018.

(5)   Where a company has a straddling period, the pre-commencement period and the post-commencement period are treated for the purposes of this paragraph as separate accounting periods.

(6)   In this paragraph—

(a)   "arrangements" includes any agreement, understanding, scheme transaction or series of transactions (whether or not legally enforceable),

(b)   "straddling period", "pre-commencement period" and "post-commencement period" have the same meaning as they have for the purposes of paragraph 44, and

(c)   "tax advantage" has the meaning given by section 1139 of CTA 2010.

COMMENTARY ON SCHEDULE 4 PART 3

Commencement

Schedule 4 generally comes into force for accounting periods starting on or after 1 April 2020, subject to the anti-forestalling rules. An accounting period straddling that date is treated as two separate accounting periods and there are rules for computing the apportionment of chargeable gains and allowable losses arising in the straddling period between the pre- and post-commencement periods. Essentially, there is no restriction on allocations of allowable losses between the two parts of the straddling period, and the new rules effectively only apply to allowable losses carried forward from before the pre-commencement period to the post-commencement period.

There is also a special rule for non-resident companies with a UK property business that are within the scope of income tax prior to 6 April 2020 but come into the corporation tax regime on 6 April 2020 and have chargeable gains subject to corporation tax in an accounting period between 1 and 5 April 2020. In such cases, no restriction arises on the use of losses arising either in that short accounting period or in the accounting period starting on 6 April 2020. Instead, the company is treated as having made an election under CTA 2010, s 269CYA (see above) in respect of each short AP between 1 and 5 April 2020, and the deductions allowances for each will be computed accordingly.

Anti-forestalling

The anti-forestalling rules apply to arrangements made on or after 29 October 2018 – the date of the original announcement of the new restriction – that have a main purpose of securing a tax advantage based on the new rule, CTA 2010, s 269ZBA, not being effective in the relevant accounting period because it has not yet come into force. It applies to accounting periods starting on or after 29 October 2018 and ending before 1 April 2020, as well as to the pre-commencement period in any straddling period.

Where this provision applies, the deductions for the relevant accounting period are restricted to 50% of the qualifying chargeable gains for the period.

This anti-forestalling provision is treated as coming into force on 29 October 2018 and the whole of CTA 2010, Pt 7ZA is also treated as coming into force on that date, so far as is necessary to give effect to these anti-forestalling rules.

It is interesting to surmise what arrangements might be caught by this rule. The obvious forestalling arrangement would be to simply accelerate a disposal by selling the asset before 1 April 2020. This could be argued to be an arrangement with a main purpose of securing a tax advantage based on CTA 2010, s 269ZBA not yet being in force. However, it is difficult to see how simply selling something earlier than might otherwise have been the case could be construed as offensive and a necessary target of an anti-forestalling rule. It is understood that, in the context of the changes to entrepreneurs' relief (see section 23 and Schedule 3), HMRC has said that arrangements to sell a trade or trading company before the commencement date do not contravene the anti-forestalling rule in those provisions, so it seems likely that HMRC would take a similar view here.

The most likely tax planning would have been to create a disposal to a connected person and to ensure that the disposal was unconditional but not completed. Then, when a real sale happens, the original disposal can complete and will be treated (by TCGA 1992, s 28) as having happened prior to CTA 2010, s 269ZBA coming into force, so there will be no restriction on using carried forward allowable losses to shelter the gain (planning that is specifically targeted by the entrepreneurs' relief anti-forestalling rules – see Schedule 3, para 3, above).

SCHEDULE 5

STRUCTURES AND BUILDINGS ALLOWANCES

Section 30

Introduction

1 CAA 2001 is amended as follows.

Research and development allowances

2 In Part 2A (structures and buildings allowances), for section 270EC substitute—

"270EC   Research and development

(1) This section applies if, at any time, a person sells the relevant interest in a building or structure to another.

(2) The total amount of the allowances under this Part by reference to the building or structure that is available to the person buying the relevant interest is reduced (but not below nil) by the amount of any Part 6 allowance to which the person is entitled by reference to the building or structure.

(3) There is another restriction on the total amount of those allowances which applies if—

    (a)   the sale in question, or a sale of the relevant interest at an earlier time, is by a person entitled to a Part 6 allowance by reference to the building or structure, and

    (b)   the amount paid for the relevant interest on any of those sales is less than the ordinary Part 2A amount (see subsection (6)).

(4) The other restriction is that the total amount of the allowances under this Part by reference to the building or structure that is available to the person buying the relevant interest may not exceed the permitted maximum.

(5) For this purpose "the permitted maximum" is—

    (a)   the lowest sum paid for the relevant interest on the sale in question or any earlier sale within subsection (3)(a), less

    (b)   the total amount of the allowances under this Part arising by reference to the building or structure since the earliest sale identified for the purposes of paragraph (a) of this subsection.

(6) In this section "the ordinary Part 2A amount" means—

    (a)   the amount of the qualifying expenditure, by reference to which an allowance can be made under this Part, incurred in relation to the building or structure before the time of the sale in question, less

    (b)   the total amount of the allowances under this Part arising before that time by reference to the building or structure.

(7) In this section any reference to allowances under this Part is to allowances to which an entitlement has arisen under this Part or would have arisen under this Part if the building or structure had been in continuous qualifying use since it was first brought into non-residential use.

(8) In this section "Part 6 allowance", in relation to a person and a building or structure, means an allowance under Part 6 in respect of expenditure incurred by the person on its construction or acquisition."

Contribution allowances

3 (1) Section 538A (contributions: buildings and structures) is amended as follows.

(2) For subsection (3)(b) substitute—

    "(b)   the building or structure were brought into qualifying use, for the purposes of the allowance in relation to the contribution, on—

        (i)   the day on which R first brought the building or structure into qualifying use, or

        (ii)   if R is a public body, the earlier of the day mentioned in sub-paragraph (i) and the day on which R first brought the building or structure into non-residential use."

(3) For subsection (4) substitute—

"(4) If, at any time in the period beginning with the day on which C made the contribution and ending with the day on which R first brought the building or structure into non-residential use, C did not have a relevant interest in the building or structure—

    (a) C is to be treated for the purposes of allowances under Part 2A as having had a relevant interest in the building or structure when that period begins, and

    (b) C is not to be treated for those purposes as ceasing to have that interest on any subsequent sale of R's relevant interest in the building or structure."

(4) After subsection (6) insert—

"(7) In determining, for the purposes of this section, the day on which R first brings a building or structure into non-residential use, ignore any use of the building or structure which is insignificant."

Minor amendments

4 In section 270AA(2) (entitlement to structures and buildings allowances), at the beginning of paragraph (b)(i) insert "on or".

5 In section 270BB (capital expenditure incurred on construction), in subsection (2)(a), for "qualifying use" substitute "non-residential use".

6 In section 270BL (apportionment of sums partly referable to non-qualifying assets), for "qualifying expenditure" substitute "expenditure for which an allowance can be made under this Part".

7 In section 270IA (evidence of qualifying expenditure etc), in subsection (4)(a), omit "written".

Commencement

8 The amendment made by paragraph 2 has effect in the case of any sale within subsection (1) of the substituted section 270EC(1) of CAA 2001 that takes place on or after 11 March 2020.

9 The amendments made by paragraph 3 have effect in relation to contributions made on or after 11 March 2020.

10 Part 2A of CAA 2001 has effect, and is to be deemed always to have had effect, with the amendments made by paragraphs 4 to 7.

COMMENTARY ON SCHEDULE 5

A new capital allowance known as the structures and buildings allowance (SBA) was introduced by regulations (SI 2019/1087) under powers conferred by FA 2019, s 30. These regulations inserted a new Part 2A (ss 270AA–270IH) into CAA 2001. This provides relief for qualifying capital expenditure on buildings and structures brought into use for the purposes of a trade, profession, vocation, property business or other qualifying activity. The SBA is available on eligible construction costs incurred on or after 29 October 2018. It is available to persons within the charge to either income tax or corporation tax.

Schedule 5, introduced by section 30, makes miscellaneous amendments to the operation of the SBA. These may be divided for convenience into three parts. Paragraph 2 of Schedule 5 deals with the interaction of SBAs and research and development capital allowances. Paragraph 3 covers SBAs due to a person who has contributed to another's expenditure ('contribution allowances'). Paragraphs 4–7 make minor amendments to ensure that various rules operate as intended.

Paragraph 2

The original legislation (CAA 2001, s 270EC) contained provision to deal with cases in which expenditure on a building potentially qualifies for both SBAs and research and development (R & D) capital allowances. A new CAA 2001, s 270EC is now substituted. It potentially applies if, at any time on or after 11 March 2020, a person sells the relevant interest in a building or structure to another person. Its intention is to prevent double relief, and it operates as follows.

The total SBAs available to the buyer of the relevant interest are reduced by the amount of any R & D allowance available to the buyer by reference to the building or structure. Additionally, if the sale in question, or a sale of the relevant interest at any earlier time, is by a person entitled to an R & D allowance by reference to the building or structure *and* the amount paid on any of those sales is less than the total remaining SBAs available at the time of sale, the total SBAs available to the buyer cannot exceed a permitted maximum.

The permitted maximum is the lowest sum paid for the relevant interest on the sale in question or any of the earlier such sales *less* the total SBAs arising since the earliest such sale.

In applying these provisions, reference to the total SBAs is to the total to which an entitlement has arisen or would have arisen if the building or structure had been in continuous qualifying use since first being brought into non-residential use.

Paragraph 3

This amendment has effect in relation to contributions made on or after 11 March 2020.

Entitlement to contributions allowances in relation to the SBA is governed by CAA 2001, s 538A. That legislation is now amended so as to ensure that a person can claim an allowance for a contribution to expenditure incurred by a public body and that the rules work correctly in this regard. Under the amended rules for such contributions, the contributor can claim an allowance when the public body brings the building or structure into qualifying use *or, if earlier, into non-residential use*. Previously, a contribution allowance would have been available only if and when the public body brought the building or structure into *qualifying* use, which may not have been possible.

It is further provided that if the recipient of the contribution does not have a relevant interest in the building or structure, the recipient is treated as having a relevant interest solely for the purposes of calculating any SBAs that may be due to the contributor. Finally, it is provided that in determining the day on which the recipient first brings a building or structure into non-residential use, one should disregard any use of the building or structure which is insignificant. 'Insignificant' is not given a statutory definition for this purpose.

Paragraphs 4–7

All the remaining amendments are treated as always having had effect.

Oddly, the original legislation (in CAA 2001, s 270AA(2)) provided for entitlement to SBAs to commence on the day *after* a building or structure first comes into non-residential use. This is amended so that entitlement begins on the day *on or after* a building or structure first comes into such use.

There is a pre-existing rule in CAA 2001, s 270BB(2), (3) involving capital expenditure incurred in relation to a building or structure after it has been brought into qualifying use and on different days (whether or not in the same chargeable period). The rule enables such expenditure to be lumped together as if it had all been incurred on the same day, thus avoiding the need to have a separate writing-down period for each and every item. Schedule 5, paragraph 5 substitutes 'non-residential use' for 'qualifying use'. This has the effect of extending this easement to persons not within the charge to tax.

CAA 2001, s 270BL(1) originally provided that wherever an item of expenditure falls to be apportioned between qualifying expenditure and other expenditure, the apportionment is to be made on a just and reasonable basis. This is now widened so as to apply to any apportionment between expenditure for which an SBA can be made and other expenditure.

Under CAA 2001, s 270IA, anyone claiming an SBA who did not themselves incur the qualifying expenditure must obtain an 'allowance statement' from any person previously entitled to a relevant interest in the building or structure. One of the items of information the allowance statement had to contain was the date of the earliest written contract for the construction of the building or structure. This is now changed so as to refer to the earliest contract, whether it be written or oral.

SCHEDULE 6

NON-UK RESIDENT COMPANIES CARRYING ON UK PROPERTY BUSINESSES ETC

Section 32

Calculation of non-trading profits and deficits from loan relationships or derivative contracts

1 In section 301 of CTA 2009 (calculation of non-trading profits and deficits from loan relationships), for the subsection (1A) inserted into that section by paragraph 15(3) of Schedule 5 to FA 2019 substitute—

"(1A)   In the case of a non-UK resident company, subsections (4) to (7) need to be read with section 5(3), (3A)(b) and (3B)(b) (territorial scope of charge to corporation tax)."

2 In section 574 of CTA 2009 (derivative contracts: non-trading credits and debits to be brought into account), for the subsection (2A) inserted into that section by paragraph 18 of Schedule 5 to FA 2019 substitute—

"(2A)   In the case of a non-UK resident company, subsection (2) needs to be read with section 5(3), (3A)(b) and (3B)(b) (territorial scope of charge to corporation tax)."

Debits referable to times before UK property business etc is carried on

3 After section 330 of CTA 2009 insert—

"*Pre-commencement debits of property businesses etc of non-UK resident companies*

330ZA   Debits referable to times before UK property business etc carried on

(1)   This section applies if—

    (a)   a non-UK resident company has debits in respect of a loan relationship to which it is a party for the purposes of its UK property business,

    (b)   the debits are referable to times ("the pre-rental times") before (but not more than 7 years before) the date on which it starts to carry on the business, and

    (c)   the debits are not otherwise brought into account for tax purposes.

(2)   If, on the assumption that the company had been carrying on the business at the pre-rental times, the debits—

    (a)   would have been recognised in determining its profit or loss for a period consisting of or including those times, and

    (b)   would have been brought into account for the purposes of this Part,

the debits are (so far as they exceed relevant credits) treated for the purposes of this Part as if they were debits for the accounting period in which it started to carry on the business.

(3)   For this purpose "relevant credits" means credits of the company in respect of the loan relationship which, on the assumption that the company had been carrying on the business at the pre-rental times—

    (a)   would have been recognised in determining its profit or loss for a period consisting of or including those times,

    (b)   would have been brought into account for the purposes of this Part, and

    (c)   would not otherwise have been brought into account for tax purposes.

(4)   This section is subject to section 327 (disallowance of imported losses etc).

(5)   This section also applies in relation to a non-UK resident company which is a party to a loan relationship for the purpose of enabling it to generate other UK property income (within the meaning given by section 5(6))."

4 After section 607 of CTA 2009 insert—

"607ZA   Debits referable to times before UK property business etc carried on

(1)   This section applies if—

    (a)   a non-UK resident company has debits in respect of a derivative contract to which it is a party for the purposes of its UK property business,

    (b)   the debits are referable to times ("the pre-rental times") before (but not more than 7 years before) the date on which it starts to carry on the business, and

    (c)   the debits are not otherwise brought into account for tax purposes.

(2)   If, on the assumption that the company had been carrying on the business at the pre-rental times, the debits—

    (a)   would have been recognised in determining its profit or loss for a period consisting of or including those times, and

    (b)   would have been brought into account for the purposes of this Part,

the debits are (so far as they exceed relevant credits) treated for the purposes of this Part as if they were debits for the accounting period in which it started to carry on the business.

(3)   For this purpose "relevant credits" means credits of the company in respect of the derivative contract which, on the assumption that the company had been carrying on the business at the pre-rental times—

    (a)   would have been recognised in determining its profit or loss for a period consisting of or including those times,

    (b)   would have been brought into account for the purposes of this Part, and

    (c)   would not otherwise have been brought into account for tax purposes.

(4)   This section also applies in relation to a non-UK resident company which is a party to a derivative contract for the purpose of enabling it to generate other UK property income (within the meaning given by section 5(6))."

5 In paragraph 40 of Schedule 5 to FA 2019 (transitional provision: imported losses in respect of derivative contracts), at the end insert—

"(7)   Section 607ZA of CTA 2009 (debits referable to times before UK property business carried on) has effect subject to this paragraph."

Duty to notify chargeability to corporation tax: exceptions

6 In paragraph 2 of Schedule 18 to FA 1998 (duty of company to notify HMRC that it is chargeable for an accounting period if it has not received a notice requiring a company tax return), in sub-paragraph (1A) (which provides an exception to that duty), as inserted into that paragraph by paragraph 6(2) of Schedule 5 to FA 2019—

    (a)   omit the "and" before paragraph (b), and

    (b)   after that paragraph insert ", and

    (c)   having deducted the income tax mentioned in paragraph (a) at the fourth step in paragraph 8 (calculation of tax payable), the amount of tax payable for the period is nil."

7 In section 55A(1) of FA 2004 (exception to duty of company to give notice of coming within the charge to corporation tax), as inserted by paragraph 7 of Schedule 5 to FA 2019—

    (a)   omit the "and" before paragraph (b), and

    (b)   after that paragraph insert ", and

    (c)   in consequence of the deduction of the income tax mentioned in paragraph (a) at the fourth step in paragraph 8 of Schedule 18 to the Finance Act 1998 (calculation of tax payable), the amount of tax payable for the period will be nil."

Period for making election under regulation 6A of the Disregard Regulations

8 In regulation 6A of the Loan Relationships and Derivative Contracts (Disregard and Bringing into Account of Profits and Losses) Regulations 2004—

    (a)   in paragraph (5)(b), after "fair value" insert "(but see paragraph (6))", and

    (b)   at the end insert—

"(6)   For the purposes of the definition of "the first relevant period" an accounting period of a company is to be ignored if—

    (a)   the accounting period begins solely as a result of a disposal of an asset by the company, and

(b) any gain accruing to the company on the disposal would be chargeable to corporation tax as a result of section 2B(4) of the Taxation of Chargeable Gains Act 1992."

9 In paragraph 44 of Schedule 5 to FA 2019, at the end insert—

"(4) In determining for the purposes of this paragraph whether, on the commencement date, a company comes within the charge to corporation tax by reason of this Schedule, no account is to be taken of any disposal made by the company before that date where any gain accruing to the company on the disposal would be chargeable to corporation tax as a result of section 2B(4) of TCGA 1992."

Commencement

10 Schedule 5 to FA 2019 has effect as if the amendments made by paragraphs 1 to 7 had at all times been incorporated into the provision made by that Schedule.

11 The amendments made by paragraphs 8 and 9 have effect in relation to disposals made on or after 6 April 2019.

COMMENTARY ON SCHEDULE 6

Schedule 6 contains a number of minor amendments to the loan relationships and derivative contracts legislation which primarily address the way in which these regimes apply to non-UK resident companies that come within the charge to corporation tax with effect from 5 April 2020 in respect of their UK property business or other UK property income (within the meaning of CTA 2009, s 5(5)).

The effect of the amendment made by paragraph 1 is to ensure that non-trading loan relationship debits and credits are included in computing the profits and losses of a UK permanent establishment of a non-UK resident company, to the extent that the company is a party to the loan relationship for the purposes of its UK permanent establishment. This amendment is deemed to have effect from 6 April 2019 (being the date that the original amendment introduced by FA 2019, Sch 5 took effect) (paragraph 8).

Paragraph 2 contains an equivalent amendment to paragraph 1 to the provisions of the derivative contracts legislation. This amendment is also deemed to have effect from 6 April 2019 (being the date that the original amendment introduced by FA 2019, Sch 5 took effect) (paragraph 8).

Paragraph 3 introduces a new CTA 2009, s 330ZA, which permits a company to obtain relief for net pre-business debits that arise in respect of loan relationships in the seven year period before it begins to carry on a UK property business or to receive other UK property income (within the meaning of CTA 2009, s 5(5)).

Paragraph 4 introduces an equivalent provision, CTA 2009, s 607ZA, to permit a company to obtain relief for net pre-business derivative contract debits that arise in the seven year period before it begins to carry on a UK property business or to receive other UK property income.

Paragraph 5 makes an amendment to FA 2019, Sch 5, para 40 to provide that the transitional rules for imported losses will take precedence over CTA 2009, s 607ZA which is being introduced by paragraph 4.

Paragraph 6 modifies the obligation of a non-UK resident company that is carrying on a UK property business, or is in receipt of UK property income, to give notice that it is chargeable to corporation tax for an accounting period. The effect of the amendment is that a company will not need to give notice to HMRC where its corporation tax liability for the accounting period is covered by income tax that has been withheld from rental payments. Paragraph 7 makes an equivalent amendment to FA 2004, s 55A.

Paragraphs 8 and 9 address a concern expressed to HMRC that if a company disposed of a property and triggered a liability to corporation tax on chargeable gains in the tax year to 5 April 2020, this could have accelerated the deadline by which it would have to elect in order to apply the Loan Relationships and Derivative Contracts (Disregard and Bringing into Account of Profits and Losses) Regulations 2004 to derivative contracts for which it is a party to the purposes of its UK property business or its business of receiving UK property income. The effect of the amendment is that the chargeable gain on or after 6 April 2019 will be disregarded in determining when the company came within the charge to corporation tax so that it will be treated as if it had come within the charge to corporation tax with effect from 6 April 2020.

Paragraph 10 provides that the amendments made by paragraphs 1–7 will be treated as if they had been included in FA 2019, Sch 5.

Paragraph 11 provides that the amendments made by paragraphs 8 and 9 have effect in relation to disposals on or after 6 April 2019.

SCHEDULE 7

CT PAYMENT PLANS FOR TAX ON CERTAIN TRANSACTIONS WITH EEA RESIDENTS

Section 34

CT payment plans

1 In TMA 1970, after section 59FA insert—

"59FB   CT payment plans for tax on certain transactions with EEA residents

Schedule 3ZC makes provision enabling a company that is liable to pay corporation tax arising in connection with certain transactions to defer payment of the tax by entering into a CT payment plan."

2 After Schedule 3ZB to TMA 1970 insert—

"SCHEDULE 3ZC

CT PAYMENT PLANS FOR TAX ON CERTAIN TRANSACTIONS WITH EEA RESIDENTS

Section 59FB

Introduction

1 This Schedule makes provision enabling a company that is liable to pay qualifying corporation tax for an accounting period to defer payment of the tax by entering into a CT payment plan.

Qualifying corporation tax

2 (1)   For the purposes of this Schedule a company is liable to pay qualifying corporation tax for an accounting period if CT1 is greater than CT2 where—

CT1 is the corporation tax which the company is liable to pay for the accounting period, and
CT2 is the corporation tax which the company would be liable to pay for the accounting period if any gains, credits, losses or debits arising in respect of qualifying transactions of the company were ignored.

(CT2 will be zero if the company would not be liable to pay any corporation tax for the period).

(2)   The amount of qualifying corporation tax which the company is liable to pay is the difference between CT1 and CT2.

Qualifying transactions

3 (1)   For the purposes of this Schedule each of the following is a qualifying transaction of a company ("the company concerned")—

    (a)   a disposal within sub-paragraph (2),
    (b)   a transaction within sub-paragraph (3),
    (c)   a transaction within sub-paragraph (4), and
    (d)   a transfer within sub-paragraph (5).

(2)   A disposal is within this sub-paragraph if—

    (a)   it is a disposal by the company concerned of an asset,
    (b)   it is a disposal to a company ("the transferee") that at the time of the disposal is resident outside the United Kingdom in an EEA state, and
    (c)   it is a disposal to which section 139 or 171 of TCGA 1992 would apply were the transferee resident at the time of the disposal in the United Kingdom instead.

(3)   A transaction is within this sub-paragraph if—

    (a)   it is a transaction, or the first in a series of transactions, as a result of which the company concerned is directly or indirectly replaced as a party to a loan relationship by another company ("the transferee"),
    (b)   at the time of the transaction the transferee is resident outside the United Kingdom in an EEA state, and

(c) it is a transaction to which section 340(3) of CTA 2009 would apply were the transferee resident at the time of the transaction in the United Kingdom instead.

(4) A transaction is within this sub-paragraph if—

(a) it is a transaction, or the first in a series of transactions, as a result of which the company concerned is directly or indirectly replaced as a party to a derivative contract by another company ("the transferee"),

(b) at the time of the transaction the transferee is resident outside the United Kingdom in an EEA state, and

(c) it is a transaction to which section 625(3) of CTA 2009 would apply were the transferee resident at the time of the transaction in the United Kingdom instead.

(5) A transfer is within this sub-paragraph if—

(a) it is a transfer from the company concerned of an intangible fixed asset,

(b) it is a transfer to a company ("the transferee") that immediately after the transfer is resident outside the United Kingdom in an EEA state, and

(c) it is a transfer to which section 775(1) of CTA 2009 would apply were the transferee resident immediately after the transfer in the United Kingdom instead.

(6) In this Schedule "transferee", in relation to a qualifying transaction of a company, means the transferee referred to in sub-paragraph (2), (3), (4) or (5) (as the case may be).

Eligibility to enter a CT payment plan

4 (1) A company that is liable to pay qualifying corporation tax for an accounting period may enter into a CT payment plan in respect of the tax in accordance with this Schedule.

(2) The CT payment plan may relate to—

(a) all of the qualifying corporation tax that the company is liable to pay for the accounting period, or

(b) only part of the qualifying corporation tax that the company is liable to pay for the accounting period.

(3) In this Schedule "deferred tax", in relation to a CT payment plan, means the qualifying corporation tax to which the plan relates.

Application to enter a CT payment plan

5 A company that is liable to pay qualifying corporation tax for an accounting period may enter into a CT payment plan in respect of the tax only if—

(a) an application to enter into the plan is made to HMRC before the end of the period of 9 months beginning immediately after the accounting period, and

(b) the application contains details of all the matters which are required by paragraph 7 to be specified in the plan.

Entering into a CT payment plan

6 (1) A company enters into a CT payment plan if—

(a) the company agrees to pay, and an officer of Revenue and Customs agrees to accept payment of, the deferred tax in accordance with paragraphs 9 to 12,

(b) the company agrees to pay interest on the deferred tax in accordance with paragraph 8(3) and (5), and

(c) the plan meets the requirements of paragraph 7 as to the matters that must be specified in it.

(2) The CT payment plan may, in the circumstances mentioned in sub-paragraph (3), contain appropriate provision regarding security for HMRC in respect of the payment of the deferred tax.

(3) Those circumstances are where an officer of Revenue and Customs considers that agreeing to accept payment of the deferred tax in accordance with paragraphs 9 to 12 would present a serious risk as to collection of the tax in the absence of provision regarding security in respect of its payment.

(4) A CT payment plan is void if any information furnished by the company in connection with the plan does not fully and accurately disclose all facts and considerations material to the decision of the officer of Revenue and Customs to accept payment of the deferred tax in accordance with paragraphs 9 to 12.

Content of CT payment plan

7 (1) A CT payment plan entered into by a company must—

    (a)   specify the accounting period to which the plan relates ("the accounting period concerned"),

    (b)   specify the amount of qualifying corporation tax which, in the company's opinion, is payable by it in respect of the accounting period concerned,

    (c)   specify the amount of the deferred tax,

    (d)   identify each qualifying transaction of the company in respect of which gains or credits arose in the accounting period concerned, and

    (e)   specify in relation to each of those qualifying transactions—

        (i)   the name of the transferee,

        (ii)   the EEA state in which the transferee was resident at the time of the transaction, and

        (iii)   the amount of the deferred tax that is attributable to the transaction.

(2) The amount of the deferred tax that is attributable to a qualifying transaction of the company in respect of which a gain or credit arose in the accounting period concerned is—

$(A / B) \times T$

where—

A is the gain or credit that arose in the accounting period concerned in respect of the qualifying transaction,

B is the total gains or credits that arose in the accounting period concerned in respect of all qualifying transactions of the company,

T is the amount of the deferred tax.

Effect of CT payment plan

8 (1) This paragraph applies where a CT payment plan is entered into by a company in accordance with this Schedule.

(2) As regards when the deferred tax is payable—

    (a)   the CT payment plan does not prevent the deferred tax becoming due and payable under section 59D or 59E, but

    (b)   the Commissioners for Her Majesty's Revenue and Customs—

        (i)   may not seek payment of the deferred tax otherwise than in accordance with paragraphs 9 to 12;

        (ii)   may make repayments in respect of any amount of the deferred tax paid, or any amount paid on account of the deferred tax, before the CT payment plan is entered into.

(3) As regards interest—

    (a)   the deferred tax carries interest in accordance with Part 9 as if the CT payment plan had not been entered into, and

    (b)   each time a payment is made in accordance with paragraphs 9 to 12, it is to be paid together with any interest payable on it.

(4) As regards penalties, the company will be liable to penalties for late payment of the deferred tax only if it fails to make payments in accordance with paragraphs 9 to 12 (see item 6ZAA of the Table at the end of paragraph 1 of Schedule 56 to the Finance Act 2009).

(5) Any of the deferred tax which is for the time being unpaid may be paid at any time before it becomes payable under paragraphs 9 to 12 together with interest payable on it to the date of payment.

The payment method: instalments

9 (1) Where a CT payment plan is entered into by a company, the deferred tax is due in 6 instalments of equal amounts as follows—

   (a)   the first instalment is due on the first day after the period of 9 months beginning immediately after the end of the accounting period to which the plan relates, and

   (b)   the other 5 instalments are due one on each of the first 5 anniversaries of that day.

(2) But see paragraphs 10 to 12 for circumstances in which all or part of the outstanding balance of the deferred tax becomes due otherwise than by those instalments.

The payment method: all of outstanding balance due

10 (1)   Where at any time after a CT payment plan is entered into by a company an event mentioned in sub-paragraph (2) occurs the outstanding balance of the deferred tax is due on the date on which the next instalment of that tax would otherwise be due.

(2) The events are—

   (a)   the company becoming insolvent or entering administration;

   (b)   the appointment of a liquidator in respect of the company;

   (c)   an event under the law of a country or territory outside the United Kingdom corresponding to an event in paragraph (a) or (b);

   (d)   the company failing to pay any amount of the deferred tax for a period of 12 months after the date on which the amount becomes due;

   (e)   the company ceasing to be within the charge to corporation tax.

All of outstanding balance attributable to particular qualifying transaction due

11 (1)   This paragraph applies where—

   (a)   a CT payment plan is entered into by a company,

   (b)   during the instalments period a trigger event occurs in relation to a qualifying transaction identified in the plan, and

   (c)   a trigger event has not previously occurred in relation to that qualifying transaction during the instalments period.

(2) A trigger event occurs in relation to a qualifying transaction if the transferee ceases to be resident in an EEA state and, on so ceasing, does not become resident another EEA state.

(3) A trigger event occurs in relation to a qualifying transaction if the company and the transferee cease to be members of the same group as one another.

(4) A trigger event occurs in relation to a qualifying transaction within sub-paragraph (2) or (5) of paragraph 3 if the transferee disposes of the asset that is the subject of the transaction.

(5) A trigger event occurs in relation to a qualifying transaction within sub-paragraph (3) or (4) of paragraph 3 if the transferee ceases to be a party to the loan relationship or derivative contract concerned.

(6) On the occurrence of the trigger event an amount of the deferred tax is due.

(7) The amount due is—

$$(A - B) \times (O / T)$$

where—

> "A" is the amount of the deferred tax that is attributable to the qualifying transaction (see paragraph 7(2)),
>
> "B" is the amount of the deferred tax that has previously become due under paragraph 12 by reason of a partial trigger event occurring in relation to the qualifying transaction,
>
> "O" is the amount of the deferred tax that is outstanding at the time of the trigger event, and
>
> "T" is the amount of the deferred tax.

(8) In this paragraph "the instalments period" means the period—

   (a)   beginning with the time the CT payment plan is entered into, and

   (b)   ending with the day on which the final instalment of the deferred tax is due under paragraph 9.

Part of outstanding balance attributable to particular qualifying transaction due

12 (1)   This paragraph applies where—

(a) a CT payment plan is entered into by a company,

(b) during the instalments period a partial trigger event occurs in relation to a qualifying transaction listed in the plan, and

(c) a trigger event has not previously occurred in relation to that qualifying transaction during the instalments period.

(2) A partial trigger event occurs in relation to a qualifying transaction within sub-paragraph (2) of paragraph 3 if the transferee disposes of part (but not all) of the asset that is the subject of the transaction.

Section 21(2)(b) of TCGA 1992 (meaning of part disposal of an asset) applies for the purposes of this sub-paragraph as it applies for the purposes of that Act.

(3) A partial trigger event occurs in relation to a qualifying transaction within sub-paragraph (3) or (4) of paragraph 3 if there is a disposal by the transferee of a right or liability under the loan relationship or derivative contract concerned which amounts to a related transaction (as defined in section 304 or 596 of CTA 2009 as the case may be).

(4) A partial trigger event occurs in relation to a qualifying transaction within sub-paragraph (5) of paragraph 3 if the transferee enters into a subsequent transaction which results in a reduction in the accounting value of the intangible fixed asset that is the subject of the qualifying transaction but does not result in the intangible fixed asset ceasing to be recognised in the transferee's balance sheet.

(5) In relation to an intangible fixed asset that has no balance sheet value (or no longer has a balance sheet value) sub-paragraph (4) applies as if, immediately before the subsequent transaction, it did have a balance sheet value.

(6) On the occurrence of the partial trigger event an amount of the deferred tax is due.

(7) The amount due is the amount that is just and reasonable having regard to the amount that would have been due had a trigger event occurred in relation to the qualifying transaction instead.

(8) In this paragraph "the instalments period" and "trigger event" have the same meaning as in paragraph 11."

Penalties

3 (1) Schedule 56 to FA 2009 (penalty for failure to make payments on time) is amended as follows.

(2) In the Table at the end of paragraph 1, after entry 6ZA insert—

| "6ZAA | Corporation tax | Amount payable under a CT payment plan entered into in accordance with Schedule 3ZC to TMA 1970 | The later of—
(a)the first day after the period of 12 months beginning immediately after the accounting period to which the CT payment plan relates, and
(b)the date on which the amount is payable under the plan." |

(3) In paragraph 4 (amount of penalty in respect of certain late payments) in sub-paragraph (1) for "6ZA" substitute "6ZAA".

Commencement

4 (1) The amendments made by this Schedule—

(a) have effect in relation to accounting periods ending on or after 10 October 2018, and

(b) are to be treated as having come into force on 11 July 2019.

(2) The condition for entering into a CT payment plan that is specified in paragraph (a) of paragraph 5 of Schedule 3ZC to TMA 1970 is to be treated as met if an application to enter into the plan is made to HMRC on or before 30 June 2020.

Power of repeal

5 (1) The Treasury may by regulations—

(a) repeal section 59FB of TMA 1970,

(b) repeal Schedule 3ZC to TMA 1970, and

(c)   amend Schedule 56 to FA 2009 in consequence of those repeals.

(2)   Regulations under this paragraph may contain savings and transitional provisions.

(3)   Regulations under this paragraph are to be made by statutory instrument.

(4)   A statutory instrument containing regulations under this paragraph is subject to annulment in pursuance of a resolution of the House of Commons.

COMMENTARY ON SCHEDULE 7

Certain asset transfers by companies are treated as effectively being free of corporation tax where both the transferor and the transferee are UK resident. Obvious examples are the rules for transfers of chargeable assets at no gain and no loss between UK group companies (TCGA 1992, s 171) or where the transfer is pursuant to a scheme of reconstruction (TCGA 1992, s 139). Where the transferee is not resident in the UK but is resident in an EEA member state, this tax favourable treatment is not available, which is arguably in contravention of EU and EEA legislation. This is something that many observers have highlighted over the last two decades or so but clearly came to the fore as a result of the First-tier Tribunal decision in *Gallaher Ltd* ([2019] UKFTT 207 (TC), TC07055), where the tribunal found in favour of the appellant company in respect of transfers of shares to the Dutch resident parent company.

The new rules permit the company to claim a deferral of the corporation tax charge relating to the relevant disposals over a period of five years. The rules are very similar to those introduced by FA 2013 to defer payments of corporation tax by companies ceasing to be UK resident.

The rules are contained in new TMA 1970, Sch 3ZC, introduced by new TMA 1970, s 59FB. The legislation comes into force on 11 July 2019 but is effective for accounting periods ending on or after 10 October 2018.

Deferrable CT and 'qualifying transactions'

The legislation requires the company to find the difference between the corporation tax the company is liable to pay for an accounting period and the amount of corporation tax that the company would be liable to pay if the gains or losses, credits or debits in respect of 'qualifying transactions' were ignored (TMA 1970, Sch 3ZC, para 2). When the actual amount of corporation tax payable is higher, the instalment payments plan can be applied to the difference.

Qualifying transactions are the following (paragraph 3):

- a disposal of an asset to a company resident in the EEA but not the UK where TCGA 1992, ss 139 or 171 (no gain / no loss transactions) would apply if the transferee company were UK resident
- transactions where the company is replaced as party to a loan relationship by a company resident in the EEA but not the UK, where CTA 2009, s 340(3) (transfer at notional carrying value of the asset or liability) would apply if the transferee were UK resident
- transactions where the company is replaced as party to a derivative contract by a company resident in the EEA but not the UK, where CTA 2009, s 625(3) (transfer at notional carrying value of the asset or liability) would apply if the transferee were UK resident
- transfers of intangible fixed assets by the company to a company resident in the EEA but not the UK, to which CTA 2009, s 775(1) ('tax neutral' transfers) would have applied, if the transferee had been UK resident.

A company can apply to enter into a CT payment plan in respect of the whole amount of the deferred tax or just part of it (paragraph 4) and the application must be made to HMRC within nine months of the end of the relevant accounting period. Where this period is already expired (given that the legislation applies to accounting periods ending on or after 10 October 2018) the election must be made on or by 30 June 2020.

Effect of a CT payment plan

Where a CT payment plan is entered into, the relevant amount of corporation tax is payable in six equal annual instalments, starting at nine months and one day after the end of the relevant accounting period (paragraph 9). While the tax remains technically due and payable, HMRC is not allowed to seek payment otherwise than in accordance with the payment plan or the legislation that otherwise requires payment of the outstanding amounts (paragraph 8).

Interest on late payment of tax is, however, due under the normal provisions and each instalment payment must be accompanied by the appropriate amount of interest. No penalties are due for late payment of tax, however, so long as the company pays the relevant amounts of corporation tax at the appropriate time (paragraph 8).

Early payment of balances

Payment of the whole of the outstanding balance will become due on the occurrence of a 'trigger event', as follows (paragraph 10):

- the company becoming insolvent or entering administration
- the appointment of a liquidator in respect of the company
- an event under the law of a country or territory outside the UK corresponding to either of the above
- the company failing to pay any amount of the deferred tax for a period of 12 months after the date on which the amount becomes due
- the company ceasing to be within the charge to corporation tax.

The result of such a trigger event is that the whole of the outstanding balance is to be paid on the next instalment payment date.

The outstanding balance relating to a specific transaction must be paid if one of the following trigger events occurs (paragraph 11):

- the transferee ceases to be resident in an EEA member state and not becoming resident in another one
- the transferor and transferee cease to be members of the same group
- where the qualifying transaction related to a disposal or transfer of chargeable assets or chargeable intangible assets, the transferee disposes of the assets
- where the asset was a loan relationship or derivative contract, the transferee ceases to be a party to that loan relationship or derivative contract

In these cases, the deferred corporation tax is due when the trigger event happens

It is also possible to have partial trigger events where, for example, there is a part disposal of a chargeable asset or part realisation of a chargeable intangible asset by a transferee company, or if a transferee company disposes of a right or liability under a loan relationship or derivative contract that amounts to a related transaction (paragraph 12). In these cases, the amount of corporation tax that would immediately become due and payable is to be calculated on a just and reasonable basis.

Administrative requirements

A CT payment plan must specify all of the following (paragraph 7):

- the accounting period to which the plan relates
- the amount of qualifying corporation tax payable in respect of the accounting period
- the amount of the deferred tax
- identify each qualifying transaction of the company in respect of which gains or credits arose in the accounting period concerned, and
- in relation to each of the qualifying transactions, state the name of the transferee, the EEA state in which the transferee was resident at the time of the transaction, and the amount of the deferred tax that is attributable to the transaction

The plan must be agreed to by both the company and HMRC (paragraph 4(1)). HMRC can also require security where an officer of HMRC considers that this is necessary where entering into the plan might pose a serious risk to the collection of the tax (paragraph 4(2) and (3)). A CT payment plan is void if the information given by the company 'does not fully and accurately disclose all facts and considerations material to the decision of [HMRC]' (paragraph 4(4)).

SCHEDULE 8

DIGITAL SERVICES TAX: RETURNS, ENQUIRIES, ASSESSMENTS AND APPEALS

Section 56

PART 1

INTRODUCTION

1 (1)   References in this Schedule—

    (a)   to the delivery of a DST return are to the delivery of a return by the responsible member for an accounting period where the return complies with the requirements of paragraph 2(2);

    (b)   to the filing date, in relation to a DST return, are to the last day of the period within which the return must be delivered.

(2)   In this Schedule—

"relevant person" has the same meaning as in section 47;

"tax" means digital services tax;

"tribunal" means the First-tier Tribunal, or where determined by or under Tribunal Procedure Rules, the Upper Tribunal.

COMMENTARY ON SCHEDULE 8, PART 1

Schedule 8 is a lengthy overview of DST administration. The Schedule covers DST returns, the enquiries, assessments, and appeals process. Much of the DST administration process mirrors that of the corporation tax process for enquiries, assessment and appeals; however, as DST is a new tax, and not within the corporation tax system, all of this repetition is legislatively necessary.

Schedule 8 does not repeat matters already covered in sections 39–72, thus matters such as the responsible member, group definition, the alternative basis of charge calculation, accounting periods and other areas already discussed are assumed knowledge in this Schedule.

PART 2

DST RETURNS

DST returns

2 (1)   A DST return for an accounting period must be delivered before the end of one year from the end of the accounting period.

(2)   A DST return must—

    (a)   be in the specified form,

    (b)   contain specified information,

    (c)   contain an assessment ("a self-assessment") of the amount of tax payable by the group for the accounting period (including a breakdown showing the amount of tax payable by each relevant person), and

    (d)   contain a declaration by the person making the return that the return is, to the best of the person's knowledge, correct and complete.

(3)   In this paragraph "specified" means specified in a notice published by HMRC.

Amendment of return by responsible member

3 (1)   This paragraph applies where a DST return has been delivered.

(2)   The responsible member may amend the DST return by notice to HMRC.

(3)   The notice must—

    (a)   be in the specified form, and

    (b)   contain specified information.

(4)   In this paragraph "specified" means specified in a notice published by HMRC.

(5)   No amendment may be made under this paragraph more than 12 months after the filing date.

COMMENTARY ON SCHEDULE 8, PART 2

Part 2 of the Schedule concerns the DST returns themselves. The responsible member of the group carries the responsibility for filing the annual DST return within one year of the end of the accounting period. It is important to remember the earlier definitions of accounting period here which ordinarily follow consolidated accounting dates. The DST returns procedure is an online self-assessment exercise, undertaken using HMRC's online portal on GOV.UK. HMRC's portal will direct the user to include the specified information. Only the responsible member may amend this return and again, this is only available online through the DST portal. Amendments may be made by the responsible member up to 12 months after the original filing date.

PART 3

DUTY TO KEEP AND PRESERVE RECORDS

Duty to keep and preserve records

4 (1) This paragraph applies in relation to a group for an accounting period if the responsible member is required by section 56 to deliver a DST return for that period.

(2) The responsible member must—

    (a) keep such records as may be needed to enable it to deliver a correct and complete DST return, and

    (b) preserve those records in accordance with this paragraph.

(3) The records must be preserved until the end of the relevant day.

(4) In this paragraph "the relevant day" means—

    (a) the sixth anniversary of the last day of the accounting period, or

    (b) such earlier day as may be specified (and different days may be specified for different cases).

(5) In this paragraph "specified" means specified in a notice published by HMRC.

Preservation of information etc

5 The duty under paragraph 4 to preserve records may be satisfied—

    (a) by preserving them in any form and by any means, or

    (b) by preserving the information contained in them in any form and by any means,

subject to any conditions or exceptions specified in a notice published by HMRC.

COMMENTARY ON SCHEDULE 8, PART 3

Part 3 of the Schedule requires the responsible member to maintain and preserve records relating to the submitted DST returns for six years following the end of the accounting period (unless specifically told otherwise that it may be earlier). HMRC may require these records at any time within that time frame.

The records which the responsible member is expected to keep are discussed further in HMRC guidance, to include transaction records, financial management reports, accounting reports and any other relevant documents used to deliver the DST return. Especially in early years, we can expect HMRC to be particularly interested in records, as this provides an insight into how groups have determined their business activities, calculated their UK digital services revenues, determined location of users, taken just and reasonable splits into account, to name just a few areas. With a risk-based approach, HMRC is likely to spend considerable time with a small pool of larger businesses understanding the detail of their returns.

PART 4

ENQUIRY INTO RETURN

Notice of enquiry

6 (1) An officer of Revenue and Customs may enquire into a DST return if, within the time allowed, the officer gives notice to the responsible member of the officer's intention to do so.

(2) The time allowed is—

    (a)   if the return was delivered on or before the filing date, up to the end of the period of 12 months after the filing date;

    (b)   if the return was delivered after the filing date, up to and including the quarter day next following the first anniversary of the day on which the return was delivered;

    (c)   if the return is amended under paragraph 3, up to and including the quarter day next following the first anniversary of the day on which the return was amended.

The quarter days are the 31 January, 30 April, 31 July and 31 October.

(3)   A return that has been the subject of one notice of enquiry may not be the subject of another, except one given in consequence of an amendment (or another amendment) of the return under paragraph 3.

(4)   A notice under this paragraph is referred to as a "notice of enquiry".

Scope of enquiry

7 (1)   An enquiry extends to anything contained in the return, or required to be contained in the return, including anything that relates—

    (a)   to the question of whether tax is chargeable in respect of the accounting period, or

    (b)   to the amount of tax so chargeable.

This is subject to the following exception.

(2)   If the notice of enquiry is given as a result of an amendment of the return under paragraph 3—

    (a)   at a time when it is no longer possible to give notice of enquiry under paragraph 6(2)(a) or (b), or

    (b)   after an enquiry into a return has been completed,

the enquiry into the return is limited to matters to which the amendment relates or that are affected by the amendment.

Amendment of self-assessment during enquiry to prevent loss of tax

8 (1)   If at a time when an enquiry is in progress into a DST return an officer of Revenue and Customs forms the opinion—

    (a)   that the amount stated in the self-assessment contained in the return as the amount of tax payable is insufficient, and

    (b)   that unless the assessment is immediately amended there is likely to be a loss of tax to the Crown,

the officer may by notice in writing to the responsible member amend the assessment to make good the deficiency.

(2)   In the case of an enquiry that under paragraph 7(2) is limited to matters arising from an amendment of the return, sub-paragraph (1) applies only so far as the deficiency is attributable to the amendment.

(3)   For the purposes of this paragraph the period during which an enquiry is in progress is the whole of the period—

    (a)   beginning with the day on which notice of enquiry is given, and

    (b)   ending with the day on which the enquiry is completed.

Amendment of return by responsible member during enquiry

9 (1)   This paragraph applies if a DST return is amended under paragraph 3 at a time when an enquiry is in progress into the return.

(2)   The amendment does not restrict the scope of the enquiry but may be taken into account (together with any matters arising) in the enquiry.

(3)   While the enquiry is in progress, so far as the amendment affects the amount stated in the self-assessment as the amount of tax payable, the amendment does not take effect in relation to any matter to which it relates or which is affected by it.

(4)   An amendment whose effect is deferred under sub-paragraph (3) takes effect as follows—

    (a)   if the conclusions in a closure notice state either—

        (i)   that the amendment was not taken into account in the enquiry, or

        (ii)   that no amendment of the return is required arising from the enquiry, the amendment takes effect when the closure notice is issued (see paragraph 14);

  (b)   in any other case, the amendment takes effect as part of the amendments made by the closure notice.

(5)   For the purposes of this paragraph the period during which an enquiry is in progress is the whole of the period—

  (a)   beginning with the day on which notice of enquiry is given, and
  (b)   ending with the day on which the enquiry is completed.

Referral of questions to the tribunal during enquiry

10 (1)   At any time when an enquiry is in progress into a DST return any question arising in connection with the subject-matter of the enquiry may be referred to the tribunal for determination.

(2)   Notice of referral must be given to the tribunal, jointly by the responsible member and an officer of Revenue and Customs.

(3)   More than one notice of referral may be given under this paragraph in relation to an enquiry.

(4)   For the purposes of this paragraph the period during which an enquiry is in progress is the whole of the period—

  (a)   beginning with the day on which notice of enquiry is given, and
  (b)   ending with the day on which the enquiry is completed.

Withdrawal of notice of referral

11 An officer of Revenue and Customs or the responsible member may withdraw a notice of referral under paragraph 10.

Effect of referral on enquiry

12 (1)   While proceedings on a referral under paragraph 10 are in progress in relation to an enquiry—

  (a)   no closure notice may be given in relation to the enquiry (see paragraph 14), and
  (b)   no application may be made for a direction to give such a notice.

(2)   For the purposes of this paragraph proceedings on a referral are in progress where—

  (a)   notice of referral has been given,
  (b)   the notice has not been withdrawn, and
  (c)   the questions referred have not been finally determined.

(3)   For the purposes of sub-paragraph (2)(c) a question referred is finally determined when—

  (a)   it has been determined by the tribunal, and
  (b)   there is no further possibility of the determination being varied or set aside (disregarding any power to grant permission to appeal out of time).

Effect of determination

13 (1)   The determination of a question referred to the tribunal under paragraph 10 is binding on the parties to the referral in the same way, and to the same extent, as a decision on a preliminary issue in an appeal.

(2)   The determination must be taken into account by an officer of Revenue and Customs—

  (a)   in reaching the officer's conclusions on the enquiry, and
  (b)   in formulating any amendments of the return required to give effect to those conclusions.

(3)   The question determined may not be reopened on an appeal, except to the extent that it could be reopened if it had been determined as a preliminary issue in that appeal.

Completion of enquiry

14 (1)   An enquiry is completed when an officer of Revenue and Customs by notice (a "closure notice") informs the responsible member that the enquiry is complete and states the conclusions reached in the enquiry.

(2)   A closure notice must either—

    (a)   state that in the opinion of an officer of Revenue and Customs no amendment of the return is required, or

    (b)   make the amendments of the return required to give effect to the conclusions stated in the notice.

(3)   A closure notice takes effect when it is issued.

Direction to complete enquiry

15 (1)   The responsible member may apply to the tribunal for a direction that an officer of Revenue and Customs give a closure notice under paragraph 14 within a specified period.

(2)   The tribunal hearing the application must give a direction unless satisfied that HMRC have reasonable grounds for not giving an enquiry closure notice within a specified period.

(3)   Paragraphs 44 (settling of appeals by agreement) and 51 (tribunal determinations) apply to an application under sub-paragraph (1) as they apply to an appeal under paragraph 33, subject to any necessary modifications.

COMMENTARY ON SCHEDULE 8, PART 4

Part 4 of the Schedule discusses the enquires process for DST. HMRC may give notice that it is opening an enquiry within the timeframes discussed, which mirror that of the corporation tax returns process: generally there is a 12 month window, but this is extended somewhat where returns are amended or filed late. Paragraph 6(3) limits HMRC's ability to enquire into separate aspects of the DST return at different times – it must enquire into the DST return once and only once (unless there are amendments).

The scope of HMRC's enquiries where a DST return has been delivered are broad and cover anything related to the DST liability in question. The scope of the enquiry into an amendment is limited to those amendments if the usual deadline for enquiry has passed.

Paragraph 8 allows HMRC to amend the DST assessment during the enquiry process where it believes that DST has been underpaid.

If an amendment to the DST return is made during the enquiry process, under paragraph 9 the amendment would be considered by HMRC but does not limit its powers of enquiry into the return. The amendment may take effect as part of the closure notice as is determined by the closure notice of the enquiry.

Paragraphs 10–13 contain a provision for a joint referral by HMRC and the taxpayer to the tax tribunal during the enquiry process. With agreement from both parties, this enables contentious issues to be dealt with on a question by question basis at the tribunal which could then inform the results of the HMRC enquiries – rather than needing to close an enquiry before taking disagreements to the tribunal. Unless the referral to the tribunal is withdrawn by either party, no closure notice may be issued during the time when the tribunal are considering the question which has been referred. This effectively pauses the HMRC enquiry on a specific point while the tribunal form a conclusion. The tribunal's conclusions are taken to be the same as those formed as a First-tier Tribunal appeals process, meaning that HMRC's determination of the enquiry must respect the conclusions drawn, and neither party may disregard the conclusions other than to appeal via the usual tribunal mechanism as if a first tier conclusion had been drawn.

The closure notice for an enquiry is the same as that for corporation tax, in that it completes the enquiry by either instructing that no amendment is required or making such an amendment. As for a corporation tax enquiry, if the responsible member wishes, they may apply to the tribunal for a closure notice to be issued by HMRC in relation to their enquiries. Whether a direction from the tribunal to close the enquiry is given to HMRC will depend on the facts and circumstances of the enquiry, including any open questions of fact or unanswered requests.

PART 5

HMRC DETERMINATIONS

Determination of tax chargeable if no return delivered

16 (1)   An officer of Revenue and Customs may determine to the best of the officer's information and belief the total amount of tax payable by relevant persons for an accounting period ("an HMRC determination") if the conditions in sub-paragraph (2) are met.

(2)   The conditions in this sub-paragraph are met if—

    (a)   no DST return for the accounting period has been delivered by the end of the filing date, and

    (b)   the officer has reasonable grounds for believing the responsible member is under a duty to deliver a DST return for the accounting period.

(3)   Notice of an HMRC determination—

    (a)   must state the date on which it is issued, and

    (b)   must be served on the responsible member.

(4)   No HMRC determination may be made more than 3 years after the filing date.

Determination to have effect as a self-assessment

17 (1)   An HMRC determination has effect for enforcement purposes as if it were a self-assessment (within the meaning of paragraph 2(2)).

(2)   In sub-paragraph (1) "for enforcement purposes" means for the purposes of provisions providing for—

    (a)   tax-related penalties,

    (b)   collection and recovery of tax, and

    (c)   interest on overdue tax.

(3)   Nothing in this paragraph affects any liability to a penalty for failure to deliver a return.

Determination superseded by actual self-assessment

18 (1)   If, after an HMRC determination has been made, a DST return is delivered for the accounting period, the self-assessment included in the return supersedes the determination.

(2)   Sub-paragraph (1) does not apply to a return delivered—

    (a)   more than 3 years after the day on which the power to make the determination first became exercisable, or

    (b)   more than 12 months after the date of the determination,

whichever is the later.

(3)   Where—

    (a)   proceedings have been begun for the recovery of any tax charged by an HMRC determination, and

    (b)   before the proceedings are concluded the determination is superseded by a self-assessment,

the proceedings may be continued as if they were proceedings for the recovery of so much of the tax charged by the self-assessment as is due and payable and has not been paid.

(4)   Where—

    (a)   action is being taken under Part 1 of Schedule 8 to F(No.2)A 2015 (enforcement of deduction from accounts) for the recovery of an amount ("the original amount") of tax charged by an HMRC determination, and

    (b)   before that action is concluded, the determination is superseded by a self-assessment,

that action may be continued as if it were an action for the recovery of so much of the tax charged by the self-assessment as is due and payable, has not been paid and does not exceed the original amount.

COMMENTARY ON SCHEDULE 8, PART 5

Paragraphs 16–18 discuss the determinations process, whereby HMRC may issue a requirement for DST to be paid in the absence of submission of a DST return. Within three years of the filing deadline, if HMRC determines that a group should have filed a DST return for an accounting period and yet have not, it may issue a determination stating the amount of DST it believes to be payable.

For the purposes of enforcing collection, recovery, interest and penalties, paragraph 17 then instructs that this determination acts as if it were a self-assessment return (yet does not remove any possible penalty for failure to deliver a return, given that the determination was not given by the taxpayer). Where a self-assessment DST return is delivered after a HMRC determination, but within a specified timeframe, paragraph 18 explains that for the most part, the determination is superseded by this late self-assessment. The impact on recovery proceedings of the late self-assessment is covered in paragraph 18(3) and (4).

PART 6

HMRC ASSESSMENTS

Assessments where loss of tax discovered

19 (1) If, in respect of an accounting period of a group, an officer of Revenue and Customs discovers that—

    (a)   an amount of tax that ought to have been assessed has not been assessed, or

    (b)   an assessment to tax is or has become insufficient,

the officer may make an assessment (a "discovery assessment") in the amount or further amount which ought in the officer's opinion to be charged in order to make good to the Crown the loss of tax.

(2) This is subject to the restrictions in paragraph 20.

Restrictions on assessments

20 (1) If a DST return has been delivered in respect of the accounting period, the power to make a discovery assessment—

    (a)   may only be made in the two cases specified in sub-paragraphs (2) and (3), and

    (b)   may not be made in the circumstances specified in sub-paragraph (5).

(2) The first case is where the situation mentioned in paragraph 19(1) was brought about carelessly or deliberately on the part of—

    (a)   a relevant person, or

    (b)   a person acting on behalf of a relevant person.

(3) The second case is where an officer of Revenue and Customs, at the time the officer—

    (a)   ceased to be entitled to give a notice of enquiry into the return, or

    (b)   completed an enquiry into the return,

could not have been reasonably expected, on the basis of the information made available to the officer before that time, to be aware of the situation mentioned in paragraph 19(1).

(4) For this purpose information is regarded as made available to the officer of Revenue and Customs if—

    (a)   it is contained in the DST return for the accounting period in question or either of the two immediately preceding accounting periods,

    (b)   it is contained in any documents produced or information provided by the responsible member for the purposes of an enquiry into any such return, or

    (c)   it is information the existence of which, and the relevance of which as regards the situation mentioned in paragraph 19(1)—

        (i)   could reasonably be expected to be inferred by the officer of Revenue and Customs from information falling within paragraph (a) or (b), or

        (ii)   are notified in writing to an officer of Revenue and Customs by the responsible member or another person acting on the responsible member's behalf.

(5) No discovery assessment may be made if—

    (a)   the situation mentioned in paragraph 19(1) is attributable to a mistake in the return as to the basis on which the tax liability ought to have been calculated, and

(b)   the return was in fact made on the basis or in accordance with the practice generally prevailing at the time it was made.

Time limits for discovery assessments

21 (1)   The general rule is that no discovery assessment may be made more than 4 years after the end of the accounting period to which it relates.

(2)   An assessment in a case involving a loss of tax brought about carelessly by a relevant person (or a person acting on their behalf) may be made at any time not more than 6 years after the end of the accounting period to which it relates.

(3)   An assessment in a case involving a loss of tax—

(a)   brought about deliberately by a relevant person (or a person acting on their behalf), or

(b)   attributable to a failure by the responsible member to comply with an obligation under section 54,

may be made at any time not more than 20 years after the end of the accounting period to which it relates.

Assessment procedure etc

22 (1)   Where notice of a discovery assessment is issued, the notice must be served on the responsible member.

(2)   The notice must state—

(a)   the tax due,

(b)   the date on which the notice is issued, and

(c)   the time within which any appeal against the assessment must be made.

(3)   After notice of the assessment has been served under this paragraph, the assessment may not be altered except as provided for by or under this Part of this Act.

(4)   Where an officer of Revenue and Customs has—

(a)   decided to make an assessment to tax, and

(b)   taken all other decisions needed for arriving at the amount of the assessment,

the officer may entrust to some other officer of Revenue and Customs the responsibility for completing the assessing procedure, whether by means involving the use of a computer or otherwise, including responsibility for serving notice of the assessment.

Liability to amounts charged by way of discovery assessment

23 (1)   This paragraph applies where—

(a)   notice of a discovery assessment has been issued under paragraph 22, and

(b)   no appeal has been brought against the assessment under paragraph 33(1)(c).

(2)   The responsible member is liable to the tax due, subject as follows.

(3)   The responsible member may make a request to an officer of Revenue and Customs for one or more other relevant persons to be liable to the tax due (or any part of it).

(4)   The request must be made within 30 days of the date of issue of the notice of assessment.

(5)   Within 30 days of receiving the request, the officer must—

(a)   either agree to the request or refuse it,

(b)   notify the responsible member of the decision, and

(c)   if the officer agrees to the request, give effect to it by making all necessary adjustments.

(6)   An officer may not agree to the request unless satisfied it is reasonable in all the circumstances.

(7)   A request or notification under this paragraph must be in writing.

COMMENTARY ON SCHEDULE 8, PART 6

HMRC may issue a discovery assessment to the responsible member to reclaim unpaid DST in a way which also mirrors the corporation tax process for discovery assessments.

A DST discovery assessment may be issued where there is careless or deliberate behaviour leading to the inferred loss of tax; or where the opportunity to open an enquiry is passed (or such an enquiry is already closed), but HMRC is subsequently party to information leading to the loss of tax that it could not reasonably have been expected to know at the time of the enquiry period from the DST return, records and other written correspondence.

A discovery assessment for DST may not be made where a DST return is submitted under generally prevailing practice and yet a mistake in the return has led to loss of tax.

Discovery assessments may be raised within a four year time limit, extended to six years for careless behaviours and 20 years for deliberate behaviours. Where a DST return has not been filed (and should have been), the 20 year time limit also applies.

Paragraph 22 covers the procedure for HMRC in making a discovery assessment, and paragraph 23 allows the responsible member to request for one or more other relevant persons to be liable for any assessment. This reflects that an assessment would be issued by HMRC to the responsible member, however the DST liability may relate to various group entities. If the amount is not appealed, and in the absence of a request to re-allocate the liability, the responsible member becomes liable for the amount of DST due from the assessment.

PART 7

RELIEF IN CASE OF OVERPAID TAX

Claim for relief for overpaid tax

24 (1)   This paragraph applies where, in relation to a group, an amount has been paid by way of tax for an accounting period which was not tax due.

(2)   The responsible member may make a claim to the Commissioners for repayment of the amount.

(3)   The Commissioners must give effect to such a claim; but this is subject to—

     (a)   paragraph 26 (cases where no liability to give effect to claim), and

     (b)   paragraph 27 (power to enquire into claims).

(4)   Except as provided for by or under this Part of this Act, the Commissioners are not liable to repay any amount paid by way of tax by reason of the fact it was not tax due.

(5)   This paragraph is to be read with paragraph 25.

Making a claim

25 (1)   A claim under paragraph 24 may not be made—

     (a)   if the amount paid is excessive by reason of a mistake in a DST return or returns, more than 4 years after the end of the accounting period to which the return (or, if more than one, the first return) relates, and

     (b)   otherwise, more than 4 years after the end of the accounting period in respect of which the amount was paid.

(2)   A claim must—

     (a)   be in the specified form, and

     (b)   contain specified information.

(3)   A claim may not be made by being included in a DST return.

(4)   In this paragraph "specified" means specified in a notice published by HMRC.

Cases in which Commissioners not liable to give effect to claim

26 (1)   If, or to the extent that, a claim under paragraph 24 falls within any of Cases A to D, the Commissioners are not liable to give effect to the claim.

(2)   Case A is where, in relation to the group, there is unpaid DST liability for the accounting period.

(3)   Case B is where the responsible member is or will be able to seek relief by taking other steps under this Part of this Act.

(4)   Case C is where the responsible member—

     (a)   could have sought relief by taking such steps within a period that has now expired, and

     (b)   knew, or ought reasonably to have known, before the end of that period that such relief was available.

(5)   Case D is where—

(a) the amount paid is excessive by reason of a mistake in calculating the amount of tax payable by the group for the accounting period, and

(b) the amount was calculated in accordance with the practice generally prevailing at the time.

(6) In this paragraph "DST liability" has the same meaning as in section 66.

Power to enquire into claims

27 (1) An officer of Revenue and Customs may enquire into a claim under paragraph 24 if the officer gives notice to the responsible member of the officer's intention to do within the time allowed.

(2) The time allowed is the period ending with the quarter day next following the first anniversary of the day on which the claim was made.

The quarter days are the 31 January, 30 April, 31 July and 31 October.

(3) A claim enquired into under sub-paragraph (1) may not be the subject of a further notice under that sub-paragraph.

Completion of enquiry into claim etc

28 (1) An enquiry under paragraph 27 is completed when the officer by notice (a "closure notice") informs the responsible member that the enquiry is complete and states the conclusions reached in the enquiry.

(2) A closure notice must either—

(a) state that in the opinion of an officer of Revenue and Customs no amendment of the claim is required, or

(b) make the amendments of the claim required to give effect to the conclusions stated in the notice.

(3) A closure notice takes effect when it is issued.

(4) The officer must give effect to any amendments made by the closure notice by making such adjustments as may be necessary whether—

(a) by way of assessment, or

(b) by discharge or repayment of tax.

(5) The adjustments must be made within 30 days of the date of issue of the closure notice.

(6) Paragraph 15 (direction to complete enquiry) applies in relation to an enquiry under paragraph 27 as it applies in relation to an enquiry under paragraph 6.

Assessment for excessive repayment etc

29 (1) This paragraph applies where—

(a) an amount has been paid by way of a repayment of tax, and

(b) the amount paid exceeded the amount which the Commissioners were liable at that time to repay.

(2) The Commissioners may—

(a) to the best of their judgment, assess the amount of the excess, and

(b) notify the amount to the responsible member.

Supplementary assessments

30 (1) This paragraph applies where—

(a) an assessment has been notified under paragraph 29, and

(b) it appears to the Commissioners that the amount which ought to have been assessed as due exceeds the amount that has already been assessed.

(2) The Commissioners may—

(a) on or before the last day on which the assessment under paragraph 29 could have been made, make a supplementary assessment of the amount of tax due, and

(b) notify the amount to the responsible member.

Further provision about assessments under paragraph 29 and 30

31 (1) An amount assessed and notified under paragraph 29 or 30 counts as a liability to digital services tax for the purposes of this Part of this Act.

(2) But sub-paragraph (1) does not have effect if, or to the extent that, the assessment has been withdrawn or reduced.

Time limits for assessments

32 An assessment under paragraph 29 or 30 may not be made more than 4 years after the end of the accounting period in which evidence of facts sufficient in the opinion of the Commissioners to justify making the assessment comes to their knowledge.

COMMENTARY ON SCHEDULE 8, PART 7

Paragraph 24 introduces a mechanism for the responsible member to request repayment of an overpayment of DST. Claims for a repayment of overpaid tax should not be made alongside the DST return but via separate process, and there is a four year time limit for making such a claim.

Paragraph 26 provides specific Cases where HMRC is not liable to repay excess DST even after a claim is made. In summary, these Cases are where there is otherwise unpaid DST for the accounting period, where other relief under this Part is available or was available but for a missed deadline, or where the DST paid was due to a mistake under prevailing practice at the time.

Paragraphs 27 and 28 contain measures for HMRC enquiry into overpayment claims and how such enquiries are managed. Paragraphs 29–32 contain measures for HMRC assessment after an excessive repayment has been made. Time limits and procedure for enquiries and assessment relating to overpayments are broadly in line with those for enquiries and assessments relating to the original DST liability.

PART 8

APPEALS AGAINST HMRC DECISIONS ON TAX

Right of appeal

33 (1) An appeal may be brought against—

    (a) an amendment of a DST return under paragraph 8 (amendment during enquiry to prevent loss of tax);

    (b) an amendment made by a closure notice under paragraph 14;

    (c) a discovery assessment (under paragraph 19);

    (d) an amendment made by a closure notice under paragraph 28;

    (e) an assessment made under paragraph 29 or 30.

(2) Any such appeal is to be brought by the responsible member ("the appellant").

(3) If an appeal under sub-paragraph (1)(a) against an amendment of a self-assessment is made while an enquiry into the return is in progress none of the steps mentioned in paragraph 36(2)(a) to (c) may be taken in relation to the appeal until the enquiry is completed.

Notice of appeal

34 (1) Notice of appeal under paragraph 33 must be given to HMRC—

    (a) in writing,

    (b) within 30 days after the specified date.

(2) In sub-paragraph (1) "specified date" means—

    (a) in relation to an appeal under paragraph 33(1)(a), the date on which the notice of amendment was issued;

    (b) in relation to an appeal under paragraph 33(1)(b) or (d), the date on which the closure notice was issued;

    (c) in relation to an appeal under paragraph 33(1)(c) or (e), the date on which the notice of assessment was issued.

(3) The notice of appeal must specify the grounds of appeal.

Late notice of appeal

35 (1) This paragraph applies in a case where—

    (a) notice of appeal may be given to HMRC under this Schedule, but

    (b) no notice is given before the relevant time limit.

(2) Notice may be given after the relevant time limit if—

    (a)   HMRC agree, or

    (b)   where HMRC do not agree, the tribunal gives permission.

(3)   HMRC must agree to notice being given after the relevant time limit if the appellant has requested in writing that HMRC do so and HMRC are satisfied—

    (a)   that there was a reasonable excuse for not giving the notice before the relevant time limit, and

    (b)   that the request has been made without unreasonable delay.

(4)   If a request of the kind mentioned in sub-paragraph (3) is made, HMRC must notify the appellant whether or not HMRC agree to the request.

(5)   In this paragraph "relevant time limit", in relation to notice of appeal, means the time before which the notice must be given (disregarding this paragraph).

Steps that may be taken following notice of appeal

36 (1)   This paragraph applies if notice of appeal has been given to HMRC.

(2)   In such a case—

    (a)   the appellant may notify HMRC that the appellant requires HMRC to review the matter in question (see paragraph 37),

    (b)   HMRC may notify the appellant of an offer to review the matter in question (see paragraph 38), or

    (c)   the appellant may notify the appeal to the tribunal.

(3)   This paragraph does not prevent the matter in question from being dealt with in accordance with paragraph 44(1) and (2) (settling of appeals by agreement).

Right of appellant to require review

37 (1)   If the appellant notifies HMRC that it requires them to review the matter in question, HMRC must—

    (a)   notify the appellant of HMRC's view of the matter in question within the relevant period, and

    (b)   review the matter in question in accordance with paragraph 39.

(2)   Sub-paragraph (1) does not apply if—

    (a)   the appellant has already given a notification under this paragraph in relation to the matter in question,

    (b)   HMRC have given a notification under paragraph 40 in relation to the matter in question, or

    (c)   the appellant has notified the appeal to the tribunal.

(3)   In this paragraph "the relevant period" means—

    (a)   the period of 30 days beginning with the day on which HMRC receive the notification from the appellant, or

    (b)   such longer period as is reasonable.

Offer of review by HMRC

38 (1)   Sub-paragraphs (2) to (5) apply if HMRC notify the appellant of an offer to review the matter in question.

(2)   The notification must include a statement of HMRC's view of the matter in question.

(3)   If the appellant notifies HMRC within the acceptance period that it accepts the offer, HMRC must review the matter in question in accordance with paragraph 39.

(4)   If the appellant does not accept the offer in accordance with sub-paragraph (3)—

    (a)   HMRC's view of the matter in question is treated as if it were contained in a settlement agreement (see paragraph 44(1)), but

    (b)   paragraph 44(3) (right to withdraw from agreement) does not apply in relation to that notional agreement.

(5)   Sub-paragraph (4) does not apply to the matter in question if, or to the extent that, the appellant notifies the appeal to the tribunal under paragraph 42.

(6)   HMRC may not take the action mentioned in sub-paragraph (1) at any time if before that time—

    (a)   HMRC have given a notification under this paragraph in relation to the matter in question,

(b)   the appellant has given a notification under paragraph 37 in relation to the matter in question, or

(c)   the appellant has notified the appeal to the tribunal.

(7)   In this paragraph "acceptance period" means the period of 30 days beginning with the date of the document by which HMRC notify the appellant of the offer to review the matter in question.

Nature of review

39 (1)   This paragraph applies if HMRC are required by paragraph 37 or 38 to review the matter in question.

(2)   The nature and extent of the review are to be such as appear appropriate to HMRC in the circumstances.

(3)   For the purpose of sub-paragraph (2), HMRC must, in particular, have regard to steps taken before the beginning of the review—

(a)   by HMRC in deciding the matter in question, and

(b)   by any person in seeking to resolve disagreement about the matter in question.

(4)   The review must take account of any representations made by the appellant at a stage which gives HMRC a reasonable opportunity to consider them.

(5)   The review may conclude that HMRC's view of the matter in question is to be—

(a)   upheld,

(b)   varied, or

(c)   cancelled.

(6)   HMRC must notify the appellant of the conclusions of the review and their reasoning within—

(a)   the period of 45 days beginning with the relevant day, or

(b)   such other period as may be agreed.

(7)   In sub-paragraph (6) "relevant day" means—

(a)   in a case where the appellant required the review, the day when HMRC notified the appellant of HMRC's view of the matter in question;

(b)   in a case where HMRC offered the review, the day when HMRC received notification of the appellant's acceptance of the offer.

(8)   If HMRC do not give notice of the conclusions of the review within the period specified in sub-paragraph (6), the review is treated as having concluded that HMRC's view of the matter in question is upheld.

(9)   If sub-paragraph (8) applies, HMRC must notify the appellant of the conclusions which the review is treated as having reached.

Effect of conclusions of review

40 (1)   If HMRC give notice of the conclusions of a review (see paragraph 39)—

(a)   the conclusions are to be treated as if they were contained in a settlement agreement (see paragraph 44(1)), but

(b)   paragraph 44(3) (withdrawal from agreement) does not apply in relation to that notional agreement.

(2)   Sub-paragraph (1) does not apply to the matter in question if, or to the extent that, the appellant notifies the appeal to the tribunal (see paragraphs 41 and 42).

Notifying appeal to tribunal after appellant has required review

41 (1)   Where HMRC have notified an appellant under paragraph 37(1)(a) of their view of a matter to which an appeal under paragraph 33 relates, the appellant—

(a)   may not notify the appeal to the tribunal before the beginning of the post-review period;

(b)   may notify the appeal to the tribunal after the end of that period only if the tribunal gives permission.

(2)   Except where sub-paragraph (3) applies, the post-review period is the period of 30 days beginning with the date of the document in which HMRC give notice of the conclusions of the review in accordance with paragraph 39(6).

(3)   If the period specified in paragraph 39(6) ends without HMRC having given notice of the conclusions of the review, the post-review period is the period that—

    (a)   begins with the day following the last day of the period specified in paragraph 39(6), and

    (b)   ends 30 days after the date of the document in which HMRC give notice of the conclusions of the review in accordance with paragraph 39(9).

Notifying appeal to tribunal after HMRC have offered review

42 (1)   Where HMRC have offered to review the matter to which a notice of an appeal under paragraph 33 relates, the right of the appellant at any time to notify the appeal to the tribunal depends on whether or not the appellant has accepted the offer at that time.

(2)   If the appellant has accepted the offer, the appellant—

    (a)   may not notify the appeal to the tribunal before the beginning of the post-review period;

    (b)   may notify the appeal to the tribunal after the end of that period only if the tribunal gives permission.

(3)   If the appellant has not accepted the offer, the appellant—

    (a)   may notify the appeal to the tribunal within the acceptance period;

    (b)   may notify the appeal to the tribunal after the end of that period only if the tribunal gives permission.

(4)   In this paragraph—

    (a)   "acceptance period" has the same meaning as in paragraph 38;

    (b)   "post-review period" has the same meaning as in paragraph 41.

Interpretation of paragraphs 36 to 42

43 (1)   In paragraphs 36 to 42—

    (a)   "matter in question" means the matter to which an appeal relates;

    (b)   a reference to a notification is to a notification in writing.

(2)   In paragraphs 36 to 42, a reference to the appellant includes a person acting on behalf of the appellant except in relation to—

    (a)   notification of HMRC's view under paragraph 37(1)(a);

    (b)   notification by HMRC of an offer of review (and of their view of the matter) under paragraph 38;

    (c)   notification of the conclusions of a review under paragraph 39(6) or (9).

(3)   But if a notification falling within any of paragraphs (a) to (c) of sub-paragraph (2) is given to the appellant, a copy of the notification may also be given to a person acting on behalf of the appellant.

Settling of appeals by agreement

44 (1)   In relation to an appeal of which notice has been given under paragraph 34, "settlement agreement" means an agreement in writing between the appellant and an officer of Revenue and Customs that is—

    (a)   entered into before the appeal is determined, and

    (b)   to the effect that the decision appealed against should be upheld without variation, varied in a particular manner or discharged or cancelled.

(2)   Where a settlement agreement is entered into in relation to an appeal, the consequences are to be the same (for all purposes) as if, at the time the agreement was entered into, the tribunal had decided the appeal and had upheld the decision without variation, varied it in that manner or discharged or cancelled it, as the case may be.

(3)   Sub-paragraph (2) does not apply if, within 30 days beginning with the date on which the settlement agreement was entered into, the appellant gives notice in writing to HMRC that it wishes to withdraw from the agreement.

(4)   Sub-paragraph (5) applies where notice of an appeal has been given under paragraph 34 and—

    (a)   the appellant notifies HMRC, orally or in writing, that the appellant does not wish to proceed with the appeal, and

    (b)   HMRC do not, within 30 days after that notification, give the appellant notice in writing indicating that they are unwilling that the appeal should be withdrawn.

(5)   Sub-paragraphs (1) to (3) have effect as if, at the date of the appellant's notification, the appellant and an officer of Revenue and Customs had agreed that the decision under appeal should be upheld without variation.

Appeal does not postpone recovery of tax

45 (1)   Where there is an appeal under paragraph 33, the tax in question remains due and payable as if there had been no appeal.

(2)   That is subject to paragraphs 46 and 47.

Application for payment of tax to be postponed

46 (1)   If the appellant has grounds for believing that the amendment or assessment overcharges a relevant person to tax, the appellant may—

    (a)   first apply by notice in writing to HMRC within 30 days after the specified date for a determination by them of the amount of tax the payment of which should be postponed pending the determination of the appeal, and

    (b)   if the appellant does not agree with a determination made by HMRC under paragraph (a), refer the application for postponement to the tribunal within 30 days from the date of the document notifying HMRC's determination.

An application under paragraph (a) must state the amount believed to be overcharged to tax and the grounds for that belief.

(2)   An application under sub-paragraph (1) may be made more than 30 days after the specified date if there is a change in the circumstances of the case as a result of which the appellant has grounds for believing that the relevant person is overcharged to tax by the decision appealed against.

(3)   If, after an application under sub-paragraph (1) has been determined, there is a change in the circumstances of the case as a result of which either party has grounds for believing that the amount determined has become either excessive or insufficient, that party may (if the parties cannot agree on a revised determination) apply to the tribunal for a revised determination of that amount.

(4)   An application under sub-paragraph (3) may be made at any time before the determination of the appeal.

(5)   Paragraphs 35 (late notice of appeal) and 44 (settling of appeals by agreement) apply to an application under this paragraph as they apply to an appeal under paragraph 33, subject to any necessary modifications.

(6)   The amount of tax of which payment is to be postponed pending the determination of the appeal is the amount (if any) by which it appears that there are reasonable grounds for believing that the relevant person is overcharged.

(7)   A decision of the tribunal under this paragraph is final and conclusive (despite the provisions of sections 11 and 13 of the Tribunals, Courts and Enforcement Act 2007).

(8)   In this paragraph "specified date" has the meaning given by paragraph 34.

Agreement to postpone payment of tax

47 (1)   If the appellant and HMRC agree that payment of an amount of tax should be postponed pending the determination of the appeal, the consequences are to be the same (for all purposes) as if the tribunal had, at the time when the agreement was entered into, made a direction to the same effect as the agreement.

This is without prejudice to the making of a further agreement or further direction.

(2)   Where the agreement is not in writing—

    (a)   sub-paragraph (1) does not apply unless the fact that an agreement was entered into, and the terms agreed, are confirmed by notice in writing given by HMRC to the appellant or by the appellant to HMRC, and

    (b)   the reference in sub-paragraph (1) to the time when the agreement was entered into is to be read as a reference to the time when notice of confirmation was given.

(3)   References in this paragraph to an agreement being entered into with an appellant, and to the giving of notice to or by the appellant, include references to an agreement being entered into, or notice being given to or by, a person acting on behalf of the appellant in relation to the appeal.

Assessments and self-assessments

48 (1)   This paragraph applies where an appeal under paragraph 33 has been notified to the tribunal.

(2)   If the tribunal decides that a relevant person is overcharged by a self-assessment or any other assessment, the assessment must be reduced accordingly.

(3)   If the tribunal decides that a relevant person is undercharged to tax by a self-assessment or any other assessment, the assessment must be increased accordingly.

(4)   In a case where neither sub-paragraph (2) or (3) apply, the assessment is to stand good.

Payment of tax where appeal has been determined

49 (1)   This paragraph applies where an appeal under paragraph 33 has been notified to the tribunal.

(2)   On the determination of the appeal, any tax overpaid must be repaid.

(3)   On the determination of the appeal, section 51 has effect in relation to any relevant tax.

(4)   The reference to "relevant tax" is to any tax payable in accordance with the determination, so far as it is tax—

    (a)   the payment of which had been postponed, or

    (b)   which would not have been charged by the amendment or assessment if there had been no appeal.

Payment of tax where there is a further appeal

50 (1)   Where a party to an appeal to the tribunal under paragraph 33 makes a further appeal, tax is to be payable or repayable in accordance with the determination of the tribunal or court (as the case may be), even though the further appeal is pending.

(2)   But if the amount charged by the assessment is altered by the order or judgment of the Upper Tribunal or court, then—

    (a)   if too much tax has been paid, the amount overpaid must be refunded, with any interest allowed by the order or judgment, and

    (b)   if too little tax has been charged, section 51 has effect in relation to the amount undercharged.

Tribunal determinations

51 The determination of the tribunal in relation to any proceedings under this Part of this Schedule is final and conclusive except as otherwise provided in sections 9 to 14 of the Tribunals, Courts and Enforcement Act 2007 (or in this Part of this Act).

COMMENTARY ON SCHEDULE 8, PART 8

As for other taxes, the taxpayer has the right to appeal any decision made by HMRC as it relates to DST, covering amendments, discovery assessments or closure notices. The responsible member should make any such appeal in writing, specifying grounds and within 30 days of receiving HMRC's decision. Late appeals may only be accepted where HMRC or a tribunal give permission (based on a reasonable excuse for missing the deadline and without unreasonable delay following that).

After an appeal notice, either the responsible member can ask for HMRC review of a matter, HMRC can notify the responsible member that it intends to do so, or the tribunal can require this. HMRC's review may be limited to a specific point or broader areas of the application of DST, as dictated by the facts and circumstances of the case. The appeal would consider the group's representations, filings, and any prior correspondence between the group and HMRC as part of an enquiry or otherwise.

Within 45 days (or an agreed longer term by both parties), HMRC's review should provide conclusion that its views should be upheld, varied or cancelled.

Where the responsible member has requested the appeal, they should not seek to refer the matter to the tribunal until the HMRC review is completed. They would have 30 days to do so following receipt of HMRC's conclusions. A similar timetable applies to where HMRC has offered the review depending on if the group accept or reject the HMRC proposals.

Any settlement agreement between the group and HMRC which is reached during the appeals process is treated as if the tribunal had provided that conclusion and settled the matter (subject to the usual 30 day cooling off period).

The general rule is that an appeal does not stop the clock ticking on due dates for either returns to be filed or DST payments to be made. The responsible member may apply to postpone payment of DST where they believe it to be excessive, stating the grounds and amount of the excess. There is generally a 30 day time limit to request such a postponement.

Paragraphs 48–51 set out the implications of a tribunal decision, which is then to be respected in the tax assessment. Any over assessed tax is to be repaid to the responsible member, and any underpaid tax is to be paid to HMRC. The First-tier Tribunal's decision is to be respected in this regard, despite any further appeal (until such time as a different conclusion is reached by the Upper Tribunal or a court).

PART 9

PENALTIES

Failure to deliver return: flat-rate penalty

52 (1) A person who is required to file a DST return and fails to do so by the filing date is liable to a penalty under this paragraph.

The person may also be liable to a penalty under paragraph 53 (tax-related penalties).

(2) The penalty is—

(a) £100, if the return is delivered within 3 months after the filing date;

(b) £200, in any other case.

(3) The amounts are increased to £500 and £1000 (respectively) for a third successive failure.

(4) For this purpose, a "third successive failure" occurs where—

(a) the duty under section 56 (duty to file returns) applies in relation to a group for 3 successive accounting periods,

(b) a person was liable to a penalty under this paragraph in respect of each of the first 2 accounting periods, and

(c) a person is liable to a penalty under this paragraph in respect of the third accounting period.

Failure to deliver return: tax-related penalty

53 (1) A person who is required to file a DST return for an accounting period and fails to do so within 18 months from the end of that period is liable to a penalty under this paragraph.

This is in addition to any penalty under paragraph 52 (flat-rate penalty).

(2) The penalty is—

(a) 10% of the unpaid tax, if the return is filed within 2 years from the end of the accounting period;

(b) 20% of the unpaid tax, in any other case.

(3) The "unpaid tax" means the total amount of tax payable by members of the group for the accounting period which remains unpaid on the date when the liability to the penalty under this paragraph arises.

Failure to deliver a return: reasonable excuse

54 (1) Liability to a penalty under paragraph 52 or 53 in relation to a failure to make a return does not arise if the person ("P") satisfies HMRC or (on appeal) the tribunal that there is a reasonable excuse for the failure.

(2) For that purpose—

(a) an insufficiency of funds is not a reasonable excuse,

(b) where P relies on any other person to do anything, that is not a reasonable excuse unless P took reasonable care to avoid the failure, and

(c) where P had a reasonable excuse for the failure but the excuse has ceased, P is to be treated as having continued to have the excuse if the failure is remedied without unreasonable delay after the excuse ceased.

Failure to keep and preserve records: penalty

55 (1) A person who fails to comply with paragraph 4 in relation to an accounting period is liable to a penalty not exceeding £3,000, subject to the following exception.

(2) No penalty is incurred if HMRC are satisfied that any facts which they reasonably require to be proved, and which would have been proved by the records, are proved by other documentary evidence provided to HMRC.

Assessment of penalty, etc

56 (1) If a person is liable to a penalty under this Part of this Schedule, HMRC must—

    (a)   assess the penalty, and

    (b)   notify the person.

(2) The assessment of a penalty—

    (a)   is to be treated for procedural purposes in the same way as an assessment to tax (except in respect of a matter expressly provided for by this Schedule),

    (b)   may be enforced as if it were an assessment to tax, and

    (c)   may be combined with an assessment to tax.

(3) A supplementary assessment may be made in respect of a penalty if an earlier assessment is based on an amount of tax due and payable that is found by HMRC to be an underestimate or insufficient.

(4) Sub-paragraph (5) applies if—

    (a)   an assessment in respect of a penalty is based on a liability to tax that would have been shown in a return, and

    (b)   that liability is found by HMRC to be excessive.

(5) HMRC may by notice amend the assessment so it is based on the correct amount.

(6) An amendment under sub-paragraph (5)—

    (a)   does not affect when the penalty must be paid;

    (b)   may be made after the last day on which the assessment in question could have been made (under sub-paragraph (7)).

(7) An assessment of a penalty must be made before the end of the period of 12 months beginning with—

    (a)   the end of the appeal period for the assessment of the liability to tax which would have been shown in the return, or

    (b)   if there is no such assessment, the date on which that liability is ascertained or it is ascertained that the liability is nil.

(8) In sub-paragraph (7) "appeal period" means the period during which—

    (a)   an appeal could be brought, or

    (b)   an appeal that has been brought has not been determined or withdrawn.

(9) A penalty must be paid before the end of the period of 30 days beginning with the day on which notification of the penalty is issued.

Special reduction

57 (1) If HMRC think it right because of special circumstances, they may reduce a penalty under this Part of this Schedule.

(2) In sub-paragraph (1) "special circumstances" does not include—

    (a)   ability to pay, or

    (b)   the fact that a potential loss of revenue from one taxpayer is balanced by a potential over-payment by another.

(3) In sub-paragraph (1) the reference to reducing a penalty includes a reference to—

    (a)   staying a penalty, and

    (b)   agreeing a compromise in relation to proceedings in respect of a penalty.

Right to appeal against penalty

58 A person may appeal against—

    (a)   a decision of HMRC that a penalty under this Part of this Schedule is payable by the person, or

    (b)   a decision of HMRC as to the amount of any such penalty.

Procedure on appeal against penalty

59 (1) Part 8 of this Schedule (apart from paragraphs 33, 45 to 47, and 49) applies in relation to an appeal under paragraph 58 as it applies in relation to an appeal under paragraph 33.

(2) On an appeal under paragraph 58, payment of the penalty is postponed pending determination of the appeal.

(3) On an appeal under paragraph 58(a) that is notified to the tribunal, the tribunal may confirm or cancel the decision.

(4) On an appeal under paragraph 58(b) that is notified to the tribunal, the tribunal may—

(a) confirm the decision, or

(b) substitute for the decision another decision that HMRC had power to make.

(5) If the tribunal substitutes its decision for HMRC's, the tribunal may rely on paragraph 57—

(a) to the same extent as HMRC (which may mean applying the same percentage reduction as HMRC to a different starting point), or

(b) to a different extent, but only if the tribunal thinks that HMRC's decision in respect of the application of that paragraph was flawed.

(6) In sub-paragraph (5)(b) "flawed" means flawed when considered in the light of the principles applicable in proceedings for judicial review.

(7) On determination of an appeal under paragraph 58, where a penalty is payable it is to be paid before the end of 30 days beginning with the day on which the determination was issued.

Payments in respect of penalties

60 (1) This paragraph applies if—

(a) a person liable to a penalty under this Part of this Schedule has an agreement in relation to the penalty with one or more companies within the charge to corporation tax, and

(b) as a result of the agreement, the person receives a payment or payments in respect of the penalty that do not, in total, exceed the amount of the penalty.

(2) The payment—

(a) is not to be taken into account in calculating the profits for corporation tax purposes of either the person or the company making the payment, and

(b) is not to be regarded as a distribution for corporation tax purposes.

COMMENTARY ON SCHEDULE 8, PART 9

Paragraphs 52–60 of the Schedule describe penalties that may be levied in respect of DST.

First are the penalties for failing to deliver a DST return as required. For the first two offences of missing the DST return deadline a flat rate £100 penalty is levied when the return is late, followed by a further £100 after three months (so in total, a £200 penalty when the return is more than three months late). For a third successive failure to deliver on time, these penalties are increased five-fold to £500 and £1,000.

Where returns are more than six months late, a tax geared penalty may also be levied. Note that the legislation refers to an 18 month deadline from the end of an accounting period, which must be interpreted with the knowledge that a group would have 12 months to file the return from the end of that period. Penalties here are levied at 10% or 20% of the unpaid tax, depending on if the returns are filed within a year of the normal filing deadline or not.

Penalties for failing to deliver a return may be waived if there is a reasonable excuse for the failure per paragraph 53. HMRC, (or the Tribunal, if the penalty were to be appealed) would need to determine whether any excuse is taken to be reasonable for these purposes.

The second penalty is that for failing to maintain appropriate records. Where a group fails to preserve, maintain and demonstrate that it has kept the appropriate records for DST purposes, a flat rate penalty of £3,000 could be levied. The penalty would not apply if the group can produce other evidence for HMRC that would have been included in the records, if they were available.

How a penalty is assessed is described at paragraph 56. It is relatively self-explanatory and covers how penalties are notified and collected. A penalty must be assessed, and notification issued, within a 12 month period after the closure of an appeal or where the liability is ascertained. Penalties must be paid within 30 days.

HMRC may reduce penalties at their discretion under paragraph 57 where the circumstances are somewhat 'special'. This does not include financial distress or mismatched payments, but could include good co-operation and a somewhat reasonable position by the taxpayer.

Penalties may be appealed in the usual way, described procedurally at paragraph 59.

The person liable to the penalty (likely to be the responsible member of the group) may wish to obtain payment for such a penalty from other group members. Paragraph 60 allows for such compensation to the responsible member without deeming that payment as a distribution or a taxable income amount.

SCHEDULE 9

DST PAYMENT NOTICES

Section 66

Introduction

1 (1)   This Schedule applies where a payment notice has been given to a person ("the recipient").

(2)   In this Schedule—

"DST liability", "payment notice" and "relevant person" have the same meaning as in section 66;

"relevant liability" means any DST liability in relation to the group for the accounting period.

Payment notice: effect

2 (1)   For the purposes of the recovery from the recipient of any unpaid digital services tax, penalty or interest (including interest accruing after the date of the payment notice) the recipient is treated as if—

    (a)   any relevant liability of a person other than the recipient were a liability of the recipient ("the deemed liability"),

    (b)   the deemed liability became due and payable when the relevant liability became due and payable, and

    (c)   any payments made in respect of the relevant liability were made in respect of the deemed liability.

(2)   Nothing in this paragraph gives the recipient a right to appeal against any assessment, determination or other decision giving rise to a relevant liability (or against the deemed liability).

Payment notice: appeals

3 (1)   The recipient may appeal against the notice, within the period of 30 days beginning with the date on which it is given, on the ground that the person is not a relevant person.

(2)   Where an appeal is made, anything required by the notice to be paid is due and payable as if there had been no appeal.

Payment notices: effect of making payment etc

4 (1)   If the recipient pays any amount in pursuance of the notice the recipient may recover that amount from the person liable to pay it.

(2)   In calculating the recipient's income, profits or losses for any tax purposes—

    (a)   a payment in pursuance of the notice is not allowed as a deduction, and

    (b)   the reimbursement of any such payment is not regarded as a receipt.

(3)   Any amount paid by the recipient in pursuance of the notice is to be taken into account in calculating—

    (a)   the amount unpaid, and

    (b)   the amount due by virtue of any other payment notice relating to the amount unpaid.

(4)   Similarly, any payment by the person liable to pay it of any of the amount unpaid is to be taken into account in calculating the amount due by virtue of the payment notice (or by virtue of any other payment notice relating to the amount unpaid).

COMMENTARY ON SCHEDULE 9

Schedule 9 of the Act contains instruction regarding payment notices.

Paragraph 2 tells us that where a payment notice is given to a taxpayer by HMRC to recover unpaid DST, penalty or interest then the recipient of that notice is treated as owing all amounts attributable to any group members within the relevant timeframes as would have applied. In essence, it provides for joint and several liability for a group's liabilities to HMRC to the person receiving the payment notice.

A payment notice may be appealed per paragraph 3 within 30 days of receiving such a notice. The amounts assessed remain payable.

Paragraph 4 allows for the party making payment under a notice to recover the amounts from other group members in a tax neutral fashion. The party making payment is taken to do so on behalf of the group members under the deeming provisions of paragraph 2.

SCHEDULE 10

DIGITAL SERVICES TAX: MINOR AND CONSEQUENTIAL AMENDMENTS

Section 70

Provisional Collection of Taxes Act 1968

1 In section 1(1) of the Provisional Collection of Taxes Act 1968 (temporary statutory effect of House of Commons resolutions affecting income tax etc) after "the apprenticeship levy," insert "digital services tax,".

FA 1989

2 (1)   Section 178(2) of FA 1989 (setting of interest rates) is amended as follows.

(2)   Omit the "and" at the end of paragraph (u).

(3)   After paragraph (v) insert—

"(w)   sections 67 and 68 of the Finance Act 2020."

FA 2007

3 (1)   Schedule 24 to FA 2007 (penalties for errors) is amended as follows.

(2)   In paragraph 1, in the table after the entry relating to accounts in connection with ascertaining liability to corporation tax insert—

"Digital services tax	DST return under paragraph 2 of Schedule 8 to FA 2020."

FA 2008

4 FA 2008 is amended as follows.

5 (1)   Schedule 36 (information and inspection powers) is amended as follows.

(2)   In paragraph 63(1) after paragraph (cb) insert—

"(cc)   digital services tax,".

6 (1)   Schedule 41 (penalties for failure to notify etc) is amended as follows.

(2)   In paragraph 1, in the table after the entry relating to diverted profits tax insert—

"Digital services tax	Obligation under section 54 of FA 2020 (obligation to notify HMRC when threshold conditions for digital services tax are met)."

(3)   In paragraph 7 after sub-paragraph (4A) insert—

"(4B)   In the case of a relevant obligation relating to digital services tax and an accounting period, the potential lost revenue is so much of any digital services tax payable by members of the group for the accounting period as by reason of the failure is unpaid 12 months after the end of the accounting period."

COMMENTARY ON SCHEDULE 10

Schedule 10 contains some minor consequential amendments required for the introduction of a new UK tax. The Schedule ensures that DST is included as a relevant tax for interest and penalties purposes where such provisions are included in other Finance Acts.

SCHEDULE 11

PRIVATE PLEASURE CRAFT

Section 89

Amendments of HODA 1979

1 HODA 1979 is amended as follows.

2 In section 6AB(4A) after "vehicles" insert "etc".

3 (1)   Section 12 is amended as follows.

(2)   In subsection (1) after "vehicle" insert "or as fuel for propelling a private pleasure craft".

(3)   After subsection (2) insert—

"(2A)   For provision relating to private pleasure craft that corresponds to subsection (2), and for the meaning of "private pleasure craft", see section 14E."

(4)   In the heading at the end insert "etc".

4 In section 13ZB(5), in paragraph (b) of the definition of "prohibited use" after "vehicle" insert "or as fuel for a private pleasure craft".

5 In section 14A for subsection (4) substitute—

"(4)   For the meaning of "private pleasure craft", see section 14E."

6 (1)   Section 14B is amended as follows.

(2)   In subsection (1)(a)—

   (a)   at the end of sub-paragraph (i) (but before the "or") insert—
               "(ia)   used as fuel for propelling a private pleasure craft,";

   (b)   in sub-paragraph (ii) for "so used" substitute "used as mentioned in sub-paragraph (i) or (ia)".

(3)   In the heading at the end insert "etc".

7 (1)   Section 14C is amended as follows.

(2)   In subsection (1)—

   (a)   at the end of paragraph (b) insert "or";
   (b)   omit the "or" at the end of paragraph (c);
   (c)   omit paragraph (d).

(3)   Omit subsection (4A).

8 For section 14E substitute—

"**14E   Restrictions on use of certain fuel for private pleasure craft**

   (1)   Restricted fuel must not—

      (a)   be used as fuel for propelling a private pleasure craft,
      (b)   be used as an additive or extender in any substance so used, or
      (c)   be taken into the fuel supply of an engine provided for propelling a vessel that is being used as a private pleasure craft.

   (2)   "Restricted fuel" means—

      (a)   rebated fuel, or
      (b)   marked oil that is not rebated fuel.

   (3)   "Rebated fuel" means rebated heavy oil, rebated biodiesel or rebated bioblend.

   (4)   "Marked oil" means any hydrocarbon oil in which a marker is present which is for the time being designated by regulations made by the Commissioners under subsection (5) below, other than marked oil which is in the fuel supply of an engine provided for propelling a vessel having been taken in to that supply in accordance with the law of the place where it was taken in.

   (5)   The Commissioners may for the purposes of this section designate any marker which appears to them to be used for the purposes of the law of any place (whether within or outside the United Kingdom) for identifying hydrocarbon oil that is not to be used as fuel for propelling private pleasure craft.

   (6)   In this Act "private pleasure craft" has the same meaning as in Article 14(1)(c) of Council Directive 2003/96/EC (taxation of energy products etc).

(7)   The Treasury may by regulations provide for cases in which a vessel is treated as not being a private pleasure craft for the purposes of this Act (which may include cases in which the vessel is used in accordance with instructions given by an officer of HMRC for the purposes of removing restricted fuel from the vessel)."

9 For section 14F substitute—

"14F   Penalties for contravention of section 14E

(1)   Conduct within any of the following paragraphs attracts a penalty under section 9 of the Finance Act 1994 (civil penalties)—

(a)   using restricted fuel in contravention of section 14E(1);

(b)   becoming liable for restricted fuel being taken into the fuel supply of an engine—

(i)   in contravention of section 14E(1), or

(ii)   having reason to believe that it will be put to a particular use that is a prohibited use;

(c)   supplying restricted fuel, having reason to believe that it will be put to a particular use that is a prohibited use.

(2)   An offence is committed if—

(a)   a person intentionally uses restricted fuel in contravention of section 14E(1),

(b)   a person is liable for restricted fuel being taken into the fuel supply of an engine, and the restricted fuel was taken in with the intention by the person that restrictions imposed by section 14E(1) should be contravened, or

(c)   a person supplies restricted fuel, intending that it will be put to a particular use that is a prohibited use.

(3)   A person guilty of an offence under this section is liable—

(a)   on summary conviction, to a fine not exceeding the maximum fine or imprisonment for a term not exceeding the maximum term (or both);

(b)   on conviction on indictment, to a fine or imprisonment for a term not exceeding 7 years (or both).

(4)   For the purposes of subsection (3)(a) the "maximum fine" is—

(a)   in England and Wales, £20,000 or (if greater) 3 times the value of the heavy oil, biodiesel or bioblend in question;

(b)   in Scotland or Northern Ireland, the statutory maximum or (if greater) 3 times the value of the heavy oil, biodiesel or bioblend in question.

(5)   For the purposes of subsection (3)(a) the "maximum term" is—

(a)   in England or Wales (subject to subsection (6)) or Scotland, 12 months;

(b)   in Northern Ireland, 6 months.

(6)   In relation to an offence committed before the commencement of section 282 of the Criminal Justice Act 2003 (increase in maximum term that may be imposed on summary conviction of offence triable either way), subsection (5)(a) has effect in England and Wales as if for "12 months" there were substituted "6 months".

(7)   Restricted fuel is liable to forfeiture if it is—

(a)   taken into the fuel supply of an engine as mentioned in section 14E(1),

(b)   supplied as mentioned in subsection (1)(c) or (2)(c) above, or

(c)   taken into the fuel supply of an engine provided for propelling a vessel at a time when it is not a private pleasure craft and remains in the vessel as part of that fuel supply at a later time when it becomes a private pleasure craft.

(8)   If rebated fuel is used or taken into the fuel supply of an engine in contravention of section 14E(1), the Commissioners may—

(a)   assess an amount equal to the rebate on like fuel at the rate in force at the time of the contravention as being excise duty due from any person who—

(i)   used the rebated fuel, or

(ii)   was liable for it being taken into the fuel supply, and

(b)   notify the person or the person's representative accordingly.

(9)   In this section—

"prohibited use" means a use that contravenes section 14E(1);

"rebated fuel" has the meaning given by section 14E(3);
"restricted fuel" has the meaning given by section 14E(2)."

10 In section 20AAA(4)(a) after "vehicle" insert "or as fuel for propelling a private pleasure craft".

11 In section 24 (control of use of duty-free and rebated oil) after subsection (3) insert—

"(3A)   Subsection (3) does not apply to heavy oil, biodiesel or bioblend used for propelling a private pleasure craft if it is proved to the satisfaction of the Commissioners that the heavy oil, biodiesel or bioblend was taken into the vessel in accordance with the laws of the place where it was taken in."

12 In section 27(1) at the appropriate place insert—

""private pleasure craft" has the meaning given by section 14E;".

13 (1)   Schedule 4 (regulations under section 24) is amended as follows.

(2)   In paragraph 19 after "vehicle" insert "or a vessel".

(3)   In paragraph 20 after "vehicle" insert "or a vessel".

(4)   In paragraph 21—

    (a)   the existing provision becomes sub-paragraph (1) of that paragraph;

    (b)   in that sub-paragraph—

        (i)   after "vehicles" insert "or vessels";

        (ii)   after "vehicle" insert "or vessel";

    (c)   after that sub-paragraph insert—

"(2)   In this paragraph "premises" includes any floating structure.

(3)   Nothing in sub-paragraph (1) enables regulations to be made authorising the examination of the interior of part of a vessel if that part is used as a dwelling."

14 (1)   Schedule 5 (sampling) is amended as follows.

(2)   In paragraph 1—

    (a)   in sub-paragraph (a)—

        (i)   for "motor vehicle" substitute "vehicle or a vessel";

        (ii)   after "the vehicle" insert "or the vessel";

    (b)   in sub-paragraph (b) for "motor vehicle" substitute "vehicle or a vessel".

(3)   In paragraph 2(3) after "vehicle" insert "or the vessel".

(4)   In paragraph 4 after sub-paragraph (6) insert—

"(6A)   In sub-paragraphs (5) and (6) "land" includes any floating structure."

(5)   In paragraph 7 after "vehicle" insert "or a vessel".

Other amendments

15 In Schedule 7A to VATA 1994, in Group 1, in Note 1(3) omit paragraph (b) (and the "or" immediately before it).

16 In Schedule 41 to FA 2008, in the table in paragraph 3(1) for the entry relating to section 14F(2) of HODA 1979 substitute—

"HODA 1979 section 14F(8) | Rebated heavy oil, biodiesel or bioblend".

17 In Schedule 9 to TCTA 2018, in paragraph 6 omit sub-paragraphs (3) and (4).

General

18 Paragraphs 1 to 17 of this Schedule come into force on such day or days as the Treasury may by regulations appoint.

19 Different days may be appointed for different purposes or different areas.

20 The Treasury may by regulations make such transitional, transitory or saving provision as they consider appropriate in connection with the coming into force of any of those paragraphs (including provision conferring functions on the Commissioners for Her Majesty's Revenue and Customs).

21 The Treasury may by regulations make such amendments of any enactment as they consider appropriate in consequence of the coming into force of any of paragraphs 1 to 17.

22 A statutory instrument containing regulations under paragraph 21 is subject to annulment in pursuance of a resolution of the House of Commons.

23 Any power to make regulations under this Schedule is exercisable by statutory instrument.

COMMENTARY ON SCHEDULE 11

In 2018, the CJEU ruled that the use of red diesel to propel private pleasure craft breached the Fuel Marker Directive, which is designed to ensure that any misuse of diesel crossing EU internal borders can be detected given the variation in duty treatment in member states. During the transition period following the UK's departure from the EU, the UK is obliged under EU law to implement the judgment or risk substantial fines.

However, private pleasure craft already pay white diesel rates for their propulsion, even though they are allowed to put red diesel in their tanks. Under this measure, private pleasure craft would have to use white diesel in their propulsion tanks. Craft with a separate fuel tank for domestic use on-board can continue to use red diesel for this purpose. Where craft have one tank for propulsion and heating, the Government will explore options that prevent them from having to pay a higher rate of duty on their heating use than they would otherwise be required to pay.

The measure was subject to a summer 2019 consultation, a response will be published later in 2020 alongside the Government's consultation on red diesel.

The Hydrocarbon Oil Duties Act 1979 (HODA) covers the UK law on the taxation of hydrocarbon oils, including diesel used on and off road. The main provisions for fuel used to propel private pleasure craft are in HODA 1979, s 14E with penalties in s 14F. They allow red diesel to be supplied to operators of private pleasure craft for all uses but compel suppliers of the fuel to collect the additional duty on the fuel used for propulsion of private pleasure craft.

Section 89 introduces the changes made in Schedule 11 which:

- amends HODA 1979, ss 12 and 14E to disallow the rebates that apply to diesel, biodiesel and bioblend that are not used for road vehicles on the fuel used for propelling private pleasure craft. In practice such craft have not been benefiting from this rebated rate on the fuel used in propulsion as they have been paying the additional duty to ensure they pay the full rate
- replaces HODA 1979, s 14F to create new penalties for using marked fuel for propelling a private pleasure craft similar to those that exist when marked fuel is used in road vehicles
- makes consequential amendments to HODA 1979, ss 6AB, 13ZB, 14A, 14B, 14C, 20AAA, 24, and 27 and Schs 4 and 5; this includes giving HMRC powers to take samples
- provides for secondary legislation to mitigate the impact of the measure on permanently moored houseboats
- amends VATA 1994, Sch 7A to provide for the removal, if necessary, of the reference to marked fuel used in private pleasure craft in respect of which a declaration has been received
- provides for the changes to be brought into force on a day appointed in secondary legislation, if necessary, and to the extent required to meet our continuing international obligations

These provisions come into force on such day or days as the Treasury may by regulations appoint. However, HMRC has stated that 'If the changes need to be brought into force, a statutory instrument would be made and laid. If they were brought into force for the whole of the UK, SI 2008/2599 would be amended in due course to remove redundant references to private pleasure craft'. Based on this statement, it is possible that the UK may never introduce the required legislation to comply with the EU ruling.

SCHEDULE 12
CARBON EMISSIONS TAX
Section 95

Introduction

1 Part 3 of FA 2019 (carbon emissions tax) is amended in accordance with paragraphs 2 to 8.

Power to set emissions allowance

2 (1)   Section 73 (emissions allowance) is amended in accordance with this paragraph.

(2)   The existing text becomes subsection (1).

(3)   After that subsection insert—

"(2)   Regulations under this section—
> (a)   may have effect in relation to the reporting period during which they are made, and
> (b)   may make provision by reference to data relating to times before they are made."

Power to make further provision by regulations

3 In section 70 (charge to carbon emission tax), at the end insert—

"(4)   The Treasury may by regulations provide that carbon emissions tax is not charged in relation to regulated installations of a specified description."

4 (1)   Section 75 (power to make further provision about carbon emissions tax) is amended in accordance with this paragraph.

(2)   In subsection (1)(d) (enforcement) after "tax" insert "(including provision for the imposition of civil penalties for failure to comply with a requirement of regulations under this Part)".

(3)   In subsection (2)(d) (review and appeal), omit "of a regulator".

(4)   In subsection (3) (regulations), for paragraph (b) substitute—
> "(b)   modify—
>> (i)   the Monitoring and Reporting Regulation;
>> (ii)   the Verification Regulation;
>> (iii)   subordinate legislation relating to the monitoring or regulation of emissions."

5 In section 76 (consequential provision), in subsection (5), for the words from "amend" to the end substitute "modify—
> (a)   any enactment (whenever passed or made);
> (b)   the Monitoring and Reporting Regulation;
> (c)   the Verification Regulation."

6 (1)   Section 78 (regulations) is amended in accordance with this paragraph.

(2)   In subsection (1)—
> (a)   in paragraph (a) (conferral of functions etc), after "discretions on" insert "HMRC, the Secretary of State,";
> (b)   in paragraph (b) (charges), after "regulations" insert "or in anticipation of the conferral of such a function".

(3)   For subsection (3) (procedure) substitute—

"(3)   A statutory instrument containing regulations under section 76(4) that make provision amending or repealing any provision of an Act of Parliament must be laid before the House of Commons after being made and, unless approved by that House before the end of the period of 40 days beginning with the date on which the instrument is made, ceases to have effect at the end of that period."

(4)   After subsection (5) insert—

"(6)   The fact that a statutory instrument ceases to have effect as a result of subsection (3) does not affect—
> (a)   anything previously done under the instrument, or

    (b)   the making of a new instrument.

(7)   In calculating the period of 40 days mentioned in subsection (3), no account is to be taken of any time—

    (a)   during which Parliament is dissolved or prorogued, or

    (b)   during which the House of Commons is adjourned for more than four days.”

Interpretation

7 (1)   Section 77 (interpretation) is amended in accordance with this paragraph.

(2)   In subsection (1)—

    (a)   after the definition of “installation” insert—

“ “modify” includes amend, repeal or revoke;”;

    (b)   for the definition of “the Monitoring and Reporting Regulation” substitute—

“ “the Monitoring and Reporting Regulation” means Commission Implementing Regulation (EU) 2018/2066 of 19 December 2018 on the monitoring and reporting of greenhouse gas emissions pursuant to Directive 2003/87/EC of the European Parliament and of the Council and amending Commission Regulation (EU) No 601/2012 (as amended from time to time);”;

    (c)   in the definition of “reporting period” omit “(subject to section 79(4))”;

    (d)   for the definition of “the Verification Regulation” substitute—

“ “the Verification Regulation” means Commission Implementing Regulation (EU) No 2018/2067 of 19 December 2018 on the verification of data and on the accreditation of verifiers pursuant to Directive 2003/87/EC of the European Parliament and of the Council (as amended from time to time).”

(3)   For subsection (4) substitute—

“(4)   For the purposes of this Part, the Monitoring and Reporting Regulation is to be treated for the purposes of section 3 of the European Union (Withdrawal) Act 2018 as if it is fully in force immediately before IP completion day (even if it is not).”

Commencement and transitional provision

8 (1)   Section 79 (commencement and transitional provision) is amended in accordance with this paragraph.

(2)   For subsection (1) substitute—

“(1)   This Part comes into force—

    (a)   for the purposes of making regulations under section 70, 73, 75 or 76, on the day after the day on which paragraphs 1 to 8 of Schedule 12 to FA 2020 come into force, and

    (b)   for all other purposes, on such day as the Commissioners may by regulations appoint.”

(3)   Omit subsections (3) to (5).

Penalty for failure to make payments on time

9 In Schedule 56 to FA 2009 (penalty for failure to make payments on time), in the Table in paragraph 1, after item 10A insert—

“10B	Carbon emissions tax	Amount payable under section 70(3) of FA 2019	The date determined by or under regulations under section 75 of FA 2019 as the date by which the amount must be paid”

Commencement

10 Paragraph 9 comes into force on such day as the Treasury may by regulations made by statutory instrument appoint.

COMMENTARY ON SCHEDULE 12

Section 95 and Schedule 12 make amendments to FA 2019, Pt 3 which established (but did not commence) a carbon emissions tax. Whether this carbon emissions tax and a standalone emissions trading system will come into force in the UK will depend on the terms of the UK's future relationship with the EU after the implementation period. Moreover, further legislation on the detailed operation of the tax is still required.

Paragraph 2 makes amendments to FA 2019, s 73 (which confers the powers to set an emissions allowance) to clarify that regulations may be made within the same year to which the emissions allowance will relate and can refer to data relating to times before the regulations are made.

Paragraph 3 provides for powers under FA 2019, s 70 for the Treasury to make regulations provide that carbon emissions tax is not charged in relation to certain regulated installations.

Paragraph 4, makes amendments to FA 2019, s 75 in relation to matters including powers for imposing civil penalties, reviews and the right to appeal.

Paragraph 5 amends FA 2019, s 76 and provides for powers to modify domesticised versions of certain EU legislation.

Paragraph 6 amends FA 2019, s 78 to clarify that functions or discretions may be conferred on the Secretary of State or HMRC and to ensure that regulators will be able to recover costs incurred in doing work connected with carbon emissions tax.

Paragraph 7 amends certain definitions in FA 2019, s 77 due to changes in other legislation since FA 2019 received Royal Assent.

Paragraph 8 deals with commencement and transitional provisions and paragraphs 9 and 10 introduce a penalty for failure to pay the tax on time.

SCHEDULE 13

JOINT AND SEVERAL LIABILITY OF COMPANY DIRECTORS ETC

Section 100

Introduction

1 (1)   This Schedule provides for an individual to be jointly and severally liable to the Commissioners for Her Majesty's Revenue and Customs, in certain circumstances involving insolvency or potential insolvency, for amounts payable to the Commissioners by a company.

(2)   Such liability arises where the individual is given a notice under—

    (a)   paragraph 2(1) (tax avoidance and tax evasion cases),

    (b)   paragraph 3(1) (repeated insolvency and non-payment cases), or

    (c)   paragraph 5(1) (cases involving penalty for facilitating avoidance or evasion).

A notice under paragraph 2(1), 3(1) or 5(1) is referred to in this Schedule as a "joint liability notice".

(3)   In this Schedule "company" has the same meaning as in the Corporation Tax Acts (see section 1121 of CTA 2010), except that it also includes a limited liability partnership.

(4)   Paragraph 18 makes provision about the application of this Schedule in relation to limited liability partnerships.

Tax avoidance and tax evasion cases

2 (1)   An authorised HMRC officer may give a notice under this sub-paragraph to an individual if it appears to the officer that conditions A to E are met.

(2)   Condition A is that a company has—

    (a)   entered into tax-avoidance arrangements, or

    (b)   engaged in tax-evasive conduct.

(3)   Condition B is that—

    (a)   the company is subject to an insolvency procedure, or

    (b)   there is a serious possibility of the company becoming subject to an insolvency procedure.

(4)   Condition C is that—

    (a)   the individual—

        (i)   was responsible (whether alone or with others) for the company entering into the tax-avoidance arrangements or engaging in the tax-evasive conduct, or

        (ii)   received a benefit which, to the individual's knowledge, arose (wholly or partly) from those arrangements or that conduct,

at a time when the individual was a director or shadow director of the company or a participator in it, or

    (b)   the individual took part in, assisted with or facilitated the tax-avoidance arrangements or the tax-evasive conduct at a time when the individual—

        (i)   was a director or shadow director of the company, or

        (ii)   was concerned, whether directly or indirectly, or was taking part, in the management of the company.

(5)   For the purposes of sub-paragraph (4)(a)(ii)—

    (a)   an individual is treated as knowing anything that the individual could reasonably be expected to know;

    (b)   an individual is treated as receiving anything that is received by a person with whom the individual is connected (within the meaning given by section 993 of ITA 2007).

(6)   Condition D is that there is, or is likely to be, a tax liability referable to the tax-avoidance arrangements or to the tax-evasive conduct ("the relevant tax liability").

(7)   Condition E is that there is a serious possibility that some or all of the relevant tax liability will not be paid.

(8)   A notice under sub-paragraph (1) must—

    (a)   specify the company to which the notice relates;

(b) set out the reasons for which it appears to the officer that conditions A to E are met;

(c) state the effect of the notice;

(d) offer the individual a review of the decision to give the notice, and explain the effect of paragraph 11 (right of review);

(e) explain the effect of paragraph 13 (right of appeal).

(9) It must also—

(a) specify the amount of the relevant tax liability, if the existence and amount of that liability have been established;

(b) if not, indicate that the amount will be specified in a further notice.

(10) Once the existence and amount of the relevant tax liability have been established in a case to which sub-paragraph (9)(b) applies, an authorised HMRC officer must give a further notice specifying that amount.

(11) A notice under sub-paragraph (10) must—

(a) be given to the individual to whom the notice under sub-paragraph (1) was given;

(b) offer the individual a review of the decision to give the notice, and explain the effect of paragraph 11 (right of review);

(c) explain the effect of paragraph 13 (right of appeal).

(12) An individual who is given a notice under sub-paragraph (1) is jointly and severally liable with the company (and with any other individual who is given such a notice) for the relevant tax liability.

This is subject to paragraph 9 (interaction with penalties).

(13) The amount of the individual's liability under sub-paragraph (12) is taken to be the amount specified under sub-paragraph (9)(a) or (10).

For provision under which the amount so specified may be varied, see—

(a) paragraph 10 (modification etc),

(b) paragraphs 11 and 12 (review), and

(c) paragraphs 13 and 14 (appeal).

Repeated insolvency and non-payment cases

3 (1) An authorised HMRC officer may give a notice under this sub-paragraph to an individual if it appears to the officer that conditions A to D are met.

(2) A notice under sub-paragraph (1) may not be issued after the end of the period of two years beginning with the day on which HMRC first became aware of facts sufficient for them reasonably to conclude that conditions A to D are met.

(3) Condition A is that there are at least two companies ("the old companies") in the case of each of which—

(a) the individual had a relevant connection with the company at any time during the period of five years ending with the day on which the notice is given ("the five-year period"),

(b) the company became subject to an insolvency procedure during the five-year period, and

(c) at the time when the company became subject to that procedure—

(i) the company had a tax liability, or

(ii) the company had failed to submit a relevant return or other document, or to make a relevant declaration or application, that it was required to submit or make, or

(iii) the company had submitted a relevant return or other document, or had made a relevant declaration or application, but an act or omission on the part of the company had prevented HMRC from dealing with it.

In sub-paragraphs (ii) and (iii) "relevant" means relevant to the question whether the company had a tax liability or how much its tax liability was.

(4) Condition B is that another company ("the new company") is or has been carrying on a trade or activity that is the same as, or is similar to, a trade or activity previously carried on by—

(a) each of the old companies (if there are two of them), or

(b) any two of the old companies (if there are more than two).

(5)   Condition C is that the individual has had a relevant connection with the new company at any time during the five-year period.

(6)   Condition D is that at the time when the notice is given—

    (a)   at least one of the old companies referred to in sub-paragraph (4)(a) or (b) has a tax liability, and

    (b)   the total amount of the tax liabilities of those companies—

        (i)   is more than £10,000, and

        (ii)   is more than 50% of the total amount of those companies' liabilities to their unsecured creditors.

(7)   An individual who is given a notice under sub-paragraph (1) is jointly and severally liable with the new company (and with any other individual who is given such a notice)—

    (a)   for any tax liability that the new company has on the day on which the notice is given, and

    (b)   for any tax liability of the new company that arises—

        (i)   during the period of five years beginning with that day, and

        (ii)   while the notice continues to have effect.

(8)   If an old company referred to in sub-paragraph (4)(a) or (b) has a tax liability on the day on which an individual is given a notice under sub-paragraph (1), the individual is also jointly and severally liable with that company (and with any other individual who is given such a notice) for that liability.

(9)   Sub-paragraphs (7) and (8) are subject to paragraph 9 (interaction with penalties).

(10)   For the purposes of this paragraph—

    (a)   an individual has a "relevant connection" with one of the old companies if the individual—

        (i)   is a director or shadow director of the company, or

        (ii)   is a participator in the company;

    (b)   an individual has a "relevant connection" with the new company if the individual—

        (i)   is a director or shadow director of the company,

        (ii)   is a participator in the company, or

        (iii)   is concerned, whether directly or indirectly, or takes part, in the management of the company.

(11)   A notice under sub-paragraph (1) must—

    (a)   set out the reasons for which it appears to the officer giving the notice that conditions A to D are met;

    (b)   state the effect of the notice;

    (c)   specify any amounts for which the individual is liable under sub-paragraph (7)(a) or (8);

    (d)   offer the individual a review of the decision to give the notice, and explain the effect of paragraph 11 (right of review);

    (e)   explain the effect of paragraph 13 (right of appeal).

(12)   The amount of the individual's liability under sub-paragraph (7)(a) or (8) is taken to be the amount specified under sub-paragraph (11)(c).

For provision under which the amount so specified may be varied, see—

    (a)   paragraph 10 (modification etc),

    (b)   paragraphs 11 and 12 (review), and

    (c)   paragraphs 13 and 14 (appeal).

4 (1)   The Treasury may by regulations made by statutory instrument—

    (a)   amend paragraph 3(6)(b)(i) by substituting a different amount for the one that is for the time being specified there;

    (b)   amend paragraph 3(6)(b)(ii) by substituting a different percentage for the one that is for the time being specified there.

(2)   A statutory instrument containing regulations under this paragraph—

    (a)   is subject to annulment in pursuance of a resolution of the House of Commons, if the regulations increase the specified amount by no more than is necessary to reflect changes in the value of money;

    (b)   otherwise, may not be made unless a draft of the instrument has been laid before and approved by a resolution of the House of Commons.

Cases involving penalty for facilitating avoidance or evasion

5 (1) An authorised HMRC officer may give a notice under this sub-paragraph to an individual if it appears to the officer that conditions A to D are met.

(2) Condition A is that—

    (a)   a penalty under any of the specified provisions (see sub-paragraph (6)) has been imposed on a company by HMRC, or

    (b)   proceedings have been commenced before the First-tier Tribunal for a penalty under any of those provisions to be imposed on a company.

(3) Condition B is that—

    (a)   the company is subject to an insolvency procedure, or

    (b)   there is a serious possibility of the company becoming subject to an insolvency procedure.

(4) Condition C is that the individual was a director or shadow director of the company, or a participator in it, at the time of any act or omission in respect of which—

    (a)   the penalty was imposed, or

    (b)   the proceedings for the penalty were commenced.

(5) Condition D is that there is a serious possibility that some or all of the penalty will not be paid.

(6) The specified provisions are—

    (a)   section 98C(1) of the TMA 1970 (penalties for breach of certain obligations relating to disclosure of tax avoidance schemes by promoters etc of schemes);

    (b)   paragraphs 2 and 3 of Schedule 35 to FA 2014 (promoters of tax avoidance schemes: penalties);

    (c)   paragraph 1 of Schedule 20 to FA 2016 (penalties for enablers of offshore tax evasion or non-compliance);

    (d)   Part 1 of Schedule 16 to F(No.2)A 2017 (penalties for enablers of defeated tax avoidance);

    (e)   Part 2 of Schedule 17 to that Act (penalties for breach of certain obligations relating to disclosure of tax avoidance schemes by promoters etc of schemes).

(7) A notice under sub-paragraph (1) must—

    (a)   specify the company to which the notice relates;

    (b)   set out the reasons for which it appears to the officer that conditions A to D are met;

    (c)   state the effect of the notice;

    (d)   offer the individual a review of the decision to give the notice, and explain the effect of paragraph 11 (right of review);

    (e)   explain the effect of paragraph 13 (right of appeal).

(8) It must also—

    (a)   specify the amount of the penalty, if sub-paragraph (2)(a) applies;

    (b)   if sub-paragraph (2)(b) applies, indicate that the amount will be specified in a further notice.

(9) Once the existence and amount of the penalty have been established in a case where sub-paragraph (2)(b) applies, an authorised HMRC officer must give a further notice specifying that amount.

(10) A notice under sub-paragraph (9) must—

    (a)   be given to the individual to whom the notice under sub-paragraph (1) was given;

    (b)   offer the individual a review of the decision to give the notice, and explain the effect of paragraph 11 (right of review);

    (c)   explain the effect of paragraph 13 (right of appeal).

(11) An individual who is given a notice under sub-paragraph (1) is jointly and severally liable with the company (and with any other individual who is given such a notice) for the amount of the penalty.

(12) The amount of the individual's liability under sub-paragraph (11) is taken to be the amount specified under sub-paragraph (8)(a) or (9).

For provision under which the amount so specified may be varied, see—

    (a)   paragraph 10 (modification etc),

    (b)   paragraphs 11 and 12 (review), and

    (c)   paragraphs 13 and 14 (appeal).

"Tax-avoidance arrangements"

6 (1)   In this Schedule "tax-avoidance arrangements" means—

    (a)   arrangements in respect of which a notice has been given under paragraph 12 of Schedule 43 to FA 2013, paragraph 8 or 9 of Schedule 43A to that Act or paragraph 8 of Schedule 43B to that Act (notice of final decision after considering opinion of GAAR Advisory Panel) stating that a tax advantage is to be counteracted under the general anti-abuse rule;

    (b)   arrangements in respect of which a notice has been given under section 204 of FA 2014 (follower notice) and not withdrawn;

    (c)   DOTAS arrangements within the meaning given by subsection (5) of section 219 of that Act (circumstances in which an accelerated payment notice may be given);

    (d)   arrangements to which HMRC have allocated a reference number under paragraph 22 of Schedule 17 to F(No.2)A 2017 (disclosure of tax avoidance schemes: VAT and other indirect taxes) or in respect of which the promoter must provide prescribed information under paragraph 23 of that Schedule;

    (e)   arrangements in relation to which a relevant tribunal order has been made;

    (f)   arrangements that—

        (i)   are substantially the same as arrangements in relation to which a relevant tribunal order has been made (whether involving the same or different parties), and

        (ii)   have as their promoter the person specified as the promoter in the application for the order.

(2)   For the purposes of sub-paragraph (1)(e) and (f) a relevant tribunal order is made in relation to arrangements if the tribunal—

    (a)   makes an order under—

        (i)   subsection (1)(a) of section 314A of FA 2004 (order to disclose), or

        (ii)   paragraph 4(1)(a) of Schedule 17 to F(No.2)A 2017 (corresponding provision for indirect taxes),

that a proposal for the arrangements is notifiable;

    (b)   makes an order under—

        (i)   subsection (1)(b) of that section, or

        (ii)   paragraph 4(1)(b) of that Schedule,

that the arrangements are notifiable;

    (c)   makes an order under—

        (i)   subsection (1)(a) of section 306A of FA 2004 (doubt as to notifiability), or

        (ii)   paragraph 5(1)(a) of Schedule 17 to F(No.2)A 2017,

that a proposal for the arrangements is to be treated as notifiable;

    (d)   makes an order under—

        (i)   subsection (1)(b) of that section, or

        (ii)   paragraph 5(1)(b) of that Schedule,

that the arrangements are to be treated as notifiable.

(3)   Section 307 of FA 2004 (meaning of "promoter") applies for the purposes of sub-paragraph (1)(f)(ii).

In that section as it so applies—

    (a)   references to a notifiable proposal are to be read as references to the proposal mentioned in sub-paragraph (2)(a) or (c);

    (b)   references to notifiable arrangements are to be read as references to the arrangements mentioned in sub-paragraph (2)(b) or (d).

"Tax-evasive conduct"

7 In this Schedule "tax-evasive conduct" means—

    (a)   giving to HMRC any deliberately inaccurate return, claim, document or information, or

    (b)   deliberately failing to comply with an obligation specified in the Table in paragraph 1 of Schedule 41 to FA 2008 (obligations to notify liability to tax, etc).

"Insolvency procedure" etc

8 (1) For the purposes of this Schedule a company is "subject to an insolvency procedure" if—

(a) it is undergoing, or has undergone, a relevant winding up (see sub-paragraphs (2) and (3));

(b) it is in administration (see sub-paragraph (4)) or is a company to which sub-paragraph (5) applies,

(c) it is in receivership (see sub-paragraph (6)),

(d) a relevant scheme (see sub-paragraph (7)) has effect in relation to it, or

(e) its name has been struck off the register under section 1000 or 1003 of the Companies Act 2006.

(2) A company is "undergoing a relevant winding up" for the purposes of this paragraph if—

(a) it is being wound up under—

(i) the Insolvency Act 1986 ("the 1986 Act"), or

(ii) the Insolvency (Northern Ireland) Order 1989 (S.I. 1989/2405 (N.I. 19)) ("the 1989 Order"),

otherwise than by way of a members' voluntary winding up,

(b) it is being wound up by way of a members' voluntary winding up under the 1986 Act, or the 1989 Order, and the period of 12 months beginning with the day on which that winding up commenced has expired without the company having paid its debts in full together with interest at the official rate, or

(c) a corresponding situation to a winding up under the 1986 Act or the 1989 Order exists in relation to the company under the law of a country or territory outside the United Kingdom.

(3) A company has "undergone a relevant winding up" for the purposes of this paragraph if—

(a) it has been wound up under the 1986 Act, or the 1989 Order, otherwise than by way of a members' voluntary winding up,

(b) it has been wound up by way of a members' voluntary winding up under the 1986 Act, or the 1989 Order, without having paid its debts in full together with interest at the official rate, or

(c) it has been wound up or dissolved under the law of a country or territory outside the United Kingdom.

(4) A company is "in administration" for the purposes of this paragraph if—

(a) it is in administration within the meaning given by paragraph 1 of Schedule B1 to the 1986 Act or paragraph 2 of Schedule B1 to the 1989 Order, or

(b) there is in force in relation to it under the law of a country or territory outside the United Kingdom any appointment corresponding to the appointment of an administrator under either of those Schedules.

(5) This sub-paragraph applies to a company in respect of which—

(a) a notice under sub-paragraph (1) of paragraph 84 of Schedule B1 to the 1986 Act (moving from administration to dissolution) has been registered under sub-paragraph (3) of that paragraph, or

(b) a notice under sub-paragraph (1) of paragraph 85 of Schedule B1 to the 1989 Order (corresponding provision for Northern Ireland) has been registered under sub-paragraph (3) of that paragraph,

unless an order has been made in relation to that notice under sub-paragraph (7)(c) of that paragraph.

(6) A company is "in receivership" for the purposes of this paragraph if—

(a) there is (or, but for a temporary vacancy, would be) a person who in relation to the company—

(i) is acting as administrative receiver in accordance with Chapter 1 of Part 3 of the 1986 Act or Part 4 of the 1989 Order, or

(ii) is acting as receiver by virtue of section 51 of the 1986 Act, or

(b) a corresponding situation under the law of a country or territory outside the United Kingdom exists in relation to the company.

(7) In this paragraph "relevant scheme" means a compromise or arrangement—

(a)   under Part 1 of the 1986 Act or Part 2 of the 1989 Order (company voluntary arrangements),

(b)   under Part 26 of the Companies Act 2006 (arrangements and reconstructions), or

(c)   under any corresponding provision of a country or territory outside the United Kingdom.

Interaction with penalties

9 The amount for which an individual is jointly and severally liable under paragraph 2 or 3 in respect of a company's tax liability is reduced by the amount of any penalty that the individual has paid in relation to that liability under any of the following provisions—

(a)   section 61 of VATA 1994 (VAT evasion: liability of directors etc);

(b)   section 28 of FA 2003 (liability of directors etc where body corporate liable to penalty for evasion of customs duty etc);

(c)   paragraph 19 of Schedule 24 to FA 2007 (liability of company officer where company liable to penalty under that Schedule);

(d)   paragraph 22 of Schedule 41 to FA 2008 (liability of company officer where company liable to penalty under that Schedule).

Withdrawal or modification of notice

10 (1)   HMRC must withdraw a joint liability notice given to an individual, by giving a further notice to the individual, if—

(a)   any of the relevant conditions were not met when the joint liability notice was given, or

(b)   it is not necessary for the protection of the revenue for the notice to continue to have effect.

(2)   In this Schedule "relevant conditions" means—

(a)   conditions A to E in paragraph 2, in the case of a notice under paragraph 2(1);

(b)   conditions A to D in paragraph 3, in the case of a notice under paragraph 3(1);

(c)   conditions A to D in paragraph 5, in the case of a notice under paragraph 5(1).

(3)   HMRC must withdraw a notice given to an individual under paragraph 3(1), by giving a further notice to the individual, if—

(a)   at least one of the old companies (see paragraph 3(3)) is a company that—

(i)   became subject to an insolvency procedure on the basis that it was being wound up by way of a members' voluntary winding up, and

(ii)   pays its debts in full, together with interest at the official rate, after the end of the period of 12 months beginning with the day on which the members' voluntary winding up commenced but before the end of that winding up, and

(b)   condition A in paragraph 3 would not have been met if that company, or each of them (if more than one), had not been subject to an insolvency procedure.

(4)   For the purposes of sub-paragraph (3)(a)(ii), the end of a members' voluntary winding up of a company happens when—

(a)   the company is dissolved in pursuance of the members' voluntary winding up, or

(b)   the members' voluntary winding up becomes a creditors' voluntary winding up.

(5)   HMRC may withdraw a notice given to an individual under this Schedule, by giving a further notice to the individual, if they think it appropriate to do so even though sub-paragraph (1) or (3) does not apply.

(6)   Where an individual has been given a joint liability notice, HMRC may by further notice to the individual vary an amount specified—

(a)   under paragraph 2(9)(a) or (10), paragraph 3(11)(c) or paragraph 5(8)(a) or (9), or

(b)   under this sub-paragraph,

if it seems to them that the amount so specified is, or has become, too much or not enough.

(7) Subject to sub-paragraph (8), a joint liability notice that is withdrawn under this paragraph is of no effect.

(8) Where a joint liability notice is withdrawn under sub-paragraph (1)(b) or (3), the withdrawal of the notice does not give the individual a right to recover any amount that the individual has already paid to HMRC in response to the notice.

Right of review

11 (1) Where—

    (a)   an individual is given a joint liability notice or a notice under paragraph 2(10) or 5(9), and

    (b)   before the end of the permitted period the individual communicates to HMRC written acceptance of the offer of a review contained in the notice,

HMRC must review the decision to give the notice.

(2) For the purposes of this paragraph "the permitted period" begins with the day on which the notice mentioned in sub-paragraph (1)(a) is given, and ends—

    (a)   with the 30th day after that day, or

    (b)   if HMRC give the individual a further notice specifying a later day (an "extension notice"), with that day.

(3) An extension notice—

    (a)   must be given before the permitted period would (but for the notice) have expired;

    (b)   must specify a day that is at least 30 days after the date of the extension notice;

    (c)   may be given even if one or more extension notices have already been given.

(4) If the individual does not accept the offer of a review within the permitted period, HMRC must nevertheless review the decision in question if—

    (a)   after the end of the permitted period, the individual gives HMRC a notice requesting a review out of time, and

    (b)   HMRC are satisfied that the individual had a reasonable excuse for not accepting the offer within the permitted period, and that the individual made the request without unreasonable delay after the excuse ceased to apply.

(5) HMRC are not required to undertake or continue a review under this paragraph if the individual appeals under paragraph 13 against the notice in question.

Reviews under paragraph 11

12 (1) This paragraph applies where HMRC are required to undertake a review under paragraph 11.

(2) The nature and extent of the review are to be such as appear appropriate to HMRC in the circumstances.

(3) HMRC must, in particular, have regard to steps taken before the beginning of the review—

    (a)   by HMRC in reaching the decision, and

    (b)   by any person in seeking to resolve disagreement about the decision.

(4) The review must take account of any representations made by the individual at a stage which gives HMRC a reasonable opportunity to consider them.

(5) But it is not open to the individual to challenge the existence or amount of any tax liability of a company to which the joint liability notice in question relates.

(6) At the conclusion of the review—

    (a)   HMRC must set aside the notice to which the review relates if it appears to them that—

        (i)   any of the relevant conditions were not met when the notice was given, or

        (ii)   it is not necessary for the protection of the revenue for the notice to continue to have effect;

    (b)   HMRC must set aside the notice or vary an amount specified under paragraph 2(9)(a), 3(11)(c) or 5(8)(a), or (as the case may be) paragraph 2(10) or 5(9), if it appears to HMRC that the amount specified is incorrect;

(c) otherwise, HMRC must uphold the notice.

(7) HMRC must give the individual notice of the conclusions of the review and their reasoning—

(a) within the period of 45 days beginning with the relevant date, or

(b) within any other period that HMRC and the individual may agree.

(8) In sub-paragraph (7) "relevant date" means—

(a) the date on which HMRC received the individual's notification accepting the offer of a review (in a case falling within paragraph 11(1)), or

(b) the date on which HMRC decided to undertake the review (in a case falling within paragraph 11(4)).

(9) Where HMRC do not give notice of the conclusions within the time period specified in sub-paragraph (7)—

(a) the notice to which the review relates is treated as upheld, and

(b) HMRC must notify the individual accordingly.

(10) Where a joint liability notice is set aside under sub-paragraph (6)(a)(ii), the setting aside of the notice does not give the individual a right to recover any amount that the individual has already paid to HMRC in response to the notice.

Right of appeal

13 (1) An individual who has been given—

(a) a joint liability notice, or

(b) a notice under paragraph 2(10) or 5(9),

may appeal against the notice to the First-tier Tribunal.

(2) An appeal under this paragraph must be made before—

(a) the end of the period of 30 days beginning with the day on which the notice appealed against is given, or

(b) if later, the end of the permitted period (within the meaning given by paragraph 11(2)).

This is subject to sub-paragraphs (3) to (5).

(3) Where HMRC are required to undertake a review under paragraph 11 in respect of a notice, any appeal in respect of that notice must be made within the period of 30 days beginning with the date of the notice under paragraph 12(7) communicating the conclusions of the review ("the conclusion date").

(4) Where HMRC are requested to undertake a review in accordance with paragraph 11(4)—

(a) no appeal may be made unless HMRC have notified the individual as to whether or not a review will be undertaken;

(b) if HMRC have notified the individual that a review will be undertaken, any appeal must be made within the period of 30 days beginning with the conclusion date;

(c) if HMRC have notified the individual that a review will not be undertaken, an appeal may be made only if the tribunal gives permission.

(5) Where paragraph 12(9) applies, any appeal must be made—

(a) after the end of the period specified in paragraph 12(7), and

(b) before the end of the period of 30 days beginning with the date of the notice under paragraph 12(9)(b).

(6) An appeal may be made after the end of the period specified in sub-paragraph (2), (3), (4)(b) or (5)(b) if the tribunal gives permission.

Appeals under paragraph 13

14 (1) On an appeal under paragraph 13—

(a) the tribunal must set aside the notice appealed against if it appears to the tribunal that—

(i) any of the relevant conditions were not met when the notice was given, or

(ii) it is not necessary for the protection of the revenue for the notice to continue to have effect;

(b) the tribunal must set aside the notice or vary an amount specified under paragraph 2(9)(a), 3(11)(c) or 5(8)(a), or (as the case may be) paragraph 2(10) or 5(9), if it appears to the tribunal that the amount specified is incorrect;

(c) otherwise, the tribunal must uphold the notice.

(2) It is not open to an individual appealing under paragraph 13 to challenge the existence or amount of any tax liability of a company to which the joint liability notice in question relates.

(But see paragraph 15, under which the individual may in certain circumstances pursue an appeal in place of the company.)

(3) Where a notice is set aside under sub-paragraph (1)(a)(ii), the setting aside of the notice does not give the individual a right to recover any amount that the individual has already paid to HMRC in response to the notice.

Appeal in respect of liability of company

15 (1) Where—

(a) an individual is made jointly and severally liable by a joint liability notice for a tax liability of a company,

(b) an appeal by the company in respect of that liability has been commenced (whether before or after the joint liability notice is given) but has not been determined, and

(c) the company is subject to an insolvency procedure,

the individual is entitled to be a party to the proceedings, and may continue the appeal if the company is unable or unwilling to do so.

(2) Where—

(a) an individual is made jointly and severally liable by a joint liability notice for a tax liability of a company, and

(b) the company is subject to an insolvency procedure and does not make an appeal in respect of that liability,

an appeal in respect of that liability may be made in the name of the individual.

(3) An appeal made under sub-paragraph (2) may be commenced within the period of 30 days beginning with the day on which the joint liability notice is given (even if a time limit for the company to appeal has expired).

Proceedings for determination of penalty to be imposed on company

16 Where an individual is given a notice under paragraph 5(1) in a case where paragraph 5(2)(b) applies (proceedings commenced before First-tier Tribunal for penalty to be imposed on company), the individual is entitled to be a party to the proceedings referred to in that provision.

Cases where company has ceased to exist

17 (1) Where a joint liability notice is given to an individual at a time when the company to which the notice relates has ceased to exist, a reference in this Schedule to the individual being jointly and severally liable with the company for an amount is to be read as—

(a) a reference to the individual being solely liable for that amount (where no other individual is given a joint liability notice in respect of it), or

(b) a reference to the individual being jointly and severally liable for that amount with each other individual who is given a joint liability notice in respect of it.

(2) The tax liability at a particular time of a company which no longer exists at that time is treated for the purposes of this Schedule as being whatever it was immediately before the company ceased to exist.

Application to limited liability partnerships

18 (1) This paragraph has effect for the purposes of this Schedule as it applies in relation to a limited liability partnership.

(2) A reference to a director or shadow director of a company, or a participator in it, is to be read as a reference to a member or shadow member of the limited liability partnership.

(3) A reference in paragraph 8 to the Insolvency Act 1986 or the Insolvency (Northern Ireland) Order 1989 is to that Act or Order as applied or incorporated by regulations under section 14 of the Limited Liability Partnerships Act 2000.

(4) A reference in paragraph 8 to the Companies Act 2006 is to that Act as applied or incorporated by regulations under section 15 of the Limited Liability Partnerships Act 2000.

Interpretation

19 In this Schedule—

"authorised HMRC officer" means an officer of Revenue and Customs who is, or is a member of a class of officers who are, authorised by the Commissioners for Her Majesty's Revenue and Customs for the purpose of this Schedule;

"company" has the meaning given by paragraph 1(3);

"contract settlement" means an agreement in connection with a person's liability to make a payment to HMRC under or by virtue of an enactment;

"creditors' voluntary winding up" has the meaning given by—

    (a)   section 90 of the Insolvency Act 1986 ("the 1986 Act") (in relation to England and Wales and Scotland), or

    (b)   Article 76 of the Insolvency (Northern Ireland) Order 1989 (S.I. 1989/2405 (N.I. 19)) ("the 1989 Order") (in relation to Northern Ireland);

"director" has the meaning given by section 250 of the Companies Act 2006;

"joint liability notice" has the meaning given by paragraph 1(2);

"HMRC" means Her Majesty's Revenue and Customs;

"insolvency procedure" has the meaning given by paragraph 8;

"limited liability partnership" means a body incorporated under the Limited Liability Partnerships Act 2000;

"member", in relation to a limited liability partnership, has the same meaning as in the Limited Liability Partnerships Act 2000 (see section 4 of that Act);

"members' voluntary winding up" has the meaning given by—

    (a)   section 90 of the 1986 Act (in relation to England and Wales and Scotland), or

    (b)   Article 76 of the 1989 Order (in relation to Northern Ireland);

"notice" means notice in writing;

"notify" means notify in writing;

"the official rate", in relation to interest, means the rate payable under section 189 of the 1986 Act or (as the case may be) Article 160 of the 1989 Order;

"participator" has the meaning given by section 454 of CTA 2010;

"relevant conditions" has the meaning given by paragraph 10(2);

"shadow director" has the meaning given by section 251 of the Companies Act 2006;

"shadow member", in relation to a limited liability partnership, means a person in accordance with whose directions or instructions the members of the partnership are accustomed to act (except that a person is not treated as a shadow member by reason only that the members of the partnership act on advice given by the person in a professional capacity);

"tax-avoidance arrangements" has the meaning given by paragraph 6;

"tax-evasive conduct" has the meaning given by paragraph 7;

"tax liability", in relation to a company, means any amount payable to the Commissioners for Her Majesty's Revenue and Customs by the company under or by virtue of an enactment or under a contract settlement;

"unsecured creditor" has the meaning given by—

    (a)   section 248 of the 1986 Act (in relation to England and Wales and Scotland);

    (b)   Article 5(1) of the 1989 Order (in relation to Northern Ireland).

COMMENTARY ON SCHEDULE 13

Schedule 13 provides for three different circumstances in which an individual can be made jointly and severally liable for the debts of a company or limited liability partnership they have been involved with. The three circumstances are: first, tax avoidance and tax evasion cases (paragraph 2); second, repeated insolvency and non-payment cases (paragraphs 3 and 4); and third, cases involving penalties for facilitating avoidance or evasion (paragraph 5) The Schedule then sets out various definitions (paragraphs 6, 7 and 8) before dealing with administrative and miscellaneous matters (paragraphs 9 to 19).

The general scheme of the three circumstances is that a notice can be served on an individual by an 'authorised HMRC officer' if it 'appears' to the officer that certain conditions are satisfied. The designation of an authorised officer will presumably mean that the person issuing the notice will specialise in this area and it will give some consistency to the circumstances in which the notices are issued.

Tax avoidance and tax evasion cases

Paragraph 2 provides for the authorised officer to give a joint liability notice to an individual if it appears that conditions A to E are met.

Condition A is that a company has entered into tax-avoidance arrangements or tax evasive conduct. These two terms are further explained in paragraphs 6 and 7. Tax-avoidance arrangements are basically cases where (i) a notice has been given under the GAAR; (ii) a follower notice has been given; (iii) DOTAS arrangements; (iv) cases where HMRC has allocated a reference number for the disclosure of a VAT or indirect tax scheme; (v) arrangements where a tribunal has made an order under certain specified statutory provisions; and as a catch all (vi) arrangements that are similar to those in (v). Tax-evasive conduct means deliberately providing an inaccurate return, claim, document or information or failing to comply with an obligation to notify a tax liability.

Condition B is that the company is subject to an insolvency procedure or there is a serious possibility of the company becoming subject to an insolvency procedure. Insolvency procedure is further explained in paragraph 8 where the different types of insolvency procedures ie administration, liquidation, CVA, receivership etc are set out. What is not explained is how a company for which there is a serious possibility of it becoming subject to an insolvency procedure is to be identified. Presumably, the fact that the notice has to be issued by an authorised officer will add some consistency to the circumstances when they will be issued and the authorised officer will have some training to identify relevant cases, remembering for condition B to be satisfied it only has to 'appear' to the officer that it is satisfied.

Condition C is that the individual was responsible, either alone or with others, for entering into the arrangements or received a benefit which to the individual's knowledge arose from those arrangements at a time when they were a director, shadow director or participator in the company. For these purposes an individual is treated as knowing anything which they ought reasonably be expected to know. The extension to participators widens considerably the ambit of the condition especially in conjunction with the objective test of knowledge. Condition C also applies where the individual took part in or facilitated the conduct at a time when the individual was a director or shadow director of the company or took part in the management of it.

Condition D is that as a result of the avoidance or evasive conduct there is likely to be a tax liability.

Condition E is that there is a serious possibility that all or some of the tax liability will not be paid.

Paragraph 2(8) sets out the required contents of the notice including why it appears to the officer that the conditions are satisfied, offering a review and setting out the rights of appeal. The notice must either specify the amount of tax or state that it will be specified in a further notice. The further notice must be given 'once the existence and amount of the relevant tax liability have been established'. This means that an individual can be made jointly and severally liable for a tax debt which it appears to the authorised officer may be due, but which may not actually exist.

An individual who is given a notice is jointly and severally liable for the relevant tax liability.

Repeated insolvency and non-payment cases

The provisions as to repeated insolvency cases are designed to combat phoenixism but appear to go much wider.

Paragraph 3 provides for an authorised officer of HMRC to give a joint liability notice to an individual if it appears to the officer that Conditions A to D are met.

Paragraph 3(2) sets out a time limit in which HMRC has to issue the notice which is two years beginning with the day on which HMRC first became aware of facts sufficient for it to reasonably conclude that conditions A to D are met; however, there is no requirement for HMRC to inform the individual as to when it became aware of the facts.

Condition A requires that there are at least two companies which the individual had a relevant connection with in the five years ending with the day on which the notice is served. For the purposes of these 'old companies' an individual has a relevant connection if they are a director or shadow director of the old company or a participator in it. Those two companies must have become subject to an insolvency procedure (which has the same meaning as for tax-avoidance and evasion cases) and at the time each became subject to that procedure the company was subject to a tax liability or had failed to submit returns in respect of those liabilities or the companies had submitted a return but prevented HMRC from dealing with it.

Condition B is that another 'new company' is or has been carrying on a trade or activity that is the same or similar to a trade or activity which was carried on by the old companies (if there were two) or at least two of them (if there were more than two).

Condition C is that the individual has had a relevant connection with the new company at any time during the five-year period. The definition of relevant connection is wider than for Condition A and includes an individual who is concerned, whether directly or indirectly, or takes part in, the management of the new company. Concerns have been expressed that this could include a turnaround specialist; however, HMRC has said that the legislation is not intended to catch such people and will issue guidance to that effect. Whether this affords sufficient protection remains to be seen.

Condition D is that at the time when the notice is given, one of the old companies has a tax liability which is more than £10,000 and is more than 50% of the total amount of those companies' liabilities to their unsecured creditors. Paragraph 4 permits the Treasury by regulations to alter the amount and the percentage.

Paragraph 3(7) and (8) contain similar provisions to paragraph 2(8) and (9) setting out the requirements for the contents of the notice which must include the reasons for the officer's belief that Conditions A to D are satisfied, the amounts for which the individual is liable, offering a review and setting out the rights of appeal.

Cases involving penalty for facilitating avoidance or evasion

Paragraph 5 is targeted at the avoidance of penalties. It provides for an authorised officer of HMRC to give a joint liability notice to an individual if it appears to the officer that conditions A to D are met.

Condition A is that either a penalty under any of the provisions specified in sub-paragraph (6) has been imposed on a company by HMRC or proceedings have been commenced before the First-tier Tribunal for a penalty under those provisions. Section 100(4) provides that this paragraph does not apply unless the penalty was imposed or the Proceedings started after 22 July 2020.

Condition B is that the company is subject to an insolvency procedure or there is a serious possibility of the company becoming subject to an insolvency procedure.

Condition C is that the individual was a director, shadow director or participator in the company at the time that the penalty was imposed, or the proceedings were commenced. Again, the inclusion of participator widens the ambit of the ability to give notice. There is no restriction on the giving of the notice if the participator was not a party to the act or omission that gave rise to the penalty.

Condition D is that there is a serious possibility that some or all of the penalty will not be paid.

Paragraph 5(7) and (8) set out the requirements for the contents of the notice.

Administrative and other provisions

Interaction with penalties

Paragraph 9 provides for the liability of the person who is jointly and severally liable under paragraphs 2 and 3 (not paragraph 5) to be reduced by specified penalties that the individual might have already paid in respect of those liabilities under paragraphs 2 and 3.

Withdrawal or modification of notice.

Paragraph 10 provides for three situations when a joint liability notice must be withdrawn. These are: first, where any of the relevant conditions (para 2, A to E; para 3, A to D; and para 5, A to D) were not met when the joint liability notice was given; second, it is not necessary for the protection of the revenue for the notice to have effect; and third, where in paragraph 3(3) one of the old companies was being wound up by way of members' voluntary liquidation ('MVL') (ie a solvent liquidation) and pays its debts within 12 months and condition A would not have been met if that company had not been subject to an insolvency procedure.

The third situation recognises that for condition A of paragraph 3 there must be at least two old companies that have gone into an insolvency procedure. Insolvency procedure includes an MVL. As the purpose of the legislation is to protect HMRC in insolvency situations, where one of the two companies turns out to be solvent and repays its debts Condition A was arguably not satisfied.

Paragraph 10(7) provides that a notice that is withdrawn is of no effect; however, paragraph 10(8) provides that where a notice is withdrawn under sub-paragraph (1)(b) (not necessary for the protection of the revenue) or sub-para-graph (3) (company pays its debts) the withdrawal of the notice does not give the individual the right to recover from HMRC any amount that has already been paid. The individual will, however, have the right under the general law to recover that amount from the company. It appears that the individual does have the right to recover from HMRC if the various conditions were not satisfied when the notice was given (sub-paragraph 10(1)(a)).

Right of review

Paragraphs 11 and 12 give a right of review similar to those found in other areas of the Taxes Acts.

Right of appeal

Paragraph 13 gives an individual who has received a joint liability notice the right to appeal to the First-tier Tribunal (FTT).

Paragraph 14 sets out the circumstances in which the FTT can set aside the notice. These are: first, that it appears to the Tribunal that any of the relevant conditions were not satisfied when the notice was given; second, the notice is not necessary for the protection of the revenue; and third, the Tribunal may set aside the notice or vary it if it appears to the Tribunal that the amount specified in the notice is incorrect. Otherwise, the Tribunal must uphold the notice. It is not open to the individual to challenge the underlying tax liability (unless paragraph 15 applies, see below).

Paragraph 14(3) provides that in the case where the Tribunal finds the notice is not required for the protection of the revenue, the individual has no right to recover any amounts already paid under the notice. Again, under the general law the individual should be able to recover from the company. In the other two cases the individual can recover the amounts paid from HMRC.

Appeal in respect of liability of company

When a company goes into administration or liquidation the management of the affairs pass to the administrator or liquidator; consequently, the former directors or participators have no standing to appeal any tax assessments on the company. Paragraph 15 provides an exception to that rule. Where the company is subject to an insolvency procedure and an appeal in respect of the liability for which the individual is sought to be jointly liable has been commenced but not determined, the individual is entitled to be made a party to the proceedings and can continue the appeal even if the company is unable or unwilling to do so. This gives the individual the ability to contest the liability and thus the liability under the notice.

Similarly, the individual can make an appeal in their own name where they are given a joint liability notice and the company is in an insolvency procedure and does not make an appeal. The time limit for appeal by the individual is 30 days after the giving of the notice and this applies whether the time limit for the company has expired.

Proceedings for determination of penalty to be imposed on company

Paragraph 16 provides for the individual to be made a party to proceedings where they are commenced before the FTT for a penalty to be imposed on the company.

Cases where company has ceased to exist

Paragraph 17 deals with the situation where the company has ceased to exist probably by being struck off or by dissolution (which may be following an insolvency procedure). In this case any reference to an individual being jointly liable with a company is to the individual being solely liable unless another individual has been given a notice in which case it refers to the individual being jointly liable with that other individual.

Paragraph 17 also provides that the tax liability of a company that has ceased to exist is treated for the purposes of the Schedule as being what it was before it ceased to be so. This means the individual cannot argue there is no debt because the debtor has ceased to exist.

Application to limited liability partnerships

Paragraph 18 applies the Schedule to limited liability partnerships and makes all the members potentially capable of being given a joint liability notice including 'shadow members' which are equivalent to shadow directors. The Schedule does not apply to limited partnerships under the Limited Partnerships Act 1907 or general partnerships under the Partnerships Act 1890.

Interpretation

Paragraph 19 gives the meaning of certain words used in the Schedule.

SCHEDULE 14

AMENDMENTS RELATING TO THE OPERATION OF THE GAAR

Section 101

Introduction

1 Part 5 of FA 2013 (the general anti-abuse rule) is amended as follows.

Protecting adjustments under the GAAR before time limits expire

2 In section 209 (counteracting the tax advantage), for subsection (6) substitute—

"(6) But—

    (a)   the effect of adjustments made by an officer of Revenue and Customs by virtue of this section is suspended until the procedural requirements of Schedule 43, 43A or 43B have been complied with, and

    (b)   the power to make adjustments by virtue of this section is subject to any time limit imposed by or under any enactment other than this Part.

The provision made by this subsection needs to be read with sections 209AA to 209AC and has no effect on adjustments so far as made otherwise than by virtue of this section."

3 After section 209 insert—

"209AA   Protective GAAR notices

(1)   An officer of Revenue and Customs may give a written notice (a "protective GAAR notice") to a person stating that the officer considers—

    (a)   that a tax advantage might have arisen to the person from tax arrangements that are abusive, and

    (b)   that, on the assumption that the advantage does arise from tax arrangements that are abusive, it ought to be counteracted under section 209.

(2)   The protective GAAR notice must be given within the ordinary assessing time limit applicable to the proposed adjustments.

(3)   But if—

    (a)   a tax enquiry is in progress into a return made by the person, and

    (b)   the return relates to the tax in respect of which the specified adjustments under the protective GAAR notice are made,

the protective GAAR notice must instead be given no later than the time when the enquiry is completed.

(4)   The protective GAAR notice must—

    (a)   specify the arrangements and the tax advantage, and

    (b)   specify the adjustments that, on the assumption that the advantage does arise from tax arrangements that are abusive, the officer proposes ought to be made.

(5)   The adjustments specified in the protective GAAR notice have effect as if they are made by virtue of section 209.

(6)   Notice of appeal may be given against the adjustments specified in the protective GAAR notice (whether or not the adjustments are also made otherwise than by virtue of section 209).

(7)   Any appeal against the specified adjustments (whether made by virtue of section 209 or otherwise) is, as a result of this subsection, stayed—

    (a)   for a period of 12 months beginning with the day on which the protective GAAR notice is given, or

    (b)   if a final GAAR counteraction notice is given before the end of that period, for a period ending with the day on which the final GAAR counteraction notice is given.

(8)   If, in the case of the specified adjustments (whether made by virtue of section 209 or otherwise)—

    (a)   notice of appeal is not given or notice of appeal is given but the appeal is subsequently withdrawn or determined by agreement, and

    (b)   no final GAAR counteraction notice is given,

the protective GAAR notice has effect for all purposes (other than the purposes of section 212A) as if it had been given as a final GAAR counteraction notice (and, accordingly, as if the GAAR procedural requirements had been complied with).

(9) In any case not falling within subsection (8)—

    (a) the specified adjustments have no effect (so far as they are made by virtue of section 209) unless they (or lesser adjustments) are subsequently specified in a final GAAR counteraction notice, but

    (b) the giving of the protective GAAR notice is treated as meeting the requirements of section 209(6)(b) in the case of that final GAAR counteraction notice."

4 After section 209AA (as inserted by paragraph 3) insert—

"209AB   Adjustments under section 209: notices under Schedule 43 or 43A

(1) This section applies in the case of any particular adjustments in respect of a particular period or matter ("the adjustments concerned") if—

    (a) a person is given a notice under paragraph 3 of Schedule 43 or a pooling notice or notice of binding under Schedule 43A ("the Schedule 43 or 43A notice") that specifies the adjustments concerned (whether or not other adjustments are specified),

    (b) the Schedule 43 or 43A notice is given within the relevant time limit applicable to the adjustments concerned, and

    (c) the adjustments concerned have not been specified in a provisional counteraction notice under section 209A, or a protective GAAR notice under section 209AA, given before the time at which the Schedule 43 or 43A notice is given.

(2) The Schedule 43 or 43A notice is given within the relevant time limit if—

    (a) it is given within the ordinary assessing time limit applicable to the adjustments concerned, or

    (b) if a tax enquiry is in progress into a return made by the person and the particular adjustments concerned relate to the matters contained in the return, it is given no later than the time when the enquiry is completed.

(3) The adjustments concerned have effect as if they are made by virtue of section 209.

(4) If, in the case of the specified adjustments (whether made by virtue of section 209 or otherwise)—

    (a) notice of appeal is not given or notice of appeal is given but the appeal is subsequently withdrawn or determined by agreement, and

    (b) no final GAAR counteraction notice is given,

the Schedule 43 or 43A GAAR notice has effect for all purposes (other than the purposes of section 212A) as if it had been given as a final GAAR counteraction notice (and, accordingly, as if the GAAR procedural requirements had been complied with).

(5) In any case not falling within subsection (4)—

    (a) the adjustments concerned have no effect (so far as they are made by virtue of section 209) unless they (or lesser adjustments) are subsequently specified in a final GAAR counteraction notice, but

    (b) the giving of the Schedule 43 or 43A notice is treated as meeting the requirements of section 209(6)(b) in the case of that final GAAR counteraction notice."

5 After section 209AB (as inserted by paragraph 4) insert—

"209AC   Sections 209AA and 209AB: definitions

(1) In sections 209AA and 209AB—

    "final GAAR counteraction notice" means a notice given under—

        (a) paragraph 12 of Schedule 43,

        (b) paragraph 8 or 9 of Schedule 43A, or

        (c) paragraph 8 of Schedule 43B,

    "GAAR procedural requirements" means the procedural requirements of Schedule 43, 43A or 43B, "lesser adjustments" means adjustments specified in the final GAAR counteraction notice which assume a smaller tax advantage than was assumed in the protective GAAR notice or (as the case may be) the Schedule 43 or 43A notice, and

"ordinary assessing time limit", in relation to any adjustments, means the time limit imposed by or under any enactment other than this Part for the making of the adjustments.

(2) Expressions which are used in section 202 of FA 2014 ("tax enquiry", and its being "in progress", and "return") have the same meaning in sections 209AA and 209AB as they have in that section (and references to completing a tax enquiry are to be read accordingly)."

6 Omit sections 209A to 209F (provisional counteraction notices).

7 In section 214(1) (interpretation of Part 5 of FA 2013), omit—

    (a)   the definition of "notified adjustments", and

    (b)   the definition of "provisional counteraction notice".

Minor amendments

8 In paragraph 11 of Schedule 43A (meaning of "equivalent arrangements"), omit "For the purposes of paragraph 1,".

9 In paragraph 5 of Schedule 43C (penalty under section 212A), for sub-paragraphs (5) and (6) substitute—

"(5) An assessment of a penalty under this paragraph must be made before the end of the period of 12 months beginning with the date (or the latest of the dates) on which the counteraction mentioned in section 212A(1)(d) becomes final (within the meaning of section 210(8))."

Commencement

10 The amendment made by paragraph 2 has effect in relation to adjustments made by an officer of Revenue and Customs by virtue of section 209 of FA 2013 on or after the commencement date.

11 The amendment made by paragraph 3 has effect in relation to notices given under section 209AA of FA 2013 on or after the commencement date (whenever the arrangements are entered into) but no notice may be given under that section in relation to any adjustments if a provisional counteraction notice has been given under section 209A of that Act before that date in respect of those adjustments.

12 The amendment made by paragraph 4 has effect in relation to notices given under Schedule 43 or 43A to FA 2013 on or after the commencement date (whenever the arrangements are entered into).

13 The amendment made by paragraph 6 does not affect the operation of sections 209A to 209F of FA 2013 in relation to provisional counteraction notices given under section 209A of that Act before the commencement date.

14 The amendment made by paragraph 9 has effect in relation to cases where a person becomes liable to a penalty under section 212A of FA 2013 on or after the commencement date.

15 In paragraphs 10 to 14 "the commencement date" means the date on which this Act is passed.

COMMENTARY ON SCHEDULE 14

By virtue of section 101 and Schedule 14, amendments are made to FA 2013, the primary legislation for the general anti-avoidance rule (GAAR). By way of background the GAAR, which initially came into effect on 17 July 2013 by virtue of FA 2013, ss 206–215 and Sch 43, targets tax avoidance arrangements which are abusive, under a double 'reasonable test' namely the arrangements in question cannot reasonably be regarded as a reasonable course of action. The taxes covered by the GAAR are income tax, corporation tax, capital gains tax, petroleum revenue tax, inheritance tax, stamp duty land tax, the annual tax on enveloped dwellings (ATED), NIC and in respect of the diverted profit tax. Under self assessment a taxpayer is required to consider whether GAAR applies. HMRC regularly provides guidance on GAAR (see www.gov.uk/government/publications/tax-avoidance-general-anti-abuse-rules) stating that the primary policy objective is to deter taxpayers from entering into abusive arrangements and to deter would-be promoters from their promotion.

The substantive procedural rules for GAAR are contained in FA 2013, Schs 43, 43A and 43B, involving a GAAR advisory panel, which considers whether the GAAR is applicable, thereafter the panel giving its opinion. If the arrangements are determined to be abusive then a counteraction notice is given, which in turn must be just and reasonable. Schedule 14 repeals FA 2013, ss 209A–209F, which covered counteraction notices, time limits and appeals, and replaces them with FA 2013, ss 209AA–209AC introducing provisional counteraction notices to replace counteraction notices and which are intended to be procedurally more simple. They allow HMRC to pursue arrangements in the event they do not wish to use GAAR, by using technical non-GAAR arguments, and are effective for provisional counteraction notices issued on or after 22 July 2020, the date of Royal Assent of FA 2020.

The new procedures include the following:

- An officer of HMRC may give a protective GAAR notice which states that an abusive tax arrangement may have resulted in a tax advantage, and that is should be counteracted;
- The notice must be given with the ordinary time limits subject to any tax enquiry being in progress for a tax return which relates to the protective GAAR notice;
- The notice must specify the arrangements and the tax advantage and the adjustments proposed by HMRC;
- A notice of appeal may be given by the taxpayer against any of HMRC's specified adjustments within 12 months of the date of the protective GAAR notice or if earlier in the case of a final GAAR counteraction notice not later than the date of that notice;
- If there is no notice of appeal, or an appeal is either withdrawn or determined by agreement between HMRC and the taxpayer and there is no final GAAR counteraction notice, then the protective GAAR notice will have effect.

SCHEDULE 15

TAX RELIEF FOR SCHEME PAYMENTS ETC

Section 102

Introductory

1 (1) This Schedule provides for the following in respect of qualifying payments—

(a) an exemption from income tax, and

(b) an exemption from capital gains tax.

(2) This Schedule also provides for a relief from inheritance tax in respect of qualifying payments (but see paragraph 5(4), which contains an excepted case).

Qualifying payments

2 (1) In this Schedule "qualifying payment" means a payment within any of sub-paragraphs (2) to (5).

(2) A payment is within this sub-paragraph if it is a payment under the Windrush Compensation Scheme.

(3) A payment is within this sub-paragraph if—

(a) it is made otherwise than under the Windrush Compensation Scheme,

(b) it is made to, or in respect of, a person who made a claim under that Scheme (which the person was eligible to make),

(c) it is made in connection with the same circumstances as gave rise to that person's eligibility to make that claim, and

(d) it is made by or on behalf of—

(i) the government of the United Kingdom,

(ii) the government of a part of the United Kingdom, or

(iii) a local or other public authority in the United Kingdom.

(4) A payment is within this sub-paragraph if it is a payment under the Troubles Permanent Disablement Payment Scheme established by the Victims' Payments Regulations 2020 (S.I. 2020/103) (as that scheme is amended from time to time).

(5) A payment is within this sub-paragraph if—

(a) it is a compensation payment of a description specified in regulations made by the Treasury by statutory instrument, and

(b) it is a payment made by or on behalf of—

(i) the government of the United Kingdom,

(ii) the government of a part of the United Kingdom,

(iii) the government of any other country or territory,

(iv) a local or other public authority in the United Kingdom, or

(v) a local or other public authority of a territory outside the United Kingdom.

(6) Regulations under sub-paragraph (5) may provide that a compensation payment of a description specified in the regulations is a qualifying payment only for the purposes of particular provisions of this Schedule.

(7) A statutory instrument containing regulations under sub-paragraph (5) is subject to annulment in pursuance of a resolution of the House of Commons.

(8) In this paragraph "the Windrush Compensation Scheme" means the scheme published by the Home Office on 3 April 2019 which provides compensation for certain categories of persons in recognition of difficulties arising out of an inability to demonstrate lawful immigration status (as that scheme is amended from time to time).

Exemption from income tax

3 (1) No liability to income tax arises in respect of a qualifying payment.

(2) A qualifying payment is to be ignored for all other income tax purposes.

(3) This paragraph has effect in relation to qualifying payments within paragraph 2(2) or (3) that are received on or after 3 April 2019.

(4) This paragraph has effect in relation to qualifying payments within paragraph 2(4) that are received on or after 29 May 2020.

(5) This paragraph has effect in relation to qualifying payments within paragraph 2(5) that are received on or after such date as is specified in the regulations concerned (which may be a date before the regulations are made).

Exemptions from capital gains tax

4 (1) A gain accruing on a disposal is not a chargeable gain if it accrues on—

    (a) a disposal arising as a result of the forfeiture or surrender of rights, or as a result of refraining from exercising rights, in return for a qualifying payment,

    (b) a disposal of the right to receive the whole or any part of a qualifying payment, or

    (c) a disposal of an interest in any such right.

(2) In sub-paragraph (1)(c) "interest", in relation to a right, means an interest as a co-owner of the right (whether it is owned jointly or in common and whether or not the interests of the co-owners are equal).

(3) This paragraph has effect—

    (a) in a case where the qualifying payment concerned is within paragraph 2(2) or (3), in relation to disposals made on or after 3 April 2019, and

    (b) in a case where the qualifying payment concerned is within paragraph 2(4), in relation to disposals made on or after 29 May 2020.

    (c) in a case where the qualifying payment concerned is within paragraph 2(5), in relation to disposals made on or after such date as is specified in the regulations concerned (which may be a date before the regulations are made).

Relief from inheritance tax

5 (1) This paragraph applies where a qualifying payment is at any time received by a person or the personal representatives of a person (but see sub-paragraph (4)).

(2) The inheritance tax chargeable on the value transferred by the transfer made on the person's death is to be reduced by an amount equal to—

    (a) the relevant percentage of the amount of the payment, or

    (b) if lower, the amount of inheritance tax that would, apart from this paragraph, be chargeable on the value transferred.

(3) The "relevant percentage" means the percentage in the last row of the third column of the Table in Schedule 1 to IHTA 1984.

(4) This paragraph does not apply in a case where—

    (a) the qualifying payment is within paragraph 2(3),

    (b) the payment is made after the death of the person mentioned in paragraph (b) of paragraph 2(3), and

    (c) the payment is made otherwise than to the personal representatives of that person.

(5) This paragraph has effect, in a case where the qualifying payment is within paragraph 2(2) or (3), in relation to deaths occurring on or after 3 April 2019.

(6) This paragraph has effect, in a case where the qualifying payment is within paragraph 2(4), in relation to deaths occurring on or after 29 May 2020.

(7) This paragraph has effect, in a case where the qualifying payment is within paragraph 2(5), in relation to deaths occurring on or after such date as is specified in the regulations concerned (which may be a date before the regulations are made).

COMMENTARY ON SCHEDULE 15
[See Commentary note for section 102]

SCHEDULE 16
TAXATION OF CORONAVIRUS SUPPORT PAYMENTS

Section 106

Accounting for coronavirus support payments referable to a business

1 (1) This paragraph applies if a person carrying on, or who carried on, a business (whether alone or in partnership) receives a coronavirus support payment that is referable to the business.

(2) So much of the coronavirus support payment as is referable to the business is a receipt of a revenue nature for income tax or corporation tax purposes and is to be brought into account in calculating the profits of that business—

    (a)   under the applicable provisions of the Income Tax Acts, or

    (b)   under the applicable provisions of the Corporation Tax Acts.

(3) Subject to paragraph 2(5), sub-paragraph (2) does not apply to an amount of a coronavirus support payment if—

    (a)   the business to which the amount is referable is no longer carried on by the recipient of the amount, and

    (b)   the amount is not referable to activities of the business undertaken at a time when it was being carried on by the recipient of the amount.

(4) If an amount of the coronavirus support payment is referable to more than one business or business activity, the amount is to be allocated between those businesses or activities on a just and reasonable basis.

(5) Paragraph 3 contains provision about when, in certain cases, an amount of a coronavirus support payment is, or is not, referable to a business for the purposes of this paragraph and paragraph 2.

(6) In this Schedule "business" includes—

    (a)   a trade, profession or vocation;

    (b)   a UK property business or an overseas property business;

    (c)   a business consisting wholly or partly of making investments.

Amounts not referable to activities of a business which is being carried on

2 (1) This paragraph applies if a person who carried on a business (whether alone or in partnership) receives a coronavirus support payment that—

    (a)   is referable to the business, and

    (b)   is not wholly referable to activities of the business undertaken while the business was being carried on by the recipient of the payment.

(2) So much of the coronavirus support payment as is referable to the business but which is not referable to activities of the business undertaken while the business was being carried on by the recipient of the payment is to be treated as follows.

(3) An amount referable to a trade, profession or vocation is to be treated as a post-cessation receipt for the purposes of Chapter 18 of Part 2 of ITTOIA 2005 or Chapter 15 of Part 3 of CTA 2009 (trading income: post-cessation receipts), and—

    (a)   in the application of Chapter 18 of Part 2 of ITTOIA 2005 to that amount, section 243 (extent of charge to tax) is omitted, and

    (b)   in the application of Chapter 15 of Part 3 of CTA 2009 to that amount, section 189 (extent of charge to tax) is omitted.

(4) An amount referable to a UK property business or an overseas property business is to be treated (in either case) as a post-cessation receipt from a UK property business for the purposes of Chapter 10 of Part 3 of ITTOIA 2005 or Chapter 9 of Part 4 of CTA 2009 (property income: post-cessation receipts), and—

    (a)   in the application of Chapter 10 of Part 3 of ITTOIA 2005 to that amount, section 350 (extent of charge to tax) is omitted, and

    (b)   in the application of Chapter 9 of Part 4 of CTA 2009 to that amount, section 281 (extent of charge to tax) is omitted.

(5) In any other case, for the purposes of paragraph 1(3)—

    (a)   the recipient of the amount is to be treated as if carrying on the business to which the amount is referable to at the time of the receipt of the amount, and

    (b)   the amount is to be treated as if it were referable to activities undertaken by the business at that time.

(6)   Where the recipient of the amount has incurred expenses that—

(a)   are referable to the amount, and

(b)   would be deductible in calculating the profits of the business if it were being carried on at the time of receipt of the amount,

the amount brought into account under paragraph 1(2) by virtue of sub-paragraph (5) is to be reduced by the amount of those expenses.

(7)   But sub-paragraph (6) does not apply to expenses of a person that arise directly or indirectly from the person ceasing to carry on business.

Amounts referable to businesses in certain cases

3 (1)   An amount of a coronavirus support payment made under an employment-related scheme—

(a)   is referable to the business of the person entitled to the payment as an employer (even if the person is not for other purposes the employer of the employees to whom the payment relates), and

(b)   is not referable to any other business (and no deduction for any expenses in respect of the same employment costs which are the subject of the payment is allowed in calculating the profits of any other business or in calculating the liability of any other person to tax charged under section 242 or 349 of ITTOIA 2005 or section 188 or 280 of CTA 2009 (post-cessation receipts)).

(2)   A coronavirus support payment made under the self-employment income support scheme is referable to the business of the individual to whom the payment relates.

(3)   Where an amount of a coronavirus support payment made under the self-employment income support scheme is brought into account under paragraph 1(2), the whole of the amount is to be treated as a receipt of a revenue nature of the tax year 2020–21 (irrespective of its treatment for accounting purposes).

(4)   But sub-paragraph (3) does not apply to an amount of a coronavirus support payment made under the self-employment income support scheme in respect of a partner of a firm where the amount is distributed amongst the partners (rather than being retained by the partner).

(5)   An amount of a coronavirus support payment made under the self-employment income support scheme in respect of a partner of a firm that is retained by the partner (rather than being distributed amongst the partners) is not to be treated as a receipt of the firm.

(6)   Accordingly—

(a)   the receipt is not to be included in the calculation of the firm's profits for the purposes of determining the share of profits or losses for each partner of the firm (see sections 849 to 850E of ITTOIA 2005 and sections 1259 to 1265 of CTA 2009), and

(b)   the receipt is then to be added to the partner's share.

Exemptions, reliefs and deductions

4 (1)   An amount of a coronavirus support payment that relates only to mutual activities of a business that carries on a mutual trade is to be treated as if it were income arising from those activities (and accordingly the amount is not taxable).

(2)   A coronavirus support payment is to be ignored when carrying out the calculation—

(a)   in section 528(1) of ITA 2007 (incoming resources limit for charitable exemptions);

(b)   in section 482(1) of CTA 2010 (incoming resources limit for charitable companies);

(c)   in section 661CA(1) of CTA 2010 (income condition for community amateur sports clubs).

(3)   A coronavirus support payment made under an employment-related scheme is to be ignored when carrying out the calculation—

(a)   in section 662(2) of CTA 2010 (exemption from corporation tax for UK trading income of community amateur sports clubs);

(b)   in section 663(2) of that Act (exemption from corporation tax for UK property income community amateur sports clubs).

(4)   No relief under Chapter 1 of Part 6A of ITTOIA 2005 (trading allowance) is given to an individual on an amount of a coronavirus support payment made under the self-employment income support scheme brought into account under paragraph 1(2) as profits of that tax year.

(5)   For the purposes of that Part, such an amount is to be ignored when calculating the individual's "relevant income" for that tax year under Chapter 1 of that Part.

(6)   Neither section 57 of ITTOIA 2005 nor section 61 of CTA 2009 (deductions for pre-trading expenses) (including as they apply by virtue of sections 272 and 272ZA of ITTOIA 2005 and section 210 of CTA 2009) apply to employment costs where an amount of a coronavirus support payment made under an employment-related scheme relates to those costs.

Charge where employment costs deductible by another

5 (1)   Income tax is charged on an amount of a coronavirus support payment made under an employment-related scheme if conditions A and B are met.

(2)   Condition A is that the amount is neither brought into account under paragraph 1(2) in calculating the profits of a business carried on by the person entitled to the payment as an employer nor treated, by virtue of paragraph 2(3) or (4), as a post-cessation receipt arising from the carrying on of such a business.

(3)   Condition B is that expenses incurred by another person in respect of the same employment costs which are the subject of the coronavirus support payment and to which the amount relates are deductible—

  (a)   in calculating the profits of a business carried on by that other person (for income or corporation tax purposes), or

  (b)   in calculating the liability of that other person to tax charged under section 242 or 349 of ITTOIA 2005 or section 188 or 280 of CTA 2009 (post-cessation receipts).

(4)   Tax is charged under sub-paragraph (1) on the whole of the amount to which that sub-paragraph applies.

(5)   The person liable for tax charged under sub-paragraph (1) is the person entitled to the coronavirus support payment as an employer.

(6)   Section 3(1) of CTA 2009 (exclusion of charge to income tax) does not apply to an amount of a coronavirus support payment that is charged under this paragraph.

Charge where no business carried on

6 (1)   Tax is charged on an amount of a coronavirus support payment, other than a payment made under an employment-related scheme or the self-employment income support scheme, if—

  (a)   the amount is neither brought into account under paragraph 1(2) in calculating the profits of a business nor treated as a post-cessation receipt by virtue of paragraph 2(3) or (4), and

  (b)   at the time the coronavirus support payment was received, the recipient did not carry on a business whose profits are charged to tax and to which the payment could be referable.

(2)   In this paragraph "tax" means—

  (a)   corporation tax, in the case of a company that (apart from this paragraph) is chargeable to corporation tax, or to any amount chargeable as if it was corporation tax, or

  (b)   income tax, in any other case.

(3)   Tax is charged under sub-paragraph (1) on the whole of the amount to which that sub-paragraph applies.

(4)   The person liable for tax charged under sub-paragraph (1) is the recipient of that amount.

(5)   Where income tax is charged under sub-paragraph (1), sections 527 and 528 of ITA 2007 (exemption and income condition for charitable trusts) have effect as if sub-paragraph (1) were a provision to which section 1016 of that Act applies.

(6)   Where corporation tax is charged under sub-paragraph (1), sections 481 and 482 of CTA 2010 (exemption and income condition for charitable companies) have effect as if sub-paragraph (1) were a provision to which section 1173 of that Act applies.

Modification of the Tax Acts

7 The Treasury may by regulations modify the application of any provision of the Tax Acts that affects (or that otherwise would affect) the treatment of—

(a)   receipts brought into account under paragraph 1(2),

(b)   amounts treated as post-cessation receipts under paragraph 2(3) or (4), or

(c)   amounts charged under paragraph 5(1) or 6(1).

Charge if person not entitled to coronavirus support payment

8 (1)   A recipient of an amount of a coronavirus support payment is liable to income tax under this paragraph if the recipient is not entitled to the amount in accordance with the scheme under which the payment was made.

(2)   But sub-paragraph (1) does not apply to an amount of a coronavirus support payment made under a coronavirus business support grant scheme or the coronavirus statutory sick pay rebate scheme.

(3)   For the purposes of this Schedule, references to a person not being entitled to an amount include, in the case of an amount of a coronavirus support payment made under the coronavirus job retention scheme, a case where the person ceases to be entitled to retain the amount after it was received—

(a)   because of a change in circumstances, or

(b)   because the person has not, within a reasonable period, used the amount to pay the costs which it was intended to reimburse.

(4)   Income tax becomes chargeable under this paragraph—

(a)   in a case where the person was entitled to an amount of a coronavirus support payment paid under the coronavirus job retention scheme but subsequently ceases to be entitled to retain it, at the time the person ceases to be entitled to retain the amount, or

(b)   in any other case, at the time the coronavirus support payment is received.

(5)   The amount of income tax chargeable under this paragraph is the amount equal to so much of the coronavirus support payment—

(a)   as the recipient is not entitled to, and

(b)   as has not been repaid to the person who made the coronavirus support payment.

(6)   Where income tax which is chargeable under this paragraph is the subject of an assessment (whether under paragraph 9 or otherwise)—

(a)   paragraphs 1 to 6 do not apply to the amount of the coronavirus support payment that is the subject of the assessment,

(b)   that amount is not, for the purposes of Step 1 of the calculation in section 23 of ITA 2007 (calculation of income tax liability), to be treated as an amount of income on which the taxpayer is charged to income tax (but see paragraph 10 which makes further provision about the application of that section), and

(c)   that amount is not to be treated as income of a company for the purposes of section 3 of CTA 2009 (and accordingly the exclusion of the application of the provisions of the Income Tax Acts to the income of certain companies does not apply to the receipt of an amount charged under this paragraph).

(7)   No loss, deficit, expense or allowance may be taken into account in calculating, or may be deducted from or set off against, any amount of income tax charged under this paragraph.

(8)   In calculating profits or losses for the purposes of corporation tax, no deduction is allowed in respect of the payment of income tax charged under this paragraph.

(9)   For the purposes of this paragraph and paragraphs 9(4) and 14, a firm is not to be regarded as receiving an amount of a coronavirus support payment made under the self-employment income support scheme in respect of a partner of that firm that is retained by the partner (rather than being distributed amongst the partners).

Assessments of income tax chargeable under paragraph 8

9 (1)   If an officer of Revenue and Customs considers (whether on the basis of information or documents obtained by virtue of the exercise of powers under Schedule 36 to FA 2008 or otherwise) that a person has received an amount of a coronavirus support payment to which the person is not entitled, the officer may make an assessment in the amount which ought in the officer's opinion to be charged under paragraph 8.

(2) An assessment under sub-paragraph (1) may be made at any time, but this is subject to sections 34 and 36 of TMA 1970.

(3) Parts 4 to 6 of TMA 1970 contain other provisions that are relevant to an assessment under sub-paragraph (1) (for example, section 31 makes provision about appeals and section 59B(6) makes provision about the time to pay income tax payable by virtue of an assessment).

(4) Where income tax is chargeable under paragraph 8 in relation to an amount of a coronavirus support payment received by a firm—

    (a)   an assessment (under sub-paragraph (1) or otherwise) may be made on any of the partners in respect of the total amount of tax that is chargeable,

    (b)   each of the partners is jointly and severally liable for the tax so assessed, and

    (c)   if the total amount of tax that is chargeable is included in a return under section 8 of TMA 1970 made by one of the partners, the other partners are not required to include the tax in returns made by them under that section.

Calculation of income tax liability

10 (1) Section 23 of ITA 2007 (calculation of income tax liability) applies in relation to a person liable to income tax charged under paragraph 8 as if that paragraph were included in the lists of provisions in subsections (1) and (2) of section 30 of that Act (amounts of tax added at step 7).

(2) For the purposes of paragraph 7(2) of Schedule 41 to FA 2008, a relevant obligation relating to income tax charged under paragraph 8 of this Schedule relates to a tax year if the income tax became chargeable in that tax year.

(3) But this paragraph does not apply to a company to which paragraph 11 (companies chargeable to corporation tax) applies.

Calculation of tax liability: companies chargeable to corporation tax

11 (1) This paragraph applies where a person liable to income tax charged under paragraph 8 is a company that is chargeable to corporation tax, or to any amount chargeable as if it was corporation tax, in relation to a period within which the income tax became chargeable.

(2) Part 5A of TMA 1970 (payment of tax) applies in relation to that company as if—

    (a)   the reference to "corporation tax" in subsection (1) of section 59D (general rule as to when corporation tax is due and payable) included income tax charged under paragraph 8 of this Schedule;

    (b)   an amount of income tax charged under paragraph 8 of this Schedule were an amount within subsection (6) of section 59F (arrangements for paying tax on behalf of group members);

    (c)   any reference in section 59G (managed payment plans) to "corporation tax" included income tax charged under paragraph 8 of this Schedule.

(3) Part 9 of that Act (interest on overdue tax) applies in relation to that company as if—

    (a)   the references in section 86 (interest on overdue income tax and capital gains tax) to "income tax" did not include income tax charged under paragraph 8 of this Schedule;

    (b)   in subsection (1) of section 87A (interest on overdue corporation tax) the reference to "corporation tax" included income tax charged under paragraph 8 of this Schedule.

(4) Schedule 18 to FA 1998 (company tax returns etc.) applies in relation to that company as if—

    (a)   any reference in that Schedule to "tax", other than the references in paragraph 2 of that Schedule (duty to give notice of chargeability), included income tax charged under paragraph 8 of this Schedule, and

    (b)   in paragraph 8(1) of that Schedule (calculation of tax payable), at the end there were inserted—

"Sixth step

Add any amount of income tax chargeable under paragraph 8 of Schedule 16 to the Finance Act 2020."

(5)   But the modifications of that Schedule are to be ignored for the purposes of the Corporation Tax (Instalment Payments) Regulations 1998 (S.I. 1998/3175).

(6)   Schedule 41 to FA 2008 applies in relation to that company as if—

(a)   the references to "income tax" in paragraph 7(2) did not include income tax charged under paragraph 8 of this Schedule;

(b)   the reference to "corporation tax" in paragraph 7(3) included income tax charged under paragraph 8 of this Schedule;

(but see paragraph 13(5) of this Schedule which has the effect that paragraph 7 of that Schedule does not apply in certain circumstances).

(7)   For the purposes of paragraph 7(3) of Schedule 41 to FA 2008 (as modified by sub-paragraph (6)), a relevant obligation relating to income tax charged under paragraph 8 of this Schedule relates to an accounting period if the income tax became chargeable in that period.

Notification of liability under paragraph 8

12 (1)   Section 7 of TMA 1970 (notice of liability to income tax and capital gains tax) applies in relation to income tax chargeable under paragraph 8 as provided for in sub-paragraphs (2) to (5).

(2)   Subsection (1) has effect as if paragraph (b) (and the "and" before it) were omitted.

(3)   Subsection (1) has effect as if the reference to "the notification period" were to the period commencing on the day on which the income tax became chargeable and ending on the later of—

(a)   the 90th day after the day on which this Act is passed, or

(b)   the 90th day after the day on which the income tax became chargeable.

(4)   Subsection (3)(c) has effect as if after "child benefit charge" there were inserted "or to income tax under paragraph 8 of Schedule 16 to the Finance Act 2020".

(5)   In relation to income tax chargeable under paragraph 8 in relation to an amount of a coronavirus support payment received by a firm, the duty in subsection (1) (as it has effect by virtue of sub-paragraphs (2) and (3)) is taken to have been complied with by each of the partners if one of the partners has complied with it.

(6)   The reference in section 36(1A)(b) of TMA 1970 (20 year period for assessment in a case involving a loss of income tax) to a failure to comply with an obligation under section 7 of that Act is not to be taken as including a failure arising by virtue of the modification of that section by this paragraph, unless the failure is one to which paragraph 13 applies.

Penalty for failure to notify: knowledge of non-entitlement to payment

13 (1)   This paragraph applies to a failure of a person to notify, under section 7 of TMA 1970 (as modified by paragraph 12), a liability to income tax chargeable under paragraph 8 where the person knew, at the time the income tax first became chargeable, that the person was not entitled to the amount of the coronavirus support payment in relation to which the tax is chargeable.

(2)   Schedule 41 to FA 2008 (failure to notify) applies to a failure described in sub-paragraph (1) as follows.

(3)   The failure is to be treated as deliberate and concealed.

(4)   Accordingly, paragraph 6 of that Schedule has effect as if the references to a penalty for "a deliberate but not concealed failure" or for "any other case" were omitted.

(5)   For the purposes of that Schedule (except in a case falling within paragraph 14 of this Schedule), the "potential lost revenue" is to be treated as being the amount of income tax which would have been assessable on the person at the end of the last day of the notification period (see paragraph 12(3)).

Penalties: partnerships

14 (1)   This paragraph applies to a failure to notify, under section 7 of TMA 1970 (as modified by paragraph 12), a liability to income tax chargeable under paragraph 8 by a partner of a firm that received the amount of the coronavirus support payment in relation to which the tax is chargeable.

(2)   For the purposes of paragraph 13(1) of this Schedule, each partner is taken to know anything that any of the other partners knows.

(3) Where a partner would be liable to a penalty under Schedule 41 to FA 2008 (whether in a case falling within paragraph 13 or otherwise), the partner is instead jointly and severally liable with the other partners to a single penalty under that Schedule for the failures by each of them to notify.

(4) In a case not falling within paragraph 13, if the failure of at least one of the partners—

    (a) was deliberate and concealed, the single penalty is to be treated as a penalty for a deliberate and concealed failure;

    (b) was deliberate but not concealed, the single penalty is to be treated as a penalty for a deliberate but not concealed failure.

(5) For the purposes of Schedule 41 to FA 2008, the "potential lost revenue" is to be treated as being the amount of income tax which would have been assessable on any one of the partners (see paragraph 9(4)(a))—

    (a) in a case falling within paragraph 13, at the end of the last day of the notification period, or

    (b) in any other case, at the end of 31 January following the tax year in which the amount of coronavirus support payment was received by the firm.

(6) Paragraph 22 of that Schedule (limited liability partnerships: members' liability) does not apply.

Liability of officers of insolvent companies

15 (1) This paragraph—

    (a) provides for an individual to be jointly and severally liable to the Commissioners for Her Majesty's Revenue and Customs for a liability of a company to income tax charged under paragraph 8, where a notice under sub-paragraph (2) is given to the individual, and

    (b) applies paragraphs 10 to 15 and 17 of Schedule 13 (joint liability notices: tax avoidance, tax evasion and repeated insolvency and non-payment) to such a notice.

(2) An officer of Revenue and Customs may give a notice under this sub-paragraph to an individual if it appears to the officer that conditions A to D are met.

(3) Condition A is that—

    (a) the company is subject to an insolvency procedure, or

    (b) there is a serious possibility of the company becoming subject to an insolvency procedure.

(4) Condition B is that the company is liable to income tax under paragraph 8.

(5) Condition C is that the individual was responsible for the management of the company at the time the income tax first became chargeable and the individual knew (at that time) that the company was not entitled to the amount of the coronavirus support payment in relation to which the tax is chargeable.

(6) Condition D is that there is a serious possibility that some or all of the income tax liability will not be paid.

(7) For the purposes of sub-paragraph (5) the individual is responsible for the management of a company if the individual—

    (a) is a director or shadow director of the company, or

    (b) is concerned (whether directly or indirectly) in, or takes part in, the management of the company.

(8) A notice under sub-paragraph (2) must—

    (a) specify the company to which the notice relates;

    (b) set out the reasons for which it appears to the officer that conditions A to D are met;

    (c) specify the amount of the income tax liability;

    (d) state the effect of the notice;

    (e) offer the individual a review of the decision to give the notice and explain the effect of paragraph 11 of Schedule 13 (right of review);

    (f) explain the effect of paragraph 13 of that Schedule (right of appeal).

(9) An individual who is given a notice under sub-paragraph (2) is jointly and severally liable with the company (and with any other individual who is given such a notice) to the amount of the income tax liability specified under sub-paragraph (8)(c).

For provision under which the amount so specified may be varied, see—

    (a)   paragraph 10 of Schedule 13 (modification etc),

    (b)   paragraphs 11 and 12 of that Schedule (review), and

    (c)   paragraphs 13 and 14 of that Schedule (appeal).

(10)   Paragraphs 10 to 15 and 17 of Schedule 13 apply to a notice under sub-paragraph (2) as they apply to a joint liability notice (see paragraph 1(2) of that Schedule) as if—

    (a)   the references in those paragraphs to "relevant conditions" were to conditions A to D in this paragraph;

    (b)   sub-paragraphs (3) and (4) of paragraph 10 were omitted (and references to sub-paragraph (3) in that paragraph were omitted);

    (c)   in paragraph 10(6)(a), after "or (9)" there were inserted "or paragraph 15(8)(c) of Schedule 16";

    (d)   in paragraph 12(6)(b) after "5(9)" there were inserted "or paragraph 15(8)(c) of Schedule 16".

(11)   Expressions used in this paragraph and in Schedule 13 have the same meaning in this paragraph as they have in that Schedule (subject to the modification made by sub-paragraph (10)(a))."

COMMENTARY ON SCHEDULE 16

[See also the Commentary note under section 106]

Paragraph 1 provides that so much of a CSP as is referable to a business is a receipt of a revenue nature to be brought into account for income tax or corporation tax purposes. 'Business' includes a trade, profession or vocation; a property business; or a business consisting wholly or partly of making investments.

Paragraph 2 deals with payments relating to a business that has ceased. In most cases they will be treated as post-cessation receipts.

Paragraph 3 provides that a CSP made under an employment-related scheme (ie the CJRS or the CSSPRS) is referable only to the business of the person entitled to the payment as an employer. An SEISS grant is referable to the business of the individual to whom the payment relates, and the whole of the amount of the grant is treated as a receipt of a revenue nature of the tax year 2020/21.

Paragraph 4 provides an exemption for CSPs relating to mutual activities of a business carrying on a mutual trade. A CSP is to be ignored in calculations for the purpose of specified limits and conditions relating to charitable activities and community amateur sports clubs. Paragraph 4 also deals with the treatment of CSPs for the purpose of the trading allowance (ITTOIA 2005, Pt 6A, Ch 1) and deductions for pre-trading expenses (ITTOIA 2005, s 57).

Paragraphs 5–7 deal with the tax charge in a case where employment costs are deductible by a person other than the employer, and the tax charge in a case where no business is carried on. It also provides HM Treasury with a power to modify any provision of the Tax Acts that affects, or would otherwise affect, the tax treatment of CSPs.

Paragraph 8 provides that a recipient of an amount of a CSP is liable to income tax if the recipient is not entitled to the amount under the rules of the relevant scheme. This tax charge does not apply to payments under the coronavirus business support grant scheme or the CSSPRS.

For the purpose of the CJRS, the reference to a person not being entitled to an amount includes a case where the person ceases to be entitled to retain the amount after it was received (a) because of a change in circumstances, or (b) because the person has not, within a reasonable period, used the amount to pay the costs which it was intended to reimburse.

The income tax becomes chargeable:

    (a)   where the person was entitled to an amount of a payment under the CJRS but subsequently ceases to be entitled to retain it, when the person ceases to be entitled to retain the amount, or

    (b)   otherwise, when the CSP is received.

The amount of income tax chargeable is 100% of so much of the CSP as the recipient is not entitled to and has not been repaid to the person who made the payment. There is no deduction for losses, expenses or allowances.

If income tax is charged on an amount under paragraph 8, then paragraphs 1 to 6 are disapplied and the amount is not treated as income charged to income tax for the purpose of ITA 2007, s 23 (calculation of income tax liability).

Paragraph 9 provides that if an HMRC officer considers that a person has received an amount of a CSP to which the person is not entitled, the officer may make an assessment (subject to the time limits in TMA 1970, ss 34 and 36) in the amount which, in the officer's opinion, ought to be charged under paragraph 8.

TMA 1970, Parts IV (assessment and claims), V (appeals etc), VA (payment of tax) and VI (collection and recovery) apply to an assessment made under paragraph 9 so that, for example, the tax will normally be payable on or before 31 January after the end of the tax year (see TMA 1970, s 59B).

Paragraph 10 adds paragraph 8 to the list of provisions in TMA 1970, s 30, so that the amount of the paragraph 8 charge is added at step 7 in the calculation of income tax liability set out in TMA 1970, s 23. Paragraph 10 also determines the tax year for which there is a 'relevant obligation' under FA 2008, Sch 41, para 7(2) (penalties for failure to notify: potential lost revenue).

Paragraph 11 deals with the calculation of tax liability for companies chargeable to corporation tax.

Paragraph 12 applies TMA 1970, s 7, with some modifications, to the income tax chargeable under paragraph 8. The effect is to require notification of liability to the paragraph 8 charge whether or not the taxpayer has received a notice to file a return.

The notification period for liability to the paragraph 8 charge begins on the day on which the income tax became chargeable, and ends on the later of the 90th day after the day on which FA 2020 was passed or the 90th day after the day on which the income tax became chargeable.

Paragraph 12(6) provides that a failure to comply with this requirement to notify a paragraph 8 charge will not trigger the 20-year assessing time limit in TMA 1970, s 36(1A) (loss of tax brought about carelessly or deliberately etc) unless paragraph 13 (see below) applies. (Note, however, that the 20-year time limit can still apply for other reasons, eg a loss of tax 'brought about deliberately'.)

Paragraph 13 applies to a person's failure to notify where the person knew, at the time the income tax first became chargeable, that the person was not entitled to the amount of the CSP on which tax is chargeable.

In that event, for the purpose of FA 2008, Sch 41 (penalties for failure to notify):

- the failure is treated as deliberate and concealed, and
- the potential lost revenue is the amount of income tax which would have been chargeable under paragraph 8 at the end of the last day of the notification period.

Paragraphs 14 and 15 respectively deal with penalties in relation to partnerships and the liability of officers of insolvent companies.

Coronavirus support schemes

The Coronavirus Act 2020, which received Royal Assent on 25 March 2020, was enacted to enable the Government to respond to the COVID-19 emergency and manage the impact of the pandemic. It includes provisions relating to HMRC functions, national insurance contributions, working tax credit and statutory sick pay.

Coronavirus Act 2020, s 76 provides that HMRC is to have such functions as HM Treasury may direct in relation to the coronavirus or coronavirus disease, in addition to HMRC's existing powers of collection and management of taxes, and Coronavirus Act 2020, s 71 relaxes requirements regarding the signature of Treasury directions.

The following Treasury directions, made under Coronavirus Act 2020, ss 71 and 76, set out the legal framework of the major grant-based support schemes administered by HMRC:

- The Coronavirus Act 2020 Functions of Her Majesty's Revenue and Customs (Coronavirus Job Retention Scheme) Direction of 15 April 2020, which was modified by further directions made on 20 May and 25 June; and
- The Coronavirus Act 2020 Functions of Her Majesty's Revenue and Customs (Self-Employment Income Support Scheme) Direction of 30 April 2020, which was modified by a further direction made on 1 July.

Coronavirus job retention scheme (CJRS)

The Coronavirus Act 2020 Functions of Her Majesty's Revenue and Customs (Coronavirus Job Retention Scheme) Direction of 15 April 2020 (https://tinyurl.com/yb6rup9h) set out the purpose of the scheme and the conditions applying to employers, qualifying costs and furloughed employees.

The direction of 15 April continued to have effect but was modified by the schedules to the 20 May and 25 June directions.

The CJRS was launched on 20 April 2020. By 19 July, 9.5m jobs had been furloughed by 1.2m employers, and the total value of claims made was estimated at £29.8bn.

The detailed conditions for the CJRS are outside the scope of this summary. There have been several changes to the published legal framework and HMRC guidance and, as the Chartered Institute of Taxation has observed, updates to the guidance 'may well impact on claims that have already been made'.

Broadly, the CJRS is intended to enable employers to keep employees on furlough, or temporary leave, between March and October 2020. Employers can claim from HMRC a grant to cover a proportion of furloughed employee's wages and related employer NIC and pension contributions.

At the time of writing, HMRC guidance set out on its CJRS 'collection' page (https://tinyurl.com/y9karxak) included the following guidance notes which were last updated on 10 and 17 July 2020:

- Check if you can claim for your employees' wages through the Coronavirus Job Retention Scheme;
- Check which employees you can put on furlough to use the Coronavirus Job Retention Scheme;
- Steps to take before calculating your claim using the Coronavirus Job Retention Scheme;
- Calculate how much you can claim using the Coronavirus Job Retention Scheme;
- Claim for wages through the Coronavirus Job Retention Scheme – including guidance on correcting errors and paying back overclaimed amounts; and
- Reporting employees' wages to HMRC when you've claimed through the Coronavirus Job Retention Scheme.

Further guidance on paying back overpaid CJRS grants was updated on 1 July 2020 (https://tinyurl.com/yby84wmz).

Job retention bonus

The Chancellor announced in his summer economic statement on 8 July 2020 a 'Plan for Jobs', including a job retention bonus for employers who keep on their furloughed employees after the CJRS is closed.

'The government will introduce a one-off payment of £1,000 to UK employers for every furloughed employee who remains continuously employed through to the end of January 2021. Employees must earn above the [NIC] lower earnings limit (£520 per month) on average between the end of the [CJRS] and the end of January 2021. Payments will be made from February 2021,' HM Treasury said in the Plan for Jobs document (https://tinyurl.com/ycqele8y).

Further details about the job retention bonus scheme would be announced by the end of July, the Treasury said. A ministerial direction to HMRC, relating to the introduction and operation of the scheme, was published on 9 July.

Self-employment income support scheme (SEISS)

The Coronavirus Act 2020 Functions of Her Majesty's Revenue and Customs (Self-Employment Income Support Scheme) Direction of 30 April 2020 (https://tinyurl.com/ybumehhh), set out the purpose of the scheme and the conditions for eligibility.

The direction of 15 April ('the SEISS direction') continued to have effect but was modified and extended by the schedule to the 1 July direction ('the SEISS extension').

The SEISS was launched on 13 May 2020. By 19 July, 2.7m claims had been made with a total value of £7.8bn.

The detailed conditions for the SEISS are outside the scope of this summary. As noted above, particular care is required because of the frequency of changes to HMRC guidance. Guidance on the meaning of 'adversely affected by coronavirus' for the purpose of the SEISS grant was developed over several weeks following the scheme's launch.

Broadly, the SEISS is intended to support self-employed people whose business has been adversely affected by coronavirus.

Applications for the first grant – worth 80% of average monthly trading profits, paid in a single instalment covering three months' worth of profits calculated on that basis, and capped at £7,500 – closed on 13 July 2020.

Those who were eligible for the first grant and can confirm to HMRC that their business has been adversely affected on or after 14 July, will be able to make a claim for a second and final grant from 17 August, HMRC said in guidance updated on 14 July (https://tinyurl.com/y9m637nq). HMRC added:

> 'HMRC will check claims and take appropriate action to withhold or recover payments found to be dishonest or inaccurate. If you know you've been overpaid or are not eligible for the grant and do not tell us you may have to pay a penalty.'

The second and final grant is worth '70% of your average monthly trading profits, paid out in a single instalment covering three months' worth of profits, and capped at £6,570 in total', HMRC said in a separate guidance note updated on 14 July (https://tinyurl.com/wmdr3q3).

Other financial support

The Chancellor also announced in his summer economic statement on 8 July 2020 that HMRC would administer a new scheme to encourage people to return to eating out after the easing of public health restrictions. 'Eat Out to Help Out ... will entitle every diner to a 50% discount of up to £10 per head on their meal, at any participating restaurant, café, pub or other eligible food service establishment. The discount can be used unlimited times and will be valid Monday to Wednesday on any eat-in meal (including on non-alcoholic drinks) for the entire month of August 2020 across the UK. Participating establishments will be fully reimbursed for the 50% discount,' the Treasury said. A Treasury direction and HMRC guidance on the Eat Out to Help Out scheme were published on 9 July.

The Chancellor also announced temporary cuts in VAT for the hospitality sector and temporary cuts in stamp duty land tax.

The Plan for Jobs document set out various other government support schemes announced since the March 2020 Budget. These included:

- access to finance – five schemes to support businesses with cashflow difficulties;
- HMRC's time to pay arrangements;
- deferral of income tax and NIC payments;
- deferral of VAT payments;
- delayed extension of the off-payroll working (IR35) rules to engagements in the private sector;
- business rates holidays and grants for retail, hospitality and leisure sectors; and
- a statutory sick pay rebate scheme.

Cessation of trade

A June 2020 update to HMRC's Business Income Manual at BIM48000 sets out how HMRC will apply legislation and case law to crisis situations, such as the coronavirus pandemic, resulting in a business changing its normal business activities by changing product lines, providing goods or services to key workers free or at significant discounts, or donating supplies to charities, hospitals and care homes.

The updated guidance also addresses the question whether a new activity should be regarded as a new trade or as an extension of an existing one, and the treatment of temporary breaks in trading activity.

INDEX